Printed Voices

The Renaissance
Culture of Dialogue

Edited by Dorothea Heitsch
and Jean-François Vallée

UNIVERSITY OF TORONTO PRESS
Toronto Buffalo London

© University of Toronto Press Incorporated 2004
Toronto Buffalo London
Printed in Canada

ISBN 0-8020-8706-X

Printed on acid-free paper

National Library of Canada Cataloguing in Publication

Printed voices : the Renaissance culture of dialogue / edited by
Dorothea Heitsch and Jean-François Vallée.

Includes bibliographical references and index.
ISBN 0-8020-8706-X

1. Dialogue – History.   2. Dialogue in literature.   3. Renaissance.
I. Heitsch, Dorothea B., 1968– .   II. Vallée, Jean-François, 1970– .

PN1551.P74 2004   809′.926   C2004-902166-4

University of Toronto Press acknowledges the financial assistance to its
publishing program of the Canada Council for the Arts and the
Ontario Arts Council.

University of Toronto Press acknowledges the financial support for its
publishing activities of the Government of Canada through the Book
Publishing Industry Development Program (BPIDP).

Contents

Acknowledgments   vii

Foreword   ix

DOROTHEA HEITSCH AND JEAN-FRANÇOIS VALLÉE

The Fate of Dialogue   1

Problematizing Renaissance Exemplarity: The Inward Turn
of Dialogue from Petrarch to Montaigne   3

FRANÇOIS RIGOLOT

The Utopia of Dialogue   25

Dialogue, Utopia, and the Agencies of Fiction   27

NINA CHORDAS

The Fellowship of the Book: Printed Voices and Written
Friendships in More's *Utopia*   42

JEAN-FRANÇOIS VALLÉE

Thomas More's *Utopia* and the Problem of Writing a Literary History
of English Renaissance Dialogue   63

J. CHRISTOPHER WARNER

Dialogue and the Court   77

The Development of Dialogue in *Il libro del cortegiano*: From
the Manuscript Drafts to the Definitive Version   79

OLGA ZORZI PUGLIESE

Pietro Aretino between the *locus mendacii* and the *locus veritatis*   95

ROBERT BURANELLO

From Dialogue to Conversation: The Place of Marie de Gournay   114

DOROTHEA HEITSCH

Dialogues with History, Religion, and Science   135

'Truth Hath the Victory': Dialogue and Disputation in John Foxe's
Actes and Monuments   137

JOSEPH PUTERBAUGH

Milton's 'Hence': Dialogue and the Shape of History in 'L'Allegro'
and 'Il Penseroso'   157

W. SCOTT HOWARD

Hobbes, Rhetoric, and the Art of the Dialogue   175

LUC BOROT

The Purpose of Dialogue   191

Francesco Barbaro's *De re uxoria*: A Silent Dialogue for a Young
Medici Bride   193

CAROLE COLLIER FRICK

Dialogue and German Language Learning in the Renaissance   206

NICOLA McLELLAND

The Subject of Dialogue   227

Renaissance Dialogue and Subjectivity   229

EVA KUSHNER

Bibliography   243

List of Contributors   275

Index Nominum   279

Index Rerum   287

Acknowledgments

The editors of this volume would like to thank all the contributors in general for their work as well as François Rigolot in particular who kindly supported the project from beginning to end. We would like to thank Suzanne Rancourt for encouraging us to submit the manuscript to the University of Toronto Press. The editors also would like to acknowledge and recognize each other's dedication throughout the lengthy electronic dialogue that made *Printed Voices* possible.

Foreword

Dorothea Heitsch and Jean-François Vallée

I will not here take notice of the several kinds of Dialogue, and the whole Art of it, which would ask an entire Volume to perform. This has been a Work long wanted, and much desir'd, of which the Ancients have not sufficiently inform'd us; and I question whether any Man, now living, can treat it accurately.

John Dryden[1]

The dialogue genre was, without doubt, one of the most prevalent forms of writing in the European Renaissance. Countless authors, no matter what their interests or special fields, appreciated the rhetorical and fictional means of representing conversations by way of the written word. Humanists especially were eager to try their hand at dialogues, imitating more or less faithfully, and sometimes conflating or adapting, ancient dialogic models, such as those of Plato, Cicero, and Lucian. In fact, dialogue was 'so widespread during the Renaissance that it seems to represent a fundamental and innovative aspect of its intellectual life,'[2] writes Eva Kushner in the concluding essay of this collection.

The sheer quantity of dialogues published in most European cultural traditions of the period is, in itself, quite impressive. According to Roger Lee Deakins, fifty-six dialogues were written in England between 1500 and 1558,[3] while John T. Day lists another 206 appearing between 1558 and 1603.[4] For the Spanish tradition, Jacqueline Ferreras – taking into account only 'conceptual' dialogues written in Castilian – compiles a catalogue of seventy-nine authors and more than 100 complete books of dialogues published in the sixteenth century.[5] Jesús

Gómez identifies 173 dialogues in the bibliography of his book on Spanish Renaissance dialogue.[6] To date, no comparable survey of French dialogue exists, but Mustapha Kemal Bénouis noted, as early as 1976, that sixteenth-century dialogues in French were 'too numerous not to attract attention' and recorded forty-nine sixteenth-century French dialogues in the – obviously incomplete – index at the end of his volume.[7] In Quattrocento[8] and Cinquecento[9] Italy – where the genre, in its neoclassical Renaissance guise, had emerged as early as the Trecento, with Petrarch – the number of dialogues written and published has not yet been established, but it certainly surpasses all other cultural traditions.[10] Much of the same may be said of neo-Latin dialogues or dialogues written in various other European languages, such as Portuguese,[11] German,[12] Polish, or Czech.[13]

More importantly, it cannot be said that dialogue was a 'minor' genre, since many of the most renowned authors of the period made prolific use of this polyvocal writing strategy. Petrarch, Bruni, Valla, Alberti, Pontano, Poggio, Ficino, Machiavelli, Bembo, Erasmus, Budé, More, Vives, Hutten, Castiglione, Aretino, Speroni, Tasso, Spenser, Campanella, Bruno, Galileo, Cervantes, Hobbes, and many others were all engaged in the composition of such texts, some of which still resist monologic interpretation today. Dialogues often also framed even narrative genres (most notably Boccacio's *Decameron* and Marguerite de Navarre's *Heptaméron*), when these were not already predominantly written in dialogue form, such as Rabelais's *Tiers Livre*, to give only one example. Furthermore, as Jon Snyder has remarked, the Renaissance was the first period in Western literary history to give rise to genuine *theoretical* attempts at defining this ubiquitous genre: 'Only in that period and in that place did literary critics or theorists recognise the full extent of the problem of dialogue and treat it as an urgent one for literary studies.'[14] Hence, it is not surprising that dialogue has been characterized as the 'humanistic genre *par excellence*,'[15] or that a general historical survey of dialogue would conclude that the Renaissance is the period in which dialogue, 'as a genre, universally triumphed.'[16]

Until fairly recently, however, dialogue had been conspicuously absent from Renaissance anthologies and scholarship.[17] The disciplinary nature of modern literary theory and nineteenth-century generic categories – based, most notably, on the distinction between poetry, narrative genres, and theatre – has perhaps blinded scholars to dialogue, which tends to blur, and bridge, the modern distinctions between fiction and nonfiction, orality and literacy, or poetry, prose, and drama. A fundamentally hybrid genre, dialogue spans not only what modernity has described as 'literature' and 'philosophy,' but also rhetoric, ethics, social history, and pedagogy. More than any other genre, it may have transformed one or several ancient genres through inversion, displacement, or combination.[18]

The study of dialogue has become increasingly more topical, particularly in the past two decades of Renaissance scholarship. One might wonder why this has happened so recently. The twentieth century seems to have reversed the historical process of the Renaissance in that philosophical and theoretical approaches to dialogue (and dialogism) – in the works of such authors as Martin Buber, Hans-Georg Gadamer, Mikhail Bakhtin, Francis Jacques, Julia Kristeva, Tzvetan Todorov, and others – have *preceded* the interest for the study of dialogical writing itself.

Conceivably, as Virginia Cox has noted, 'this awkwardly hybrid genre,' that had 'slipped through the gap between philosophy and rhetoric which was already beginning to open up' during the Renaissance has become more visible given that this gap is now 'beginning to close.'[19] It might be that the disciplinary nature of the modern epistemology made it difficult to study a genre that was used for so many different purposes in such diverse fields of knowledge and culture: from literature to architecture, from gardening to political satire, from eroticism to speculative philosophy or religious controversy.

One could also allege that the rise of theory as modern academic discourse may have promoted scholarly interest in the texts of an epoch that is marked by a similar theoretical restlessness.[20] Finally, it is equally possible that the recent revolutions in communication technologies and media, which have dramatically unsettled the foundations of the 'Gutenberg galaxy,' have simultaneously made us aware of this fundamentally communicative and rhetorical genre, set on the threshold of orality and literacy. Nevertheless, whatever the causes for the belated contemporary interest in dialogue, it seems obvious that a great deal of work remains to be done if we are to have a clear image of the genre's importance and influence in the period.

Most of the extant publications on the subject have confined themselves to limited studies of single works, authors, or, at best, one national tradition. Among these contributions to the study of the genre, a few should be mentioned here. The scholarly interest in the tradition of Renaissance dialogue gradually emerged in the seventies.[21] One of the contributors to this volume, Eva Kushner, was without doubt the most active and insightful pioneer at the time. Her numerous essays set the course for the theoretical exploration of the genre, as well as for the analysis of the French tradition.[22] Another early contribution to the study of sixteenth-century French dialogue is Mustapha Kemal Bénouis's previously quoted *Le dialogue philosophique dans la littérature française du seizième siècle*, which cites and classifies French Renaissance dialogue, defining dialogue as a 'self-reflexive' text and as an instrument of intellectual investigation.

At the beginning of the eighties, a more rewarding decade for dialogue studies, David Marsh made an important contribution to the scholarship in English on Quattrocento humanistic dialogue. Establishing the death of classical dialogue with Augustine and its revival with Petrarch (whose *Secretum* anticipates the relativity and freedom of discussion in the Italian tradition of the fifteenth century), Marsh analyses dialogues – modelled for the most part on Cicero – by Bruni, Poggio Bracciolini, Valla, Alberti, and Pontano.[23] A rare comparative encounter with Renaissance dialogue should also be mentioned here: two conferences held in Paris in 1983 and 1984.[24] The following year, Kenneth Wilson, referring mainly to classical theory and poetics in his book on the formation of English Renaissance dialogue, describes the genre as a 'medial art' and goes on to examine Tudor dialogue with a focus on Ascham, Elyot, and especially Thomas More.[25] Jon Snyder was the first to concentrate on the theories of dialogue. His analysis of the late sixteenth-century definitions and conceptualizations of dialogue in Italy by Sigonio, Speroni, Tasso, and Castelvetro portrays the intricacy of the genre and its import in the epistemological and disciplinary upheavals of early modernity.[26]

In the last decade, dialogue studies have flourished in many European languages. Virginia Cox, for one, adopted a socio-historical approach to examine dialogue as an 'act of communication.' She explores several Cinquecento works in order to show the many facets of the genre, before charting its decline in Italy at the end of that century due, most notably, to the rise of the increasingly visual print culture.[27] The same year, Suzanne Guellouz published, in French, the first contemporary attempt at defining the dialogue genre throughout its history from antiquity to the present, including of course the Renaissance.[28] A collection of articles edited by Colette Winn followed in 1993, introducing a formal aspect to the definition and classification of dialogue, and concentrating in particular on late sixteenth- and early seventeenth-century French dialogue.[29] Another contributor to this volume, Olga Pugliese, published a book on the labyrinthine structure of humanistic dialogue.[30] Ruxandra Irina Vulcan made the most of a much needed rhetorical approach to dialogue in order to analyse the multiple forms of the genre in the first half of sixteenth-century France.[31] More recently, Anne Godard, in a commendable comparative approach, has endeavoured to discuss the fifteenth and sixteenth century in Europe as an age of the dialogue. Humanism, according to her, practises a 'cultural dialogism' that attempts to fuse the literary models of the genre with their contemporary representations in a self-reflexive manner that produces a unique interaction of literature, linguistics, philosophy, and religion.[32]

As one can easily gather from this cursory survey, Renaissance dialogue studies are gaining momentum. But serious comparative and theoretically well-informed studies of the dialogue's importance in the context of early modern Europe are still required, especially in English.[33] This volume seeks to contribute to and intensify the international and interdisciplinary scholarly dialogue that should be broadened if we are to have a better knowledge of this still too frequently neglected genre of the Renaissance canon. Many important works have yet to be unearthed (and made available in modern editions). Many others ought to be reexamined from a dialogical perspective. Comprehensive theoretical and historical studies should be carried out if we wish to have a better portrait of the epistemological and cultural roots of dialogue's immense popularity in the Renaissance.

Our cross-cultural and interdisciplinary discussion of Renaissance dialogue purports to make a contribution in this respect. Bringing together the work of scholars with different linguistic, cultural, and disciplinary backgrounds, this collection of essays offers a truly comparative outlook on dialogue: Italian, French, German, neo-Latin, and English works are discussed by both young and established scholars in the field of Renaissance studies.[34] The authors examine the genre from many different perspectives, taking into account various factors that are linked to the upsurge of dialogue in the Renaissance: the emergence of a complex and multifarious subjectivity, the advent of modern utopias, the social and political importance of courtliness, the rise of print culture, religious and scientific controversy, the prevalence of pedagogy and rhetorical culture, the *ethos* of humanism, the 'gendering' of dialogue, and Renaissance 'logocentrism.' The various methodological and theoretical approaches that have been drawn on by our thirteen contributors span comparative literature, new historicism, rhetoric, gender studies, historical analysis, genetic theory, linguistics, philosophy, theology, and philology. All the essays, though often based on theoretical premises, avoid theoretical jargon and constitute what we would term 'serious scholarship,' based on careful scrutiny of original sources.

The collection begins with a historically ambitious and thought-provoking essay by François Rigolot, on the 'inward turn' of dialogue throughout the Renaissance, and culminates with a similarly sweeping, and truly comparative, article by a pioneer in the field of dialogue studies, Eva Kushner, on the issue of early modern subjectivity in its relation to the genre. The eleven other essays have been arranged in four thematic sections that represent some of the key areas intersecting with dialogue: The Utopia of Dialogue, Dialogue and the Court, Dialogues with History, Religion, and Science, and The Purpose of Dialogue.

The Fate of Dialogue

In his opening essay, 'Problematizing Renaissance Exemplarity: The Inward Turn of Dialogue from Petrarch to Montaigne,' François Rigolot revisits the development of dialogical techniques and intentionality in a selective but highly representative sample of literature spanning almost three centuries. Concentrating on seminal Italian, French, and neo-Latin texts (Petrarch's *Secretum*, Bruni's dialogues, Erasmus's *Colloquies*, Castiglione's *Cortegiano*, Marguerite de Navarre's *Heptaméron*, and Montaigne's *Essais*), he argues that, although the playful twists and turns of Petrarch's successors are not alien to the dialogical Ciceronian tradition, they also increasingly serve as a vehicle for problematizing the authority of exemplary models, and point to a gradual 'inward turn' of Renaissance dialogue culminating in Montaigne's essays. This overview of our topic demonstrates eloquently how crucial the study of dialogue is, most notably for our understanding of the constitution of modern subjectivity and self-consciousness.

The Utopia of Dialogue

In our first thematic section, we have brought together three essays that deal, in very different ways, with the decisive relationship of dialogue and utopia. Indeed, it is certainly not a coincidence that many utopias, such as Plato's *Republic*, were written in dialogue form. But the Renaissance, starting with Thomas More's exemplary *Utopia*, provides most certainly the basis of the modern fictional incarnation of the genre. More's most celebrated of dialogues and its progeny have had a powerful effect on the social, political, and literary history of the following centuries.

In 'Dialogue, Utopia, and the Agencies of Fiction,' Nina Chordas discusses many utopian texts of the sixteenth and seventeenth centuries, such as More's *Utopia*, Campanella's *City of the Sun*, Bacon's *New Atlantis*, J. Valentin Andreae's *Christianopolis*, Cavendish's *Blazing World*, and Spenser's *A View of the Present State of Ireland*. She develops an original thesis on this obviously critical, yet seldom examined, relationship between utopia and dialogue. In probing the ambiguous connection of both genres to fiction, she attempts to demonstrate how 'early modern utopia, enabled by the dialogue, is closely allied with nascent imperialism in the period.'

Jean-François Vallée, in 'The Fellowship of the Book: Printed Voices and Written Friendships in More's *Utopia*,' shifts the focus in order to show that the utopia of More's work might also be seen to reside in the written dialogue itself. Through a close analysis of the dialogical structure of the text and of its relationship to the circle of Northern humanists, the essay illustrates how the notions and values of dialogue and friendship are intricately linked, and textually incarnated, in the 'dialogocentric' *ethos* of the humanistic book. *Utopia* can thus be read as a dialogical manifesto, a truly utopian embodiment of the friendly dialogue that humanists so highly regarded, and so often only represented – at a distance – through the technologies of writing and printing.

Christopher Warner, in 'Thomas More's *Utopia* and the Problem of Writing a Literary History of English Renaissance Dialogue,' courageously endeavours to confront the much less utopian incarnations of English dialogue 'after' *Utopia*. Warner questions both the traditionally romanticizing and the contemptuous critical views of most of the three hundred prose dialogues published in England during the sixteenth and seventeenth centuries. Adopting a broad literary historical perspective, he seeks to give a better account of the literary sophistication of these works' engagements in specific political and theological controversies by concentrating on the rhetorical dialogue 'between the dialogues' themselves. He proposes a novel approach to this corpus by way of its social context. The fruitfulness of such a methodological course is illustrated by a study of three different specific political and religious controversies that gave rise to 'clusters' of dialogues: Henry VIII's dispute with Rome over his marriage to Catherine of Aragon (1529–34), the years following the Spanish Armada's defeat (1588–90), and, finally, the period of the Exclusion Crisis (1679–82).

Dialogue and the Court

As Warner's essay demonstrates, dialogues were not only written or held in utopian contexts or for utopian goals. They were often closely related to the very pragmatic nature of the public, political, and social conversations that were held in, and out of, the Renaissance courts. The question of the nature of public and private dialogue, which is also the subject of debate in the dialogue of counsel of More's *Utopia*, becomes crucial in a court setting where power dwells.

The most famous courtly dialogue of the Renaissance is, of course, Baldassare Castiglione's *Libro del Cortegiano*, at once a model of courtly interaction and the ultimate model of the written genre of the courtly dialogue. A specialist of Castiglione and of the dialogue genre, Olga Pugliese, in her essay 'The Development of Dialogue in *Il libro del cortegiano*: From the Manuscript Drafts to the Definitive Version,' proposes an original, genetic perspective on this most celebrated dialogue of the sixteenth century. Through a collation of the various versions found in the autograph drafts of the Castiglioni Archive of Mantua and the fair copies of the Vatican, Pugliese examines the structural development of the treatise, thus giving us a rare glimpse of the very process of composition of dialogues by Renaissance authors. This rigorous study also traces the evolution of Castiglione's thought on various topics, such as the political role of the courtier and the portrayal of women.

The courtly dialogical model, however, was not universally admired. Pietro Aretino, for one, wrote dialogues that promoted a provocative alternative to the court for the sixteenth-century *letterato*. Thus, in his essay 'Pietro Aretino between the *locus mendacii* and the *locus veritatis*,' Roberto Buranello develops a very different picture of the Cinquecento dialogue, its setting, and its politics. He particularly illustrates how the edifying courtly setting of Castiglione's dialogue was openly challenged by Aretino's infamous *Sei giornate* (a dialogue in the company of whores) and, in a different manner, by his *Ragionamento delle corti* (*Dialogues of the Court*) set in the calm of a humanist Venetian residence. Via Bakhtin's concept of the chronotope and through a close analysis of the setting, the characters, and their interactions (in the latter work especially), Buranello maps out the fuller dimensions of Aretino's satirical dialogues and of his proposed alternative forum.

Dorothea Heitsch transports us from the Italian court of the early sixteenth century to its French incarnation in the seventeenth century. In 'From Dialogue to Conversation: The Place of Marie de Gournay,' she focuses on the transformation of dialogue at the end of the French

Renaissance and its reemergence in baroque salon culture. She identifies and documents a crucial paradigm shift in the very conception and practice of dialogue at the time. It is against this shifting historical, literary, and social background that Heitsch presents Marie de Gournay, Montaigne's adoptive daughter, shown here as she uses the growing possibilities of print culture, which enable her to partake in a complex literary dialogue, to strategically reedit her texts, and to assert her voice in contemporaneous conversations.

Dialogues with History, Religion, and Science

The third thematic section of this volume deals with three different, but vital, areas that intersect with the rhetorical power of dialogue as a genre and as a mode of exposition and/or controversy, that is, religion, history, and science.

In '"Truth Hath the Victory": Dialogue and Disputation in John Foxe's *Actes and Monuments*,' Joseph Puterbaugh underlines the importance of dialogue for Protestant polemics in sixteenth-century England. He notes that the genre was appealing to Protestants and Puritans, on the one hand, 'because dialogue can disguise the source of controversial opinion,' thus enabling authors to 'deflect direct responsibility for provocative points of view.' On the other hand, dialogue is the perfect genre to represent reconciliation and order: 'it dramatizes the movement of the individual into a wider circle of believers, a movement which is at the center of Protestant conceptions of spiritual cooperation and godly community.' More importantly, Puterbaugh shows how the dual written/ 'oral' nature of dialogue allows these writers to explore the movement of the Word and thus to represent the very process of religious identity formation. Having examined a few typical examples of religious dialogues and controversies, he undertakes an analysis of John Foxe's use of dialogue and debate in his *Actes and Monuments*. Here he concentrates on two evocative sections of Foxe's work (the Oxford martyrs and the William Hunter episode) and then demonstrates 'how the *act* of disputation [*was*] crucial in the formation of Protestant identity.'

Scott Howard, in his essay 'Milton's "Hence": Dialogue and the Shape of History in "L'Allegro" and "Il Penseroso,"' brings us to the next century and shifts the perspective from the religious to the literary and historical significance of dialogue. Howard shows how Milton's celebrated 'twin poems' of mirth and melancholy constitute a hybrid genre and he proposes to examine them in relation to 'the one Renaissance literary form that epitomizes both the mixing of genres and the dramatization of intertextuality: the dialogue.' Situating the texts in the English tradition of poetic dialogue, he demonstrates how they engage with the mode of dialectical dialogue as a means to imagine a pattern for history. As Howard maintains, 'that pattern, which traces formal and thematic crossings between and within the poems, outlines Milton's idea of history as a dynamic, often violent, cultural process shaped by contiguous cycles of degeneration and contrary a-cyclical paths toward progress.' This essay refers to both the theoretical and the literary tradition and hinges on a spatial and temporal understanding of Milton's use of the word 'hence,' thus reading the companion poems as inherently sociable, dialogic texts.

Luc Borot, in 'Hobbes, Rhetoric, and the Art of the Dialogue,' conveys us to the historical and epistemological final stages of the Renaissance, when the dialogue genre in its humanistic guise had long begun its decline. Borot, a specialist and translator of the English philosopher, observes that Thomas Hobbes was educated at the very end of the sixteenth century in an academic culture still dominated by rhetoric and dialectic. In many ways, he can be seen as one of the last true humanists. However, in middle life, 'he converted to the new science under the influence of Euclid and Galileo,' and 'wrote his works on first philosophy and political philosophy according to their methods.' Why then did he, in later life after *Leviathan*, undertake to write several dialogues? After a presentation of Hobbes's relationship to humanism and rhetoric, the essay discusses the position of this author's dialogues in the history of the genre and proposes an interpretation of his particular use of dialogue, through a close study of *Behemoth* and of the *Dialogue of the Common Laws*. Combining extensive knowledge of Hobbes, of the political, rhetorical, historical, and scientific aspects of his works and of the context of their publication, this essay sheds new light at once on Hobbes and on the fate of late Renaissance dialogue.

The Purpose of Dialogue

Dialogue, in the Renaissance, was used not only for lofty philosophical or speculative pursuits. It also had some very obvious, though sometimes subtle, pragmatic purposes. The last thematic section of our collection offers two very different examples of the many potential 'practical' uses of dialogue.

The first essay by Carole Frick, 'Francesco Barbaro's *De re uxoria*: A Silent Dialogue for a Young Medici Bride,' illustrates how dialogue was exploited for the imperious task of fashioning a wife in Quattrocento Italy. Through a historical reading of a *trattato* written by the Venetian humanist Francesco Barbaro as a gift on the occasion of Lorenzo de' Medici (Il Vecchio)'s wedding to Ginevra Cavalcanti in 1416, Frick describes how a young Florentine upper-class woman was taught to develop 'a self-conscious dialogue with herself,' so as to learn how to exercise self-control over body and mind. The solitary dialogue with oneself, proposed by Barbaro, would serve at least two purposes according to Frick: 'continual refinement, and a silent, inward preoccupation with one's self-reflection,' thus safeguarding the crucial, but utterly passive, role of these fifteenth-century 'sacred dolls,' within the families of the upper class in Renaissance Italy.

Nicola McLelland's essay, 'Dialogue and German Language Learning in the Renaissance,' presents a very different, and less monological, instance of dialogues being used for didactic ends. McLelland examines the widespread use of the genre as a tool for linguistic instruction during the European Renaissance. The dialogue was admirably well suited for language practitioners, writes McLelland, since it 'imitates, more or less convincingly, the form of a spoken exchange, so that unlike other written forms, it not only presents ideas, but also *represents* the means – the linguistic forms – that communicate those ideas.' After describing the major types of dialogues and documenting the predilection for the genre in theoretical discussions (and defences) of vernacular languages, McLelland, concentrating especially – though not exclusively – on the German-language context, identifies 'a wider dialogue, between two traditions of language learning,' the 'humanist renewal in the teaching of Latin, and the birth of teaching foreign vernaculars as part of formal schooling.' This wide-ranging comparative study of diverse works of the fifteenth and sixteenth centuries belonging to these two traditions – from Donatus's *Ars minor* and Juan Luis Vives's Latin dialogues to various little-known but fascinating examples of *Sprachbücher* (German language manuals made for foreign tradesmen especially) – brings to light the emergence of visually oriented methods at the end of the Renaissance. This essay gives an enticing indication of the diversity of as yet uncharted territories of dialogue studies.

The Subject of Dialogue

The vast corpus of dialogues in the Renaissance is rivalled only by the weightiness of the underlying and manifold issues related to the genre's immense popularity. And one of the chief implications of the prevalence of dialogue in the period is certainly its importance for the contemporaneous conceptions of the subject. In this respect, Eva Kushner's analysis 'Renaissance Dialogue and Subjectivity' provides a fitting conclusion to our volume. Indeed, asks Kushner, what does the prevalence of dialogue in the Renaissance mean for our understanding of early modern subjectivity? Should we espouse the Burckhardtian view of the period as the birthplace of the modern autonomous individual or should we rather adopt the more sceptical view of a Greenblatt or a Foucault concerning the unlikely existence of 'subjectivity in the modern sense' before Descartes? Kushner begins her essay by highlighting one of the main characteristics of dialogue: that is, 'the author's initial self-projection into two voices, preceding more complex fragmentation to come.' She then traces the multiple facets and possibilities of this self-fragmentation by way of mimetic dramatization through a series of relevant texts: dialogues by Petrarch (including his *Secretum*, arguably the first example in the Western canon that textualizes the self's division), Marguerite de Navarre's *Dialogue en forme de vision nocturne*, More's *Dialogue of Comfort against Tribulation*, Erasmus's *De pueris*, Latin dialogues of Juan Luis Vives and, finally, Pontus de Tyard's *Premier curieux*. With regard to this last dialogue, she notes that the 'dialogue is process rather than affirmation of elusive truths; that is why it expresses an inner plurality,' and so she concludes that this 'plurality announces for the dialogues to come a role of semaphore among subjects no longer limited to communicate only, or mostly, within the "universe of resemblance."'

This last essay of our volume points to the opening contribution, echoing François Rigolot's analysis of the inward turn of dialogue in the course of the Renaissance. Our collective study of this important genre, and concept, of Renaissance Europe thus takes the form of a circular journey: having travelled through *Utopia* and its (sometimes dystopian) satellites, paid a considerate visit to the French and Italian courts, survived religious, historical, and epistemological storms of controversy, been subjected to the patriarchal monologue of the Florentine upper class and to language lessons through written conversation, we have once again landed before ourselves, in the company of our plural twenty-first century identities. Ever so eager to enter into a (written) dialogue with our fellow early-modern humanists, we, like them, are submitted to important technological changes in the way we communicate and interact, are forced to reassess our notion of self, the world, and God, and are confronted with seismic epistemological, cultural, political, religious, and communicational transformations that are perhaps matched only by their own contemporaneous upheavals. Hence, the interhistoricity of dialogue as a cultural phenomenon might still be of value to our allegedly 'post-humanist' civilization. We wish to add our modest contribution to this continuing dialogue.

NOTES

1 Dryden, 'The Life of Lucian,' 222.
2 Other periods, of course, also produced dialogues, most notably Greek and Roman antiquity, and perhaps the European Enlightenment, but never to the same extent as the Renaissance. For a monumental survey of ancient dialogue, see Hirzel, *Der Dialog, ein literarhistorischer Versuch*. Hirzel, however, devotes only a few pages to Renaissance dialogue.
3 Deakins, 'The Tudor Dialogue as a Literary Form.'
4 Day, 'Elizabethan Prose Dialogue.' See also Wilson, *Incomplete Fictions*, ix, n. 1.
5 Ferreras, *Les dialogues espagnols du XVIe siècle*, 5. Ferreras does not count independent dialogues, dialogues written in Latin, or theatrical dialogues.
6 Gómez, *El diálogo en el Renacimiento*, 217–30.
7 Bénouis, *Le dialogue philosophique dans la littérature française du seizième siècle*, 207.
8 See especially Marsh, *The Quattrocento Dialogue*.
9 See Cox, *The Renaissance Dialogue*.
10 Cox's bibliography lists no less than ninety-nine authors of dialogues writing between 1500 and 1650; many of these authors wrote more than one dialogue.
11 Preto-Rodas, *Francisco Rodrigues Lobo: Dialogue and Courtly Lore in Renaissance Portugal*.
12 Niemann, *Die Dialogliteratur der Reformationszeit*. Nieman's historical approach presents Ulrich von Hutten as the rediscoverer of antique dialogue (especially in its Lucianic form), as one of the promoters of humanistic-rhetorical dialogue in Latin, and as one of the first to use German in the context of his critique of Rome.
13 Jechova, 'Le dialogue dans les littératures tchèque et polonaise entre le Moyen Âge et la Renaissance.'
14 Snyder, *Writing the Scene of Speaking*, 2. Deakins had also observed that 'the

sixteenth century was as seminal for the theory of dialogue as it was for the writing of dialogues' ('The Tudor Dialogue as a Literary Form,' 6).

15 Vulcan, *Savoir et rhétorique dans les dialogues français*, 1.

16 Guellouz, *Le dialogue*, 166. Our translation.

17 In 1992, Virginia Cox could still write: 'Though it is generally acknowledged to be one of the most characteristic literary forms of the Renaissance, the dialogue remains curiously invisible in the literary history of the period' (*The Renaissance Dialogue*, xi).

18 Todorov, *Les genres du discours*, 49.

19 Cox, *The Renaissance Dialogue*, xi.

20 Guillén, *Literature as a System*, 108.

21 Apart from the already mentioned survey of (mostly classical) dialogue by Rudolf Hirzel (1895), the only previously published book-length studies are one on English dialogue by Merrill (*The Dialogue in English Literature* [1911; reprint, 1970]) and one on the German tradition (Gewerstock, *Lucian und Hutten*. [1924; reprint 1967]).

22 Her first article on the subject was published as early as 1972 ('Réflexions sur le dialogue en France au XVIᵉ siècle'). In English, see, for example, 'The Dialogue of the French Renaissance: Work of Art or Instrument of Inquiry?' and 'The Renaissance Dialogue and Its Zero-Degree Fictionality.'

23 Marsh, *The Quattrocento Dialogue*. Marsh also takes into account the Lucianic model of dialogue.

24 The proceedings were edited soon after the conference by Jones-Davies: *Le dialogue au temps de la Renaissance*. Most contributions are in French and are transcriptions of the talks given at the two conferences.

25 Wilson, *Incomplete Fictions*.

26 Snyder, *Writing the Scene of Speaking*. We should also mention here a stimulating and sweeping article by Burke, 'The Renaissance Dialogue.'

27 Cox, *The Renaissance Dialogue*.

28 Guellouz, *Le dialogue*.

29 Winn, *The Dialogue in Early Modern France*.

30 Pugliese, *Il discorso labirintico del dialogo rinascimentale*. In previous years, no less than three Italian scholars had published books on Renaissance dialogue: Girardi, *La società del dialogo*; Forno, *Il 'libro animato'*; and Vianello, *Il 'giardino' delle parole*.

31 Vulcan, *Savoir et rhétorique dans les dialogues français*. In another book, Véronique Zaercher undertakes an analysis of Rabelais's *Tiers livre*, first with a view to France and then within the theoretical context of Renaissance dialogue: *Le Dialogue rabelaisien*.

32 Godard, *Le dialogue à la Renaissance*. Reinier Leushuis, finally, analyses mar-

riage and courtly friendship in their socio-historical and theological context during the first half of the sixteenth century with a view to the form of dialogue as well as to the realism of marriage and to contemporary endeavours for its reform: *Le Mariage et l''amitié courtoise' dans le dialogue et le récit bref de la Renaissance.*

33 Among all the previously mentioned studies, only five are available in English: Marsh, Snyder, and Cox on the Italian tradition, Wilson on early sixteenth-century English dialogue, and the Winn collection on French dialogues of the late Renaissance. To date, no comparative book-length studies have been published in English.

34 The 'Printed Voices' project was inspired by a panel on Renaissance dialogue organized by Jean-François Vallée for the 1997 MLA convention in Toronto. Three of our contributors, François Rigolot, Christopher Warner, and Olga Pugliese, read earlier versions of their current essays at this session. A group of eight contributors met in two panels organized by Dorothea Heitsch and Jean-François Vallée at the 2003 conference of the Renaissance Society of America in Toronto. It should be made clear, however, that the project did not emerge as a conference volume.

The Fate of Dialogue

Problematizing Renaissance Exemplarity: The Inward Turn of Dialogue from Petrarch to Montaigne[1]

François Rigolot

Do not try to go outside; come back into yourself; for truth dwells within the human being.

Augustine[2]

Plato seems to me to have favored this form of philosophizing in dialogues deliberately, to put more fittingly into diverse mouths the diversity and variation of his own ideas.

Montaigne[3]

In the beginning was Petrarch's *Secretum,* a literary form of conversation which took place between two exemplary characters, Francis and Augustine, and proved to have an immense impact on later humanist sensibility. Arguably, for the first time in the European tradition, the search for truth was powerfully rooted in a scenario characterized by a doubling of the self. Dialogue served to dramatize the value attached to the 'inward turn' of the psyche, a notion that has remained profoundly associated with Renaissance Geistgeschichte. No matter how excessively idealized Burckhardt's version of humanist individuality may have been,[4] it was certainly a crucial step in the right direction, by granting a central place to interiority in the formation of early modern self-consciousness.

Leonardo Bruni's early Quattrocento dialogues followed a much similar path in a different format.[5] Two lively conversations, one recalls, are held on successive days at the patrician homes of Coluccio Salutati and Roberto de' Rossi. In the convivial, friendly atmosphere of the humanist *brigata,* a bright young man, Niccolò Niccoli, argues successively *against and in favour* of the singular achievements of modern Florentine culture. In the history of Renaissance criticism, from Hans Baron to David Quint and Christine Smith, this paradoxical 'double talk' has usually been interpreted as a sophisticated variation on the classical mode of arguing *in utramque partem*, on both sides of the question.[6] This intellectual technique was borrowed from the Academic sceptics – and especially Cicero, who had himself borrowed it from Aristotle.

Under Salutati's beneficial influence, the new Florentine setting and atmosphere (the practice of meeting in private homes to discuss ideas) completely transformed a dialogical structure which had been the basis of much dialectical gamesmanship in the age of scholasticism. Through the Ciceronian ideal of civic participation (*De oratore* I.viii.32–4), the medieval art of disputation was dramatically revived.[7] By foregrounding 'friendly conversation' as society's most desirable goal, Leonardo Bruni skilfully displayed his ability to compose aesthetically pleasant and mimetically defensible arguments in the culture of his own society. No matter how excessive his young spokesman might have been, Bruni's aim was to develop a model of anti-imperial history that could validate the civic morality of early modern Italian communities.

Generally speaking, the development of Renaissance dialogue has been interpreted as a healthy reaction against the increased specialization of learning in the 'waning years' of the Middle Ages:[8] a move away from the subservience to scholastic categories of thought; a reaction, as Brian Vickers has put it, against the 'dismemberment' of rhetoric into mutually exclusive *artes*, which fed treatises of specialized, technical nature.[9] Clearly the Italian Renaissance dialogue was a mixture of rhetorical art and civic humanism. As enlightened disputation, it was meant to address the problems of republican city-states in a constructive and eloquent way – an ideal that was repeatedly stressed by Italian humanists, from Lorenzo Valla to Francesco Patrizi.[10]

Besides its usefulness as a rhetorical tool for political gains, dialogue also played an increasingly important role as a mode of philosophical investigation. In the Neoplatonic culture of Quattrocento Italy, the Renaissance art of dialogue, as exemplified by Florentine humanist practices, also served to appropriate and question some of the exemplary modes of oratory inherited from classical antiquity, and, by doing so, experiment with new forms of expressivity that might challenge the basic assumptions underlying Aristotelian essentialism. If, as David Quint has shown, Bruni's dialogues already exhibit a clear sense of historical rupture with classical culture, and if the difference between antiquity and modern humanism is felt to be unbridgeable, then one can understand why the 'intellectual hero' of the Renaissance might be tempted to retreat into the private sphere of self-doubt and self-knowledge.[11]

Yet, in the golden age of Florentine humanism, this retreat away from human affairs into self-absorbed interiority cannot be adequately documented. Indeed, scepticism was not a threatening but a liberating force, a welcomed occasion for action. But, as we move from Quattrocento Florence to Cinquecento Urbino (with Castiglione) and Northern Europe (with Erasmus and Montaigne), the belief in the possibility of responsible persuasion through dialogue becomes increasingly problematized. A new, vibrant brand of Socratic irony, cut off from civic participation and stemming from a self-directed questioning impulse, gradually replaces the static, ahistorical Ciceronian model which had held its sway over Republican ideals.

In this article, I will attempt to revisit the development of dialogical techniques and intentionality in a selective sample of Cinquecento literature. Although I fully realize that much has already been written on dialogue in the literary canon of Renaissance,[12] I nevertheless propose to reexamine a few neo-Latin, Italian, and French texts and argue that, although the playful twists and turns of Niccoli's successors were not alien to the followers of the Platonic, Ciceronian, and even Lucianic tradition, they also increasingly served as a vehicle for problematizing the authority of exemplary models, pointing to what I propose to call a gradual 'inward turn' of the dialogic mode.[13]

Erasmus's *Colloquies*: Exemplarity through Dialogic Equality

Petrarch's *Secretum*, along with the satirical dialogues of Lucian, was to inspire Erasmus and many others to write similar informal *colloquia familiaria*.[14] As Craig R. Thompson has noted, the Erasmian colloquium is 'an admirable medium for expressing, freely and informally, his observations on current issues, institutions, ideas, customs, and even individuals.'[15] Their intentionality is based neither on Ciceronian 'double talk' nor on scholastic dialectical reasoning, but on a free-flowing exchange in which participants question preconceived models of authority on the basis of practical acts of charity. As such, the colloquies appropriate the virtues of dialogic art, namely transparence and plasticity, which also belong to other works by the humanist of Rotterdam.[16]

The function of the Erasmian colloquy was aptly described by Dennis

Costa as a 'sacramental economy' based on the theological notions of
oikon and *oikonomia*.[17] For instance, in the famous 'Shipwreck' – a controversial text which inspired generations of students – dialogue is used
to test the passengers' attitudes in the face of seafaring perils. Adolph
and Anthony do not openly question the efficacy of the saints as exemplary models; they simply leave it to the reader to pass judgment on the
scene they witness: the panicked travellers who invoke Venus and fran-
tically mumble prayers on their rosaries, and 'the poor little woman
with her baby' who confesses silently to God and implores His divine
mercy.[18]

  The same thing could be said, although in a more complex way, of
the *Convivium religiosum* (Godly Feast) which, like Bruni's and many
other dialogues, takes place in the setting of a country house. Yet, with
Erasmus, the fictional conversation over dinner moves to the subject of
evangelical freedom. As one of the guests, Eulalius, puts it in a controversial passage (actually condemned by the Sorbonne), 'all things are
permissible – that is a matter of gospel liberty; but one may abstain
from what is permitted, and prefer to yield to the welfare of a neighbor
rather than exercise one's liberty.'[19]

  In this new dialogic situation the onus of interpretation is placed
solely and squarely on the reader. The protagonists are still debating
successively *pro et contra* à la Niccolò Niccoli, in the convivial, friendly
atmosphere of a humanist *brigata*. Yet their double talk has lost the
intellectual disengagement of traditional sceptics. The freedom it seeks
has nothing to do with academic gamesmanship: it lies beyond the
technical art of arguing *in utramque partem*. At the same time, there is
no authority on the scene to make you select the proper moral lesson:
the ultimate exegetical gesture must come from the reader. As Victoria
Kahn puts it: 'Absence is required in order to make room for the practice of interpretation and the ethical praxis that constitutes the true *imitatio Christi*.'[20]

  Yet it would be disingenuous to argue that Erasmus did not have a
specific ideological agenda. Among all the literary genres at his disposal, he selected the dialogic form because it best fitted his purpose,
that is, to convince his readers of his worthy cause while, at the same
time, enlisting them through a pleasurable experience in debates of a
controversial and combative nature.[21] After all, his purpose was clearly
the advancement of learning and of the Christian faith. The familiar,
dispassionate, or, at times, sarcastic tone may be deceiving: contrary to
what P.S. Allen thought, his colloquia are not trifles which he threw off

to amuse himself.[22] And the self-deprecatory remarks the humanist made about his work are actually meant to ingratiate the reader, serving as a *captatio benevolentiae* to reinforce the powerful impact of a so-called minor genre. In other words, although through their form the colloquies seem to deny all exemplary status, they retain, by the way they are set up, an intentional didactic purpose which places them squarely within the rhetoric of exemplarity.[23]

Throughout the early modern period, the Latin word *exemplum* continued to refer to a specific rhetorical practice: that is, an illustrative anecdote with a moral point, although it may not have always meant to serve a definite demonstrative purpose.[24] In the Erasmian humanistic oratory, the allegation of examples never imposes upon the reader, and therefore never looks authoritarian. Only for better elocutory purposes are graphic case stories used in dialogic form to make the speech more appealing and enjoyable.[25] In the colloquies, *exemplars* (Latin *exemplaria*) are never used to provide the audience with models of conduct to imitate. In the new epistemological context, dialogue becomes a much wanted vehicle to investigate and test the applicability of canonical stories and eventually question their exemplary status. The famous quarrel about 'Ciceronianism,' in which Erasmus took an essential part, constitutes a significant chapter in the history of exemplarity. Recent scholarship has demystified not only Erasmus's but also, more generally, the humanists' idealistic claims, and pointed to the gap between their emphasis on preparation for active political responsibility and the disappointing consent of their pedagogical programs.[26]

In Erasmian colloquies an active coexistence of humanist and scholastic cultures can be traced in the way exemplarity becomes invested with the resilient spoils of dogmatism in the guise of freedom of conscience.[27] The writer's self-authorizing liberality may be ascribed to some sort of reenactment of God's freedom in the creation of a contingent universe.[28] *Exempla* are no longer the only initiative models for literary creation, which is no longer predetermined by a condition outside the writer. In this light, the discussion of free will becomes crucial to our understanding of the representation, through dialogue, of contingency and singularity, two central elements in the questioning of exemplarity.

Castiglione's *Cortegiano*: Dialogic Equality with Exemplarity

Diversity of opinions is a central feature of Baldassare Castiglione's *Libro del Cortegiano*, published in Venice in 1528. The sophisticated conversational game, staged at the court of Urbino, is made possible because the aristocratic *amorevole compagnia* shares similar values and shows mutual respect. By choosing the dialogical form, the author gives up his right to impose his preferences, a decision tempered, of course, by the residual presence of a narrator who controls the flow of discourse in a discreet way.[29]

For one thing, the book of the *Courtier* is not presented as a 'book,' with a didactically organized structure, at all, but as a freewheeling conversation, at times verging on 'self-subversion,' between aristocratic equals united by a common education, similar goals, and friendship.[30] In the opening paragraph of the first book, the author's *persona* makes this point indirectly to the reader by addressing Messer Alfonso Ariosto:

> In these books we shall follow no fixed order or rule of distinct precepts, such as are usually employed in teaching anything whatever; but after the fashion of many ancient writers, we shall revive a pleasant memory and rehearse certain discussions that were held between men singularly competent in such matters ... (8)[31]

In his *Apologia dei dialogi* Sperone Speroni will develop a theory of dialogue based on similar arguments. If you follow the path of dialogue ('il sentiero dei dialogi'), you will stroll leisurely through a delightful garden ('un giardin dilettevole') and enjoy the diversity and novelty of arguments ('la varietà e novità [delli] ragionamenti' [274]).[32] In Castiglione's *Cortegiano* the count also used the metaphor of the garden to celebrate the copiousness and fertility of the courtier's appropriate speech: 'and if it [language] were not pure old Tuscan, it would be Italian, universal, copious, and varied, and in a way like a delightful garden of various flowers and fruits' (46).[33] Dialogue, Speroni argued, makes you linger within a pleasurable labyrinth ('piacevole labirinto' [286]). This *labirincità* is meant to be set against the useful, rational, and straightforward way generally associated with Aristotelian modes of speech: 'la strada utile aristotelica, molto aspra e severa' (273).[34]

Although women do not play as important a part as men do in the dialogue, their subtle influence is strongly felt, especially in the case of the duchess, who presides over the debate with gentle firmness. As Peter Burke remarked, 'Greek and Roman dialogues had no place for women (except for courtesans, who were given a voice by Lucian'). The case was different, of course, in Boccaccio's *Decameron*, one of Castiglione's models; Pietro Bembo, Castiglione's friend, had also inserted three young ladies in his *Asolani*. Burke further remarks that, although the role of women in the *Cortegiano* may be judged minor by our standards, 'at the time it was seen as prominent enough to be edited out of the Polish and Portuguese adaptations of the text, because the adapters thought that, in their own countries women had nothing to say on topics such as these.'[35]

In the *Cortegiano* the dialogic intentionality is clear: this is not a treatise on good manners, written by a scholastic clerk, imparted with scholarly authority, pedagogical skills, and didactic purposes. In his conversation with Magnifico Juliano, the count uses the term 'clero' (from the French 'clerc') to describe this kind of studious man ('uomo di studio') who was generally despised in France: 'They [the French] hold all men of letters most base, and think they speak very basely of any man when they call him a *clerk*' (56).[36]

In the 'Lettera dedicatoria' to Don Michel de Silva, the *Libro* limits its claims to being 'un ritratto di pittura della corte d'Urbino' (25), a vivid depiction of a specific courtly atmosphere. As Carlo Ossola puts it, the move ('la traslazione') from *trattato* (treatise) to *ritratto* (portrait) preserves the lifelike presence of real voices, not allegorized substitutes, even after death has silenced them for ever.[37] This does not mean that the characters share the same ideas or agree on all matters they discuss. On the contrary: diversity of opinions pervades the atmosphere of the *Cortegiano* and offers a sharp contrast to the basic uniformity of manners. This is no Abbey of Thélème where all the participants are patterned after the same model ('les Thélémites') and react in the same way, which precludes any possibility for true dialogue. One could hardly imagine a more variegated set of characters: Bernardo, Gasparo, and Ottaviano express feelings and personal convictions about love and women, ranging from the idealist feminist position to the most caricatural forms of traditional misogyny.

Yet, realism rarely comes to mind here. The ideal aristocratic society the book tries to represent suggests a world almost entirely removed from daily necessities.[38] Just as in Bruni's Florentine prose, the reader is expected to accept the highly contrived dialogues as transparent reproductions of those that actually took place at the court of Urbino. Contrary to most medieval didactic debates, we are no longer presented with allegorical characters, representing truth and falsehood, and arguing against each other with strictly defined opposite views. We have moved away from fictional abstraction to conversational actuality. The dialogues are meant to issue forth from a set of 'real' characters, known to and loved by the author himself. They are individualized and recognizable; they speak their minds and are not afraid to show disagreement or poke fun at their friends.

In other words, regardless of its fictional form and stylistic sophistication, Castiglione's project is meant to be historically grounded.[39] From the start the author clearly defines his intentions with his prefatory insistence on the truthfulness of his writings. In the 'Lettera dedicatoria' to Don Michel De Silva, Castiglione claims that he has faithfully reproduced life scenes at Urbino and preserved them as they originally took place, 'senza adornar la verità ... o far per arte ... quello che non è' (25) (without embellishing truth ... or using art [meaning artifice] ... to make believe something that never happened [3]). Castiglione's notion of artless art is rooted in the aesthetic wisdom of classical antiquity. True art consists in concealing its artfulness: *ars latet arte sua*.[40] This means that dialogue mimics real exchange so effectively that readers will feel that they are witnessing a series of court life scenes as if they were actually present.[41] The master-disciple type of relationship has been dismissed, and the exemplary model has also been displaced. Dialogic *dispositio* no longer serves to hide an authoritarian voice. Enlightened readers are invited to join the open-ended discussion as new, full-fledged members of an honourable and joyful *amorevole compagnia*.

Marguerite de Navarre's *Heptaméron*: Dialogic Equality as Exemplarity

A similar situation can be observed in Marguerite de Navarre's *Heptaméron*, composed a few years after the first French translation of the *Cortegiano* had been published in 1537.[42] The unfinished work gives extended space to conversations and makes an even stronger claim to truth. Although, as we are told in the prologue, the new collection of tales looks superficially similar to Boccaccio's *Decameron*, it is actually patterned after a 'real' literary project that had been proposed at the French court but never actually completed. Like the members of Castiglione's *brigata*, the French fictional characters are storytellers ('devisants'), but with an equal number for each sex (five men and five women). Although modern critics have debated their real identity, they were meant to be *recognizable* courtiers in the sixteenth century. Moreover, unlike Boccaccio, who, according to his French imitator, had made up his *novelle* as he pleased, Navarre did not allow her 'devisants' to tell a story that was not 'truthful.' In the prologue to the *Heptaméron* Parlamente, Navarre's spokesperson, declared:

> I don't think there is one of you who hasn't read the hundred tales by Boccaccio, which have recently been translated from Italian into French. [Several people at court] made up their minds to do the same as Boccaccio but with one difference – that they should not write any story that was not truthful. (68)[43]

Much as in Castiglione's *Cortegiano*, rhetorical ornaments were not permitted, not because of the writer's inability to emulate trained artists but because 'art' itself might be an impediment to truthfulness. Castiglione, we recall, had presented himself as a 'humble painter,' unlike Raphael or Michelangelo, who knew only how to make rough drawings and was unable to capture the true essence of his characters. To Michel de Silva he declared:

> I send you this book as a picture of the Court of Urbino, not by the hand of Raphael or Michelangelo, but by a humble painter, who knows only to trace the chief lines, and cannot adorn truth with bright colouring, or by perspective art make that which is seem to be. (2–3)[44]

Castiglione insisted on the inadequacy of his style and the failure of his imagination in rendering the qualities and character of his personages ('non solo il mio stile non è sufficiente ad esprimerle, ma pur l'intelletto ad imaginarle' [25]).

Navarre's Parlamente gives a different reason to justify a similar attitude. When the French court decided to promote an imitation of Boccaccio's *Decameron*, she recalls, scholarly writers were excluded because one feared their very expertise might spoil the job:

> Together with Monseigneur the Dauphin the ladies promised ... to get together a party of ten people who were qualified to contribute something, excluding those who studied and were men or women of letters. For Monseigneur the Dauphin didn't want their art brought in, and he was afraid that rhetorical ornament would in part falsify the truth of the account. (68–9)[45]

Paradoxically the lack of learning and expertise is not seen as a drawback but as an advantage in fashioning a lifelike work of art. The *devisants'* easy-going conversations after each novella will therefore be based on real case stories, told 'naïvely,' that is 'naturally' by trustworthy aristocrats. The dialogue's claim to truthfulness will not be based on its inner logic and coherence but on the prediction that artlessness is synonymous with veracity.

One troubling element here, of course, is the fact that these comments are not made by the author herself but by a character of hers named Parlamente. Although Parlamente shares several features with Marguerite de Navarre, she is not a real person but a fictional construct – never to be confused with the authorial voice in the book. This may problematize the author's textual claim to truth but not the principle of reality upon which the very conception of the dialogue following each story is based. No matter who says that the original courtly project 'must now be completed' (estre mise à fin [10]), the goal is clear: exemplarity is not to be found in an objectively higher sphere defined by rules of aesthetics but in the reader's ability to engage mimetically in the open-ended discussion of unadorned and verifiable facts.

Thus, both in the *Cortegiano* and the *Heptaméron* the problem of Boccaccio's foundational model lurks in the distance. Exemplarity is never openly challenged, probably because it is inseparable from the doctrine of *imitatio*, which prescribes the sacrosanct recourse to inherited cultural models. At the same time, the appeal of *mimesis*, characterized by the stress on actual experience of the real world, can be read as a humanist reaction to scholastic insularity, which greatly problematized the reception of revered models. Whereas a long-held reverence for the imitative power of traditional *exempla* offered compelling patterns of moral conduct, the new attractiveness of a more 'natural' mimetic discourse tended to turn the study of models away from reduplication.[46]

Nowhere more clearly than in Navarre's imitation of the *Decameron* can we find expressed the principle of equality through diversity. When the time comes to choose a pastime to relieve the company, stranded by the floods in the Pyrenees, from boredom, the *devisants* propose different ideas. Oisille, the devout dowager, prescribes the reading of the Holy Scripture; Hircan, the down-to-earth male chauvinist, prefers the kind of 'physical exercise' that, as he crudely puts it, 'requires only two participants.' Parlamente, Hircan's wife, objects to her husband's sexual fantasies, and proposes a more literary pastime, in which all the participants 'will tell a story which they have either witnessed themselves, or which they have heard from somebody worthy of belief' (69). Yet, in the end, a consensus is reached, and even Hircan, the most uncompromising character, concedes that 'where games are concerned everybody is *equal*' (70) (car au jeu nous sommes tous *esgaulx* [10]).

At the same time, equality of status never entails giving up one's opinions to please others. In fact, the *devisants'* strongly opposite views are maintained and never substantially changed through dialogue. Indeed Dagoucin's idealism stands to the end in stark contrast to Hircan's entrenched antifeminism; Oisille's contemplative devotion never supersedes Parlamente's down-to-earth pragmatism. The fundamental disagreement, which occurs between the *devisants* at the end of novella XXXII, also reflects well-known polarized positions in contemporary humanist circles. John Fisher, the chancellor of Cambridge University,[47] and Jacques Lefèvre d'Etaples, the scholar and Bible translator, did not argue *in utramque partem* but took sides in heated philological debates.[48] Yet, Navarre's own ideological position cannot be identified with certainty.[49] Even to a greater degree than the author figure in the *Cortegiano*, by choosing the dialogical form, she gives up her right to imposed preferences: there is no narrator left to control the flow of discourse, even in a discreet way. At no point in the *Heptaméron*, not even in the Prologue, can we find clear authorial markings of intentionality: there is no ultimate voice to deliver a univocal message of truth.[50] In the absence of a narrator figure, no attempt can be made to resolve the tensions that arise between various shades of sensibility: they coexist side by side and interact with one another in an inconclusive, open-ended conversation and it is up to the reader to formulate his or her opinion about the issues at stake.[51]

Montaigne's *Essais*: Exemplarity Crisis and Dialogic Conscience

Finally, the evolutionary pattern I have traced finds its ultimate *telos* in Montaigne's *Essais*, characterized by what I have called a gradual 'inward turn' of the dialogical mode. It is a well-known fact that Etienne de La Boétie's premature death deprived Montaigne of the unique friend with whom he loved to converse freely. Their lively discussions are nostalgically alluded to in many passages of the *Essais*, which pass themselves off as poor substitutes for the highest form of a vanished dialogue. In the third book, a whole chapter is devoted to 'l'art de conferer' – the art of discussion. 'The most fruitful and natural exercise of our mind in my opinion,' Montaigne writes, is 'la conference' (III 8, 922b), 'the art of discussion' (III 8, 704). He whole-heartedly welcomes a vigorous, pungent engagement with kindred minds that are willing to wrestle intellectually with him. He writes:

> [b] So contradictions of opinions neither offend nor affect me; they merely arouse and exercise me ... I like a strong, manly fellowship and familiarity, a friendship that delights in the sharpness and vigor of its intercourse, as does love in bites and scratches that draw blood. [c] It is not vigorous and generous enough if it is not quarrelsome, if it is civilized and artful, if it fears knocks and moves with constraint. (705)[52]

With his intimate friend's death, Montaigne is left alone. His thought process is no longer interrupted by the sharp, contentious voice that brought 'vigor' – even against the rules of civility – to intellectual exchanges in the name of 'truth and liberty' (720). In Quintilian's terms, *altercatio* is no longer possible; it has to yield to monological *oratio perpetua* (uninterrupted speech).[53] Yet, Montaigne will try to preserve that dialogical dimension in his *Essais*, by bringing together contradictory opinions, and making them wrestle with each other. On the scene of writing, conflicting ideas become internalized: *altercatio* reappears in the form of a feisty dialogue within his own lonely self.

Take Montaigne's stand in the hot debates of his time over political and religious issues. Montaigne declared himself in favour of the monarchy and the succession to the throne. At the same time, he also criticized several extreme Roman Catholic 'Ligueurs' and praised the virtues he perceived in some Huguenot leaders: 'In the present broils of this state, my own interest has not made me blind either to the laudable qualities in our adversaries or those that are reproachable in the men I have followed' (774b).[54]

As a lawyer, magistrate, and elected official – he served twice as mayor of Bordeaux – Montaigne respected the law and was paid to ask others to do the same. He felt he had a duty to uphold the fundamental principles of political order and social conduct. By definition, civil servants are conservative: they exist to maintain the smooth functioning of the city. The mayor of Bordeaux, however, cannot completely eclipse Michel, the private man, painter of the 'passage' and believer in the relativity of things. In the *Essais* he consistently draws a line between his official position (he upholds the legitimacy of the monarchy) and his personal opinions:

> The Mayor and Montaigne have always been two, with a very clear separation. (774b) ... I adhere firmly to the healthiest of the parties, but I do not

seek to be noted as especially hostile to the others and beyond the bounds of the general reason. (774c)[55]

Montaigne refuses the generalizing statements wherein the public figure speaks for the private conscience. He wants to remain in tune with daily experience in a period of confusion, when one must often accept uncertainty and contradiction or suffer even greater moral disintegration. He admits: 'I do not know how to involve myself so deeply and so entirely' (III, 10, 774b) [Je ne sçay pas m'engager si profondement et si entier (1012b)].

Hence the necessity of the dialogic conscience, that is one which requires a complementary world view in constant response to that which denies it. In the area of political ruminations, it may be beneficial to let antagonistic forces play themselves out. Why couldn't the admirer of Henri de Guise (the Catholic extremist) also be the friend of Henri de Navarre, the head of the Huguenots?

> I condemn extraordinarily this bad form of arguing: 'He is of the League, for he admires the grace of Monsieur de Guise.' 'The activity of the King of Navarre amazes him: he is a Huguenot.' 'He finds this to criticize in the king's morals: he is seditious in his heart.' (774–5c)[56]

To be sure, dialogue has become synonymous with a sane appeal to rationality. Unfortunately, it is totally alien to polemical rhetoricians whose twists and turns are only meant to sway their audience to their side. In the public sphere, political engagement can never lend itself to subtle distinctions, because the art of persuasion requires 'clear separations' that remove all doubt or hesitation. In the opening chapter of the second book one reads:

> If I speak of myself in different ways, that is because I look at myself in different ways. All contradictions may be found in me by some twist and some fashion ... I have nothing to say about myself absolutely, simply, and solidly, without confusion and without mixture, or in one word. *Distinguo* is the most universal member of my logic. (242)[57]

The open-ended form of the essay invites recurrent questions, objections, or reservations. Reflexive operations are grafted onto the main logical thread of the discourse. Montaigne follows his exemplary model, Socrates, who would always ask questions and stir up discussion, 'never concluding never satisfying' (II, 12, 377c) [tousjours demandant et esmouvant la dispute, jamais l'arrestant, jamais satisfaisant (II, 12, 509c)]. In our perverse and inflated world of public affairs, the private subject must turn to his inner self to find, through dialogic disquisition, the true richness of moral conscience. Montaigne's movement toward interiority is also a movement toward the truth of things.[58]

Montaigne's obsessive scrutiny of ancient historical stories eventually prompted him to challenge their exemplary status. In the face of the inexhaustible diversity and unpredictability of human behaviour, how could we choose a proper model after which to pattern our own actions? Even in the absence of an ideal interlocutor, dialogue has turned 'inward' but has not 'decayed.' It has remained a master form of inquiry, a productive method for problematizing exemplarity, and, in the face of social turmoil and political corruption, for controlling the humanist's disenchantment with the traditional symbols of moral conduct.

Some considerations need to be made, at this point, about Ramist methodology and criticism. Ever since Walter Ong's ground-breaking study was published some forty years ago,[59] Renaissance scholars and historians of rhetoric have generally espoused the Jesuit's brilliant thesis. Ong held Ramus largely responsible for what he thought to be the ultimate 'decay of dialogue' in the mapping of universal knowledge. According to Ong, communication through lively speech was gradually thought to be undesirable, and it eventually disappeared. It was to be replaced with Ramus by 'diagrammatically grounded concepts.'[60] Rhetoric came to be basically reduced to *elocutio*, which was itself limited to tropes and figures. *Actio* was nominally salvaged but, in fact, played an insignificant role: in the end, 'oral delivery perished of neglect.'[61]

Walter Ong was a great scholar (his *Ramus and Talon Inventory* is a masterpiece of scholarship), but he had a truncated view of Ramus's theory. He did not heed the Ramists' insistence on separating the *artes* in theory but reconnecting them in practice. In other words, he overlooked the difference of levels in the complex interaction between dialectic and rhetoric. More recently, Kees Meerhoff has shown that Ramus and his collaborators neither neglected the theory of *actio* nor underestimated the importance of orality. Sound patterns actually play a crucial part in Ramus's *Rhetoricae Distinctiones*.[62] Very early in his works, Ramus declared that dialectic and rhetoric were sisters meant to be taken together because they were bound by a natural conjunction.[63] Contrary to Ong's claims, I myself fail to see in Ramist theory any 'declaration' against dialogue 'in favor of (silent) thought.'[64] And I propose to replace Ong's wrong-headed notion of 'decay' with that of an 'inward turn' of dialogue, as the Renaissance moved from Italy to Northern Europe.

More than fifty years ago, one recalls, Mikhail Bakhtin argued that Rabelais's own brand of *dialogism* provided an escape from the 'official' cultural order and represented a pattern of life shaped by an open, unstable, and 'polyphonic' world view.[65] One of the problems, however, with using Bakhtin's terminology and reference, is that 'polyphony' for him typified modernity and presupposed a divided subject, which is hardly recognizable in the Renaissance. At about the same time, in his stimulating study on the history of Western narrative, Erich Kahler, a lesser-known German scholar of great distinction, showed how Western fictional discourse had gradually evolved from a theologically oriented perspective to an inward-looking search for fictionalized selves. In all cultures, Kahler argued, sooner or later, the bracing magical power of epic poems and heroic romances was bound to make room for less uplifting and more humane concerns, as psychology somehow moved upstage and forced the gods and their spokespersons to recede to the wings.[66]

In this article I have simply meant to suggest that emerging modes of self-consciousness and subjectivity could be traced to a gradual 'inward turn' of dialogical questioning by reexamining a few canonical works of the Italian and French Renaissance. In England the humanist rhetoric of argument will eventually be used to break down the readers' confidence in a universally accepted set of rules, the ultimate avatar of exemplarity. As the traditional faith in *consensus omnium* is shaken, Bacon and Hobbes will try to demonstrate the necessity of promoting arbitrary standards of judgment and the impossibility of making decisions through dialogic confrontation and the shared exercise of practical reason.[67]

NOTES

1 A first version of this essay was presented in December 1997 at a special session entitled 'Printed Voices: A Comparative Outlook on Renaissance Dialogue,' at the Modern Language Association meeting in Toronto. I wish to thank Dorothea Heitsch, Reinier Leushuis, Olga Pugliese, and Jean-François Vallée for their comments and suggestions.

2 'Noli foras ire, in te redi; in interiore homine habitat veritas' (*De vera religione*, XXXIX, 72). My translation.

3 'Platon me semble avoir aymé cette forme de philosopher par dialogues à
   escient, pour loger plus decemment en diverses bouches la diversité et variation de ses propres fantasies' (*Essais*, II, 12, 509c; 377c). Roman and arabic
   numerals refer to books, chapters and pages of the *Essais* (Book II, chapter
   12, page 509 of the French text, page 377 of the English translation). References to the French text are to the Pierre Villey edition of *Essais*. The
   English translation is taken from Donald M. Frame's edition of *The Complete Essays*. Letters a, b, and c refer to the editions of 1580 (a), of 1588 (b),
   and to manuscript additions to Montaigne's copy of the 1588 edition (c).
4 Burckhardt. *Die Cultur der Renaissance in Italien.*
5 The original Latin text of Bruni's *Dialogi ad Petrum Histrum* is from *Prosatori
   latini del Quattrocento*, ed. by Garin. The English translation is taken from
   The Humanism of Leonardo Bruni, ed. by Griffiths, Hankins, and Thompson,
   19–52.
6 Baron, 'The Genesis of Bruni's *Dialogi*'; Quint, 'Humanism and Modernity';
   and Smith, *Architecture in the Culture of Early Humanism, Ethics, Aesthetics,
   and Eloquence*, chapters 7 and 8.
7 See Michel, 'L'Influence du dialogue cicéronien sur la tradition
   philosophique et littéraire.'
8 See Murphy, *Rhetoric in the Middle Ages*, 320ff.
9 Vickers, *In Defence of Rhetoric*, 236.
10 Martines, *Power and Imagination*, 195. Rhetorical and moral imperatives
   compel the historian to write for future generations in eloquent composi-
   tions. See also Watkins, *Humanism and Liberty*, 27–96.
11 Quint, 'Humanism and Modernity,' 424–5.
12 For a refreshing, synthetic presentation see Burke, 'The Renaissance Dialogue.' Burke identifies four main types of Renaissance dialogues or, at
   least, 'four positions on a spectrum': catechism, drama, disputation, and
   conversation. He also makes the point that the rise of the dialogue in the
   Renaissance cannot simply be accounted for as another case of the 'imitation of antiquity,' but, rather, that it should be investigated as a specific
   'response to a need' (7). Among recent important studies on the same topic
   are Kushner, 'Le dialogue en France au XVIe siècle: quelques critères
   génologiques'; Marsh, *The Quattrocento Dialogue*; Snyder, *Writing the Scene
   of Speaking*; Cox, *The Renaissance Dialogue*; Carron, 'La Renaissance du dialogue'; and Pugliese, *Il discorso labirintico del dialogo rinascimentale*. I am
   much indebted to these and several others.
13 I borrow this expression from Kahler's *The Inward Turn of Narrative*.
14 Thomas More, a great friend of Erasmus, could be counted among these
   imitators. We may recall that Book I of his *Utopia* is written in the form of a

dialogue. Marc'hadour, 'Thomas More: de la conversation au dialogue.'
We should also remember that both Erasmus and More translated Lucian
of Samosata and were influenced by his so-called Dialogues of the Dead.
See Thompson's Introduction to Thomas More, *Translations of Lucian*, and
to Erasmus's *Colloquies*.

15 Erasmus, *Ten Colloquies*, Introduction, xx.

16 Some of Erasmus's works carry the word 'dialogus' in their titles: *Dialogus,*
Julius exclusus e coelis; Dialogus de recta latini graecique sermonis pronuntia-
tione, and, of course, the *Dialogus Ciceronianus*. See Margolin, 'L'Art du dialogue et de la mise en scène dans le *Julius Exclusus*,' 213.

17 In his study of the *Convivium religiosum* Dennis Costa quotes Rom. 16:5, 1
Cor. 16:19, and Eph. 1:10; 3:2; 3:9. 'Domesticating the Divine Economy.'

18 Erasmus, *Ten Colloquies*, 8–9.

19 Ibid., 152

20 Kahn, *Rhetoric, Prudence and Skepticism in the Renaissance*, 92.

21 Or, as Jean-Claude Margolin puts it, 'convaincre le lecteur de la justesse de
sa cause tout en le divertissant et en le faisant participer au débat, qui se
mue assez souvent en combat' ('L'Art du dialogue,' 213).

22 Quoted by Thompson, *Ten Colloquies*, xiii.

23 On the rhetoric of exemplarity, see Lyons, *Exemplum*. See also the special
issue of the *Journal of the History of Ideas* 59, no. 4 (October 1998), devoted to
'The Renaissance Crisis of Exemplarity,' introduced by François Rigolot,
with seminal articles by Karlheinz Stierle, François Cornilliat, Timothy
Hampton, and Michel Jeanneret.

24 To the extent that choosing an *example* necessarily involves some form of
selective process from a larger quantity, every instance is bound to entertain a metonymic relation with a greater whole. But, etymologically, an
example is a *sample – essample*, in Old French spelling – one thing merely
alleged to resemble another one, not a demonstrative tool. Yet in his *Dictio-*
narie of the French and English Tongues (London, 1611), Randle Cotgrave
gave polysemous English equivalents for *exemple* and *exemplaire*:

> *Exemple*: 1) An example, *sample*, patterne, or president [*sic*] to follow; 2)
> a copie or counterpane of a writing; 3) one thing alleged *to prove*, or
> *inforce* another that resembles it.
> *Exemplaire*: 1) A patterne, *sample*, or *sampler*, 2) an example, president
> [*sic*] or precedent, for others to follow, or to take heed by; 3) also, the
> copie, or counterpane of a writing.

There is an odd mixture of demonstrative and nondemonstrative connotations. The two seemingly interchangeable words receive tripartite defini-

tions, with the meanings 1) 2) 3) of *exemple* corresponding to 1) 3) 2) of *exemplaire*.

25 This practice is clearly inherited from Plato, as Montaigne will discover: 'Platon me semble avoir aymé cette forme de philosopher par dialogues à escient, pour loger plus decemment en diverses bouches la diversité et variation de ses propres fantasies' [Plato seems to me to have favored this form of philosophizing in dialogues deliberately, to put more fittingly into diverse mouths the diversity and variation of his own ideas] (*Essais*, II 12, 509c; 377c).

26 See Grafton and Jardine, *From Humanism to the Humanities*, xii–xvi.

27 On freedom of conscience in the sixteenth century, see Lecler, 'Liberté de conscience'; and, more recently, Guggisberg, Lestringant, and Margolin, *La Liberté de conscience*.

28 See Langer, *Divine and Poetic Freedom in the Renaissance*. He offers interesting parallels between theological concepts and narrative strategies in major sixteenth-century literary texts. Certain traits of Pulci's *Morgante*, Aristo's *Furioso*, or Rabelais's *Pantagruel* and *Gargantua* can be explained, often productively, in terms of the distinction between absolute and hypothetical necessity. In the same way, the political problem of the 'gratuitousness of reward' can be significantly illuminated by reference to the nominalist theory of 'condign' and 'congruous' merit, which helps fashion the emergence of arbitrariness and unmotivatedness in modern literature.

29 As Piero Floriani puts it, Castiglione 'rigidly holds in his own hand and keeps for himself the direction [of the narrative] with a discreet but continuous presence' ('Il dialogo e la corte nel primo cinquecento,' 91). My translation.

30 See Greene, '*Il Cortegiano* and the Choice of a Game.'

31 'Noi in questi libri non seguiremo un certo ordine o regula di precetti distinti, che 'l più delle volte nell'insegnare qualsivoglia cosa usar si sole; ma alla foggia di molti antichi, rinovando una grata memoria, recitaremo alcuni ragionamenti, i quali già passarono tra omini singularissimi a tale proposito ...' (I, 1, 32). All references to *Il Libro del Cortegiano* are to the edition provided by Ettore Bobora. References to the book (in roman numerals), paragraphs, and pages (in arabic numerals) are inserted between round brackets in the text. English translations are from *The Book of the Courtier*, translated by Leonard Eckstein Opdycke.

32 Speroni, *Dialogo della rettorica e Aplogia dei dialogi*, 274.

33 'e se ella [lingua] non fosse pura toscana antica, sarebbe italiana, commune, copiosa e varia, e quasi come un delicioso giardino pien di diversi fiori e frutti' (I, 35, 74).

34 On the concept of *labirincità* see Pugliese, *Il discorso labirintico*, 28ff. Several modern critics, including Virginia Cox and Jon R. Snyder have commented on Speroni's defence of the 'piacevole labirinto.' See Pugliese's bibliography on the subject in *Il discorso labirintico*.
35 'Burke, 'The Renaissance Dialogue,' 9.
36 'Tutti i litterati tengon [i Francezi] per vilissimi omini; e pare lor dir gran villania a chi si sia, quando lo chiamano *clero*' (I, 42, 84).
37 Ossola, *Dal 'Cortegiano' all''Uomo di mondo,'* 29. I wish to thank Reinier Leushuis for this reference.
38 For instance, the 'donna di palazzo' is the perfect court lady who gives the tone to the conversations. True, there is little evidence of sensual excess, such as Johan Huizinga's 'waning' or 'autumn' of the Middle Ages (*Herfsttij der middeleeuwen*); nor do we find the kind of 'kreatürlicher Realismus' that Erich Auerbach attributed to some late medieval conceptual patterns (*Mimesis*, 216ff). Yet, if by *realism* we mean a concern for lifelike reality, its eloquent presence can evidently be found here.
39 See Alain Pons's introduction to Gabriel Chappuis's sixteenth-century translation of Castiglione, *Le Livre du Courtisan*, xiii.
40 Ovid, *Metamorphoses*, X, v.252.
41 See Rigolot, 'The Rhetoric of Presence.'
42 Castiglione, *Le Courtisan, nouvellement traduit de langue italique en françois*, 1537). Most scholars agree today that the *Heptaméron* was composed between 1542 and 1545. See Salminen's critical edition (1997), vol. 2, 'Genèse du recueil,' 33.
43 'Je croy qu'il n'y a nulle de vous qui n'ait leu les cent Nouvelles de Bocace, nouvellement traduictes d'ytalien en François. [Plusieurs courtisans ...] se delibererent d'en faire autant, sinon en une chose differente de Bocace, c'est de n'escrire nulle nouvelle qui ne soit veritable histoire' (9). All references to the French text are to *L'Heptaméron*, ed. by Michel François. The English translation is from *The Heptameron*, trans. by P.A. Chilton, with a fair degree of modification. Page numbers will be placed between round brackets in the text. Unfortunately Chilton's translation contains many small errors (here: 'nulle de *vous*' is rendered by 'one of *us*').
44 'Mandovi questo libro come un ritratto di pittura della corte d'Urbino, non di mano di Rafaello o Michel Anglelo, ma di pittor ignobile e che solamente sappia tirare le linee principali, senza adornar la verità de vaghi colori o far parer per arte di prospettiva quello que non è' (25).
45 'Et prosmirent les dictes dames et monseigneur le Dauphin ... d'assembler jusques à dix personnes qu'ilz pensoient plus dignes de racompter quelque chose, sauf ceulx qui avoient estudié et estoient gens de letters: car mon-

seigneur le Dauphin ne voulloit que leur art y fut meslé, et aussy de paour que la beaulté de la rethoricque feit tort en quelque partye à la verité de l'histoire' (9).

46 On Renaissance imitation, see Cave, *The Cornucopian Texte*; Greene, *The Light in Troy*; and Greenblatt, *Renaissance Self-Fashioning*. The complex relationship between Renaissance *imitatio* and *mimesis* was carefully studied by Michel Jeanneret in his *A Feast of Words*, 259–83.

47 A symposium on Bishop Fisher was held at Cambridge in 1985, on the 450th anniversary of his death. What emerges from the volume of proceedings is a troubling multifaceted personality: conservative and controversialist, mystically pacifist and insurrectionist, persecutor and martyr. See Bradshaw and Duffy, *Humanism, Reform and the Reformation*.

48 About Jacques Lefèvre d'Etaples, see Renaudet, *Préréforme et humanisme à Paris pendant les premières guerres d'Italie (1494–1517)*, and Bedouelle, *Lefèvre d'Etaples et l'intelligence des Ecritures*, as well as Rice's edition of *Prefatory Epistles of Jacques Lefèvre d'Etaples and Related Texts*. Rigolot, in 'The *Heptaméron* and the Magdalen Controversy,' examined the relation between Marguerite de Navarre's *Heptaméron* and the controversy over the 'three Marys.'

49 For instance, Oisille and Parlamente speak in favour of a philological *distinguo*, whereas Ennasuite sides with the defenders of the traditional consensus. See Rigolot, 'The *Heptaméron* and the Magdalen Controversy,' 225–6.

50 Parlamente, not Marguerite, sets the rules of the game in the Prologue of the *Heptaméron*. About Marguerite's ambivalence, as reflected in the composition and design of her book, see Tetel, *Marguerite de Navarre's Heptaméron*. On the problematic status of exemplarity in the Renaissance, see Stierle, 'L'Histoire comme exemple, l'exemple comme histoire,' and, more specifically on Marguerite, Lyons, *Exemplum*, chapter 2. In her 'La nouvelle exemplaire ou le roman tenu en échec,' Cazauran notices an interesting tension between 'le souci d'un sens exemplaire' and 'l'exégèse jamais achevée des devisants.'

51 This may partly reflect Navarre's own interior debate as she was herself torn between her deep respect for popular religious rituals and her active intellectual support of evangelical humanists who criticized them.

52 '[b] Les contradictions donc des jugemens ne m'offencent ny m'alterent; elles m'esveillent seulement et m'exercent ... J'ayme une societé et familiarité forte et virile, une amitié qui se flatte en l'aspreté et vigueur de son commerce, comme l'amour, és morsures et esgratigneures sanglantes. [c] Elle n'est pas assez vigoureuse et genereuse, si elle n'est querelleuse, si elle est civilisée et artiste, si elle craint le hurt et a ses allures contreintes' (III, 8, 924).

53 See Goyet, *Le Sublime du lieu commun*, 692–3.

54 'Aux presens brouillis de cet estat mon interest ne m'a fait mesconnoistre ny les qualitez louables de nos adversaires, ny celles qui sont reprochables en ceux que j'ay suivy' (III, 10, 1012b).

55 'Le Maire et Montaigne ont tousjours esté deux, d'une separation bien claire.' (III, 10, 1012b) ... 'Je me prens fermement au plus sain des parties, mais je n'affecte pas qu'on me remarque specialement ennemy des autres, et outre la raison generalle' (III, 10, 1013c).

56 'J'accuse merveilleusement cette vitieuse forme d'opiner. Il est de la Ligue, car il admire la grace de Monsieur de Guise. L'activeté du Roy de Navarre l'estonne: il est Huguenot. Il treuve cecy à dire aux moeurs du Roy: il est seditieux en son coeur' (III 10, 1013c).

57 'Si je parle diversement de moy, c'est que je me regarde diversement. Toutes les contrarietez s'y trouvent selon quelque tour et en quelque façon. ... Je n'ay rien à dire de moy, entierement, simplement, et solidement, sans confusion et sans meslange, ny en un mot. *Distinguo* est le plus universel membre de ma Logique' (II, 1, 335b).

58 Starobinski, *Montaigne en mouvement*. See also Fumaroli, 'Montaigne et l'éloquence du for intérieur.'

59 Ong, *Ramus, Method, and the Decay of Dialogue*.

60 Ibid., 270.

61 'Within the two-part rhetoric, the spatial and visual carries the day still further. The second half of rhetoric, *oral* delivery, perishes of neglect, and the first half, *elocutio*, is, by the appearance of the later *Rhetoric*, resolved in terms of tropes ("turnings" – a diagrammatically grounded concept) and figures ("shapes" – another visually based notion) ... Hence, shying away instinctively from sound and thus from figures, Ramist rhetoric will declare in favor of tropes when a choice between tropes and figures has to be made. This is a declaration against sound in favor of (silent) thought; but thought is conceived in terms of (ornamental) structure, with the aid of a spatial model ("turnings")' (Ibid., 281).

62 Meerhoff, *Rhétorique et poétique au XVIᵉ siècle en France*, 213, quotes Ramus, *Rhetoricae Distinctiones*, 92–3.

63 'Rhetorica ... naturalem sororis dialecticae coniunctionem libenter audiet' (Ramus, *Dialecticae Institutiones*), f. 58 and f. 54, quoted by Meerhoff, ibid., 183, note 21.

64 Ong, *Ramus, Method, and the Decay of Dialogue*, 281.

65 Bakhtin, *Rabelais and His World*, written during the Second World War, was published in Moscow only in 1965, and translated into English and French in 1968 and 1970. Although for almost twenty years this study was received

favourably, in the last decade it has been harshly criticized by a new generation of critics. See Berrong, *Rabelais and Bakhtin* [reviewed by F. Rigolot in *Renaissance Quarterly* 40, no. 2 (summer 1987), 354–7].

66 Kahler, *The Inward Turn of Narrative.*
67 See Stanley Fish's analysis of Bacon's use of the *in utramque partem* argument in *Self-Consuming Artifacts,* and Victoria Kahn's analysis of Hobbes's first two books of *Leviathan* in her *Rhetoric, Prudence, and Skepticism in the Renaissance,* 155ff.

The Utopia of Dialogue

Dialogue, Utopia, and the Agencies of Fiction

Nina Chordas

Dialogue and utopia in the early modern period have not traditionally been discussed in terms of each other. Yet the two arguably greatest utopias of the Renaissance – Thomas More's paradigmatic *Utopia* and Tommaso Campanella's *City of the Sun* – are written as dialogues; and, though later utopias of the period no longer employ dialogue directly, I would suggest that the form continues to haunt them. Clearly, then, a connection exists between early modern dialogue and the texts that elaborate the alternative worlds staged by their authors as demonstrable improvements over the social orders of their day: a connection that is grounded in the problematic standing of both dialogue and utopia in relation to fiction. This relationship generates many questions: How do the dialogue form and utopia interact with each other? What is the cultural work performed by this interaction? I will argue here that early modern utopia, with its affinity for dialogical settings, is a quintessentially humanist production; that the recent availability of the New World as an arena for the possible staging of utopian projects gives them an urgency that exceeds the more subjunctive presentation of Plato's *Republic*; and finally, that early modern utopia, enabled by the dialogue, is closely allied with nascent imperialism in the period. In addition to the utopian texts that are written in dialogue form, I will briefly address some later examples that do not use this form, concluding with the discussion of a document – Edmund Spenser's *A View of the Present State of Ireland* – that, though written in dialogue form, is not generally considered a utopian text, but for which I will argue the necessity of a utopian reading if we are to understand the nature of the reciprocity between dialogue, utopia, and imperialism during the Renaissance.

Both dialogue and utopia are what might be called quasi-fictional genres, and this shared hybrid status constitutes what is perhaps the main axis of their relationship. Though both are often thought of and discussed as fictional genres, this status is complicated in that each has a purchase on what we experience as extrafictional reality: both insist on being accepted as entities with some agency in the actual, material world – dialogue as recorded discussion, utopia as a geographical place (albeit one of vague locale) or, alternately, a space created within the reader. It is probably well to remember that the labels 'fiction' and 'nonfiction' do not operate in the early modern period in the same sense that they do for us today; although I avoid the term 'nonfiction' for precisely this reason, the term 'fiction' as I use it here should be broadly understood to mean 'invention' in its early modern sense as denoting a product of the human imagination, and falling under the category of what was then termed 'poesy.'[1] In the early modern period, however, the relationship of dialogue and utopia has to be understood also within the context of a general distrust of imaginative literature, with its potentially seductive effect on the rational mind: an anxiety about the nature of fiction that is at least partly the result of what Ronald Levao describes as a growing Renaissance view of culture as relativistic, 'not as structured by eternal categories, but as a distinctly human artifact.' With such an unmooring, 'the pleasures of feigning are often linked to the darker possibilities suggested by sixteenth-century usage, an equivocation suggested by its etymology: "fingére," to shape, fashion, or contrive, is the root of both "fiction" and "figment."'[2] It is in this climate of distrust that Sidney produces his *Defence of Poetry*.

At the same time, certain urgent factors present in the early modern period lend to both dialogue and utopia – and particularly when the two are conjoined – an aspect of verisimilitude that throws into doubt their fictional aspect while not entirely negating it. These factors include the fairly recent discovery of the New World, and a didactic humanist outlook that believes in the perfectibility of man and values discourse as both a means of teaching and arriving at what is true. To Oskar Kristeller's characterization of humanism as 'a broad cultural and literary movement,' one of whose major contributions was the humanists' firm belief 'that in order to write and to speak well it was necessary to study and to imitate the ancients,' I would add that the humanist interest in *imitatio* included the appropriation, through trans-lation, of classical rhetoric to contemporary cultures and vernaculars.[3] Because humanism replicated itself through its great influence on higher education throughout Europe, and humanists frequently served as advisers and aides to figures of state, the movement is not without political connections. While neither the novelty of discovery nor the influence of humanism remain static over the course of the period, both inform the utopian texts of the time, and play an important part in their employment of both the dialogue form and its traces, contributing to the play of a fictional construct that begs the question of its own fictionality. In order to understand the powerful impetus of this pull between the fictive and the actual in early modern utopias, particularly when conjoined with dialogue, it may help to first focus on each component alone.

Dialogue has a long and venerable history both as a tool of analysis and as a fictional medium; its eclipse in our time often blinds us to the immense popularity it enjoyed for centuries, perhaps in part because we have ceased to find the form entertaining. Its fictionality (despite its ostensible 'reporting' of actual conversation) gets a knowing wink from Philip Sidney in his *Defence of Poetry* when he observes that 'even [in] Plato whosoever well considereth shall find that in the body of his work, though the inside and strength were philosophy, the skin, as it were, and beauty depended most of poetry: for all standeth upon dialogues, wherein he feigneth many honest burgesses of Athens to speak of such matters, that, if they had been set on the rack, they would never have confessed them.'[4] Indeed, Jon R. Snyder, in *Writing the Scene of Speaking*, tells us that 'dialogues are never transcriptions of conversations or debates that actually occurred (although this is one of their enabling fictions); no unmediated traces of orality can be discovered in dialogue, except in the form of a carefully constructed illusion.'[5] Traditionally, then, and despite its pretensions to the contrary, dialogue has been viewed as a form of mimesis, an art which Sidney attributes to 'poesy,' or fiction: 'poesy therefore is an art of imitation, for so Aristotle termeth it in his word *mimesis*, that is to say, a representing, counterfeiting, or figuring forth – to speak metaphorically, a speaking picture – with this end, to teach and delight.'[6] The didacticism of the dialogue form is perhaps exactly what lessens its appeal for us today; nevertheless, as Sidney's famous characterization makes clear, didacticism was not always considered a liability, particularly when sweetened with mimetic art.

The Italian Renaissance poet, Torquato Tasso, elaborates on the mimetic aspect of dialogue and extends it in his *Discourse on the Art of the Dialogue*:

We have said that dialogues are imitations of discussions and that the dialectical dialogues imitate disputations. It follows that those who are involved in discussing and disputing will reveal both their opinions and their character, and these – opinions and character – are the essential parts of the dialogue. The writer of a dialogue must be an imitator no less than the poet; he occupies a middle ground between poet and dialectitian.[7]

Tasso here makes a claim for dialogue as a hybridized form, part fiction and part philosophy. In addition to the subject under disputation, the superior dialogues – of which Cicero and Plato were generally considered the premier models – incorporated elements of characterization, setting, and plot. Richard A. Preto-Rodas points out that in the dialogues of the sixteenth-century Portuguese courtier, Francisco Rodrigues Lobo, considerations of plot actually reveal the hybrid nature of the dialogue in that the plot may be said to be 'about' the disputation and the interlocutors as they engage in their debate. 'Hence,' he adds, 'an attempt to judge the dialogue as essentially dramatic or substantially expositional does violence to the dual character of the genre as a philosophical enquiry in dramatic form.'[8] The process which produces this dual character is elaborated by Snyder, who contends that even in such highly 'literary' dialogues as Castiglione's *Il Cortegiano* and More's *Utopia*, the 'restricted narrative structure that mimics real-life conversation and its marked tendency toward an expository prose bordering on documentary fiction' prevents the 'complete literarization' of the dialogue form. He concludes that 'even in its most sophisticated form, dialogue shuttles between the literary and the extra-literary, disrupts the boundaries between fiction and nonfiction, and explores the tension between figure and statement.'[9] It is precisely this hybridity of what we today term 'fiction' and 'nonfiction' that dialogue shares with utopia; Snyder seems to ascribe the quasi-fictionality of a text such as *Utopia* directly to the effect of the dialogue form (however attenuated) at work within it. I would suggest that other factors contribute toward establishing the utopian text in its ambiguous place between fiction and reality as well.

   If, as Virginia Cox suggests, 'dialogue reflects on its own process of communication and the response it will elicit,'[10] the fact that it is a prose medium also signals what some of its protocols will be; among them are a distancing from the overt fictionality of poetry, and an adaptability for conducting metadiscourses on its own processes. The fact that it is conducted in prose, in other words, tends to mitigate the fictionality of dialogue; as Roland Greene and Elizabeth Fowler put it in their introduction to *The Project of Prose*, prose is 'a medium that offers itself as a virtual approximation of reality itself.'[11] Thus, in spite of its status as fiction, dialogue is the medium Plato uses to banish poets from his Republic: the obverse of dialogue's fictionality, as I have suggested, is its tendency to lend an air of verisimilitude to its subject matter, as of a conversation overheard.

Utopia too is a genre whose status as fiction is not as clear-cut as might seem at first glance: in spite of being considered fictional, it has a long and well-documented career in the material world, beginning with More's *Utopia* itself. The risk of implementation is a hazard faced by all utopias, no matter how patently fictive: someone, somewhere, will always be willing to put them to the test. In the same year that More was beheaded for his opposition to the break of the English church from Rome, the humanist Bishop Vasco de Quiroga was seeking to implement the features of utopian society among the indigenous population of New Spain, in what is now Mexico City.[12] James Holstun, in fact, characterizes Quiroga's project of making a praxis out of Utopia as a 'misreading' of More: mistaking a bit of humanist fiction for an actual blueprint. It must be said, conversely, that other utopias begin their existence with the full intent of being realized in actual praxis; for instance, the social and religious projects of the Puritans in New England, as well as the French Jesuits in what is now Canada, may be termed utopian for their idealistic visions of perfected societies.[13] At the same time, these real-world utopian projects take shape on paper every bit as much as their fictional counterparts; because they start life as an imaginary projection they retain a relationship with fiction that most quotidian reality does not share. It is this reciprocal relationship between the real and the imaginary that characterizes utopia both on paper and out in the 'real' world. Moreover, utopia is characterized by discourses that carry authoritative cultural and historical weight (all of them, it might be pointed out, conducted in prose); labelling *Utopia* a piece of prose fiction completely elides the legal, political, anthropological, historical, and other kinds of discourses it incorporates. These discourses give utopia an authority in the world that eludes most fiction. In this sense, utopia subverts the view that posits Renaissance fiction as a site for the working out of real-world problems; rather, in the implementation of utopia, the real is made to work for the imaginary.

One of the factors increasing the believability of More's text is precisely the placement of his fictional society in the New World, initially encountered by Columbus a mere twenty-four years before *Utopia's* publication. Unlike Plato's *Republic*, whose construction among Socrates and his interlocutors is conjectural and located within their discourse rather than being assigned a specific geographical place, Utopia is presented as having a material existence in the world, albeit in a part of it still 'new' to Europeans, largely unknown and therefore subject to speculation. If we take the general Renaissance anxiety about the nature of fiction to be at least partly the result of what Ronald Levao describes as a growing Renaissance suspicion that culture might be a human construction rather than the result of fixed and eternal categories, the location of a fiction in the New World could potentially deflect some of this anxiety: perhaps eternal categories applied differently there, or appeared in different guises. These possibilities, combined with humanism's didacticism and belief in man's potential for perfectibility, are the strains which converge in early modern utopian visions, which gain momentum particularly when coupled with a perception of the Americas as a vast tabula rasa, or empty stage upon which to project such visions. When presented in the course of a dialogue including an interlocutor who is introduced as having actually been to the New World, these imagined societies acquire a purchase on truth that is potentially more than hypothetical. This is perhaps why the New World, as much as the dialogue form, continues to hover in the wings of utopian texts produced in the period, even after the novelty of discovery has worn off, and perhaps part of the reason the New World is so often perceived as a venue for the staging of utopian projects. It is also in the articulation of utopian agendas (often in the guise of conversation through the dialogue form or its later manifestations), and in their implementation (particularly when envisioned with indigenous Americans as the foil for or object of these social experiments), that humanism becomes implicated in the nascent imperialism that takes shape in the Renaissance. I will have more to say about this implication later in the essay.

   Both dialogue and utopia, then, have a foot in the fictional and extra-fictional worlds. In their reciprocity they affirm each other's fictionality, and at the same time undermine it by insisting on an agency in the material world. More's singular text, *Utopia* (1516), may be used as a case in point. We know that Book II, in which the description of Utopian society is given, was written prior to Book I, an extended dialogue between three interlocutors, two of them representations of actual historical figures; moreover, there is little dialogue in Book II, most of which is taken up with Raphael Hythloday's description of Utopia. It is only near the end of Hythloday's exposition on the Utopians that the More character breaks in, and then to express scepticism about the feasibility of such a society, at least in contemporary Europe.[14] It is primarily Book I that gives *Utopia* its dialogic character, not only by staging its own protracted dialogue on the advisability of counselling princes, but by allowing the monologue of Book II to read like an extension of that dialogue, carrying over with it both the speaker and his implied audience.

Staging itself in the context of an actual, historically verifiable diplomatic mission, and incorporating a dialogue that airs not only humanist but specifically English concerns, Book I furnishes its readers with the set of social, political, and philosophical issues that will provide the touchstones in negotiating between the known reality of England and Europe, and the fictional society of Utopia. In his discussion of the adaptation of classical dialogue form in England in the sixteenth century, K.J. Wilson notes that dialogues of this period are often concerned with 'expressions of English nationalism ... reflections of peculiarly English social, religious, and other preoccupations in their literary art.'[15] In fact, More prepares his English (and, of course, Continental) readers for their exercise in negotiation between the worlds of fiction and historical reality. Fictional examples creep into the serious dialogue of Book I, prefiguring and indeed naturalizing the existence of Utopia itself; Polylerites and Achorians are discussed alongside Persians, Venetians, French, and other peoples whose existence is well known to More's audience.

What is required of the reader here is nothing less than the ability to sift through the fiction being presented and glean from it whatever is applicable and even desirable in the real world.[16] More plants his text thick with signposts that signal its fictionality – not the least of which is his narrator who, in spite of being established as a wise and reasonable speaker in Book I, bears a name that identifies him as a purveyor of nonsense.[17] At the same time, its grounding in historical issues and events, conveyed in the form of a dialogue in which a persona representing its author is a participant (despite the fact that this persona is named Morus, which means 'Fool' in Latin), lends to the entire work an aura of possibility that actually fooled some of its readers, as we have seen with the example of Bishop Quiroga. The accompanying half-earnest, half-jesting correspondence concerning Utopia between More and his Continental humanist friends further blurs the line between fiction and reality, at the same time extending the dialogue within the work into an epistolary context that moves the discussion from one merely reported to one taking place in real time. Michael Ames, on a different topic, speaks of 'how popular events and institutions through their daily work can ... turn ideology into common sense and thereby increase its hegemonic power.'[18] He describes here the process of making ideology seem natural, a matter of normal daily affairs, unquestioned because invisible. The presentation of the utopian project as a topic of humanist discourse thus helps to naturalize a phenomenon which Holstun characterizes as 'something done to others,' one actually going 'beyond an act of individual or collective self-fashioning to an act of fashioning selves for others, whether they like it or not.'[19] Nowhere is this imposition of a naturalized humanist ideology upon populations, silenced both by conquest and in their status as patients operated upon by that ideology, more evident than in the various utopian agendas carried out by Europeans in the New World.

We can see the process adumbrated in More's description of the conquest of Abraxa by Utopus, who not only renames the territory as a feminized version of himself, but actually reshapes it according to his own vision. In *Utopia* this entire violent episode is briefly summed up:

> They say (and the appearance of the place confirms this) that their land was not always an island. But Utopus, who conquered the country and gave it his name (it had previously been called Abraxa) brought its rude and uncouth inhabitants to such a high level of culture and humanity that they now excel in that regard almost every other people. After subduing them at his first landing, he cut a channel fifteen miles wide where their land joined the continent, and caused the sea to flow around the country.[20]

Visions of bringing a 'rude and uncouth' population to 'a high level of culture and humanity' thus justify the violent means of bringing about such a desirable result; the casual elision of the violence attending this process in the course of a reported conversation once again helps to make of the utopian agenda an unquestioned matter of course for the conquering and reshaping entity. The humanistic residue of the operation begun in violence, the resulting ideal society, effaces the means by which it has been brought into being.

We see violence casually glossed over in another great utopian text of the period. Like *Utopia*, Tommaso Campanella's *City of the Sun* (ca. 1600) is presented as a dialogue. Written nearly a century after More's, this text bears the signs of a form in decline: both setting and character development are minimal (the two interlocutors, the Hospitaler and the Genoese, are so perfunctory they may as well be labelled Q and A), and the dialogue is presented in an 'ordered' mode, controlled by a visual representation of the speakers, whose words are preceded by their designations in capital letters rather than arising naturally in the course of discussion.[21] Although the City of the Sun appears to be located somewhere in South Asia, the Genoese's account of what happens upon his arrival in the vicinity echoes New World tropes:

HOSPITALER: Tell me, please, all that happened to you on the voyage.

GENOESE: I have already told you how I sailed around the world and came to Taprobana, where I was forced to put ashore, how I hid in a forest to escape the fury of the natives, and how I came out onto a great plain just below the equator.

HOSPITALER: What happened to you there?

GENOESE: I soon came upon a large company of armed men and women, and many of them understood my language. They led me to the City of the Sun.[22]

The Genoese, described as 'one of Columbus's sailors,' presumably is familiar with the ways by which native fury may be aroused. As in *Utopia*, once the violence of initial encounter has been quickly glossed over, the dialogue dwells instead on ethnographic details.

While early print culture had retained a conception of knowledge as an essentially discursive activity, and had therefore been an ideal medium for the humanist dialogue, the progressive development of what Cox calls the 'solipsistic mental habits of print culture' gradually separated thought from the world of discourse.[23] Without this grounding in speech as intrinsic to the process of reasoning, dialogue began to lose its raison d'être. Later utopias of the early modern period reflect this shift. Francis Bacon's *New Atlantis* (1626), for example, is typical of these later utopias in its use of dialogue to enhance the narrative, rather than vice versa. At the same time, the location of the island is still given in distinctly geographic terms ('We sailed from Peru,' the narrative begins), without an interlocutor to mediate the receiving of information, the reader directly shares in the consternation and bewilderment of the mariners, somewhere in this as yet to be discovered corner of the globe, and learns with them about the mysteries of Bensalem. In the course of their instructions, the Bensalemites reveal an extraordinary feature of their society: they know the world, but the world does not know them. The situation mirrors an increasing interiority in the pursuit of knowledge, as discussion and disputation cease to be primary ways of discovering what is true and are replaced by an ever more formalized empiricism. This retreat to an inner space, from which the subject apprehends the rest of the world, is articulated by Francis Barker:

> The very writing, which as its epistemological principle grasps the outer world as an accessible transparency, recedes from that world towards an inner location where the soul – or, as the modern terminology has it, positionality in discourse – apparently comes to fill the space of meaning and desire. The boundaries of the outer context, designated as much by discourse as by a physical separation of space, are clearly defined, and the real energies and interests of the text then locate themselves within these frontiers.[24]

This new interiority, and the profound epistemological reorganization implied by it, are historically determined phenomena whose consolidation coincides more or less with the consolidation of bourgeois hegemony in the seventeenth century, in England specifically during the revolutionary period.[25] In the context of the sort of interiority described above, which begins to be represented in New Atlantis as an early instance, dialogue becomes superfluous: 'When the mariners try to reciprocate the information they have received by telling the officials something about their own country, they are told not to bother, for nothing the mariners tell them can possibly be new: the officials already know all about Europe through their secret intelligence, both what the mariners tell them and more.'[26] Although the mariners will communicate what they have learned in Bensalem (the narrator is in fact doing just that), they will do so by replicating the monologism of the original instruction.

As the novelty of the New World wears off and the earth's geography becomes increasingly documented, early modern utopias retreat, along with dialogue, into an interior space. Though filled with discourse, this is no longer represented in the form known as 'dialogue'; rather, dialogue becomes (as in Bacon) speech reported as part of the narrative, no longer constituting the narrative in itself. Because this kind of speech is so intrinsic to these utopias – as though their authority depends on reporting what was told to the narrator – I would argue that dialogue, whether directly represented or not, permeates the very way of thinking about utopia in this period. Within this framework I would like to take note of two early modern utopias – *Christianopolis* (1619) by Johann Valentin Andreae,[27] and *The Blazing World* (1666) by Margaret Cavendish[28] – that, though not written in dialogue form, are nevertheless so heavily permeated with its vestiges that they may almost, in whole or in part, be considered dialogues. No longer located in geographical space, these utopias instead find their locus within the mind of the reader; still shadowed by a New World that is no longer new, they displace the act of geophysical discovery with a recognition and creation, respectively, of interior worlds.

If utopia uses ideal societies instrumentally for imposing a fictional construct on the material world, we have seen that dialogue aids the process of imposition by naturalizing the utopian agenda as a subject of discourse. A text that serves as a ready example of this process is Edmund Spenser's *A Vewe of the Present State of Irelande*.[29] Written in 1596 from the standpoint of an English colonial subject in Ireland, this polemical tract seeks to persuade Spenser's queen, Elizabeth I, to employ extreme means toward the goal of finally subjugating Ireland to English rule. Though not considered a utopian text, *A Vewe* fits the rubric suggested here: it proposes the forcible imposition of an ostensibly 'better' ideal (the model of an idealized English countryside, complete with English laws and customs) on an 'other' material reality (the Irish land, with its own people, customs, and traditions). Moreover, this proposal is made in dialogue form: two characters named Eudoxus and Irenius discuss the barbaric state of the Irish people, and how this unfortunate situation may be remedied through the application of English law, with or without Irish cooperation. Although it may be argued that both characters employ a similar style of diction, we could say that Eudoxus functions as the representative of central and moderate (English) order, while Irenius, for all his superior knowledge of Irish customs, represents a rough and passionate advocate of extreme measures against the Irish.[30] Thus, while grudging admiration is accorded to certain features of Irish custom and history, approximately two-thirds of *A Vewe* is taken up with delineating a scheme for bringing the Irish to a 'love of goodnes and Civilityc' through a brutal policy combining military force and famine. This harsh course is intended to relieve the Irish of the suffering caused by their backwardness, stubbornness, and Irishness, while allowing the English to appropriate their lands. I have argued that the New World informs most (if not all) utopian texts of the early modern period, and Spenser's is no exception, as the 'savage' Irish become conflated with the cannibalistic 'savages' of America; Spenser boasts (through Irenius) that if his proposal is implemented, the end will be 'verye shorte ... they would quicklye consume themselves and devour one another.'[31] In fact, the very term 'savage' (or 'salvage') connotes first and foremost the indigenous Americans, to whom it is consistently applied throughout the course of this period.

Although Spenser's *Vewe* has an overtly real-world political purpose, the status of dialogue as a fictional form is foregrounded here instead, using the fictive interlocutors to create a space into which the author might disappear. Spenser's choice of the dialogue form, however, need not have been the result solely of his wish to distance himself from the views put forth in *A Vewe*; clearly, dialogue presented a method through which the author could anticipate the questions and reactions of his audience. Attending to these in the course of the discussion, he makes a better case for the drastic measures proposed by Irenius, reinforcing their logic according to Irenius's arguments. If Irenius is engaged in a project of diplomacy as he attempts to persuade his audience – represented by Eudoxus – of the rectitude of his plan, there is no room for diplomacy within the plan itself. Ireland and England are not to coexist on the same plane, unless Ireland can be subsumed into an English order. In the course of his polemic against the Irish, Spenser actually records Irish customs and traditions that his plan will eventually be instrumental in destroying, perhaps unintentionally preserving them for posterity.[32] The Ireland of *A Vewe* may thus be read as destined to be subdued by the civilizing force of English law and custom, in the process bringing the 'rude and uncouth' Irish (the ones who survive the transformation) to 'the high level of culture and humanity' represented here by England.

Spenser's choice of the dialogue form may have been informed at least in part by his intended audience; as suggested earlier, the use of fictional interlocutors allows an author to distance himself, if necessary, from some of the opinions expressed by them. At the same time, Spenser is able to establish authority in his text through his use of the form: the classized names of his fictional debaters, the ability to ventriloquize both points of view being presented in the dialogue, the clever rhetorical strategies for demonstrating Ireland's dire need for English intervention, the recourse to various authors ancient and modern to bolster his arguments all serve to establish the qualifications and credibility of the author as an educated humanist. Furthermore, the presentation of two opposed viewpoints – that is, the moderation of Eudoxus versus the extremism of Irenius – allows Spenser to demonstrate what he believes to be the superiority of both his intimate knowledge of Irish customs and the proposal he is making for bringing Ireland under English subjection once and for all. In Spenser's text, the complicity of humanism with the imperialist aspect of the utopian project is fully revealed, as is the utility of the dialogue form in articulating this project, which is presented in the course of a rational conversation with full humanist trappings. Through their status as fictional genres that will not remain confined to the realm of fiction, then, both dialogue and utopia may be thought of as fictions that achieve a degree of agency in the world of reality. The combination of dialogue and the utopian vision naturalizes such imposition of fictional constructs, with consequences in the material world that have only recently been recognized, and that continue to play themselves out in the Americas, in Ireland, and indeed in every corner of the globe.

NOTES

1 See Philip Sidney, *A Defence of Poetry*, ed. by van Dorsten, for a sense of the term 'poetry' (that is, 'poesy') and the stakes surrounding it.
2 Levao, *Renaissance Minds and Their Fictions*, xvii, xxiii.
3 Kristeller, *The Classics and Renaissance Thought*, 86–7, 13. For more on appropriation through translation, see Copeland, *Rhetoric, Hermeneutics, and Translation in the Middle Ages*.
4 Sydney, *Defence of Poetry*, 19.
5 Snyder, *Writing the Scene of Speaking*, 17.
6 Sydney, *Defence of Poetry*, 25.
7 Tasso, *Discourse on the Art of the Dialogue*, 33.
8 Preto-Rodas, *Francisco Rodrigues Lobo*, 30.
9 Snyder, *Writing the Scene of Speaking*, 9.
10 Cox, *The Renaissance Dialogue*, 5.
11 See Fowler and Greene, *The Project of Prose in Early Modern England and the New World*, 1. This is a collection of essays discussing the protocols and peculiarities of prose writing in this period. See also Godzich and Kittay, *The Emergence of Prose*. While their study focuses specifically on the emergence of prose in France during the medieval period, the questions they raise about the 'natural' status prose has come to acquire in Western societies have some

interesting implications when considering the real-world aspirations of
those prose genres, dialogue and utopia.

12 Details of Quiroga's project may be found in Zavala, *Thomas More in New
    Spain*, and in Warren, *Vasco de Quiroga and His Pueblo-Hospitals of Santa Fe*.
13 Holstun, *A Rational Millennium*, 1–8. In his study Holstun makes an espe-
    cially strong case for the real-world agency of Puritan utopias of the seven-
    teenth century.
14 More, *Utopia*, trans. and ed. Adams, 84–5. All quotations are taken from
    this edition. There are many discussions on the function of dialogue in
    More's *Utopia*, as well as numerous speculations about More's purpose in
    writing the text. See, for example, Schoeck, 'A Nursery of Correct and Use-
    ful Institutions'; Skinner, 'Sir Thomas More's Utopia and the Language of
    Renaissance Humanism'; and Bevington, 'The Dialogue in *Utopia*.'
15 Wilson, *Incomplete Fictions*, 54.
16 Greene, 'Fictions of Immanence, Fictions of Embassy,' identifies certain lit-
    erary protocols operative in early modern fiction that have some interesting
    bearing on utopias produced in the period. Space does not permit a full dis-
    cussion either of these protocols as described by Greene, or of their correla-
    tion with utopian texts; I am indebted to the essay, however, for informing
    some of the suggestions I make regarding the operation of specific utopias
    upon the reader, as well as for pointing out broad changes seen in such
    texts over the course of the sixteenth and seventeenth centuries.
17 More, *Utopia*, 5, note 9.
18 Michael M. Ames, *Cannibal Tours and Glass Boxes: The Anthropology of
    Museums* (Vancouver: University of British Columbia Press, 1992), 10.
19 Holstun, *A Rational Millennium*, 7.
20 More, *Utopia*, 31.
21 Cox, *The Renaissance Dialogue*, 101–4.
22 Campanella, *The City of the Sun*, 27. See also Headley, 'Campanella, Amer-
    ica, and World Evangelization,' for a discussion of Campanella's vision of
    world evangelization in the wake of Columbus's encounter with the
    Americas.
23 Cox, *The Renaissance Dialogue*, 103–4.
24 Francis Barker, *The Tremulous Private Body: Essays on Subjection* (Ann Arbor:
    University of Michigan Press, 1995), 7.
25 Ibid., 62. The epistemological interiority in question here is sometimes
    referred to as the Cartesian split and arises with the historical and philo-
    sophical phenomenon we broadly call the Enlightenment. On the same
    page, Barker warns against conceiving of historical moments teleologically;
    historical phenomena have historical causes, but 'just as every beginning is

not an Origin, so not every outcome is a teleological goal.' I might say the same for the conjunction of dialogue, utopia, humanism, and nascent imperialism that I am outlining in this essay: I am describing a convergence of events and phenomena that arguably produce a specific result.

26 Boesky, 'Bacon's *New Atlantis* and the Laboratory of Prose,' 148.

27 Andreae, *Christianopolis*, 1619, ed. Thompson in 1999. Prior to this edition, the text was available in English only in the 1916 translation of Felix Emil Held, whose introduction (unfortunately unavailable in the Thompson edition) links it causally to the discovery of America, which 'opened the mind of all Europe to a realization of the narrowness of its former point of view ... A feeling developed that civilization could only be redeemed by stripping it of all useless and vain conventionalities; and in order that this might be done, primitive man would have to furnish the model' (4). While there may be more than a tinge of Rousseau in this early twentieth-century assessment of the impetus for utopian writing in the early modern period, Held is essentially correct for citing the New World as a primary influence. See his introduction to Andreae, *Christianopolis: An Ideal State of the Seventeenth Century*.

28 Cavendish, *The Description of a New World, Called The Blazing World*. Although the territory occupied by the Blazing World is ostensibly cerebral, this Restoration utopia is still informed by the discovery of the New World, as William Newcastle's prefatory poem suggests.

29 Quotations are from the Variorum edition. Perhaps more conveniently available is the recent edition by Hadfield and Maley, *A View of the State of Ireland*.

30 For a discussion of dialogue in *A Vewe*, see Coughlan, '"Some secret scourge which shall by her come unto England": Ireland and Incivility in Spenser.'

31 Spenser, *A Vewe of the Present State of Irelande*, 158. But see Shuger, 'Irishmen, Aristocrats, and Other White Barbarians,' for an argument that the Irish 'savages' are rather modelled on classical descriptions of northern Germanic tribes.

32 Spenser, *A Vewe of the Present State of Irelande*, 109, and Commentary, 283, 341–2.

The Fellowship of the Book: Printed Voices and Written Friendships in More's *Utopia*

Jean-François Vallée

To my friend Bill Readings (1960–94)

Books, once remarked the poet Jean Paul, *are long letters to friends*. One could not define with more elegance the nature and function of humanism: it is, in its essence, a telecommunication, a means of creating friendships at a distance through the technology of writing. What Cicero termed *humanitas*, in its narrowest and broadest sense, is one of the consequences of literacy.

Peter Sloterdijk[1]

Amicorum communia omnia

Erasmus[2]

'The whole Renaissance cherished that wish of reposeful, blithe, and yet serious intercourse of good and wise friends in the cool shade of a house under trees, where serenity and harmony would dwell,' wrote Johan Huizinga.[3] This idyllic conversational image illustrates eloquently the passionate predilection of Renaissance scholars and writers, especially humanists, for 'friendly dialogue.' Yet, this dialogical proclivity seems to have been more often mediated through the written page than enacted in actual oral interaction. It is indirectly reflected in the humanist fondness for 'communicative' forms of writing: letters, declamations or orations and, of course, most notably, dialogues per se.

As this collection of essays and other volumes published in the past two decades demonstrate, the study of the prevalence of the dialogue genre in the Renaissance has been growing. The conceptual and ethical importance of what P.O. Kristeller has termed the 'cult of friendship'[4] in the Renaissance has also generated an increasing number of historical and literary studies.[5] However, the – perhaps too obvious – link between the written dialogue genre and the topos of friendship is still in need of study.

Of course, this relationship has its roots in classical literature and philosophy, where friendship was a pivotal concept and value.[6] Many studies have commented on the centrality and the various conceptions of friendship in antiquity.[7] None, however, seem to have touched on its relationship to the concomitant popularity of the dialogue genre. Yet three of the most interesting classical works on friendship were composed as dialogues: Plato's *Lysis* (*On Friendship*), Cicero's *Laelius* (or *De amicitia*) and Lucian of Samosata's *Toxaris*. These works – written by the three most influential classical authors of dialogues – espouse different approaches to friendship, but all three do so through the active use of dialogical interaction between characters who represent friendship in different guises.

The choice of the dialogue genre to 'discuss' friendship is fitting: dialogue, as a textual strategy that represents an oral conversation, is a fundamentally relational mode of writing that works on two levels, that of the simulated oral exchange between the characters in the dialogue, and that of the *in absentia* relationship between the author and the reader. The written representation of a friendly conversational encounter illustrates performatively, albeit through writing, the intellectual and/or ethical theses developed on friendship within the utterances of the characters. Thus, the Renaissance 'rediscovery' of friendship concurrently with the reemergence of the dialogue genre is not very surprising. What is remarkable is that this fascinating issue does not seem to have been the object of much critical inquiry.

In the case of Northern humanism, we can begin to understand how the dialogue genre and the value of friendship interact through a study of Thomas More's *Utopia*, a work that, in my opinion, constitutes one of the most sophisticated and accomplished attempts of the early sixteenth century at using the printed book to create a reading experience that attempts to emulate a morally and intellectually stimulating dialogue between literate friends. As we shall see, More's work can be read as a dynamic manifesto, a performative textual incarnation of the profoundly 'dialogocentric'[8] ideology of humanism. Through a close reading of *Utopia*, I will attempt to show that the notions of dialogue, friendship, writing, and reading were intricately intertwined in the ethical and rhetorical outlook of this Renaissance 'literate sect'[9] traditionally identified as Northern humanism.

We must begin by saying a few words on the friendship of More and
Erasmus, perhaps the most famous literary and historical illustration
of *amicitia* of the Renaissance.[10] Their relationship, as E.E. Reynolds,
echoing many others, has stated, 'quickly passed into legend.'[11] It has
now become a centrepiece – and a commonplace – of the representation of Northern humanism. But, however overly 'mythologized' this
friendship may have been then and now,[12] it is crucial for our understanding of the genealogy and the very structure of *Utopia*.

The central importance of the notion of friendship in Erasmus's work
is well known,[13] but, for the purpose of this essay, it is especially imperative to highlight the opening *adagia* of his celebrated, oft-reprinted and
augmented[14] *Chiliades*: 'Between friends all is common.'[15] This adage,
and its commentary, could be said to contain, in a nutshell, the entire
program of Christian humanism. Erasmus first ascribes the saying to
Socrates, and then goes on to identify instances in Euripides, Terence,
Menander, Cicero, Aristotle, Plato, Martial, and Plutarch, before finally
attributing its origin to Pythagoras (based on the authority of Cicero,
Timaeus, and Aulus Gellius!). This massive recourse to the *auctoritas* of
– and intertextual dialogue with – the 'friends' of antiquity is, of course,
typical of Renaissance humanism and of the revival of classical learning. The attempt to link this ancient wisdom to Christianity, however,
is generally considered more specifically emblematic of Northern
humanism: 'nothing was ever said by a pagan philosopher which
comes closer to the mind of Christ,' writes Erasmus, in reference to
Plato's view on 'common ownership.'[16] This has led at least one scholar
to hypothesize that the adage constitutes a blueprint for More's *Utopia*:
indeed, according to John C. Olin, More's *Utopia* could be read as nothing less than 'a dramatic commentary on this adage.'[17]

The relationship of More and Erasmus is also vital because *Utopia* is
in many ways an answer or, more precisely, a complementary work to
Erasmus's *Praise of Folly* (*Utopia* supposedly being an *encomium* of wisdom). The editorial dialogue between these two books was initiated in
part by the famous *incipit* (and title) of Erasmus's work, written while
he was living at More's home in 1508. The dedication is, unsurprisingly, an ode to More, friendship, and dialogue:

> Recently when I was on my way from Italy to England, instead of wasting
> all the time I had to spend on horseback in idle chatter and empty gossip,
> I tried occasionally to think over some of the things we have studied
> together, and to call to mind the conversation of my most learned and

agreeable friends from whom I was then separated. Among those friends, you, my dear More, were the first whose name occurred to me, since I find just as much pleasure in thinking of you when we are apart as I do in your company when we are together. And, upon my soul, nothing in life has ever brought me more pleasure than your friendship.[18]

Moreover, and more importantly as we shall make clear later, the friendship of More and Erasmus plays a very active role in the whole process leading to the actual publication of *Utopia*.[19] But we must first examine the role of dialogue and friendship within the text of *Utopia* itself, since the idyllic figure of the 'friendly dialogue' – and its written representation – play a major role at every level of this sophisticated work. Too many studies – concentrating often on the monologue of Book II – have tended to read *Utopia* as a straightforward political treaty[20] (or, to the contrary, 'simply' as a work of literature).[21] Some have also observed that only Book I of *Utopia* is a dialogue per se, and that the work is therefore no more than a 'half dialogue.'[22] But the genealogy and general structure of the work tend to support a much more radical dialogical view.

As a number of scholars have demonstrated, *Utopia* was written in more than one phase. J.H. Hexter[23] was the first to show that *Utopia* had been conceived in at least two separate stages: Raphael Hythloday's description of the island of Utopia and its society (including the introductory part of the first book), composed when More was in the Netherlands in 1515, and the rest of the first book – the dialogue – written later when More was back in England.[24] More recently, Brian O'Brien established that *Utopia*'s genesis was, in fact, even more complex and included at least four, if not five, phases.[25]

However, what is most important in this genealogical perspective on *Utopia* is the 'general tendency' of the composition process: O'Brien sees it as one of 'increasing ambiguity and indirection.'[26] Indeed, each new phase of the genealogy of the work seems to make Raphael's oration of Book II more ambivalent, as it becomes encased in many layers of paradoxical, ironic or contradictory textual artefacts. In my opinion, this process would be better described as one of progressive *dialogization*. A simple declamation (delivered to an unidentified audience as in Erasmus's *Moria*) was first adorned with the fiction of a traveller's tale (that of Raphael Hythloday); it was then inscribed within a complex and unresolved dialogue between Raphael and two 'fictional' humanists ('Thomas More' and 'Peter Giles') who thus become the audience of

Raphael's oration of Book II (this dialogue includes a second embedded dialogue at the court of Cardinal Morton); this polyvocal ensemble within the fiction of *Utopia* is then rendered even more dialogical with the addition of a paradoxical prefatory letter by More (to Giles), accompanied by an epistolary, iconic, and poetic 'metadialogue' between different ('real' and historical) humanists (Erasmus, Budé, Lupset, Desmarais, Busleyden, etc.);[27] finally, there is also the anonymous 'paradialogue' of the *marginalia*[28] that introduces another axis of equivocal 'dialogue'[29] with the main text. The extreme sophistication of this multidimensional textual dialogue has given rise to many contradictory interpretations and cannot be addressed adequately in the context of a short essay. But I will at least attempt to correlate this dialogical complexity with the question of friendship that plays a crucial role at all levels of the dialogue.

First of all, let us examine the beginning of Book I just before the onset of the dialogue as such, when the narrator 'Thomas More' describes his 'perfect friend' – an alleged virtuoso of dialogue – Peter Giles:

> a young man distinguished equally by learning and character, for he is most virtuous and most cultured, to all most courteous, but to his friends so open-hearted, affectionate, loyal, and sincere that you can hardly find one or two anywhere to compare with him as the perfect friend on every score ... in conversation [*sermone*] he is so polished and so witty without offence that his delightful society and charming discourse largely took away my nostalgia.[30]

'Giles's' *ethos* is very similar to that of 'More's': both represent the 'active-civic-ciceronian' humanist type; learned and literate, but nonetheless pursuing important diplomatic business, involved in their community, in close contact with their friends and family, etc. This fact is important because it is what sets them apart from the more 'contemplative-Christian-platonic' humanist type Raphael, who later admits to having severed all links with his friends and family (he uses this excuse to justify that he need not, for their sake, enter 'into servitude to kings').[31] 'More' and 'Giles' constantly emphasize the necessity of maintaining 'relations' (with one's church, country, family, friends, etc.), while Raphael, the philosopher-traveller, opts for individual isolation ('I live as I please').[32] He cuts off all relations, just as King Utopus is said to have eliminated the isthmus that linked the ex-peninsula of Utopia to the mainland, thereby converting it into an island.[33]

More important for us, the very conception and manner of dialogue of 'Giles' and 'More,' on the one hand, and of Raphael, on the other, are also significantly different. One could even argue that the most important underlying issue of the dialogue of Book I is the question of dialogue itself, be it in private (i.e., friendly) or public (i.e., political) contexts. Of course, the manifest object of the debate that opposes the 'More-Giles' tandem and 'Hythloday' is the question of counsel: 'Why, my dear Raphael, I wonder that you do not attach yourself to some king?' asks 'Giles' at the outset of the dialogue.[34] Again, we cannot study in detail all the intricacies of the ensuing discussion, but it is important to emphasize a few relevant, and crucial, elements for our discussion of dialogue and friendship.

One notices, to begin with, that the dialogue between the three humanists is quickly led astray by Raphael who, to prove his point that it is useless to counsel kings, launches into a dialogical tirade relating (in dramatic mode) a conversation he had many years ago in the court of Cardinal Morton. This embedded dialogue is very long and, as do many of Raphael's lengthy utterances in the first-level dialogue, it foreshadows the final monologue of Book II, where Raphael completely cuts himself off from the dialogue of Book I to embark on his lengthy 'insular' *oratio*.[35]

The most fascinating part of the dialogue of Book I comes somewhat later, however, when Raphael and 'More' both make explicit their view of the nature of private and public dialogue. This is also the high point of the opposition between these two characters. Raphael has just recounted one of his failed attempts at counselling a king. He complains that his suggestion fell on 'deaf ears.' To this, 'More' retorts by attacking the very mode of 'dialogue' (*sermo*) used by Raphael (though the unfortunate translation of *sermo* by 'idea' in the Yale edition obscures this):

'Deaf indeed, without doubt,' I agreed, 'and, by heaven, I am not surprised. Neither, to tell the truth, do I think that such ideas [*huiusmodi sermones*] should be thrust on people, or such advice given, as you are positive will never be listened to. What good could such novel *ideas* [*sermo tam insolens*] do ...? In the private conversation of close friends [*Apud amiculos in familiari colloquio*] this academic philosophy is not without its charm, but in the council of kings, where great matters are debated with great authority, there is no room for these notions.'[36]

In his next utterance, 'More' rejoins with a description of his own view on the type of 'dialogical' approach that one should adopt for counselling kings (though *sermo* is once again inaccurately translated by 'idea'):

'There is another philosophy, more practical for statesmen, which knows its stage, adapts itself to the play at hand, and performs its role neatly and appropriately ... you must not force upon people new and strange *ideas* [*insuetus & insolens sermo*] which you realize will carry no weight with persons of opposite conviction. On the contrary, by the indirect approach you must seek and strive to the best of your power to handle matters tactfully.'[37]

Thus, in matters of public and political intervention, 'More' opposes a theatrical and more polite or 'decorous' model of dialogue that uses an indirect approach to Raphael's 'scholastic philosophy' and abrupt and/or strange mode of speech (*sermo tam insolens*) – said to be acceptable only in the context of a private and familiar dialogue among friends. These two conceptions of dialogue couldn't be more different. The unambiguous opposition is confirmed in Raphael's next utterance:

'By this approach,' he commented, 'I should accomplish nothing else than to share the madness of others as I tried to cure their lunacy. If I would stick to the truth [*uera loqui uolo*], I must need speak in the manner I have described. To speak falsehoods, for all I know, may be the part of a philosopher, but it is certainly not for me. Although that speech [*sermo*] of mine might perhaps be unwelcome and disagreeable to those councillors, yet I cannot see why it should seem odd even to the point of folly ... But, apart from this aspect [the question of the superiority of common over private property], what did my speech [*Mea uero oratio/sermo*] contain that would not be appropriate or obligatory to have propounded everywhere?'[38]

As Gerard Wegemer has demonstrated, through a detailed rhetorical analysis of 'More' and Raphael's utterances, the antagonism of the characters is also reflected in their *ethos* and in their actual modes of speech, that confirm – performatively – their conceptual and ethical opposition on public dialogue. 'More,' for example, adopts a 'polite' argumentative style and 'mitigates the possibility of personal offence often engendered by such strong disagreement through the use of the parable, antanagoge, understatement, and litotes ... The structure of his reply as a whole reveals [his] polite, civil, and Christian *ethos*.'[39] Raphael, on the other hand, 'places clarity and candor before charity, making little effort to mitigate the harsh effect of his radical proposals.' He 'speaks in an unpolite, blunt, and unpleasantly long-winded manner' and 'also uses exaggeration and *ad hominem* arguments to sharpen the effect of his rather virulent attacks.'[40]

As many commentators have noted, the debate between Raphael and 'More' is inconclusive: 'Opponents, arguments, and rhetoric are evenly matched,' writes Robert C. Elliott. 'From the text of *Utopia* itself it is impossible to say who "wins" in the Dialogue of Counsel.'[41] Hexter also declares that the dialogue is a 'draw,'[42] since 'they are so evenly matched that it is impossible to tell on the face of them which represented More's own belief at the time he wrote.'[43] Thus, the tension between the contradictory conceptions of dialogue of 'More' and Raphael remains unresolved.

One fact that is seldom emphasized, however, is that even if they are radically opposed on the matter of the best mode of public dialogue (for counsel), both 'More' and Raphael share the same conception of dialogue amongst friends in a private setting. This is not only confirmed by 'More's' explicit approval of Raphael's abrupt dialogical manners (his *sermo tam insolens*) in the context of 'familiar dialogue among friends' (*apud amiculos in familiari colloquio*), but also by their dialogue itself. Indeed, while the friendly conversation between 'More,' 'Giles,' and Raphael on the 'bench covered with turfs of grass'[44] of 'More's' private garden at his Antwerp home may not be consensual, and is even at times heated, it is in fact a perfect textual representation of the ideal humanist dialogue described by Huizinga at the beginning of this essay. As Catherine Demure has observed, these three characters are the very incarnation of the essential relation that holds '*humanitas* together at its highest level: *friendship*.'[45]

The problem, of course, and the crux of the debate, resides in the status of dialogue in a public and political context with 'non-humanists' and 'non-friends.' This issue is obviously related to the separation between the public and the private spheres, as well as to the opposition between the notions of private and common property. It is consequently interesting to observe that the question of personal friendship is almost totally evacuated from the Utopian society described by Raphael in his monologue of Book II. Utopian citizens have absolutely no individual identity,[46] only social or familial roles, and apparently no significant amicable relationships. Interestingly, almost all the occurences of the word 'friend' in Book II are situated in the section on 'military affairs,' where the term is used to describe nations allied to the Utopians. Thus, 'friend' is most often used here to describe collective entities rather than persons.⁴⁷ Hence, in Book II of More's *Utopia*, dialogue and (personal) friendship seem to share a similar fate, they recede in favour, respectively, of monologue (*oratio*) and of undifferentiated collective or communal relationships.

There is, however, a short but important section of Book II that warrants closer scrutiny in this respect. It comes at the end of Hythloday's monologue, where we are brought back to the scene of speaking and to its audience, 'More' and 'Giles.' The dialogue per se is not resumed, at any rate not in the direct mode: even though 'many things came to [his] mind which seemed absurdly established in the customs and laws of the people described,' 'More' the narrator refrains from criticizing Hythloday's discourse because he feels Raphael 'was wearied with his tale.' Moreover, 'More' 'was not quite certain that he could brook any opposition to his views.'⁴⁸ Thus, after sharing his thoughts with the reader through an interior monologue, 'More' relates his reply to Hythloday in indirect speech: 'I therefore praised [*the Utopians'*] way of life and his speech [*ipsius oratione*] and, taking him by the hand, led him in to supper. I first said, nevertheless, that there would be another chance to think about these matters more deeply and to talk them over with him more fully. If only this were some day possible!'⁴⁹

The ending of *Utopia* has given rise to an extremely abundant (and exceptionally contradictory) body of critical literature that I do not wish to comment on here. However, the less often noted 'performative' and dialogical nature of this last scene is important for the sake of my argument. It is indeed noteworthy that 'More' opts for a 'friendly' gesture towards Raphael instead of launching into a new dialogue for the sake of debating the aspects of Utopian life which he purports (however ambiguously and ironically) not to agree with in his interior monologue. The fact that 'More' defers the dialogue on Raphael's oration to another time is also significant because it puts us on the path of another possible reading of this passage. Indeed, the (weary?) reader could also be seen as someone who should reflect upon the issues raised by Raphael's speech, and perhaps even 'talk them over' (within himself). In a way, it is also the reader who is, metaphorically, taken by the hand at the end of this dizzyingly paradoxical book.

Indeed, in reading a written dialogue, one must never forget the complex interpretative 'dialogue' that takes place at the level of the reading experience. Dialogue, as a genre, is interesting in this respect since, by representing different voices in a 'pseudo-conversation' through writing, it positions the reader as a spectator, a witness, or even an eaves-dropper in relation to a private dialogue. Thus, the interaction between the characters is replayed, somewhat differently, at the level of the reader's interaction with the author's text. This other level of interpretative interaction is sometimes mediated, or even guided, by the nature of the dialogue itself, by a narrator or by supplementary material (letters, prefaces, etc.).

Within the dialogue of Book I of *Utopia*, one could demonstrate, for example, that through the narrative introduction of 'More,' the presentation from the outside of this strange philosopher-traveller Hythloday ('sayer of nonsense'), and the visual representation of the dialogue, the reader is placed in a position which is similar to that of 'More' and 'Giles.' As Ann Astell has observed 'the reader only learns the lesson More teaches if he plays the part of Raphael's auditor in company with More and Giles.'[50] The reader is thus virtually inserted within the 'familiar dialogue amongst friends' that takes place in Book I. Consequently, the question of audience and of the reception of Raphael's utterances in Book I becomes crucial for the interpretation of Raphael's monologue to 'More' and 'Giles' (and their 'friend,' the reader) in Book II.[51]

But the attitude and position of the reader is also meant to have been prepared through the reading of all the prefatory material (which is, unfortunately, sometimes partly or completely omitted in modern editions of *Utopia*). At this early and crucial stage of the reading sequence,[52] the reader encounters a series of letters and poems that answer, question, and extol each other, the author More, and the text of *Utopia* in a complex ballet of written addresses. Astell notes that the 'writings of the *parerga*, which according to More's wish accompany *Utopia* into print, provide a guide for reader response and remind us that artefact and audience, structure and rhetorical strategy, must be considered together.'[53] This is what I have previously termed the 'metadialogue' of the *parerga* and it could be considered yet another (more obviously *written*) 'familiar dialogue amongst friends.'

In this respect, it is important to keep in mind that for Renaissance humanists the difference between letters and dialogue was not so marked. As Lisa Jardine has noted, Erasmus, in the tradition of other classical and patristic writers, had a very 'dialogical' conception of the familiar letter. In his treaty on the art of letter writing, for example, he advocated the definition provided by pseudo-Libanius (through Jerome): '"As the comedian Turpilius aptly wrote, the *epistola* is a kind of mutual exchange of speech [*sermo*] between absent friends."'[54]

This dialogue *in absentia* that is the humanist familiar letter under-scores at once the continuity that these rhetorically minded writers envisioned between oral and written forms of speech, and the radically dialogocentric *ethos* that governed their writing. Peter Allen captures eloquently how the *parerga*, which framed the text of *Utopia* in the first editions, creates the semblance of an international textual dialogue among literate friends:

> With the first letter we move into a world of scholarly discussion. Every one knows every one else; the names in the group recur throughout. A letter from a Dutch scholar to a German-Swiss printer appears next to one from a French Hellenist to an English student; the letters thus foreshorten space and, in their one language, create the sense of a small, friendly group of humanists, whose conversation revolves around the central sub-ject of *Utopia* ... [the book] ends with further dialogues and leads us on to yet another letter and two more poems. Thus the world of *Utopia* becomes an incident in a long discussion; it is not a separate book but the central subject of the conversation – a rather lengthy anecdote told to a group of humanists, all of whom listen to it and comment on it. Not only does the atmosphere begin outside *Utopia* and penetrate into it, but the story itself penetrates into real life and spreads out through the rest of the book.[55]

Accordingly, the idea, value, and humanistic commonplace of friend-ship are everywhere present in the *parerga*. In the letter addressed to the publisher Froben, that opens the two most accomplished 1518 editions of *Utopia*, Erasmus, from the very beginning, evokes his 'very close friendship' (*arctissimam inter nos amicitiam*) with More. In his letter first published in the 1517 Paris edition, Budé pledges his friendship to More and Giles and lays claim to an 'association of friendship' with Erasmus. More himself ends his prefatory letter to Giles with 'loving' words of friendship: 'In the matter of publishing which remains I shall follow my friends' advice and yours first and foremost. Good-by, my sweetest friend, with your excellent wife. Love me as you have ever done, for I love you even more than I have ever done.'[56]

Of course, one must not take everything at face value in this very sociable epistolary *colloquium*. Many of the hyperbolic proclamations of friendship scattered throughout the epistolary dialogue of the *parerga* are somewhat contrived. For instance, as Elizabeth McCutcheon has noted, 'Peter Giles ... was not quite as close a friend as More's language and stance seem to suggest.'[57] Moreover, the famous French humanist Guillaume Budé, in his letter to Thomas Lupset, admits to the indirect nature of his friendship with More and to the essentially 'literary' (and mostly epistolary) quality of the amicable relationships of the various humanists that gravitated around the central figure of Erasmus:

> It was the testimony of Peter Giles of Antwerp which caused me to have full faith in More, who of himself carries weight and relies on great authority. I have never known More in person – I am now passing over the recommendation given his learning and character – but I love him on account of his sworn friendship with the illustrious Erasmus, who has deserved exceedingly well of sacred and profane letters of all kinds. With Erasmus himself, I have long ago formed an association of friendship [*societatem amicorum*] sealed by an exchange of letters.[58]

Many of the poets, artists, and humanists (Geldenhauer, Cornelius Grapheus, Desmarais, Holbein, etc.) were arguably summoned by Erasmus and/or Giles to buttress the prestige of More's publication. Nowhere is this more obvious than in the process leading to the addition of Busleyden's letter. More had explicitly requested the contribution of such a 'statesman' in a letter to his friend Erasmus.[59] Hence, Erasmus asked Giles to write a preface to *Utopia*, but to address it to Busleyden rather than to himself: 'I am getting the Nowhere ready; mind you send me a preface, but addressed to someone other than me, Busleyden for choice. In everything else I will act as a friend should.'[60] Busleyden was thus strongly encouraged to contribute his own letter to More. The Dutch statesman later sent his letter addressed to More ... to Erasmus, with a note in which he complained about the difficulty he had composing it.[61]

Thus, one could read the *parerga* as a manifestation of the editorial marketing skills of Erasmus and his circle of humanist 'friends,' the *societatem amicorum*. Lisa Jardine does just that in her study on Erasmus, who she describes as the first true European 'man of letters.' Her chronological description of the intercontinental preparation for the first instalment of what she calls the 'coterie correspondence' of the *parerga* leads her to conclude that 'the self-consciousness of the "packaging" of *Utopia* is evident. At this crucial moment, Erasmus and More join forces to produce, in Louvain, a volume heavy with authority, whose author was conveniently both prominent and distant from the Louvain circle, whilst a publicly acknowledged long-standing friend of Erasmus's.'[62] Jardine also provides a historically and iconographically virtuoso analysis of the correspondence and circumstances surrounding the famous Quentin Metsys diptych (representing Erasmus and Giles) that was sent to More as a gift in the year following the first publication of *Utopia*. Her conclusion illustrates the self-referential, and multilevelled, artfulness of this pictorial, epistolary, and ultimately 'bookish' ode to friendship and learning in the age of the new print culture:

> When the panels [of the painting] are united, we have a fresh composition
> – a teacher and his pupil, a pair of friends, a letter writer and one of his
> familiar correspondents. Now the representation is of *amicitia* (friend-
> ship), in the deepened, classical sense – a relationship of intimacy, trust,
> and mutual service, captured in the literary heritage with the stories of
> Theseus and Pirithous, Pylades and Orestes. The graphic representation
> of intimate friendship is bestowed *in* friendship on the third member of
> the trio – Thomas More – as a token *of* friendship – testifying to the 'most
> distant ages' the friendship of Erasmus. And at the center of this testa-
> ment to friendship rests a book.[63]

This book, according to Jardine, is *Utopia*, 'a symbol indeed of the three men's *amicitia*.' Thus, the whole editorial process leading to the publication of *Utopia* illustrates vividly how the circle of Northern humanists related to Erasmus made use of writing and of the technol-ogy of printing to further their aims of creating – at a distance – an international network of literate 'friends,' what Robert Mandrou has labelled a *sodalitates litterarum*.[64]

One can view this movement in factual, hard-nosed historical or sociological terms as Jardine does for Erasmus's works. She does dem-onstrate, compellingly, that the publication of *Utopia* was based on an artful process of what we could term 'early modern networking,' in which Erasmus played the foremost role. But we must recall, even if it may seem ingenuous, that this whole enterprise was, in fact, based on at least one *genuine* friendship, that of More and Erasmus, however partly overblown or purposefully crafted for the sake of posterity it might have been. We must also not be misled by the somewhat anach-ronistic modern conceptions of authenticity, sincerity, and spontaneity that had no real meaning for the more rhetorically minded ('self-fash-ioned') humanists. Furthermore, as R.J. Schoeck has noted:

> [We] must understand that friendship among humanists was not merely
> a rhetorical *topos* handed down from Cicero and made popular in numer-
> ous intermediary writers. It was also a *habitus* developed over time from
> close study, a living development in Petrarch and Ficino especially. In the
> *Respuplica literarum* it was a practical virtue which one learned from the

studia humanitatis and then cultivated in that world in which the humanist taught, wrote and offered council.[65]

Finally, and more important for the sake of this essay, we should not let biographical and socio-historical issues prevent us from looking at the ultimate textual objectives and effects of all these 'dialogocentric' efforts to place friendship and amicable dialogue at the heart of written communication. Indeed, the very fact that friendship was so self-consciously 'advertised' in print simply confirms that humanist notions and values of friendship and dialogue permeated not only their moral outlook but their whole conception of reading and writing, thus shaping their 'utopian' conception of the printed book as a means of communication.

In the case of *Utopia*, this becomes obvious in the dialogue of Book I, where, as we have seen, the reader is urged to sit beside the humanist characters of 'More' and 'Giles' and to (mutely/visually) participate in the familiar dialogue among friends with this strange messenger, Raphael Hythloday, at once 'guide' and 'sayer of nonsense,' who launches into a lengthy utopian monologue in Book II about an insular society where everything is, *literally* 'held in common' (and not only 'literarily,' as it is for the humanist writers themselves.) What's more, as we have seen earlier, the reader's position – and disposition – had already been tweaked through the reading of the *parerga* and, especially, of the prefatory letter addressed by More to his friend Peter Giles, a letter which is an integral part of the text of *Utopia*.[66] Elisabeth McCutcheon has observed that this familiar letter to Giles is addressed to more 'friends' than its intimate tone might lead us to believe at first glance: 'But at the same time that More addresses one dear friend in his prefatory letter, and indirectly addresses another even better friend, Erasmus, he addresses other potential readers of the *Utopia*. So this letter is more public and less personal than it appears to be.'[67]

Indeed, the letter, full of irony and paradoxes, is clearly intended for the reader. Toward the end, More spends a lot of time denigrating different types of 'bad' readers who might be, for example, too ignorant or too ungrateful to appreciate the 'banquet' that he is offering them. As we have seen, he concludes his letter with loving words for his 'sweetest friend,' Giles. We must agree again with McCutcheon's reading of these final words:

> Finally we must contrast the characterization of the carping critic and bad readers with the portrayal of the sweet friend with which More ends his

letter, his historical, authorial, and reportorial selves wholly coalescing ... Formally these last two lines are the *conclusion* of the letter ... despite its brevity it daringly outweighs the sentences devoted to the ungrateful readers in the power of its feeling ... Modestly, courteously, but invoking perhaps the strongest and surely the most resonant of all humanistic themes – friendship – ... More asks only for steadfastness in an ongoing relationship ... This is, in part, a rhetorical plea to all readers for sympathetic understanding, for reading at once knowledgeably and *con amore*.[68]

Thus, *amicitia* is seen as the model of the ideal reading disposition, just as it is said to govern the familiar (and private) exchanges of Book I. For these humanists, reading should, and perhaps even *could*, emulate the dynamics of a familiar dialogue among friends.[69] Furthermore, such a 'dialogue' was, I believe, sincerely thought by humanists to have the potential to literally transform the reader intellectually and, above all, ethically or even spiritually. Erasmus, in his foreword to his translation of the New Testament, published the same year as *Utopia*, aspires to an eloquence whose power 'not only tickled the ears with momentary pleasure, but which fixed a stinging dart deep in the mind of the hearer, pulling him out of himself, transforming him utterly, and sending him away a different person than he came.'[70] In the same fashion, the playful, paradoxical, unresolved nature of the multilayered and sophisticated dialogical text that is *Utopia* was artfully meant to destabilize, provoke, and transform the friendly reader. Thus, the ultimate object of all these complex dialogical literary layers and rhetorical strategies is even more radically ambitious than that of metaphorically equating the reading experience with a familiar dialogue among friends. It purports to bring about a 'metamorphical' reading experience, an intellectual and/or ethical transformation of the reader through a multidimensional dialogical encounter with a radically dialogocentric conception of the printed book. Therefore, the 'no place' of Utopia is not an island; it is, first and foremost, a *book*, a written utterance in the continuing – and perhaps currently endangered[71] – dialogue of the humanist Republic of Letters.

NOTES

1 This is my translation of the opening lines of Sloterdijk's 'Regeln für den Menschenpark: Ein Antwortschreiben zum Brief über den Humanismus,' a

paper first delivered by Peter Sloterdijk in Basel on 15 June 1997. An edited version of this controversial talk was published in Germany: Sloterdijk, *Regeln für den Menschenpark.*

2 'Between friends all is common' is the first of Erasmus's oft-reprinted and augmented *Adagia.* Adages [i] *to Iv100*, 29.

3 Huizinga, *Erasmus of Rotterdam*, 104.

4 Kristeller, 'Thomas More as a Renaissance Humanist,' 14.

5 On friendship in the early Renaissance, see Hyatte, *The Arts of Friendship.* There are also individual studies of major authors: Erasmus (Charlier, *Érasme et l'amitié d'après sa correspondance*); Spenser (Smith, *Spenser's Theory of Friendship*); Montaigne (Defaux, *Montaigne et le travail de l'amitié*); and Shakespeare (Shannon, *Sovereign Amity*).

6 Kristeller, for one, notes how the humanists imitated the ancients in this aspect as in many others: 'The friendship between scholars is one of the characteristic features of Renaissance humanism, and as so many other things, it is an inheritance from classical philosophy and literature where friendship appears a prominent topic of moral discussion in Plato, Aristotle, Epicurus, Cicero and others' ('Thomas More as a Renaissance Humanist,' 14).

7 On the classical notions of friendship, see, for example, Fraisse, *Philia*; Price, *Love and Friendship in Plato and Aristotle*; Bolotin, *Plato's Dialogue on Friendship*; and Stern-Gillet, *Aristotle's Philosophy of Friendship.*

8 I borrow here, and 'dialogically' modify, Gérard Defaux's luminous characterization of the fundamental nature of Northern humanism. I have shown in my dissertation ('Les voix imprimées de l'humanisme') that this moral and intellectual movement is not only 'logocentric,' as Defaux has aptly demonstrated, but *dia*logocentric. For humanists like Erasmus and More, *logos* is always considered in an interactive, *dialogical* context. For Defaux's description of the logocentric nature of humanist writing, see his *Marot, Rabelais, Montaigne*, and, in English, 'Against Derrida's "Dead letter."'

9 It is Sloterdijk who refers to humanists (in general) as 'die Sekte der Alphabetisierten' (*Regeln für den Menschenpark*).

10 It is rivalled only, perhaps, in the French canon, by the *amitié* of Montaigne and La Boétie.

11 Reynolds, *Thomas More and Erasmus*, ix.

12 For a critical appraisal of this friendship, see White, 'Legend and Reality.'

13 See, for example, Charlier, *Érasme et l'amitié d'après sa correspondance.* Numerous passionate passages from Erasmus's early letters to Servatius Rogerus, his apologia of friendship in the *Praise of Folly*, and his countless letters to various 'friends' scattered throughout Europe could illustrate

this, but it is perhaps a passage from the *Dulce bellum inexpertis* that best captures his quasianthropological view of *amicitia*: 'If any one considers a moment the organization and external figure of the body, will he not instantly perceive that nature, or rather the God of nature, created the human animal not for war, but for love and friendship ... man is an animal born for that love and friendship which is formed and cemented by the mutual interchange of benevolent offices ... For what is more agreeable than a friend? What so necessary?' Erasmus, *Antipolemus*, 432–5.

14 The first edition of the *Adages* in 1500 (in Paris) contained 818 adages; the last edition in Erasmus's lifetime (in 1536 in Basel) contained 4151.

15 Erasmus, *Adages [i] to Iv100*, 29.

16 Ibid., 30.

17 Olin, 'Erasmus's *Adagia* and More's *Utopia*,' 60. Erasmus's commentary on the first *adagias* was, for the most part, added for the 1515 Froben edition, often called the 'Utopian edition' because of its temporal proximity to the *editio princeps* of More's book in 1516.

18 Erasmus, 'The Praise of Folly,' in *The Praise of Folly and other Writings*, 3. After the publication of *Utopia*, Erasmus further added to the mythology of his friendship with More by writing an oft-quoted 'word-picture' of the English humanist in a letter to Ulrich von Hutten where More is, unsurprisingly, described as an exceptional conversationalist and the 'perfect model of friendship' ('To Ulrich von Hutten,' Letter 999, 23 July 1519, *The Correspondence of Erasmus*).

19 Erasmus's editorial patronage of More's work was evident from the very first edition in 1516, even though he only provided an official introductory letter for the two 1518 Froben editions of *Utopia*, in which he contends that he previously 'distrusted [his] own judgement ... on account of [his] very close friendship' with More (*The Yale Edition of the Complete Works of St. Thomas More*, vol. 4: *Utopia*, 3 (English)/2 (Latin). (Henceforth, I will refer to this edition of *Utopia* as CWM IV.)

20 A classic example of this approach would be Karl Kautsky's Marxist reading of *Utopia*, *Thomas More and His Utopia*.

21 The most famous statement to this effect belongs to C.S. Lewis: '[*Utopia* is] a book whose real place is not in the history of political thought so much as in that of fiction and satire ... It becomes intelligible and delightful as soon as we take it for what it is – a holiday work, a spontaneous overflow of intellectual high spirits, a revel of debate, paradox, comedy and (above all) of invention, which starts many hares and kills some' (*English Literature in the Sixteenth Century*, 167–71).

22 '*L'Utopie*: demi dialogue' (Marc'hadour, 'Thomas More: de la conversation au dialogue,' 42).

23 Hexter, *More's 'Utopia': The Biography of an Idea*. There is a 'concentrated' version of this thesis in Hexter's introduction to the Yale edition of *Utopia* (CWM IV, xv–xxiii).

24 Hexter identifies the 'seam' linking these two phases 'just before the point where Book I assumes its characteristic form of a dialogue' (Hexter, CWM IV, xix). In fact, there is also some dialogue in the original introduction to Book I, but, significantly, it is narrated indirectly by the character 'More,' whereas the rest of the dialogue in Book I is in the dramatic (i.e., direct) mode.

25 O'Brien, 'J.H. Hexter and the Text of *Utopia*.' What was first called the *Nusquama* (underway perhaps as early as 1510) was originally a simple declamation, the previously evoked apologia of wisdom which was supposed to become the complementary element to Erasmus's *Praise of Folly*. It is only later that the traveller's tale and the character of Raphael were added. Thus Hexter's first phase is constituted of two distinct phases. The third phase is constituted of the dialogue(s) of Book I. The fourth comes with the addition of the *parerga*, to which I would add a fifth phase: the appending of the *marginalia*. Albert Prévost, the editor of an important critical edition of *Utopia* in French, comes to similar conclusions through a different process and with different arguments. See his 'Avant-propos,' in *L'Utopie de Thomas More*.

26 O'Brien, 'J.H. Hexter and the Text of *Utopia*,' 28.

27 The documents and authors of the *parerga* vary depending on the editions. There are four early editions of *Utopia*. The *editio princeps* was published by Martens in Louvain in 1516, and the second edition by Gourmont in Paris in 1517. The editions generally considered to be the most authoritative are the Froben editions published in Basel in March and November of 1518 (Yale uses the March edition, Prévost the November one). The *parerga* vary from one edition to another (though not between the two 1518 editions). There were no other Latin editions of *Utopia* in More's lifetime (aside from an incomplete Florentine edition in 1519).

28 On the *marginalia*, see McKinnon, 'The Marginal Glosses in More's *Utopia*.' The 'paternity' of the *marginalia* is uncertain. Giles claims to have written them (or at least some of them) in his prefatory letter to Busleyden, but they are attributed to Erasmus on the title page of the 1517 Paris edition.

29 According to Andrew McLean, 'the marginal glosses which accompany the *Utopia* carry on a dialogue with the text' ('Thomas More's *Utopia* as Dialogue and City Encomium,' 94).

30 CWM IV, 49 / 48.

31 Ibid., 55.

32 Ibid., 57.

33 Utopus is said to have 'ordered the excavation of fifteen miles on the side where the land was connected with the continent and caused the sea to flow around the land' (ibid., 113).

34 Ibid., 55. More scholars generally refer to this part of Book I as the 'Dialogue of Counsel.'

35 Interestingly, Raphael's reported dialogue set at Morton's court actually contradicts the point he wanted to make: the cardinal is shown, in fact, to be a model of the thoughtful prince who pays very careful attention to Raphael's counsel.

36 CWM IV, 97, 99 /96, 98. Emphasis mine. We should also highlight another arguable translation, that of 'sermo tam insolens,' since 'insolens' is only partially rendered by the word 'novel': of course, 'insolens' can have the meaning of 'new' or 'unusual,' but it can also mean 'insolent' (arrogant, excessive) in the modern sense. To me, it is obvious that More is playing on this double entendre, especially since 'insolens' qualifies Raphael's speech ['sermo'] which is shown to be abrupt.

37 CWM IV, 99 / 98.

38 CWM IV, 101 / 100. The word *oratio* in the March 1518 edition is replaced by the more dialogical *sermo* in the November 1518 edition. It seems possible that More himself was responsible for this eloquent revision. Prévost comments on the 'dialogical' importance of this word change (*L'Utopie de Thomas More*, 434, note 3).

39 Wegemer, 'Ciceronian Humanism in More's *Utopia*,' 13.

40 Wegemer, 'The Rhetoric of Opposition in Thomas More's *Utopia*,' 293.

41 Elliott, 'The Shape of Utopia,' 185.

42 Hexter, 'Thomas More and the Problem of Counsel,' 64.

43 Hexter, *More's Utopia*, 132.

44 CWM IV, 51.

45 Demure, 'L'Utopie de Thomas More,' 165. The translation is mine.

46 The only citizen of Utopia who has a name is King Utopus.

47 Eight of the ten occurences I have identified have this collective-national meaning. Interestingly, the only two 'personal' occurences of the word 'friend' in Book II (CWM IV, 145 / 144 and 225 /224) are related to absent friends who either live at a distance or are ... dead.

48 CWM IV, 245 / 244.

49 Ibid. In the last lines of Book II, 'More' once again comes back to his interior monologue (and to the ambiguous statements that have so divided the critical literature): 'Meanwhile, though in other respects he is a man of the most undoubted learning as well as of the greatest knowledge of human affairs, I cannot agree with all that he said. But I readily admit that there are

very many features in the Utopian commonwealth which it is easier for me to wish for in our countries than to have any hope of seeing realized [*optarim uerius, quam sperarim*]' (CWM IV, 245, 247 / 244, 246).

50 Astell, 'Rhetorical Strategy and the Fiction of Audience in More's *Utopia*,' 306.

51 According to Astell, this is the *only* plot in *Utopia*: 'The hero Hythloday is in search of an audience that will pay heed to his message. Indeed, there is no other plot' (ibid., 306). McCutcheon also insists on the centrality of this issue: 'For really, within *Utopia*, only one simple question remains. Will these good men hear his message, or will they be too deaf? Will Peter Giles, the young, virtuous, open-hearted humanist? Will the More of the narrative, a man devoted to his country, his family, and God?' (McCutcheon, 'Thomas More, Raphael Hythlodaeus, and the Angel Raphael,' 36).

52 On the importance of prefaces, preliminary letters, etc. in Renaissance printed works, see Jeanneret, 'La lecture en question.' According to Jeanneret, the prefatory material played the role of an 'instruction manual' (a 'mode d'emploi') for the new readers (and writers) of printed books.

53 Astell, 'Rhetorical Strategy and the Fiction of Audience in More's *Utopia*,' 303.

54 'Est enim [quod scite scriptum est a Turpilio comico] epistola absentium amicorum quasi mutuus sermo.' Quoted by Jardine, *Erasmus, Man of Letters*, 150. Jardine is quoting Erasmus's *De conscribendis epistolis*.

55 Allen, '*Utopia* and European Humanism,' 100. McLean reads the *parerga* as a final stage in the 'dialogisation' of *Utopia*: '[The] prefatory letters draw the reader into the ironic point of view which is the foundation of *Utopia* and they are, in effect, a final refinement of the dramatic and dialogic techniques initiated by the *declamatio* of Book 2' (Thomas More's *Utopia* as Dialogue and City Encomium,' 94).

56 CWM IV, 45 / 44.

57 Elizabeth McCutcheon, *My Dear Peter*, 14.

58 CWM IV, 13, 15 (12, 14).

59 'Some time ago I sent you my *Nowhere*; I am most anxious to have it published soon and also that it be handsomely set off with the highest of recommendations, if possible, from several people, both intellectuals and distinguished statesmen. I want this principally because of one individual [Busleyden], whose name, I think, will occur to you even without my mentioning it ... Handle this matter as you think is for my own good' (Letter to Erasmus, 20 September 1516, *Selected Letters*, 76).

60 To Pieter Gillis, Letter 477, 17 October 1516, *The Correspondence of Erasmus, Letters 446–593 (1516–17)*, 98.

61 From Jerôme de Busleyden, Letter 484, 9 November 1516, ibid., 120.

62 Jardine, *Erasmus, Man of Letters*, 121. McCutcheon also describes the members of this 'in-group' as 'conspirators' (*My Dear Peter*, 10).

63 Jardine, *Erasmus, Man of Letters*, 38. More himself furthers the myth through a prosopopeic epigram: 'The painting speaks. I represent Erasmus and Giles as close friends as once were Castor and Pollux. More, bound to them by as great a love as any man could entertain for his own self, grieves at his physical separation from them. So the measure they took, in response to the yearnings of the absent friend, was that loving letters should make their souls present to him, and I [the painting] their bodies' (quoted by Jardine, *Erasmus, Man of Letters*, 28).

64 Mandrou, *Des humanistes aux hommes de science*, 44.

65 Schoeck, 'Telling More from Erasmus,' 18.

66 This is made obvious by the fact that there are some marginal notes already in this part of the book.

67 McCutcheon, *My Dear Peter*, 16.

68 Ibid., 66–7.

69 Yvonne Charlier, at the end of her work on Erasmus and friendship, concludes that 'Belles Lettres,' and books themselves, were probably Erasmus's true best friends: 'Les Belles Lettres sont sans doute la plus grande amitié d'Érasme ... Ses chers livres sont ses meilleurs amis parce qu'ils sont immuables et bien tels qu'il les désire ... Érasme a vécu pour son œuvre et par son œuvre. L'amitié devait avant tout l'aider dans une tâche qui fut son destin.' (*Érasme et l'amitié d'après sa correspondance*, 350–1).

70 Erasmus, *The Praise of Folly and Other Writings*, 119.

71 According to Sloterdijk, we are now facing the ('dangerous') end of this 'literary humanism, conceived as a utopia of the upbringing of man through writing and reading, which render tolerant and bring about moderation in judgement and the development of listening abilities' (Sloterdijk, 'Postface à l'édition française,' 54); my approximate translation of a special 'postface' to the French edition of *Regeln für den Menschenpark*.

Thomas More's *Utopia* and the Problem of Writing a Literary History of English Renaissance Dialogue

J. Christopher Warner

Treatments of English Renaissance dialogue are few, but they all begin with the same landmark event: the publication of Sir Thomas More's *Utopia* in 1516, even though *Utopia* did not really become a dialogue in English until Ralph Robinson's 1556 translation. No matter that *Utopia* was originally written in Latin and first printed in Louvain, nor that only the first part of the work, Book I, is in dialogue form: *Utopia* gives us exactly what we value most in the genre. Thomas More drew deeply on the classical and Continental humanist traditions for inspiration and clever, richly-layered allusions and figures – dazzling ornaments not in the modern sense but as Cicero would applaud, in that they are integral to the construction of fully reasoned arguments on either side of difficult questions that are at once practical, philosophical, and moral. Better yet, the arguments *in utramque partem* do not merely promote two opposing viewpoints on these questions. The recurring ironies and multivalent allusions generate paradoxes and ambiguities that prompt us to continue the dialogue ourselves, in moments of private reflection and in conversation, in the pages of journals and books, at conferences and in classrooms.[1] These features of the text challenge us to decide between the positions of Hythloday and More not once and for all but here and there, with the result that we find ourselves leaning now toward Hythloday and away from that 'fool' More, now toward More and away from that 'purveyor of nonsense' Hythloday, while at every stage we are also being urged to imagine alternative possibilities that would transcend the wisdom of either speaker. There is, moreover, the added bonus of a dialogue within a dialogue, in Hythloday's long account of his dinner conversation at Cardinal Morton's house. We could not ask for a more promising start.

Our enthusiasm wanes, however, when we begin to survey England's dialogue output after *Utopia* to the end of the Renaissance. For the purposes of this essay, let us mark this end with a dialogue that was published just on the other side of the period but that deliberately invokes its genre's glorious ancestor: *A Pleasant Battle Between Two Lap Dogs of the Utopian Court* (1681). Despite the advertisement of its title, this anonymous tract is not pleasant at all, nor anything like what Raphael Hythloday would have us expect of dialogue in the land of Utopia, among its people or its pets. It is a nasty yipping match between vulgar-mouthed lapdogs ostensibly belonging to two mistresses of Charles II – Nell Gwyn, the former London actress, and Louise de Kéroualle, better known by her title the duchess of Portsmouth. Unlike earlier specimens of Renaissance dog-dialogues,[2] this debate never rises above the scurrilous. 'Me-thinks,' says the duchess's Snapshort, 'tis strange, your open-arse Lady, who came lately from selling ripe Oranges and Lemons about the streets ... should be so forgetful of her former Mechanic Condition.' 'If anything raise my Lady's Fortune, let me tell you,' retorts Nell's Tutty, ''tis her being a Protestant, who shall be protected, when your Romish Bitch shall be pull'd Limb from Limb' (3). In the end, the whole thing degenerates into growls and barks and ear-biting, with Nell Gwyn, the duchess, and a crew of simpering courtiers rushing into the room to wage bets on the outcome. Regrettably, and despite its nod toward Thomas More's masterpiece, *A Pleasant Battle Between Two Lap Dogs of the Utopian Court* seems too crude to invite much critical attention.

More discouraging still, among the several hundred English dialogues that were printed in the years between *Utopia* and *A Pleasant Battle Between Two Lap Dogs*, there is nothing else that comes close to *Utopia*'s rhetorical complexity. Two valuable studies of the genre make this clear.[3] English Renaissance dialogues are all in simple master-pupil mode, or team-teaching mode, or like Tutty and Snap-short's dispute, combative mode. Such comparative simplicity has made it difficult for scholars thus far to do much more than catalogue common themes and lowest common denominators. We have learned, for example, that there are dialogues on religion and politics, dialogues for and against the new-fangled faith, dialogues for and against an alliance with France; there are educational dialogues, teaching music or French; there are moral dialogues that condemn gambling, dancing, or the latest fashions from France; some dialogues are between social or religious types – a Soldier and a Merchant, a Priest and a Lawyer, a Papist and a Presbyterian; others are between symbols or abstract ideas – Mercury and Virtue, the Belly and the Head, Velvet Breeches and Cloth Breeches; others are between the author and a fictional friend, or between two actual persons who are objects of the author's admiration, or who are targets of his satire. Identifying these various types does provide a useful survey of the genre, to be sure. But we are eager now to discover whether new approaches to the study of English dialogues can make possible, and make rewarding, the kind of sustained critical attention that scholars give to *Utopia* and works in other genres.

Indeed, the study of English Renaissance dialogues has been at an impasse precisely because More's *Utopia* is so good that we want later dialogues to be just like it. By starting with an analysis of *Utopia* that enumerates its qualities, supplemented with encomiums to the virtues of dialogue from classical and Renaissance treatises on rhetoric and dialectic, we encumber ourselves with a romanticized conception of the form as humanism's open-ended vehicle of choice for combining play with serious philosophical inquiry.[4] When we then turn to examine the few specimens that, to all appearances, seem like *Utopia* to be drawing on classical and humanist tradition, we are all too likely to attribute to them the qualities we wish they possessed. There are seven dialogues in particular that tempt us in this way: Thomas More's *Dialogue concerning Heresies* and *A Dialogue of Comfort against Tribulation*; Thomas Elyot's *Pasquil the Plain* and *Of the Knowledge which Maketh a Wise Man*; Thomas Starkey's *A Dialogue between Pole and Lupset*; Roger Ascham's *Toxophilus*; and Edmund Spenser's *A Vewe of the present state of Irelande*.[5] When these works are discussed in the terms indicated by their content rather than by their genre – as theological polemic, spiritual *consolatio*, political philosophy, educational philosophy, and colonial strategy, primarily – they have rewarded study. But I would make the generalization that attempts to discuss them *as dialogues*, in something like a 'developing English dialogue tradition,' have only managed to underscore just how un-utopian that tradition is. Their main speakers, More, Anthony, Pasquil, Plato, Pole, Toxophilus, and Irenius, know all the answers, and they impart them to the Messenger, Vincent, Gnatho and Harpocrates, Aristippus, Lupset, and Eudoxus. The arguments are on the whole straightforward, the conclusions explicit. They barely, or do not, argue on either side of a question, and if they do generate ambiguity as an invitation to independent inquiry, it does not seem to be on purpose. By this measure, the utopian measure, our most 'humanistic' English Renaissance dialogues are really just longer, more learned versions of our hundreds of 'crude' English Renaissance dialogues.[6]

Scholars have been reluctant to concede this state of affairs, even when they confront it head on. For example, after distinguishing between 'genre dialogues,' which sustain thought-provoking dialectical inquiry, and 'anti-genre dialogues,' which are one-sided conversations on the master-pupil model, Roger Deakins concludes that only two sixteenth-century English dialogues are of the first type, *Utopia* and Thomas Elyot's *Of the Knowledge which Maketh a Wise Man*.[7] All 'the other two hundred and twenty-odd Tudor dialogues' belong to the dreary second category.[8] But Deakins does not explain how Elyot's one-sided dialogue between Plato and Aristippus can be defined, alongside *Utopia*, as a 'genre dialogue'; he only asserts that it is one. A similar instance of wishful thinking occurs in K.J. Wilson's book, *Incomplete Fictions: The Formation of English Renaissance Dialogue*. In the epilogue Wilson reviews his distinction between 'eiristic dialogue, the method of question and answer used for scholastic debate or religious controversy,' and 'peirastic dialogue, which is experimental, tentative, and speculative,'[9] and then claims that 'the peirastic mode won favor with the humanists as more rhetorically effective and aesthetically satisfying than the scholastic form.' This version of history would make a neat plot, but it is not actually available in Wilson's prior chapters on More's *Dialogue concerning Heresies* and *A Dialogue of Comfort*, on Elyot's *Of the Knowledge which Maketh a Wise Man*, and on Ascham's *Toxophilus*. The case that these are 'peirastic' rather than 'eiristic' dialogues is barely ventured in these chapters, clearly because the texts would defy the attempt.

That judgment would seem to consign us to a gloomy outlook for English Renaissance dialogue studies. If it is all downhill after *Utopia*, then we will need to look elsewhere – in the dramatic literature of the Elizabethan and Jacobean periods, most obviously – for the dialogical complexity that we value. I hope not to leave us at our present impasse, however, but to give an account of English Renaissance dialogues that will bring into focus rhetorical dimensions of these works that are overlooked when analysed from the perspective of a presumed classical, continental, or utopian 'literary heritage.' This requires us to approach English dialogues by way of their social context. When we do so, we discover that they are nearly always artefacts of specific political and religious controversies, and that they tended to appear in clusters, in response to specific crises. The fact that some crises elicited numerous dialogues while others generated only a few, or none, may be the result of changing tides of government censorship during this period, but we will also find that the circumstances of certain crises were such that the process of dialogue itself was under scrutiny by the culture. When reading dialogues and other tracts published during the years of such a crisis, we encounter a general perception that dialogue is suspect, if not dangerous, in its current form, or even if ostensibly allowed or encouraged, it is subject to manipulation or constraint, so that the properly transparent relation between private conscience and public speech is being muddied if not corrupted. To some degree, therefore, it was this very consciousness of a 'problem with dialogue' that in turn generated dialogues. Virginia Cox, in the introduction to her study of Renaissance Italian dialogues, has already advanced this claim as one that applies generally to the form: 'Every dialogue,' she argues, 'from the most vividly "dialogical" to the most drably "monological," shares the generic trait of self-consciously embodying a conception of the relation between language, social practice and cognition'; thus, she continues, 'it seems reasonable to assume that, when any age adopts on a wide scale a form which so explicitly "stages" the act of communication, it is because that act has, for some reason, come to be perceived as problematic.'[10]

This understanding of dialogues – that they appear in clusters and, within each cluster, participate in a society's effort to think through and resolve a perceived 'problem with dialogue' – best positions us to take the next crucial step: to define a particular cluster of dialogues for analysis and to observe and articulate how these dialogues comprise something like a 'dialogue between dialogues,' each one complementing or opposing not just the arguments and conclusions of the previous dialogues, but also their strategies of staging dialogue. Imagine, in other words, pairs of speakers in a sequence, speakers whose identities have been selected and whose dialogues have been scripted by their authors according to challenges posed by the dialogues that came beforehand. Our goal, in this case, is to explicate the rhetorical dynamic of these dialogues, not as we readily see it in the simple and explicit interaction between their two speakers but rather as we must work to interpret this dynamic in the more sophisticated, implicit interaction between pairs or groups of speakers of successive dialogues.

This is an approach that I have adopted elsewhere in a study of dialogues related to Henry VIII's dispute with Rome over his marriage to Catherine of Aragon, in the period 1529–34.[11] Much of the royal propaganda against the validity of the king's marriage, and against the Catholic Church's traditional jurisdiction and taxation privileges, took the form of anonymous prose dialogues published by Thomas Berthelet, printer to the king. These are *A Dialogue between a Knight and a Cleric* (Latin edition published in 1531; English translation published in 1533), *A Glass of the Truth* (English and Latin editions in 1531 and 1532), the series of *Doctor and Student* dialogues (1530–1), and *Salem and Bizance* (1533).[12] The publication of these works was accompanied by Henry's repeated verbal and printed professions that his pursuit of the truth was disinterested: he was encouraging open debate on the question of his marriage because his conscience was troubled by the possibility that his marriage to Catherine, his brother Arthur's widow, was incestuous in the eyes of God. The dialogue form on the one hand seemed to confirm Henry's sincere wish to hear open discussion of his 'great matter'; on the other hand, it enabled him to present his case against the marriage, and against the church's authority to decide it, while still retaining the privilege of deniability. These were not the king's words but a lawyer's, or priest's, or soldier's.

The rhetorical features of these dialogues become interesting once we begin to compare them, for as the crisis stretched on, Henry's increasing impatience was manifested in the changing relations between their speakers. Whereas, for example, the early dialogues between the Doctor of Divinity and Student of the Law are complementary – with each speaker contributing equally to the explication of England's laws – in the later *Additions to Doctor and Student* the only expert is the Student of the Law. The role of the Doctor of Divinity has diminished to that of a troublesome objector. His occasional protests against the Student's view that the pope and the Convocation of Bishops lack authority to make or enforce laws within England are answered with sharp rebukes and threats. In this steadily shifting relationship between the *Doctor and Student*'s two speakers we are able to trace Henry's developing conception of the changing relations between social groups in his realm, well before these relations were codified in the acts of supremacy.[13]

In the year of the Spanish Armada's defeat, and the period just afterwards (1588–90), we see another cluster of dialogues that merits similar comparative study. Several have the predictable aim of rallying the realm against the Spanish enemy, such as two by Edward Daunce: *A Brief Discourse Dialoguewise, Showing How False and Dangerous their Reports Are which Affirm the Spaniards intended Invasion to be for the Reestablishment of the Romish Religion*, and *A Brief Discourse of the Spanish State, with a Dialogue annexed entitled Philobasilis* (both 1590). Interestingly, it was probably William Cecil, Baron Burghley, Elizabeth's Lord Treasurer and the most powerful member of the Privy Council, who first utilized the dialogue form in a tract on the attempted Spanish invasion. Titled *A Pack of Spanish Lies Sent Abroad in the World*, this tract was published in 1588 by Christopher Barker, printer to the queen, and in a sense it mimics the exhaustive lists of *pro et contra* arguments on either side of a question for which Burghley's personal notes are so famous. Each page of the tract is divided into two columns: on the left, the text of the offending report 'from Spain' is printed in black letter, or 'gothic,' type; on the right, 'a condemnation of the Spanish lies' is printed in Roman pica. Sentence by sentence, the description of Spanish victory on the left is matched by denials and description of Spanish defeat on the right. The impression is very much of a combative dialogue between two abstractions – Spain and England – which brings *A Pack of Spanish Lies* right into line with the numerous dialogues of religious controversy printed that year and the next. For not only did the Spanish threat elicit a fresh wave of anti-Catholic tracts, but this was the period of the Martin Marprelate controversy in England, in which a series of Presbyterian satires on the bishops provoked a cascade of countertracts, most of them attacking Presbyterians and Catholics together as like enemies of good order in the realm. Dialogues were employed by both sides in this controversy. Criticism of the church and its bishops is voiced in John Udall's *The State of the Church of England laid open in a Conference between Diotrephes a Bishop, Tertullus a Papist, Demetrius a Usurer, Pandochus an Innkeeper, and Paul a Preacher of the Word of God* (1588), and the anonymous *Dialogue wherein is Plainly Laid Open, the Tyrannical dealing of L. Bishops against God's Children* (1589), between a Puritan, a Papist, a Jack of Both Sides, and a Minister. The church is defended in the 1588 reprint of John Rainolds, *The Sum of the Conference between John Rainolds and John Hart Touching the Head and the Faith of the Church*; in *Sophronistes: A Dialogue persuading the People to Reverence and Attend the Ordinance of God, in the Ministry of their Own Pastors* (1589); and in Charles Gibbon's *Not So New as True, Being a Very Necessary Caveat for All Christians to Consider Of* (1590).

Examining the back-and-forth, tract-by-tract progress of this battle between dialogues would not only yield an understanding of the various theological and political issues involved in this particular crisis of church and state; it would offer, as well, an opportunity to perceive and attempt to account for significant features of these dialogues that might otherwise go unremarked. For example, one compelling and recurring feature of many of the second, 'pro-government' dialogues is an apparent concern that their own participation in religious controversy could be counterproductive in these times of external danger to the realm, despite their confidence that they were defending what they knew to be right. Ironically, given both the genre and published format in which this concern appears, it is betrayed by a fear of public talk generally, on either side of the question. The dialogue that we might say takes the first step in this direction, though it seems obliviously, is William Averell's *Marvelous Combat of Contrarities* (1588), a dialogue between the Belly, the Back, the Hands, the Feet, and the Tongue. The speakers draw numerous analogies between themselves and the Body Politic (the Belly at one point laments, 'O tempora, o mores!' [B1r]) as they accuse each other of ruining the health of the whole, but eventually it is the Tongue that is identified as the source of all trouble. 'You know, dear brethren,' says the Belly, 'that the tongue is but a little member, but it is nimble, and quickly slideth, yea, hardly may it be restrained, and therefore hath it no measure in talking, for of a spark it will make a flame, and of one coal kindle a great fire ... She is the causer of all discord, she is more slippery than an eel, more piercing than an arrow, she delighteth to make strife between friends, and to make all men enemies' (C2r–v). The Belly seems completely innocent of the irony that it takes a tongue, his and the others in this dialogue, to condemn the tongue for its mischief. Here is a dialogue that self-reflexively condemns dialogue.

By 1589, ambivalence even toward the wagging of the most loyal tongues is quite pronounced in some dialogues. *Temporis Filia Veritas* is a dialogue in which Bennion the Button-maker and Balthesar the Barber discuss a meeting of Parliament in which a quarrel between a Catholic, Protestant, and Puritan is finally appeased by a Plowman, who urges mutual toleration as an alternative to endless wrangling. One of a series of anti-Martin Pasquil tracts formerly attributed to Thomas Nash, *The Return of the Renowned Cavaliero Pasquil of England* (1589), has Marforius several times interrupting Pasquil to warn him against too loudly speaking his mind in public, even though Pasquil is clearly defending Elizabeth's church: 'Speak softly, Cavaliero, I perceive two or three lay their heads at one side, like a ship under sail, and begin to cast about you; I doubt they have over-heard you. This Exchange is vaulted and hollow, and hath such an Echo, as multiplies every word that is spoken by Arithmetic, it makes a thousand of one, and imps so many feathers into every tale, that it flies with all speed into every corner of the Realm' (B3r). Remarkably, we even encounter such expressions of ambivalence toward dialogue in one from this period that is a translation of an earlier work: *The Sack of Rome, Executed by the Emperor Charles' Army* (1590), an English version of *Diálogo de las cosas acaecidas en Roma* by Alfonso de Valdés (1527). Here, the speaker Lattantio explains to his archdeacon friend that it was the wrong living of the clergy and worldly pretensions of the pope that brought this vengeance upon Rome, but most of their discussion is conducted in a church 'where we may talk, and none hear us' (B1r).[14] Nonetheless, a Porter comes upon them and scolds, 'What now my masters, the Church was made to pray in, and not to prate in' (K3r),[15] and he ends their meeting by shooing them out of doors. In sum, the period 1588–90 saw a cluster of dialogues that in various ways conveyed the idea that there is too much dialogue in the world.

We should, finally, reconsider *A Pleasant Battle Between Two Lap Dogs of the Utopian Court*, the 1681 dialogue that seems so greatly to discourage scholarly interest in its genre. It, too, is one of a cluster of dialogues, this one spanning the years 1679–82, the period of the Exclusion Crisis, when the Whigs and Tories first took shape as rival political parties. The Whigs, led by the earl of Shaftesbury, controlled the House of Commons and were calling for the exclusion of Charles II's Roman Catholic brother, James, from the royal succession. Charles refused to allow Parliament to meddle in the rightful succession of the crown to James, and the Tories, who controlled the House of Lords, supported him. From 1679 to 1681 Parliament met three times, and in each the Whigs ignored Charles's instructions not to send up an exclusion bill. The king therefore prorogued and dissolved the three Parliaments very shortly after they convened. The last one, which Charles ordered to meet in Oxford, he dissolved after just eight days. The Whigs knew they had a great deal of popular support for their bill, so they characterized their battle with Charles and the Tories in terms of a contest between country and court: the voice of the people was being stifled by corrupt and Catholic ministers and mistresses, who were advising the king not to allow Parliament to do its patriotic work. The Whigs engineered an impressive nation-wide petition campaign to urge Charles to allow full sessions of Parliament, and they published such tracts as *Vox populi: or, The People's Claim to their Parliament's Sitting* (1681), which deplored the 'surprising and astonishing Prorogations and Dissolutions' of Parliaments.

It is only to be expected, then, that a large number of dialogues would be published just at this time when so many concerned English subjects felt that their voices were being silenced. The debates that could not be conducted in Parliament found articulation in print; or, as I would argue is the strategy of *A Pleasant Battle Between Two Lap Dogs at the Utopian Court*, dialogues appeared that reflected on the absence of proper, meaning Parliamentary, dialogue. 'Utopian court' is an oxymoron, after all. We are meant to register the gap between the sober-minded dialogue that Hythloday says occurs in the wards of Utopia, and this mean-minded squabble at the court of Charles II. The latter represents the discursive environment in which the king has chosen to immerse himself.

We may observe, too, that *A Pleasant Battle Between Two Lap Dogs* participates in a number of specific conversational contests of the period that draw on the notions of inverted utopias and dog-talk as the court's alternative to open debate. In the Tory tract *The Deliquium: or, The Grievances of the Nation Discovered in a Dream* (1681), for example, Lucifer is described presiding as a 'Chairman, or rather Speaker' of his 'Democratic State,' and he gloats with souls who have descended from the 'Eutopia' on earth, where the earl of Shaftesbury rules 'an exact true Pattern' of the devil's republic. *Dialogue upon Dialogue: or L'Estrange, No Papist nor Jesuit but the Dog Towzer* (1681), meanwhile, is an attack on Roger L'Estrange, who was both a prolific Tory polemicist and the court-appointed censor.

A Pleasant Battle Between Two Lap Dogs is also one of several tracts printed during this period that represent a conflict between Nell Gwyn and the duchess of Portsmouth (another in dialogue form is *A Dialogue between the Duchess of Portsmouth and Madam Gwyn at Parting* [1682]). Rhetorically these are quite odd, because though they are designed to satirize conversation at court by depicting petty quarrels between the two royal mistresses, paradoxically they extol Nell Gwyn as an English Protestant foil to the French and Catholic duchess. One senses that the authors champion Nell hesitantly, even apologetically, because they cannot forget that she is a low-born former actress and a mistress of the king. The result is a tentativeness between the lines of the Nell Gwyn vs. Portsmouth dialogues that reflects the Whig's negative argument during the Exclusion Crisis. They wanted to prevent James from succeeding to the crown, but in the absence of a legitimate royal heir they had no one else to recommend. The only choice was Charles's illegitimate son, the duke of Monmouth. He was a Protestant, and he enjoyed a great deal of popularity in the country, but because he was illegitimate the Whigs were loath to be his champion. This difficult political position underlies several Whig dialogues in which the authority of those who speak for the Whig cause, such as Nell and her pet Tutty in *A Pleasant Battle between Two Lap Dogs,* is in some manner qualified, as if their authors were unable even to imagine themselves out of their awkward rhetorical corner. Another example is *A Dialogue at Oxford between a Tutor and a Gentleman, formerly his Pupil, concerning Government* (1681), in which the proponent of an exclusion bill is the young gentleman debating his former master. The gentleman's birth and moral character are without reproach, and his master offers no real counterarguments, so unmistakably this is Whig polemic. But the gentleman seems always aware of his junior position in this meeting, at times even betraying, subtly, a self-consciousness that he may be too ready to lecture his betters, too quick to embrace an exclusion bill as the answer to England's troubles – a 'Monsieur Expedient,' as his Tutor calls him at one point.

Consequently, we see the Tories gradually get the upper hand as we trace their successive dialogues through 1680–1. At first they conceded the Whigs' definition of the conflict as one between country and court, and they adopted the strategy of portraying the Whigs as unscrupulous commoners stirring up dissension. In Roger L'Estrange's *Citt and Bumpkin in a Dialogue over a Pot of Ale, concerning Matters of Religion and Government* (1680), it takes a third speaker by the name of Trueman to enter the conversation and set the yokels straight. The point is, the issue of the royal succession is not one for the general public to debate and decide. The low-born overreach themselves. We get this message again in L'Estrange's *The Casuist Uncas'd in a Dialogue betwixt Richard and Baxter, with a Moderator Between Them for Quietness Sake* (1680).

The Tories must have perceived that this was not the best tactic for their propaganda. Besides being condescending toward many in its target audience, it could be answered by Whig dialogues that depict the court alternative – petty squabbles between the king's mistresses, their lapdogs, and Frenchified courtiers. In comparison, bumpkins in an alehouse might well appear the more virtuous and trustworthy counsellors. So the Tories changed their tactic. In their later dialogues of the period, such as *A Dialogue between Two Porters* (1681), *A Pleasant Discourse Between two Sea-men* (1681), and *A Dialogue betwixt Sam the Ferriman, Will a Waterman, and Tom a Bargeman upon the King's calling a Parliament to meet at Oxford* (1681), we listen in on the sober-minded conversations of ordinary men who lament the fanaticism of the Whig position because it smacks of the 'Good Old Cause' that brought such disaster forty years before.

My hope is that this brief survey of three different clusters of dialogues has demonstrated that English dialogues merit additional study by scholars in the field of Renaissance studies. I will close with two final observations. First, it is not only the short, crude, polemical dialogues that become more interesting when we view them as dialogues between dialogues. The better-known philosophical or humanistic dialogues may also have been participating in the controversies that fuelled the polemical ones, and their rhetorical features would thus be better understood in light of this participation. Thomas Elyot's *Pasquil the Plain* and *Of the Knowledge which Maketh a Wise Man*, for instance, were published by the king's press in a year that Henry VIII's propaganda for the divorce was still in full swing (1533). I have argued that their rhetorical idiosyncrasies only become intelligible when they are viewed in that context.[16] Very likely another example is Henry Neville's *Plato Redivivus*, a lengthy master-pupil dialogue published in 1681 that proposes a new form of government for England. Certainly, we cannot discuss Neville's political philosophy without reference to his intellectual debts to Plato, Cicero, More, and Harrington. But to venture a rhetorical or literary study of *Plato Redivivus*, as a dialogue, we would position ourselves best, I am sure, by attending to its participation in the dialogue of its times – the very dialogue between dialogues that includes *A Pleasant Battle Between Two Lap Dogs at the Utopian Court*.

Second, the study of Renaissance dialogues as sequential components within different 'dialogues between dialogues' should reopen the possibility of writing a truly revelatory history of the genre. Starting with the frank concession that More's *Utopia* is something of an exotic island in English literature, such a history would focus on the numerous, mostly forgotten dialogues that were published in clusters across the span of the sixteenth and seventeenth centuries, and it would combine the explication of textual features with comparative cultural analyses of the different periods in which the clusters appeared. Probably this history would not describe a 'development' or an 'evolution,' as in one mode of the dialogue form 'winning favour' over another mode, comparable to our accounts of the rise of the novel or the progress from 'drab' to 'golden' lyric poetry. But that is a requirement that we can afford to discard. Our higher aim is the formulation of a general theory of English Renaissance dialogue: one that attempts to make explicable the genre's extraordinary attraction, and its function, in early modern English culture.

NOTES

1 For excellent analyses of *Utopia*'s dialogue form, see Schoeck, '"A Nursery of Correct and Useful Institutions'"; Altman, *The Tudor Play of Mind*, 79–87; Elizabeth McCutcheon, *My Dear Peter;* and Kinney, *Humanist Poetics*, 57–88.

2 Compare the learned and moral discourse between two dogs, named Scipio and Berganza, in Cervantes, 'Dialogue of the Dogs,' or Périers's allegory of the Inquisition vs. Protestant reformers in 'A Dialogue between Two Dogs: Hylactor and Pamphagus,' whose interlocutors formerly belonged to Acteon and acquired the power of speech by having bitten out their master's tongue (the fourth dialogue in *Cymbalum Mundi*, 65–74).

3 Deakins, 'The Tudor Dialogue as a Literary Form,' and Day, Jr, 'Elizabethan Prose Dialogue.'

4 Cf. Eva Kushner's perceptive question, in 'Epilogue: The Dialogue of Dialogues': 'Did dialogue permit unrestrained discussion? Or is it the case that we, in the twentieth century, simply tend to credit it with that capacity, and link it with a certain image of the Renaissance mentality?' (260). For twentieth-century studies of English Renaissance dialogues see Merril, *The Dialogue in English Literature;* Crawford, 'The Non-Dramatic Dialogue in English Prose'; Deakins, 'The Tudor Dialogue as a Literary Form'; McLean, 'Early Tudor Prose Dialogues'; and Wilson, *Incomplete Fictions*. Most of these draw upon insights from the standard nineteenth-century study of dialogues by Hirzel, *Der Dialog*, and presume that a survey of the classical models, the Platonic, Ciceronian, and Lucianic, for example, will provide the terms for analysing English dialogues.

5 Studies of More's later use of the dialogue form include Day, Jr, 'Elizabethan Prose Dialogue,' 137–75, and Pineas, 'Thomas More's Use of the Dialogue Form as a Weapon of Religious Controversy'; on Elyot's and Ascham's dialogues, see Wilson, *Incomplete Fictions*, 75–135; on Spenser's, see Bruce, 'Spenser's Irenius and the Nature of Dialogue'; Breen, 'Imagining Voices in *A View of the Present State of Ireland*'; Hadfield, 'Who Is Speaking in Spenser's *A View of the Present State of Ireland*?' and Maley, 'Dialogue-Wise.'

6 The same statement holds true of Thomas Lupton's dialogue, *Too Good to Be True* (1580). Though clearly invoking More's *Utopian* wordplay by staging a meeting between Someone from England and Nobody from Nowhere (reading backwards and translating Siuqila from Ailgna and Omen from Mauqsun), this work turns out to be an unremittingly one-sided and astoundingly unironic description of the rigorous enforcement of laws that makes Mauqsun, as Omen says and as Siuqila agrees, an ideal commonwealth.

7   Deakins, 'The Tudor Prose Dialogue,' 16.

8   Ibid., 18.

9   Wilson, *Incomplete Fictions*, 178. Cf. Burke's discussion, in 'The Renaissance Dialogue,' of a similar distinction made by Carlo Sigonio in *De dialogo* (Venice: Giardano Ziletti, 1562). Sigonio 'divided dialogues into two types, the *dialogi tentativi*,' which are '"experimental dialogues" (or "essays" in Montaigne's sense of the term), and the *obstetrici dialogi* or "midwife dialogues" of the Socratic type,' a contrast that Burke notes may also be likened to the classification that 'contrasts the "open" or skeptical dialogue with the "closed" or didactic form' (3).

10 Cox, *The Renaissance Dialogue*, 6, 7.

11 Warner, *Henry VIII's Divorce*.

12 *A Knight and a Cleric*, originally *Disputatio inter clericum et militem*, is a late thirteenth-century work. The authorship of *A Glass of the Truth* is uncertain, but at the time it was rumoured to be Henry's own composition. The *Doctor and Student* dialogues and *Salem and Bizance* were written by Christopher St. German.

13 See Warner, *Henry VIII's Divorce*, 27–46. For parallel analyses of dialogues published in opposition to the royal press campaign, see 56–8, 89–111, 134–8.

14 'Pues estamos aquí donde no nos oye,' says the speaker Arcidiano. I quote from the edition by Montesinos, which adopts the dialogue's alternative title, *Diálogo de las cosas ocurridas en Roma*, 11.

15 Ibid., 'Mirad, señores: la iglesia no se hizo para parlar, sino para rezar' (155).

16 See Warner, *Henry VIII's Divorce*, 69–81.

Dialogue and the Court

The Development of Dialogue in *Il libro del cortegiano*: From the Manuscript Drafts to the Definitive Version

Olga Zorzi Pugliese

Il libro del cortegiano may be considered the masterpiece of the Renaissance genre of books of conduct.[1] This dialogic treatise, which met with much international success from the sixteenth century on, displays a highly evolved and complex structure that distinguishes it from many other literary dialogues of the period. The author Baldessar Castiglione surpassed his contemporaries in his ability to make the conversations, purportedly occurring at the Montefeltro court of Urbino, appear natural and spontaneous – an achievement which may be due in part to the painstaking care with which he revised and rewrote the work. *Il libro del cortegiano* evolved from the embryonic form it displays in the earliest manuscript drafts, passing through three principal redactions, and ultimately acquiring its characteristic fullness and multidimensionality in the vulgate edition of 1528. Critics who have dealt with the dialogic structure of Castiglione's treatise during its fifteen-year period of gestation have generally dealt with the layering of the text from the point of view of the organisation of the materials – the placing of the section on love,[2] for example – and the varying division into books. Structured at one time in four and then three parts, the work acquired at a later stage of composition a fourth book in which the section on politics was added and the discussion on love was fully worked out as the climax of the work with the hymn to love as its peroration.

The rearrangement and insertion of topics is certainly an essential feature of the development of the final *dispositio* of the work, but there are other aspects of the text's evolution that still warrant attention, namely the manner in which, early on in the *inventio* phase of the composition process, Castiglione assembled and reworked the specific materials for his masterpiece and gave them their final shape. By collating the various versions one can find clues as to how the author created the single components of his dialogue and eventually fashioned them into a multifaceted whole. A close textual analysis reveals the changes that affected the structure of the dialogue and also some of the anomalies[3] that pressures of time did not allow the author to eliminate before he sent the work to press.

The early manuscripts of the *Cortegiano* still extant are the autograph sketches (known as A) in the private collection of the Castiglioni family of Mantua (Ms. II 3 b), and the two drafts of the first redaction found in the Vatican Library (Mss. Vatican lat. 8204 and 8205 usually designated as B and C). There are, as well, the second redaction published in a separate edition by Ghino Ghinassi thirty years ago on the basis of Ms. Vatican lat. 8206, and the manuscript in the Laurentian library in Florence (Ms. Ashburnham 409) used for the third and last redaction which was published in 1528, but the latter two manuscripts are referred to here only marginally. The first two Vatican manuscripts indicated above as B and C have often been cited by modern critics like José Guidi and Piero Floriani; the early drafts from Mantua instead have been examined to date only by a few modern readers, namely, as far as I can tell, Vittorio Cian and Ghino Ghinassi, and more recently by Amedeo Quondam. The earlier scholars, Cian and Ghinassi, in their edition and essays, respectively, did not deal with *all* the variants. Having had the good fortune to be able to consult the Mantua manuscript in person, and after collating the Vatican manuscripts, I have found that a number of interesting facts, some quite new, emerge concerning the composition of the treatise – an aspect not dealt with specifically by Quondam in his book which appeared in 2000.

First of all the early manuscripts reveal that Castiglione began composing his masterpiece by drafting brief outlines for the various sections of it. He wrote the sketches not in the Italian vernacular used for the fully written-out vulgate version but rather, and perhaps surprisingly, in Latin; moreover, the original formulation was not in full-fledged dialogue form but rather in expository prose, at times with brief indications in indirect discourse of what the eventual speakers might be made to say. Other important revisions modifying the form of the treatise may be classified as follows: changes in the roles assigned to the various interlocutors; rejection of the Boccaccian model; the addition of expressions of courtesy and other forms of attenuation, designed to smooth over expressions that were too polemical or impolite; the elimination of erudite allusions that in the early formulations were explicit; and, finally, a reduction in the borrowing of terms and phrases from other languages, especially Spanish.

To begin with, the initial use of Latin sketches is a compositional technique for which there are corresponding examples in other Castiglione documents, namely the autograph Latin notes found in the State Archive of Mantua that Guido La Rocca examined and published in his essay of 1980.[4] In his discussion La Rocca points out how these notes represent an early stage of composition of *Il cortegiano* and were eventually expanded in the treatise. Touching upon subjects pertaining to women, love, and language, they consist mainly of lists of names and words, series of sayings and brief phrases, some of which only begin to assume embryonic dialogue form and name Cesare Gonzaga, Bernardo Bibbiena, and others as the intended speakers.

To these preparatory notes first examined by La Rocca one must add an interesting document, found among the early autograph sketches in the private Castiglioni collection; namely, folio 84r of Ms. A.[5] It contains a fragment of a passage, lacking a beginning and written in Latin, representing the nucleus of the discussion on politics that eventually occupies the first part of Book IV of *Il libro del cortegiano*.[6] It is essentially an outline of some of the main political concepts later presented in greater detail. Briefly it enunciates the following views: that the end of the courtier is to use the means at his disposal to ingratiate himself to the prince, in order to instruct him and teach him virtue; and that the public font must not be contaminated.

> ... so that with respect to this purpose, the courtier is good. Therefore, through these means, he must engage and seek the prince's ear ... not use these means for the ruin of the prince and of the people ... but by teaching justice and other virtues. For no one amongst so many does so much good as he who makes the prince good, just as no one does so much harm as he who makes the prince evil, like he who contaminates a fountain with poison.[7]

A distinction is made between innate and acquired virtues, and there is also mention of the myth of Jupiter, the god who bestowed virtue on mankind through Mercury. The passage containing these ideas, and found on the single folio in question, is written in indirect discourse and bears an indication (through the phrases 'Dicentem Gaspar' and 'respondet Ott[avianus]') that Gasparo Pallavicino and Ottaviano Fregoso will be the main speakers on the subject when the passage is worked out in full.

Why, we might ask, is this the sole passage of consequence in Latin remaining among the folios of manuscript A? A direct examination of fol. 84r proves that the fragmentary document was preserved because, after reelaborating the Latin passage in the Italian vernacular, Castiglione did not destroy the sheet. Instead he used the verso (84v) for the successive stage of composition in the vernacular, repeating in Italian, through the first-person direct discourse of the character Ottaviano (cf. C 187v), the basic notion that the courtier must use his talents as a means to enter into his master's good graces, thereby winning his trust and teaching him virtue:

> I say therefore that the courtier, who is graced with the qualities bestowed upon him by count Ludovico and *messer* Federico, must use those qualities and by means of them try to enter into the good graces of his lord and become his confidante so as to be able subsequently to teach him the good habits and virtues that are suitable for him.[8]

One must consider the significance of Castiglione's recourse to Latin as he first penned his ideas on politics. According to La Rocca, because of his humanist education, the author used Latin as a deliberate personal choice, but not necessarily because he was consulting classical sources at the moment.[9] In the passage that is being examined here, though, Castiglione is, in fact, echoing ideas from Plutarch and Plato.[10] Another of La Rocca's conclusions about the Latin notebook in the State Archive of Mantua is that Castiglione wrote separate units and then brought them together to form his work – a method which the scholar aptly describes as an 'open process of collecting thematic units into a whole.'[11] This is diametrically opposed to what is generally considered to be the normal approach of writers of treatises, who, we surmise, begin with fundamental principles upon which they then build deductions according to logical reasoning. Castiglione's peculiar method of composing by aggregation instead is significant inasmuch as it probably contributes to the uneven structure of his treatise.

Folio 84r of manuscript A owned by the Castiglioni family is important for another reason too, for it throws new light on the dating of the various manuscripts and redactions. One cannot accept in full the chronology proposed by La Rocca (and Ghinassi) who believe that the State Archive notebook represents the veritable nucleus of the whole work.[12] On the basis of internal proof, one observes that the lists of names of famous women found in the notebook[13] cannot date back to the very first phase of composition, as was thought, since only some of the names cited (eight to be exact, including Camma, Artemisia, Telesilla, and the Celtic women) are found in C, the final version of the first redaction which was composed just before 1520, but almost all of them (totalling approximately thirty) are found instead in the second redaction of 1521. This fact demonstrates that the part of the notebook in question represents the first formulation not of the whole work, but rather of a particular section of it, the section on women, that is, which was composed fairly late, not early as is commonly believed.[14] As my collation has demonstrated, in manuscript A we find a collection of preparatory fragments of *various* versions of parts of the treatise, not necessarily the very first formulations of them or of the work as a whole. What is indisputably clear, though, is that Castiglione probably did begin composing with brief sketches and notes in Latin as he worked out the single units of his treatise.

An analysis of the drafts points to another phenomenon, that is, Castiglione's reassigning of the roles of the speakers. In some of the sections in the early drafts that are already fully formed dialogues, the names of the participants are often actually missing. Castiglione left numerous blank spaces in the manuscripts and only later filled in the gaps with indications of the interlocutors' identities. These omissions occur in the Mantua fragments in the case of the narrators of jokes (e.g., A 13v, 22r, 24r–v, 28r), and in Vatican Ms. 8204 in references to the objectors who contradict the main speaker or ask for further clarification (e.g., B 44v, 74r, 116r, 119r, 131r). During a discussion on a suitable manner of dress, for instance, the author formulates an objection, but leaves the name of the speaker blank ('Then, said ____, this would not bother me very much'),[15] clearly because he had not yet decided who would utter certain quips and statements. Only in a few examples is it evident that Castiglione simply could not recall the name of the person he had in mind, as in the case of the brother of the Great Turk,[16] specified as 'Gein Ottomani' only later as a gloss to C 139v. Although these gaps are very frequent in the first Vatican manuscript (B), even in the more fully formed manuscript C containing the complete first redaction, the author left many blank spaces in which he later inserted the appropriate names. The final decision on the identity of the speaker was often made at an advanced stage of the composition process.

This procedure proves that, in the *inventio* stage of composition, Castiglione sketched the fundamental concepts for each topic. But only later did he add the contradictions and definitively assign the various roles to specific characters. One may conclude that indeed the ideological premises preceded the actual dialogue, although the author did have a dialogic structure in mind from the beginning. This order corresponds to the theoretical views on the nature of literary dialogue advanced by other writers of the Renaissance. Lorenzo Valla who, in a passage of his *Antidotum* against Fazio of 1447, had declared well before Castiglione's time that dialogues should be constructed on principles of debate and conflict, had also stated that in dialogic writings, unlike historical works, the characters are to be adapted to the discourse and not the ideas to the person. What counts is *what* is said, wrote Valla, not *who* says it.[17] After Castiglione's time too, Sperone Speroni, the author of numerous dialogues, mentioned in his *Apology of Dialogues* (1574–5) that, at a certain stage in the composition of his dialogue on love, the specific setting and the names of the characters had yet to be determined.[18] There is an obvious parallel between, on the one hand, the theoretical notions of Valla and Speroni expressed in different periods of the Renaissance, one early and the other late, and, on the other hand, Castiglione's literary practice in a period in between. With three different phases of the Renaissance thus represented, it becomes clear that the composition of dialogues in the Renaissance tended to follow this pattern: authors first conceived the ideas and then assigned them to the interlocutors. In sum the discourse evolved from logical reasoning and not according to the development of a story line, in spite of the narrative fiction that underlies the texts.

Castiglione often changed the names of the interlocutors who were engaged in the conversations at Urbino that he purports to record. He eliminated some, added others, carrying out the modifications probably on the basis of the relations he had with his contemporaries, and also in accordance with the changing political situation. In the case of the late substitution of Giuliano de' Medici as the defender of women for the original Bolognese humanist Camillo Paleotto, whose name still appears in the second redaction, it has been argued that the Medici family member was preferred because he was a more important personage.[19] Could it not also be that Giuliano's reputation for gallantry[20] was a consideration and that Castiglione was concerned with verisimilitude too?

In other instances Castiglione undoubtedly conceded to the wishes of his friends, as his letters prove, and removed their names when they objected to being portrayed as narrators of impolite jokes or as participants in undignified pranks. In a letter to Pietro Bembo of 21 September 1518, Castiglione states that he is willing to make any change that the addressee desires if what he has been made to utter in the text does not please him.[21] In a letter of 23 June 1520 to another cardinal – Ippolito d'Este, in this case – Castiglione asks whether there are any passages that offend him in the manuscript.[22] Indeed the cardinal must have taken exception to an analogy that the author had drawn between him and the other cardinals who were said to be guilty of stupidity and senseless awkwardness ('sciochezza e gofferia insensata' C 25r and second redaction, p. 25) since the whole passage was expunged in the definitive redaction, as Ghinassi pointed out.[23] Other revisions too, such as the deletion of the criticism of Ottaviano's extravagant style of dress (B 124v), the eventual substitution of messer Roberto for Ottaviano on the question of lack of dancing ability (C 38v), and that of the servant Golpino for Giuliano de' Medici in the anecdote about a thin man being swept up a chimney (C 142r), must have been motivated by the desire not to offend his associates.

On the other hand, one character who was present in the text from the very beginning of the composition process, through all the redactions, is Gasparo, a descendant of the noble Pallavicino family of Cortemaggiore.[24] A good friend of Castiglione's (and the character who, according to the fiction of the treatise, relayed all the discussions at Urbino to the author), the marquis is characterized by a penchant for strong contradictions. Contrariness colours his interjections right from the earliest sketches of the work on issues concerning the importance of nobility, for example, a notion which he challenges quite vigorously in A 4r–v and B 106r, 126v. A few significant changes do occur, however, affecting his fate in the text. In the elaboration of Castiglione's treatise Pallavicino eventually loses his role as defender of republics, a role he had in the preparatory fragments, where he had praised freedom given by God as a supreme gift.[25] More appropriately this assignment later falls to the Venetian Pietro Bembo (e.g., C 199v). In spite of this change, though, Gasparo acquires, in the last stages of composition, a strong presence and strident voice as chief misogynist of the company – a role originally assigned to Ottaviano. Although he had died at a young age, as Castiglione ruefully acknowledges in the introduction to Book IV, Gasparo was thus given a memorable role in the text.

Another revision concerning Gasparo is to be noted: in the final version of the first redaction (C 25r and passim) in all occurrences of his name, the title preceding his name is altered. The simple *messer*, used in the first two manuscripts (A and B), is deleted in favour of the more noble *signore*. This change was probably due to Castiglione's wish to respect the dictates of social hierarchy as, over time, he became increasingly aware of the importance of political expediency. Later in the sixteenth century, it is interesting to note, during a period of even greater pressures to conform and remain orthodox, the writer Giovanni Della Casa was to advise a correct use of titles citing precisely the choice between these same two titles that correspond to the English Mister and My Lord.[26]

One of the more fundamental name changes that actually affects the basic structure of the text relates to Emilia Pia, who by the second redaction[27] acquired the role of lieutenant ('locotenente') for the duchess Elisabetta, thereby assuming the direction of the proceedings on the four evenings. Originally Castiglione had referred to her in the text as the *regina* (or queen), as Cian had noted.[28] In the final draft of the first redaction (C), instead, all occurrences of the term *regina* to describe Emilia are changed to 'madonna Emilia.' The frequency with which the queen (whose name was not always specified) was mentioned shows how Castiglione had begun with Boccaccio's *Decameron* as his model. In the earlier version of the first redaction he had specified that for the conversations of each evening there was to be a king or queen who would keep order (B 12v). The decision to eliminate this Boccaccian structure has been assessed convincingly by Guidi, who observes that, by abandoning the model provided by the *Decameron*, Castiglione showed that the rotating monarchical system which in Boccaccio's text had allowed for a different queen or king on each day, was no longer advisable in the less democratic days of the sixteenth century.[29]

As Castiglione's text developed, some fundamental narrative techniques were also modified. The most important of these perhaps was the point of view adopted by the writer. The personal pronoun adopted frequently in the first formulations of the work, both by the authorial narrator in the frame, as well as by some of the characters in the dialogues, was eventually eliminated, as the examples cited below illustrate. It would appear that at the outset the first-person authorial narrator represented himself as having been present at the conversations but then, probably following the example of Cicero,[30] he claimed that he had been away ('benché io non vi fosi presente' B 12r) and added references to his visit to England (C 6v, 219v) to explain his absence.[31] Thus his role was limited to that of transcriber and extradiegetical narrator. On this subject Guidi has conjectured that, wishing to avoid problems, Castiglione had tried to create the impression that the work was the result of a group effort[32] and thus that the ideas were not necessarily his own, but rather those of the whole court. In the manuscripts we find many instances where the pronoun *noi* (we) is deleted and the third person is substituted. In one case a phrase providing an opening to a tale refers to the discussions that *we* have heard ('noi havemo uditi' B 35v); eventually the phrase in the manuscript about the discussions was corrected to read 'were rehearsed' (forno recitati). Similarly, the harmony existing at the court of Urbino which, in the earlier version, was like a chain holding all of *us* united ('una catena che tutti *ci* tenea uniti' B 19r) and a heartfelt love which existed among all of *us* ('amor cordiale ... [che] tra tutti *noi* era') becomes more impersonally that which held *everyone*, not all of us, together, as the personal pronouns *ci* and *noi* are cancelled. In another part of the description of the court and its distinguished membership the phrase 'la casa *nostra*' (B 21r) (*our* home) is changed to 'la casa' without the possessive adjective (C 11v).

Other strategies adopted by Castiglione make the overall structure and tone of the work less personal and compromising, but also confer on the dialogue a more natural air and greater *sprezzatura*. Witty remarks are inserted more frequently in the midst of serious discussions to lighten the tone. In the discussion on care of the body and its subordination to care of the soul, already touched upon in B 62v, Ottaviano in jest interjects a request to consult a *plumper* authority on the subject.[33] In addition to such use of humour as part of the movement toward a more serene tone, there is also considerable attenuation of the aggressiveness shown at first by some speakers. This is evident in the first phases of composition and especially in the introductory part of the text where suggestions are made for the topics to be discussed. In the early versions the character Bernardo Bibbiena had acted in a rather disorderly and rebellious fashion. Not only did he ask questions instead of providing contradictory views, as the established rules prescribed (B 51v); not only, furthermore, did he express the wish to suggest four topics instead of one topic for discussion (he manages to propose only two in actual fact); but he also tells one of his female associates quite bluntly that the ladies must not speak this evening ('le donne questa sera non hanno da parlare' B 29v). In the first drafts, in fact, the ladies are silenced several times and in a manner that is brusquer than the one used in the vulgate where the injunctions are couched in more courteous terms.

In the early redactions the poet Unico Aretino too displays rudeness with none other than the duchess when he utters the following order to her: 'Do not speak ... because it is not now your turn to speak.'[34] Although he was her senior by a number of years and may have felt it his prerogative to treat her in such a condescending manner, it is shocking nonetheless that he should call her 'figliola bella' (my dear girl) not 'Signora' (My Lady), as in the definitive version of the treatise (Book I, chapter 9).

Castiglione makes a number of revisions to his text in order to reduce such elements of conflict, especially where the women are involved. Even in passages where the original impolite remarks are retained, he adds along the way one narrative tag in particular to lessen the impact of the impudent remark. He inserts the gerund 'ridendo' (laughingly) in the manuscripts many a time for this purpose. For example, when Emilia decides to halt the discussion on language and issues a warning (C 50r), the author adds an explanation that these words were spoken 'ridendo.' We find this attenuating term used seventeen times in the draft of the first redaction (B), almost three times that number in the final version of the first redaction (C), and sixty-six times in the vulgate. In all cases it qualifies a verb indicating speech and serves to soften the utterances recorded. Even if the definitive version of *Il cortegiano* is a considerably longer text and therefore could potentially have included more occurrences of the word, the increase in frequency is quite striking.

In addition to wishing to establish a cordial atmosphere for the conversations he narrates, Castiglione was concerned, of course, with achieving *sprezzatura* and avoiding an affected style. Perhaps it was in order to create greater naturalness that he also attempted to veil the erudite allusions in his text. In the Mantuan drafts he had originally cited Ovid in connection with the art of deceiving women (A 79r). In the following version, instead, the classical author's name disappears and the author refers simply to someone who had cleverly composed tracts and made great efforts to teach his readers how to deceive women.[35] Another explicit reference to Ovid in connection with Troy in A 77r is also suppressed in C 288v. Castiglione deletes Aristotle's name too on the question of the fundamental difference between men and women. In the Mantua fragments he had quoted the philosopher in relation to women's physical weakness with respect to man's greater strength and aggressiveness,[36] but later the statement is softened considerably: 'although it seems that nature has produced them [women] with a weaker body and serene soul.'[37] Ironically, the explicit references to his classical sources decrease – except when he is discussing literature – while his actual usage of ancient lore and his borrowing of philosophical concepts in the text increase. There is evidence in Castiglione's letters that even at a fairly late date, he continued to consult books from which he could glean information and ideas for his treatise,[38] but with *sprezzatura* he attempts to veil the erudite foundation of his writing.[39]

His overriding concern for *sprezzatura* affected the evolution of the text in another way too, namely a reduction in the use of Latin (and Spanish) terminology. In the fragmentary sketches there is a reference in Latin to the golden age. The phrase 'aurea ... secula' appears on A 90v, although we find 'età d'oro' in Italian immediately afterwards on A 91r. In the next redaction, however, the corresponding passage contains no Latin, but merely an allusion to the 'etate d'oro' when Saturn reigned (C 198r). In many of the witticisms quoted too, some Spanish phrases used originally for the narrative parts are eliminated, while the punchline uttered by the Spanish characters involved is kept in a few instances.[40]

The last category of revisions to be dealt with in this essay includes those that, instead of generally improving the work, actually complicate the narrative or obfuscate it, at least from the point of view of the literal meaning of the text. Some jokes are shortened, for example, and for one anecdote the abbreviated rendition found in Book II, chapter 78 of the vulgate actually results in a lack of clarity. When a man asks how he should disguise himself in order not to be recognized, he is told to dress like a learned man (A 47v). A modern critic, who failed to grasp the irony, has noted for this passage that intellectuals tended to be poor and shabbily dressed.[41] In the original version Castiglione had added that a learned man's attire would have been the best disguise for the individual involved ('la maggior tramutione che possi fare' A 47v), thus highlighting his intention to ridicule the foolish person and at the same time praise intellectuals. The shorter version lacking the explicit elucidation may be more succinct, but it does lead to ambiguity. Even the tale told in Book II, chapter 93 about the horns sketched at the entrance to signora Boadiglia's home, said by the principal interlocutor Bibbiena to be rather risqué, contains some anomalies. In its first formulation the narratee to whom the anecdote is addressed was the queen, but in the definitive text the witticism is told to a third person (the countess of Castagneto). Nevertheless the initial reference to the unidentified queen is retained in the definitive text. It is said that she was accompanying the narrator along the street and passed in front of the house – a narrative detail that is completely gratuitous and makes sense only in the first drafts of the passage in question. Clearly, when he recast his work in a less Boccaccian framework, the author forgot to delete the reference to the queen at this point in the story.[42]

There are other revisions too that produce discrepancies in the text. The phrase 'suspetto fuggitivo' (a suspect and fugitive)[43] which closes the treatise seems to be vague and perhaps deliberately so; it can even prompt the reader to devise strange symbolic interpretations as, I must confess, I have done myself in the past.[44] In an early version of the text, before the author trimmed the passage, namely in the fully worked-out first redaction C (but not in A or B), the meaning was transparent. The misogynist Ottaviano was to be handed over to the prefect and held as a captive under guard, since there was the danger that he might attempt to flee. In the Latin notebook studied by La Rocca too we find in one of the lists an annotation referring to this episode in the narrative plot: 'Custodiatur ut fugitivus' (He is to be guarded as a fugitive).[45] The cryptic phrase in the closing words of the treatise about Gasparo's being 'suspetto fuggitivo' instead is certainly less transparent.

Castiglione must have been acutely aware that such discrepancies still marred his work, which he was being pressured to release for publication. They may very well account for the deep regret that he expressed, in the prefatory letter of the vulgate edition, over the fact that his cherished book was being published before he could make final revisions. The strong desire he strenuously expressed to have more time to do so was probably more than a mere expression of modesty, as is generally thought. Content to leave the linguistic and grammatical editing to others, he must have wished to correct the more substantial flaws himself.

The discussion contained in this essay does not constitute by any means an exhaustive treatment of the evolution of the structure of the *Libro del cortegiano*, but it should serve to explain how certain formal aspects of the text developed. We must be grateful to Castiglione who was always very jealous of his papers and preserved the first drafts of his masterpiece. Although some parts have undoubtedly been lost over the centuries, the considerable number of manuscripts and sketches that are extant allows us to trace the development of many parts of the treatise and also the growth of the author's ideas on various topics. As I have discovered in my research to date, quite radical revisions are to be found in Castiglione's observations on politics and the role of the courtier, in the portrayal of women, and even in the repertory of witticisms he includes in the text. From the formal point of view too, the manuscripts provide a glimpse into the manner in which one of the classics of Renaissance literature was composed and, more pertinently, what the inner mechanisms of the dialogue genre were in that age.

NOTES

1 See the assessment by Patrizi, 'Il libro del cortegiano e la trattatistica sul comportamento.' A shorter version of this paper was presented at the meeting of the Modern Language Association in Toronto in December 1997. An essay on the same subject written in Italian has appeared in the proceedings of a conference on Renaissance dialogue held in Antwerp in February 1997 (see Pugliese, 'L'evoluzione della struttura dialogica nel *Libro del cortegiano*'). In the present essay I report on the results of a research project that is still underway and has been funded by the Social Sciences and Humanities Research Council of Canada. I have already presented orally some of the results of my research on various occasions and at various venues in North America, Europe, and South Africa.

2 See Ghinassi, 'Fasi dell'elaborazione del *Cortegiano*,' and Floriani, 'Dall'amore cortese all'amor divino.'

3 Ghinassi, 'Fasi dell' elaborazione del *Cortegiano*,' 174–6, speaks in general terms of the gaps and imbalance in the text.

4 La Rocca, 'Un taccuino autografo per il *Cortegiano*.'

5 The references are to the second series of fragments in the Mantua manuscript.

6 I wish to thank Professor Gian Carlo Alessio of the University of Venice for the suggestions he generously gave me in connection with the transcription and interpretation of this difficult passage in the manuscript.

7 ' ... sicut ad hunc finem, bonus est curialis. Debet igitur his mediis ingredi et aucupari aurem principis ... non uti illa ad perniciem principis et populorum ... sed ad docendum iustitiam et alias virtutes, nam nemo tam bene meretur de multis quam qui bonum facit principem, sicut etiam male qui malum, ut si quis veneno fontem viciet ...' (my own translation).

8 'Dico adonque che 'l corteggiano ornato de le qualitati dategli dal conte Ludovico e messer Federico deve usarle e per meggio di esse procurare d'entrare in gratia del suo signore e farseli charo et intrinseco per poter poi ... formarlo di quelli boni costumi e virtuti che se gli convengono.' This passage is found in C 187v and the speaker is Ottaviano. On fol. 85v of manu-

script A the discussion continues with the statement that a good prince is the supreme universal good while an evil prince is the worst universal evil ('non è bene alchuno che così universalmente giovi come il bon principe, né male che così universalmente noccia, come el mal principe'). Evil princes infect the whole populace with fatal poison, not like a pitcher from which only one person drinks, but like a public fountain used by all the people ('non un vaso dove un solo habbia da bere, ma el fonte publico dil quali usi tutta la gente di un paese, infettano di mortal veneno').

9   La Rocca, 'Un taccuino autografo per il *Cortegiano*,' 354–5.

10 Cf. Plutarch's 'Maxime cum principibus philosopho esse disserendum' in *Moralia* on virtue and the contamination of the public fount (Plutarch, *Moralia*, 365), and Plato's *Protagoras*, sections 320C–322A, on the myth of Prometheus (Plato, *Protagoras and Meno*, 52–3).

11 'Un processo aperto di aggregazione tematica' (La Rocca, 'Un taccuino autografo per il *Cartegiano*,' 359).

12 'Il vero germe grafico di *tutta* la celebre opera [emphasis mine]' (ibid., 348).

13 Ibid., 363–6.

14 There is also extratextual proof: in an undated letter addressed to a certain 'Paolo' (Castiglione, *Lettere inedite e rare*, 109–10), Castiglione asked for information on the Sibylls and other famous women. Guido Ghinassi ('Postille sull'elaborazione del *Cortegiano*,' 172–3) advances the hypothesis that the Paolo in question was Paolo Canale who died in 1508 and that, therefore, Castiglione began to work on the topic of the defence of women very early. But it could be that another Paolo is involved here and that the letter was written much later. As Ghinassi himself states, reference to the Sibylls is first found in the first redaction, but, it should be pointed out, only in the *final* version of the redaction (C 244v), and consequently quite late, long after Paolo Canale had died.

15 'Allhor disse   , questo a me daria poca noia' (B 125v).

16 'fratello del gran turco' (A 37v).

17 'Neque enim historiam, sed dialogum scribis, ubi pro nostro arbitratu sermonem cui volumus attribuimus, ubi non orationem persone, sed personam orationi accommodamus, ubi nihil admodum refert quis, sed quid loquatur' (II, ix, 11); passage quoted by Mariarosa Cortesi, in the introduction to her edition of Lorenzo Valla, *De professione religiosorum*, lxxix.

18 Speroni, *Apologia dei dialogi*, 692, states that his dialogues on love were at one time without a specific setting and without the names of the persons later introduced ('li dialogi dell'amore ... allora senza alcun luogo determinato e senza i nomi delle persone che vi sono ora introdotte'). I have dealt elsewhere with the Renaissance theory of dialogue (see Pugliese, *Il discorso*

labirintico del dialogo rinascimentale, 7–51, and 'Sperone Speroni and the Labyrinthine Discourse of Renaissance Dialogue.'

19 Floriani, 'I personaggi del Cortegiano,' 167.

20 Cian, 'Dizionarietto biografico,' 521, speaks of Giuliano's licentious life style.

21 Castiglione, *Le lettere*, 384.

22 Ibid., 547.

23 Ghinassi, 'Fasi dell'ellaborazione *del Cortegiano*,' 179–80.

24 Cian, 'Dizionarietto biografico,' 524.

25 'La libertà data da Dio per supremo dono' (A 91r).

26 In *Galateo*, chapter 16, Della Casa insists on the need to use the proper title and not to address with the title 'messer' those who are accustomed to being called 'signore.'

27 Castiglione, *La seconda redazione del* Cortegiano, 11.

28 *Il libro de cartegiano del conte Baldesar Castiglione*, ed. Vittorio Cian, 4th ed. Florence: Sansoni, 1947, 273n.

29 Guidi, 'Le jeu de cour et sa codification dans les différentes rédactions du *Courtisan*,' 104.

30 See Cicero, *De oratore*, III, iii, 16, where the narrator is not present at the conversation but receives a report about it. Castiglione had requested his own annotated copy of *De oratore* in a letter of 5 October 1514 addressed to his steward (*Le lettere*, 364).

31 As Freccero states in 'Politics and Aesthetics in Castiglione's *Il cortegiano*,' 265, there is a 'near-total effacement of the author-narrator.' Her explanation for this technique is a political one: 'This strategy, the claim to representational accuracy, seeks to "refashion" reality, to cope with, perhaps resolve, the political tensions of the context.'

32 Guidi, 'Baldassar Castiglione et le pouvoir politique,' 259.

33 '"Dimandatine," respose el signor Ottaviano ridendo "a questi che lo nutriscono bene e sonno grassi e freschi, ché 'l mio, come vedete, non è troppo ben curato"' (C 209 v).

34 'non parlate ... ché non è il loco vostro hora di parlare' (B 27r).

35 'chi habbia ingegnosamente composto libri e postoli ogni studii per insegnare di che modo ... s'habbiano ad ingannare le donne' (C 275r).

36 'secondo Aristotile, come l'homo per fortezza è più pugnace e bellicoso, la donna, per le imbecillità del corpo è più cauta' (A 76r–v).

37 'benché para che la natura le habbia produtte del corpo debile e de animo placido ...' (C 232v).

38 Ghinassi, 'Postille sull'elaborazione del *Cortegiano*,' 176n7.

39 Castiglione's explanation of the concept of *sprezzatura* includes the Ovidian

notion of concealing one's art. See Pigman, 'Versions of Imitation in the Renaissance,' 11–14, on the phenomenon of dissimulative imitation in the Renaissance.

40 Essays of mine on the role of Latin in the use of Spanish in the composition of *Il cortegiano* are forthcoming in volumes to be published in the United Kingdom and Mexico.

41 See the note by Nicola Longo in *Il libro del cortegiano*, Introduction by Amedeo Quondam, 228: 'Gli intellettuali, per le loro scarse risorse economiche, vestivano in modo trasandato' (Intellectuals, because of their limited financial resources, used to dress in a shabby manner).

42 The various versions of the tale are found in A13r, 63r; C168r; *Seconda redazione*, p. 175. There are three references to the queen in the first instance, two in the second, and then only one in C and subsequent versions.

43 The phrase is translated thus in *The Book of the Courtier*, trans. Charles S. Singleton, 360.

44 Pugliese, 'Love and Death and Their Function as Frames in *The Book of the Courtier*,' 142.

45 La Rocca, 'Un taccuino autografo per il *Cortegiano*,' 370.

Pietro Aretino between the *locus mendacii* and the *locus veritatis*

Robert Buranello

In every area, the capacity to do what is appropriate is a matter of art and natural ability, but to know what is appropriate at each time is a matter of intelligence.

Cicero, *De oratore*, III 212

Pietro Aretino has long been recognized as a harsh satirist, yet an intriguing one with undeniable talent and far-reaching influence. While this may be due primarily to the success of his works of theatre and his famous letters, attention must also be paid to his dialogues for these works reveal much in terms of the literary innovation that accompanied his satire. Although he is most famous for his *Dialogues* regarding whoredom (*Sei giornate* [1534]), his other dialogical works are also deserving of careful consideration.[1] These are the *Dialogue of the Courts* (*Ragionamento delle corti* [1538]) and *The Talking Cards* (*Le carte parlanti* [1543]).[2] The main focus of this study is the dialogical production of Pietro Aretino, and primarily the *Dialogue of the Courts*. The aim is to shed light on the ways in which the dialogue genre was an effective tool in Aretino's literary arsenal.[3] His dialogues offer not only mordant satire but also a provocative alternative to life in the courts of sixteenth-century Italy. Aretino accomplishes this by inhabiting an ambiguous middle ground, a dialogical one, between the setting of truth and that of mendacity.

Pietro Aretino's *Dialogue of the Courts* has long been regarded as a scathing attack on court life, particularly directed against the court of Rome. This is primarily achieved through the juxtaposition of conflicting images and interpretations. As in his earlier comedy *The Courtesan*

(La cortigiana), where Rome is denigrated from the traditional *caput mundi* (summit) to *coda mundi* (bottom)[4] and Venice is exalted as 'the Holy City and Terrestrial Paradise,' in the *Dialogue of the Courts* the chaos of the Roman court is contrasted to the calm of Francesco Marcolini's Venetian residence.[5] Further, the secular courts are judged against the celestial court.[6] The former are seen as the location of falsehood and the latter of truth or, in other words, the *locus mendacii* is juxtaposed to the *locus veritatis*. Alessandro Fontana and Jean-Louis Fournel have identified the interpretation of the socio-political situation of the time as one of contrasting opposites in these terms as particularly appropriate. According to these critics, it is by means of the court that the polysemic value of the state is communicated. The underlying principle is fraud, seen not only as a means of dissimulation and the concealment of significant information, but of simulation, of lies, and of confession. The court is indicative of the spectacle of symbolic power and the eclipse of real power; further, the first is, in fact, an indication of the latter.[7]

The *Dialogue of the Courts* is Pietro Aretino's attempt to find the most suitable environment for the early sixteenth-century man of letters who, due to socio-historical forces and circumstances, must inevitably navigate between truth and falsehood and endeavour to find an appropriate niche. Through numerous literary and historical references to the society of his day, Aretino proposes an intriguing alternative to the court for the sixteenth-century *letterato*. By analysing the *Dialogue of the Courts* and other parallel texts from the points of view of the setting, the characters, and their interactions, I intend to explore the fuller dimensions of Aretino's proposed ideal forum for the contemporary *letterati*.

Conversations occur in a place, whether real or fictitious and, in the case of literary dialogues, this place is described either explicitly by means of diegetic description or through mimetic implication. Except for the purely hypothetical ones, most conversations occur in a social space.[8] The dialogue is, in general, a tactful combination of artistic and philosophical considerations in which the immediacy, vividness, and 'situationality' (general situational background) of the dialectical tendencies of the exchange of ideas form the 'plot' of the work. Unlike the epic or narrative, the dialogue does not tell the story; like theatre, it shows the activity of thought, with attention to setting. Albert William Levy's statement regarding the importance of the dialogue's particular nature for philosophy is especially revealing for the light it sheds on the role of the setting. He sees it as a contributing factor toward what he calls the 'situationality' and 'characterological embodiment' of the discourse.[9]

The issue of the function of the setting in an analysis of dialogical exchange is therefore of central concern. Terry Comito has observed the etymological link between the concept of place and the recorded settings in which certain activities occur. The setting indicates a physical place, but also an opportunity or occasion and, consequently, a situation, state, or condition. He concludes that the 'word that begins by pointing to where ends by specifying what.'[10] The importance of 'situationality' and deictic markers in dialogues strengthen 'characterological embodiment' and are therefore important complementary elements of the effectiveness of the dialogue's discourse.

This is certainly the case with Aretino's *Dialogue of the Courts* where the spatio-temporal referent is imbued with meaning from literary tradition. This mimetic dialogue takes place in a garden setting, referred to with Petrarchan echoes as 'Marcolino's little garden' (45). As Carla Forno reminds us, this setting is the 'location of conversation, par excellence' whose symbolic importance, beyond the ability to convey the idea of perfection and harmony, also extends to the implied reconciliation of art and nature.[11]

In relation to Aretino's discussion of the courts, two other dialogues stand out in particular. One is Baldassare Castiglione's *Book of the Courtier* of 1528 and the other is Aretino's own *Dialogues* of 1534.[12] Differing from Castiglione, Aretino remains pointedly parodistic and, at times, even provides mordant criticism of the courts in the *Dialogues*. Though they share certain thematic similarities, the *Dialogues* and the *Dialogue of the Courts* also have important distinguishing factors. The *Dialogues* are an intentionally ironic rewriting of *The Book of the Courtier*; the *Dialogue of the Courts* is a much more direct attack on the concept of court, and in particular that of Rome. As Giulio Ferroni has correctly pointed out, the *Dialogue of the Courts* is truly ambitious in its scope for it is intended as the culmination of his dialogical treatment of a 'science of the world' and proof of the author's ability to identify and faithfully convey the structures and behavioural characteristics of the inhabitants of the courtly world in their totality.[13]

Despite the somewhat divergent treatments of the subject matter, both the *Dialogue of the Courts* and the *Dialogues* can be seen as complementary works that provide keen insight into the setting of the court as a dialogic scene of speaking. The *Dialogues* maintain the same strict coherence between characters, place, occasion, and subject matter that characterizes the dialogues of Pietro Bembo and Baldesar Castiglione.[14] Here, however, there is a very strong comic and even obscene tone that inverts the sense of decorum that informs Bembo's *Asolani* and Castiglione's *Courtier*.[15] The *Dialogues* are a discussion between Nanna and Antonia in which the former, a successful prostitute, instructs her interlocutor on the three possible pursuits available to women: to become a nun, a married woman, or a whore. Part II of the *Dialogues* is dedicated to a discussion of the art of being a whore. The *Dialogues*'s decorum is found in the appropriateness of speech, interaction, and subject matter with relation to the characters. Like the speakers in the dialogues of Bembo and Castiglione, the interlocutors of the *Dialogues* are all culled from a homogeneous social milieu.[16]

The decorum, therefore, is first displayed by the main character, Nanna. She is a successful whore who has passed through each of the three vocations open to women. Rather than being relegated to a secondary role, as in the *Courtier*, the women in Aretino's dialogue are the protagonists because only they have first-hand knowledge of the subject. Antonia determines the topic for discussion as being particularly appropriate and she encourages Nanna to pursue the profession by reminding her that it is 22 July, the feast of St Mary Magdalene, patron saint of sinful women:

ANTONIA: Tell me, I beg you, since in any case this is the feast day of Magdalene, our patroness, when our particular work is not done, and even if it were, I have enough bread, wine and cured meat to last us for three days.[17]

As can be seen, Aretino has established the appropriateness of the characters, the topic, and the occasion for the dialogue. Certainly not lost on the readers of this passage is the parodistic fashion in which Aretino plays on the classical concept of *otio*. The setting of the dialogues is also of fundamental importance for it, too, coincides with the general purpose of the work and must contribute to the 'homogeneity' of the picture. In diametrical opposition to the harmoniously designed garden of Bembo's *Asolani*, and the perfect symmetry of Urbino and the impressive palace of Castiglione's *Courtier*, the discussions in Aretino's *Dialogues* take place in a setting that reinforces the potential for discussion of an 'uncivilized' topic. Both outdoor settings, the first being under the fig tree and the second under the peach tree of Nanna's garden, reveal the metaphorical potential for obscenity.

Then, after stuffing their bellies as a lodger does at his own sweet will, they returned to the vineyard and sat down in the same place they had before, under the fig tree; and since the hour had come when one chases the heat with the fan of chitchat, Antonia spread her palms on her knee-caps, stuck her face right into Nanna's, and said: 'Now I am really clear about the nuns, and after my first catnap I wasn't able to shut an eye, just thinking of those crazy mothers and foolish fathers who believe that their daughters who become nuns do not have teeth to bite with, like the girls who get married; but I do pity them! They ought to know that these girls are also made of flesh and bone and that nothing whets the desire so much as forbidding it.'[18]

The next day they arrived as planned and sat down under the peach tree. The midwife sat between the wet nurse and Nanna, while like a gallant Pippa sat opposite the midwife. Just at that point a large peach, which had remained on the tree, fell on the midwife's head, and the wet nurse said, while laughing: 'Now you can't deny that when men made you give up the peaches of your ass, you didn't like to.' 'I admit that I didn't,' she answered.[19]

As Nuccio Ordine reminds us, the fig tree and the peach tree are met-aphorically associated with the practices of whores. While the peach tree is an explicit reference to the practice of sodomy, the fig tree goes beyond the more obvious allusion to the female genitalia to allude to patristic literature. It was, in fact, under a fig tree that St Augustine experienced his miraculous conversion to Christianity and renuncia-tion of the temptation of the flesh. Instead, with Aretino, the fig tree is the witness to the conversion of the innocent Pippa to the vices of the flesh, or rather, 'from conversion to perversion, from the pleasures of the spirit to those of the flesh.'[20] The garden setting, as established by Bembo, is therefore 'assaulted and degraded in the obscene image of Nanna's garden.'[21] It is a key element to understanding the full dimen-sions of the parodistic potential of the dialogue.[22] Similarly, the spatio-temporal referent in the *Dialogue of the Courts* plays a significant role in that dialogue's treatment of the subject matter.

Aretino's *Dialogue of the Courts* is a mimetic dialogue divided into two books. The discussions in this entirely mimetic work take place in the garden outside the Venetian house of the publisher Francesco Marcolini[23] which, given the objective of the work, serves as an ideal setting. It is a *locus amoenus*. However, it receives no detailed description beyond the initial words of the interlocutors at the beginning of Part I and Part II. Dolce opens the dialogue with the following *exordium*:

DOLCE: We may consider Marcolini's pleasant little garden a kind of summer fan because to draw in its gentle breeze, the shade of its trees, the sweet perfume of its flowers and the song of its Petrarchan birds is so refreshing, enriching, delightful and relaxing. It is so much better to stroll here than to be out in the heat of today's, or even yesterday's boiling August afternoon sun. So, we will sit and wait here for Piccardo who is due to arrive.[24]

The interlocutors of the *Dialogue of the Courts* are Lodovico Dolce, Francesco Coccio, and Pietro Piccardo, but the latter is replaced by Giovanni Giustiniani in the second part of the dialogue. The choice of characters is determined as much by their personal friendships with the author, as by what they represent as active members of the higher intellectual circles of the time. Lodovico Dolce was the famous polygraph and translator with ties to the productive book industry in Venice;[25] Francesco Coccio was a *letterato*, translator, and poet who was one of Aretino's literary disciples; Pietro Piccardo, an older prelate with first-hand knowledge of the environment of the Roman court; and Giovanni Giustiniani, a poet and translator of Cicero's *Second Philippic*. As Fulvio Pevere has pointed out, the choice of these interlocutors is directly linked to the fundamental theme of the dialogue, that is, the way in which the intellectual must present himself to those in power. In other words, with the first three characters we are presented with a group that represents various aspects of Aretino's own personal tribulations at the Roman court: there is the *poligrafo* with professional ties to the printing industry; the young *letterato* (as Aretino had been) who is enchanted by the enticements of the illusory and treacherous court; and the more mature and removed character who knows the secrets and baseness of that kind of life.[26]

The discussions concern Francesco Coccio's intention to abandon his university studies in favour of trying his fortunes at the court of Rome.[27] That this dialogue is intended as an invective against life at court is made obvious from the very beginning:

COCCIO: Now, let's drop the fairy tales. What do you think of my intention to *withdraw* from my studies and *give myself over* to the courts?
DOLCE: I think you are a beast, if such is the firmness of your convictions.
COCCIO: *Madonna*, yes, it certainly is.

DOLCE: *Messere*, you meant to say. There, in the *error* of the gender of your
   choice of word, is proof of the folly that you, a wise man, consider commit-
   ting. Beyond that, it is a bad omen to *corrupt* language when making a
   decision.[28]

This exchange is characterized by such opposites as 'withdraw' against
'give myself over,' 'Madonna' against 'Messere,' and further distinguished as examples of 'error' and 'corruption.' It underlines the fundamental point that one cannot 'give oneself over to the courts'
without first 'withdrawing from one's studies,' implying not only a
lack of intellectual freedom but also a sense of prostituting oneself for a
presumed good that will, in the end, only lead to a profound moral
corruption of the individual and an abandonment of higher ideals. Piccardo is unequivocal in his depiction of the court. It is referred to as,
for example, 'school of fraud,' 'market of mendacity,' 'terra firma of
flattery,' 'paradise of vice,' and 'purgatory of uprightness and the
limbo of light heartedness' (49–50).

   The corrupted perception of the courts that informs these juxtaposi-
tions is made clear by Piccardo in the following exchange:

PICCARDO: Oh God, Why isn't mendacity truth? Why is she not God?
COCCIO: What would be the point?
PICCARDO: It would be that the truth, a serpent unanimously despised, would
   become a lie, a universal remedy sought by everyone.
COCCIO: He who knows how to lie knows how to rule; whoever does not lie,
   does not rule.[29]

The arrival of Piccardo marks the beginning of the concerted effort
on the part of the two older men to dissuade Coccio from his expressed
plan of abandoning his studies for the court. Piccardo's many years of
first-hand experience make him an authority on the issue, and it is
therefore difficult to dispute his claims.

PICCARDO: Now believe me that nobody, except messer Fabrizion da Parma,
   could inform you better than I regarding the goings-on at court.[30]

Just prior to his agreeing to speak on the topic of courts, Piccardo
also comments on the absence of Marcolini and, interestingly, declares
it to be a positive factor. With a direct reference to their involvement in
the Venetian world of publishing, he states that he will try to talk sense
into Coccio only if he is sure that Marcolini is not home:

PICCARDO: I'll do just that, if you assure me that Marcolini will not make a copy of my idle words and publish them.[31]

An important distinguishing factor is established right at the beginning of the dialogue that will ensure its success and, at the same time, strengthen its goal of achieving an appropriate forum for *letterati*: namely, the absence of Francesco Marcolini. Just as the author is absent from this mimetic dialogue, so too is the publisher. As the above passage illustrates, the characters feel that they can safely discuss their topic without the slightest worry of having their opinions transcribed. Amedeo Quondam refers to Marcolini as the double of Aretino, the author, in that the function of editor furthers the notion of doubling through the transcription of their conversations and their publication.[32]

The portrayal of Francesco Marcolini's garden as a *locus amoenus* goes beyond the use of the familiar literary *topos*.[33] It is intended to symbolize Aretino's ideal space where, far from the court and the church, intellectuals and artists may pursue their goals in an autonomous society that cultivates and provides for their respective talents.[34] This garden, representative of cultural production that is free of the fetters of the other two environments, is tied to the world of book production of which Venice was the centre.[35] In fact, the characters are all related to the book production of the publishing house of Marcolini, either as writers or translators. Venice in general, and the group surrounding Marcolini in particular, form Aretino's ideal society.[36]

Throughout this dialogue the interlocutors are always conscious of the importance of Venetian print culture to their lives and make reference to it. In the opening exchange of Part II, there is a sly allusion to the transcription of the discussions of the day before.

GIUSTINIANI: So, Marcolini isn't home?

COCCIO: No, he isn't and he won't be back until evening.

DOLCE: It is rather appropriate that he not be here and that he not return today.

GIUSTINIANI: I wanted to see that letter that he had reprinted because I'd like my *Philippics* to be printed with the same fonts.

COCCIO: You're quite right to use those fonts because they are truly outstanding.

DOLCE: Outstanding would characterize our discussions yesterday with Piccardo regarding the courts of the priests, if one were to collate them.

GIUSTINIANI: Outstanding would characterize those regarding the courts of princes, if one were to discuss them.

COCCIO: You've touched a sore point.[37]

This self-reflexive act constitutes a literary 'wink' to the dialogue's readers and reveals yet more of the author's intentions. Although it disturbs the dialogue's guiding fiction of orality, it strengthens Aretino's point that Marcolini and the Venetian press play an important role in the lives of this circle of *letterati*.

Significantly, entrance to Marcolini's house is not permitted until the intellectual values expounded by Dolce and Giustiniani convince Coccio who, incapable of rebutting their sound argumentation, signals his reversal in the following exchange:

COCCIO: Since I do not know how to respond to you, I must force myself to obey you.

GIUSTINIANI: You would know how to answer me and you will know how to obey me by giving yourself over to hours of study with your mind and, collecting your thoughts into one, endure the hardship. If it happens that you are hard pressed by poverty due to what is requested of you, take comfort in fortitude, the source of every virtue. The student must be like the soldier who sleeps on the hard ground, tolerates hunger, puts up with thirst, endures lack of sleep, allows himself to be totally consumed by the effort and, that not being enough, spills his own blood and risks his own life in order to achieve fame.[38]

In fact, Part II of the dialogue, and the role of Giustiniani in particular, are instrumental in the development of the *Dialogue of the Courts* as a response to the dialogues of Bembo and Castiglione that upheld the court as the ideal space for a courtier.[39] Rather than presenting a satire of the *Courtier* in the same way as in the *Dialogues*, in Part II of the *Dialogue of the Courts* Aretino attempts to qualify his previous statements about the courts through the words of Giovanni Giustiniani.

GIUSTINIANI: Just so you know, the courts are all different yet the same in terms of the recognition of effort and the compensation of merit. Their nature is also the same with regards to the treatment of servants, even if they vary in manner.[40]

As Pevere points out, Giustiniani, a poet, speaks of the courts without the same authority as Piccardo. As an artist, he speaks of them from the outside, from the point of view of someone who, despite refusing their corrupt norms, must nonetheless deal with them in order to get by.[41] Also significant is the fact that, at the end of the work, it is Giustiniani who introduces into the discussion a reference to the celestial court ('Corte di Giesù') that is intended to contrast with the corruption of the terrestrial courts. The main criterion for acceptance in this ideal court is faith. It is the residence of the exact opposite qualities that inhabit instead the terrestrial court. All of the negative qualities associated with the courts of this world are far removed from the home of the 'courtiers of Christ' (117).

What is also particularly striking about the passage is the route that is taken to arrive at these considerations. Giustiniani's discourse omits references to terrestrial courts and points to the heavens (the court of Heaven) in a way that is reminiscent of Bembo's rhapsodic ascent to the contemplation of Platonic love in the *Courtier*. After having discussed at length the negative aspects of the terrestrial courts when compared to the celestial courts, the latter are described by Giustiniani as the ultimate place of truth in all its seraphic glory. With reference to the results of their discussions, Coccio declares 'who would think that the beginning and middle of our discussions could bring us to such a good ending' (119).[42]

Giustiniani's ascent may also be seen as an attempt to escape, however momentarily, the difficult reality of the corruption that characterizes the terrestrial court. Pevere views Giustiniani's discourse as a return to a 'Paradise Lost,' or a kind of retreat to a utopia whose internal contradictions melt away. Strengthening the parallel with Bembo, the celestial court is further likened to a kind of ideal Platonic model against which the courts of this world represent a version based on a distorted and completely inverted perception.[43]

Nevertheless, similar to the ideal space created by Bembo in Castiglione's dialogue, we are left with the impression that Giustiniani's celestial court remains an unattainable ideal. The dialogue closes with the following exchange:

GIUSTINIANI: ... May the omnipotent Father fill our souls with His mercy and His compassion so that we may love Him as He loves us, removing pride and ingratitude from our vain intentions.

DOLCE: Such a litany of warm and vehement words would not be out of place at the end of a sermon.

COCCIO: I hear the door opening.

DOLCE: That's Marcolini. I recognize him from the knock.

GIUSTINIANI: Let's go to him.[44]

While the celestial court has not been realized at the end of the dialogue, there is the striking symbolism of the closing moments. Giustiniani and Dolce have satisfactorily dissuaded Coccio from trying to find his niche at court and persuaded him to dedicate himself to more 'lofty' pursuits. They have convinced their interlocutor that the secular courts with all their lies and corruption pale absolutely in comparison with the court of Jesus. It is only by abandoning all aspirations to the *locus mendacii* and through acceptance of aspiring to the ideal of the *locus veritatis* that Coccio and his interlocutors may progress. In effect, Coccio undergoes a transformation, a cleansing, that allows him and the others to cross the threshold.[45]

As Olga Zorzi Pugliese has pointed out, much Renaissance literature shares this feature of the *topos* of liminality where the sacredness of religion is replaced by the sacredness of culture.[46] It is revealing to note that, despite the religious overtones of Giustiniani's closing speech, the group of *letterati* do not enter a church or any more overtly religious or holy place; rather, they cross the threshold to Marcolini's Venetian residence. Rather than a rhapsodic ascent to a Platonic realm of Truth, there is the symbolic crossing of the threshold to a secular abode whose owner is dedicated to the secular pursuit of publishing the humanist works of the group waiting outside his doors. Rather than being merely cynical, it seems to signal a more realistic view of the possibilities of the sixteenth-century man of letters for considering the production and publication of his literary works. Giustiniani's lofty words are regarded as more appropriate to a homily and are therefore set aside as they cross into the house of the printer. The mendacity of the courts is replaced not with the unattainable truths of a higher realm but with the veracity of secular possibilities. These would be the pursuit of knowledge for the sake of secular recognition and independence. By means of the literary experimentation of the dialogue, Aretino maximizes the potential for ambiguity and creates a space for the sixteenth-century *letterato* to engage in the culture of the times through interpretation and debate.

NOTES

1 In *The Renaissance Dialogue*, 17, Virginia Cox slots Pietro Aretino in with the *poligrafi*, the 'literary odd-job men who swarmed hopefully around the Venetian printshops in the middle decades of the sixteenth century.'

2 *Giulia and Madalena* is a dialogue that predates the *Sei giornate*. It could be

seen as a 'draft' to the late dialogue. Please see note 24. Although still debated regarding the date of composition (and possible authorship), where appropriate, reference will be made to Pietro Aretino's *Il Piacevol Ragionamento de l'Aretino. Dialogo di Giulia e di Madalena*, ed. Galderisi. This text will be referred to as the *Dialogue of Giulia and Madalena* in subsequent references.

3 With reference to Aretino as a *poligrafo* and explicit mention of the *Dialogue of the Courts*, Cox, *The Renaissance Dialogue*, 18, has the following to say regarding the importance of this group of dialogists: 'They tend, almost to take the dramatic format of the Lucianic tradition, rather than the more "respectable" narrative, Ciceronian form. Their scene-setting is generally minimal, their language colloquial – even slangy, at times – and their speakers, even if identified contemporary figures, unceremoniously drawn. When contrasted, say, with the dialogue production of native Venetian patricians of the period, the challenge they offer to the norms of the neo-Ciceronian tradition is striking.' Aretino's experimentation in dialogue writing is perhaps nowhere clearer than in the following passage of *The Talking Cards*: 'CARDS: So keep quiet about that and in so doing don't find flaw in us if we go beyond the rules of those who write dialogues since our form of decorum is to jump from one topic to another while encouraging the whims that move the thoughts of our followers, those who adapt their dance to the music that is played. What were we talking about?' (Aretino, *Le carte parlanti*, 59).

4 Though he first drafted it in 1526, the year 1534 witnessed the completion and performance of Aretino's comedy *The Courtesan* (La cortigiana), another influential work that provides a contemptuous portrayal of the court of Rome. The play opens with the character Maco who declares, 'In fine Roma è coda mundi,' thereby overturning the more commonly held notion of Rome as *caput mundi* (Aretino, *La cortigiana*, in *Tutte le commedie*, 121).

5 The original text refers to 'la città Santa et il Paradiso terrestre.' Unless otherwise indicated, all translations from the original Italian are mine. For a thorough discussion of the relationship between Aretino's *Dialogue of the Courts* and Venice, see Cairns, *Pietro Aretino and the Republic of Venice*, 69–98. In *The Talking Cards* Venice is also referred to in similar terms: 'What a pious city! What a just city! Queen of all other cities!' (240). As in the other dialogues, Venice's elevated status is due to its dedication to letters and publishing.

6 Aretino, *Ragionamento delle corti*, ed. Pevere, 16. This is the edition cited in all references.

7 Fontana and Fournel, 'Piazza, Corte, Salotto, Caffé,' 656.

8 Walzer, 'A Critique of Philosophical Conversation,' 185. As M.M. Bakhtin asserts, verbal communication and its context are integrally united, for

whatever the 'moment of the utterance-expression we may consider, it will always be determined by the real conditions of its uttering, and foremost by the *nearest social situation'* (Bakhtin and Voloshinov, *Marxism and the Philosophy of Language*, 101). Therefore, the situation and location inform the nature of the internal dynamic of the dialogue and must be taken into consideration in any analysis of dialogical interaction. Certain dialogical settings often have traditional literary implications or *topoi* associated with them, especially Renaissance literary dialogues.

9 Levy, 'Philosophy as Literature,' 17–18: 'Thus the dialogue model which is so eminently suited to mirror the precipitation of an opposition of meanings in discourse has an added advantage in this respect, and we may finally say in summary that the intrinsic appropriateness of this literary form lies in its reproduction of the *situationality* of philosophizing, in its exhibition not of philosophic doctrines, but of *philosophic activity*, and in the possibilities which it provides for *characterological embodiment* of the oppositional factors in the life of thought' (Levy's emphasis).

10 Comito, *The Idea of the Renaissance Garden*, 51.

11 Carla Forno, *Il 'libro animato,'* 278.

12 The edition used here is Aretino. *Aretino's Dialogues*, trans. Rosenthal. This is the edition cited in all subsequent references and English quotations. The Italian edition originally consulted is Pietro Aretino, *Ragionamento-Dialogo*, ed. Forno.

13 Ferroni, 'Pietro Aretino e le corti,' 34.

14 See Ordine, 'Le *Sei giornate*,' in Lettieri, Bancheri, and Buranello, *Pietro Aretino e la cultura del Rinascimento*, 685. On the other hand, I refer to the existence of 'decorum' precisely in terms of the direct correspondence between the setting, characters, and circumstance of the conversation.

15 The parodistic treatment of the tradition is made clear in the dedication of the book to his monkey: 'Pietro Aretino to his darling monkey' (11).

16 As the dialogues progress, the characters discuss all of the qualities that a whore should possess in order to succeed in this environment. From table manners, speech, and dress, to particular 'talents,' all are developed to ensure success in the profession. These discussions establish the parodistic treatment that Aretino gives of *Courtier*-like treatises.

17 Aretino, *Dialogues*, 17. The original passage is taken from *Ragionamento delle corti*, 79:

ANTONIA: Dimmelo, io te ne prego: a ogni modo è la Madalena nostra avvocata che non si fa niente; e quando ben si lavorasse, io ho pane e carne insalata per tre di.

18 *Dialogues*, 59. The original reads as follows: 'Dipoi alzato il fianco come lo

alza uno alloggiato a discrezione, ritornaro alla vigna; e riposte nel luogo dove sederno il dì inanzi e sotto la medesima ficaia, sendo ora di cacciare il caldo col ventaglio delle ciance, Antonia posato le palme sopra le ginocchia, fitto il viso nel volto di Nanna, disse: "Veramente son chiara delle suore: dopo il primo sonno non ho mai più potuto chiudere occhio, solo pensando alle pazze madri e ai semplici padri che si credono che le figliuole che fanno moniche non abbiano denti da rodere come quelle che maritono; poveretta la vita loro! dovrebbero pur sapere che son di carne e d'ossa anche esse, e che non è cosa che accresca più il desiderio che il vietare una cosa [...]"' (157).

19 *Dialogues*, 309. The original passage is as follows: 'Non si disse né rispose altro fra loro; ma vennero secondo l'ordine, e assettatesi a sedere sotto il pesco, la Comare toccò lo stare in mezzo de la Balia e de la Nanna, e a la galante Pippa al riscontro de la Comare. In questo una pesca grossa, la quale sola era rimasa nel pesco, cadde in sul capo de la Comare; onde la Balia disse ridendo a più potere: "Tu non puoi negare che il farti dar le pesche non ti sia piaciuto"; "Cotesto no" rispose ella ...' (478–9).

20 Ordine, 'Le *Sei giornate*,' 679–81 (my translation). Compare Augustine's claim to abandon all 'provision for the flesh in concupiscence' of *Confessions* 8.12.29 with Aretino's depiction of Pippa's 'conversion.' See Augustine of Hippo, *Confessions*, 100. Of course, the fiction of sitting under a tree and discussing issues brings us back to Plato's *Phaedrus* in which the discussions take place under the 'lofty and spreading plane-tree' (see Plato, *The Dialogues of Plato*, 434). Cicero makes a very direct reference to this commonplace in his *De oratore* where the embedded dialogue has Scaevola say: 'Say, Crassus, why don't we follow the example of Socrates as he appears in Plato's *Phaedrus*? For your plane tree here suggests this to me, by spreading its broad boughs to shade this place exactly like that of the other plane tree whose shade Socrates sought – which seems to me to have grown not so much because of that little stream described there as owing to Plato's own words' (see Cicero, *On the Ideal Orator* (*De oratore*), trans. James M. May and Jokob Wisse, 63–4.

21 Ordine, 'Le *Sei giorante*,' 683 (my translation).

22 Regarding Aretino's highlighting of the ambiguity and impracticality of Castiglione's ideal, as well as the important role of opinion and verisimilitude in the courtly environment, see Paternoster, *Aptum*, 24–5. For further development of these observations, see her analysis of Aretino's *Dialogues* (ibid., 243–52). Particularly intriguing is the importance she places on the textual references to the opposition of the external to the internal qualities, like honesty against dishonesty, at court (247).

23 In this dialogue, Francesco Marcolini is referred to as Francesco Marcolino and Giovanni Giustiniani as Giovanni Giustiniano. Despite this discrepancy, I have chosen to leave the names as they appear in the original text. I have made the adjustments in my translations.

24 The original text reads:

> DOLCE: Noi potremmo chiamare questo giardinetto del Marcolino ventaglio de la state, poiché il respirare del suo vento, l'ombra del suo verde, la soavità dei suoi fiori et il canto dei suoi augelli petrarchevoli rinfresca, ricopre, diletta et adormenta e tanto più giova il passegiarci ora, quanto meno il caldo del suo agosto fa bollire la nona d'oggi che quella d'ieri; perciò sedendo aspetteremo il Piccardo, che dee venire qui. (45)

The image of Marcolini's garden as a fan (*ventaglio*) is particularly appropriate since it conjures the garden's possible physical arrangement while, at the same time, conveying the metaphorical meaning as a place of reading and learning that provides a fresh 'Petrarchan' breeze. The reference to the afternoon is based on the Italian 'nona,' the ninth hour after six o'clock in the morning, therefore at approximately three o'clock in the afternoon. The next mention of the setting is made at the beginning of Part II, when Giustiniani comments on how they must wait outside for Marcolini to return (85). See also Aretino's erotic dialogue entitled *Dialogue of Giulia and Madalena* (58) for an example of a similar *locus amoenus* setting. According to the contemporary editors, this text was probably written between 1521 and 1525 (37–8) and therefore becomes an interesting text not only as a potential precursor to his famous *Dialogues* but also as a possible link between that work and the *Dialogue of the Courts*. In the description of Marcolini's little garden there are unmistakable echoes of the description of the setting of the *Phaedrus*.

25 In 1557 Lodovico Dolce published his dialogue on painting entitled *L'Aretino* with Gabriel Giolito de'Ferrari. For a thorough discussion of the relationship between Dolce and Aretino see Roskill, *Dolce's Aretino and Venetian Art Theory of the Cinquecento*, 5–62.

26 Pevere, '"Vita è il non andare in corte,"': 238.

27 For the actual inspiration for the *Dialogue of the Courts*, see Aretino's letter of 24 December 1537 to Francesco Coccio in which many of the major themes developed in the dialogue are already present (*Lettere*, 452).

28 My emphasis. The original text reads:

> COCCIO: Or lasciamo andare le favole; che vi pare del mio volere tormi agli studi per darmi a le Corti?

DOLCE: Parmi che siate una bestia, se la resoluzione dei vostri pensieri è sì fatta.

COCCIO: Madonna sì, che ella è tale.

DOLCE: Messere voleste dire. Ecco la parola che errando nel genere mostra la pazzia che voi, savio, pensate di fare. Oltra ciò, è di pessimo augurio il traviare de la lingua nel prendere i partiti. (45)

29 The passage in the original is:

PICCARDO: O Iddio, perché la menzogna non è verità? Perché non è ella Dio?

COCCIO: Che sarebbe poi?

PICCARDO: Saria che il vero, che è un serpente schifato da ognuno, diventerebbe bugia, che è mandragola donneata da tutti.

COCCIO: Chi sa mentire sa regnare, e chi nol fa non ha. (55)

30 The original lines are:

PICCARDO: Ora credetemi che niuno, eccetto messer Fabrizion da Parma, può informarvi degli andamenti de la Corte meglio di me. (49)

31 In the original text, the line is:

PICCARDO: Così farò, se mi assicurate che il Marcolino non pigli la copia de le mie chiacchiere stampandole. (49)

32 Quondam, 'Nel giardino del Marcolini,' 76. See Forno, *II 'libro animato,'* 289–90.

33 Of particular interest regarding the relationship between the *locus amoenus* and the settings of the Renaissance dialogue is the article by Eva Kushner entitled 'Le role structurel du "locus amoenus" dans les dialogues de la Renaissance.' In particular, see the intriguing suggestion made regarding 'les circonstances de l'entretien' (41).

34 Quondam, 'Nel giardino del Marcolini,' 77.

35 Pevere, '"Vita è il non andare in corte,"' 240.

36 Quondam, 'Nel giardino del Marcolini,' 95–9. A list of the literary collaborators in Marcolini's enterprises and their relation to Aretino is provided by Quondam on 95, note 41.

37 The exchange in the original is:

GIUSTINIANO: Adunque il Marcolino non è in casa?

COCCIO: Non ci è, e non tornerà fino a sera.

DOLCE: Ci viene molto a proposito il suo non esserci e non ci tornare oggi.

GIUSTINIANO: Io voleva vedere quella lettera così bella che egli ha fatto gittare di nuovo, perciò che di cotale carattero desidero che si stampino le mie *Filippice*.

COCCIO: Avete ragione di metterle in sì fatta stampa, perché sono lodatissime.

DOLCE: Lodati sarebbono i discorsi che facemmo ieri col Piccardo de la Corte dei preti, se si mettessero insieme.

GIUSTINIANO: Lodati sarieno quegli de la Corte dei principi, se si facessero.

COCCIO: Voi ci date dove ci duole. (85)

38 The passage in Italian is:

COCCIO: Poiché io non vi so rispondere, mi sforzerò di ubidirvi.

GIUSTINIANO: Voi sapreste rispondermi e saperete ubidirmi ridandovi a l'ore debite degli studi con tutta la mente, e ricogliendo i pensieri in uno sofferite il disagio; se avviene che egli ve gli disturbi con la carestia di ciò che si richiede, usate per commodità la fortezza, alimento de ogni virtù. Lo studente dee essere come il soldato, il quale dorme in terra, tolera la fame, sofferisce la sete, pate il sonno, struggesi ne la fatica e, non bastando ciò, sparge il sangue et arrischia la vita solo per venire ne la cognizione de la fama. (114–5)

39 The dissemination of Castiglione's ideas regarding the courtier predates even the publication of the book since copies circulated in manuscript form for some time. This is even mentioned explicitly in the text. For background regarding this and other issues surrounding the publication of *The Book of the Courtier*, see Quondam, 'On the Genesis of *The Book of the Courtier.*'

40 The original version:

GIUSTINIANO: Le Corti, perché sappiate, sono diverse, ma d'una medesima qualità nel ricompensare dei meriti e de le fatiche, e tutte di uguale animo inverso i servitori, se bene variano nel procedere. (87)

41 Pevere, '"Vita è il non andare in corte,"' 254.

42 In the original, the line is: 'Chi crederebbe che il principio et il mezzo del favellare nostro riuscisse a sí buon fine?' (119)

43 Pevere, '"Vita è il non andare in corte,"' 258. For the Erasmian influences on these religious ideas, see Cairns, *Pietro Aretino and the Republic of Venice*, 80–96.

44 The exchange in the original Italian text is:

GIUSTINIANO: ... Perciò piova il Padre omnipotente nel seno de le nostre anime de le sue misericordie e de le sue compassioni, sí che potiamo

amar lui come egli ama noi, togliendoci il superbo e lo ingrato de le
vanità de le intenzioni.

DOLCE: Non si disdirebbe sí fatta striscia di parole calde e veementi ne la
chiusa di qualche predica.

COCCIO: Sento che s'apre la porta.

DOLCE: Egli è il Marcolino, io l'ho conosco al battere.

GIUSTINIANO: Andiancene a lui. (120)

45 The significance of this rite of passage has been noted by Eliade: 'The
threshold that separates the two spaces also indicates the distance between
two modes of being, the profane and the religious. The threshold is the
limit, the boundary, the frontier that distinguishes and opposes the two
worlds – and at the same time the paradoxical place where those worlds
communicate, where passage from the profane to the sacred world
becomes possible' (*The Sacred and the Profane*, 25). It is important to note
that, as explained below, there is a particular interpretation of 'sacred' at
work here.

46 Pugliese, 'Liminality and Ritual in the Renaissance Attitude Toward
Antiquity.'

From Dialogue to Conversation: The Place of Marie de Gournay

Dorothea Heitsch

Truly, Saint Jerome wrote wisely in his Letters that with regard to serving God, the spirit and the doctrine must be considered – not a person's sex. This pronouncement should be applied generally so as to allow to women, on still stronger grounds, all other branches of knowledge and all the most excellent and soundest actions, to put it in a word, of the most exalted kind.[1]

Much research has focused on Marie de Gournay's relationship to Montaigne.[2] That we owe at least one authoritative edition of the *Essais* to her (1635) and that she played a major role in the preparation of the first posthumous edition (1595) has been given full credit only recently.[3] Moreover, the kindred spirit, friend, and admirer of Montaigne employs certain reading practices in her preface to the 1595 edition of the *Essais* that she will regret as well as defend in the reprints that she prepares of this work and in her own texts. Marie de Gournay thus makes very good use of the possibilities of print culture, enabling her to participate in a literary dialogue and to re-edit her texts with additions and changes. It becomes evident in 'Grief des dames' ('The Ladies' Complaint') that this is of utmost importance to her, one of her goals being the unequivocal integration of women in social events from which they have been barred, such as conversations.

The importance of conversation and/as dialogue for an early modern woman writer is the topic of my analysis: conversation as a mode of being, as a means of self-discovery, as social validation, as rhetorical means, and as a literary genre. I then discuss a paradigm shift at the end of the sixteenth and the beginning of the seventeenth century and, finally, the implications of this paradigm shift for some of Marie de

Gournay's texts. I intend, first, to underline the extremely restrictive literary and socio-historical context in order to then emphasize the courage and sophistication of Marie de Gournay's dialogical reading and writing strategy. As a result, it is possible, in addition to contributing to the 'recuperative' efforts that have been made with regard to this author, to attribute to her a 'pioneering' role in the emerging Quarrel of the Ancients and the Moderns.[4]

I. Marie de Gournay: Dialogue and/as Conversation

Marie de Gournay considers the human being as a being of dialogue and writes in order to perpetuate her literary union with Montaigne and with her readers.[5] This statement gains even more importance if we take into account her unfortunate defence of the Jesuits (1610)[6] or her role as one respondent in defence of women in the 'Querelle des Femmes' rekindled by Jacques Olivier's (i.e., the Franciscan Alexis Trousset's) *Alphabet de l'imperfection et malice des femmes* (1617). Her own voice, at the beginning of her career, when she is still unknown and without financial means or social assistance, emerges by consciously imitating Montaigne's style, as he does in the 'Apologie de Raimond Sebond,' where he protects a father figure against critics who become personal opponents.[7] Yet Marie de Gournay, who chooses a male model,[8] is very aware of the problem of difference in her reading and decides to frame it in moral rather than gender-related terms. This helps her to avoid the pitfalls of a male teacher-female pupil relationship. It can be said that this strategy plays with the concepts of friendship and eroticism and enables Gournay to keep alive sentiments by circumwriting them.[9] Or one could say that in order to make her adoptive father known and to become known herself as the daughter of her father, Marie de Gournay decides to replay the textual friendship on a grand scale in the preface.[10] I, for one, would like to state that her inherited task, be it ever so fictitiously bestowed, as has been recently explained,[11] constitutes an efficient act of gift giving reaching back to La Boétie and including the entire Montaigne family as well as Justus Lipsius, Anna Maria van Schurman, and La Mothe Le Vayer. I then approach the problem of imitation by analysing a paradigm shift that the concept of conversation undergoes at the turn of the sixteenth to the seventeenth century.

In this context, it will be helpful to link the literary genre of dialogue as conversation to the humanistic tradition. Dialogue is the recorded conversation of two or more people, especially as an element of drama or fiction. It is a literary form, and it is a carefully organized exposition by means of invented conversation, or of contrasting philosophical or intellectual attitudes. It represents an exchange of thoughts or ideas in question and answer. One of the forms of dialogue in the Renaissance is the conversation which develops meaning through the interaction between different characters.[12] This is the subgenre preferred by Montaigne in his *Essais*. In Montaigne's time, 'conferer' means 'converser,' 'conferendi,' 'controverser,' 'disputer,' as well as 'dissertatio in utramque partem.' Castiglione, Guazzo, and ultimately Plato are the models for this author. For him, as for Marie de Gournay, the human being is a dialogical being. He affirms that 'it is only words which bind us together and make us human.'[13]

What is conversation and who participates in it? In Marie de Gournay's 'Grief des dames' (1626), Montaigne's *Essais* are mentioned as the perfect example: 'for concerning the art of conversation in general, and its perfections and defects, the *Essays* deal with this to the point of excellence.'[14] In his essay on conversation, Montaigne says: 'To my taste the most fruitful and most natural exercise of our minds is conversation.'[15] Similarly, in her *Avis*, Marie de Gournay mentions a preference that confirms her kinship with Montaigne: 'If I do not have the virtues of my second father I do have some of the vices he admits to, above all this one to be quickly impatient of a disorderly conversation.'[16] This statement reminds us of those passages in Montaigne's essay 'De l'art de conferer' where he discusses his preference for order.[17] For the author, order is synonymous with the rejection of pedantic style, which places rhetoric above content. He himself prefers to emulate the arguments of shepherds and shop assistants or the disputes at inns and taverns. It is this natural conversation that he opposes to the artifice of scholastic discourse. The ideal lack of artifice is illustrated in the image of the chase or hunt, where the hunters follow their way in apparent disorder and without design, but never losing sight of their prey.

What Montaigne thinks about women and conversation can be found in 'Des trois commerces' (III, 3), where he derides the pretentiousness he sees in fashionable learned conversation, because he prefers naturalness:

Nowadays they have funnelled so much of it [learning] into the ears of the ladies in their drawing-rooms that, even though those ladies of ours have retained none of the substance, they look as though they have: on all sorts of topics and subjects, no matter how menial or commonplace, they employ a style of speaking and writing which is newfangled and erudite.[18]

All that is needed is a little arousing and enhancing of the qualities that are in them. When I see them saddled with rhetoric, judicial astrology, logic and such-like vain and useless trash, I begin to fear that the men who counsel them to do so see it as a way of having a pretext for manipulating them. For what other excuse can I find for them? ...

Should it nevertheless irk them to lag behind us in anything whatsoever; should they want a share in our books out of curiosity: then poetry is a pastime rightly suited to their needs: it is a frivolous, subtle art, all disguise and chatter and pleasure and show, like they are. They will also draw a variety of benefits from history; and in philosophy – the part which helps us to live well – they will find such arguments as train them to judge of our humours and our attributes, to shield them from our deceptions, to control the rashness of their own desires, to cultivate their freedom and prolong the pleasure of this life, and to bear with human dignity the inconstancy of a suitor, the moroseness of a husband and the distress of wrinkles and the passing years. That sort of thing. That – at most – is the share of learning that I would assign to them.[19]

For this humanist, learning constitutes, at the very most, an asset, an ornament, and an enhancement of a woman's natural graces in amicable talk, and should by no means be encouraged as an end in itself. Such an attitude may be questioned in the frame to Marie de Gournay's novella *Proumenoir*, where she presents herself as a worthy interlocutor.

II.1 Conversation and the Court

How is conversation defined by writers of the seventeenth century? Numerous contemporary manuals give extensive definitions, such as Nicolas Pasquier's *Le Gentilhomme* (1611), Jacques Du Bosc's *L'honneste Femme* (1633–6), François de Grenaille's *L'honneste Garçon* (1642) and *L'honneste Fille* (1639–40), or Nicolas Faret's *L'honnête homme ou l'art de plaire à la cour* (1636). The latter's manual is particularly interesting, because it develops some prescriptive rules that should enable the (bourgeois) reader to succeed in society. According to Faret, an interlocutor should be conscious of his personality and social position. He constantly must check his behaviour and compare himself to his interlocutors so as not to expose himself unduly. He should avoid pride and a too high consideration of his own person as well as too much talk and the desire to listen to himself. Faret classifies interlocutors as people of a superior, an equal, and an inferior rank, as friends, and as strangers. He stresses that it is difficult to talk to a prince, mentions the problem of remaining attentive while talking to an equal or to an inferior, and criticizes the habit of keeping one's defaults only for one's friends.

In the passage 'Maximes générales de la conversation' Faret advises that one should vanquish one's passions and moods, display suppleness and moderation of spirit, and, above all, obligingness which enables the interlocutor to be pleasing and adaptable.[20] The section on women's conversation describes Anne of Austria's circle that Faret considers as the model environment for conversation: with this circle in mind, he thinks women's conversation to be the softest and most agreeable, but therefore also the most difficult and the most delicate of all.[21] Men's conversation is more vigorous and free, full of serious and solid subjects: they pay less attention to the mistakes that are made than women do, who, since they are eager and not so impressed by important issues, realize more those small mistakes and are more ready to point them out.[22] They also are quick to take offence at negligent attire; Faret therefore recommends clean rather than ornate clothes.[23] He admits that the presence of so many well-dressed and agreeable ladies who are ready to engage others in conversation entices men to become gentlemanly, if only to then be remarked and served by women.[24] Yet he criticizes the evenings instigated by the queen in the passage 'De la conversation du Louvre et de ses incommodités,' maintaining that in this theatre of women's conversation the strange social mix of people is so importunate that even the best exchanges suffer from it.[25]

Though Faret presents some of Montaigne's ideas in his text, such as moderation, the ease with which different opinions are discussed, the critique of categorical affirmation, the sense of what is appropriate, the love of prudence and good judgment, this author restricts himself to the social realm and to those aspects that may guide his courtier in society. He disregards the philosophical component of Montaigne's text by reducing it to simple precepts for friendly talk. This may be due to Faret's position as a member of the bourgeoisie, for whom morality and religion are important means in social climbing, and for whom the 'honnête homme' means 'homme de bien,' 'courtisan vertueux,' a man who pursues virtue, that is, the love and respect of God.[26] His description of Anne of Austria's circle, the queen to whom Marie de Gournay dedicates *Egalité des hommes et des femmes*, helps to raise a series of questions. Which conversational theories exist? What are the social realities of conversations – their increasing political importance, the change of language and esthetics, the preferred spaces? What is a conversation in the 1620s as opposed to one in 1595? What is its social function? Who participates? Who would have an interest in excluding women from it?

II.2 Anne of Austria's Conversation

Anne of Austria loves conversation, has learned to speak French like a Parisian, and organizes a circle that becomes a brilliant assembly. Around 1620 the queen regularly holds evening meetings in the Louvre, then goes to visit a convent, and at her return dedicates more time to the princesses and ladies who come to pay their respects. At the beginning of the Fronde even, when Parliament is threatening her authority, she holds these gatherings.[27] Yet it seems that the queen's circle is not stimulating intellectually, because the participants' level of education is below hers and their interests tend to be light. Therefore the meetings represent an endeavour to raise the level of education among courtiers and ladies; and, for the first time in the seventeenth century intellectual pastimes are being organized at court.[28] Faret's description is based on these gatherings, where the ladies compete in a display of their wealth and magnificence. Yet it is difficult to enjoy their conversation, because of the many different social ranks present in a heterogeneous crowd, those high up preventing communication from developing freely, court spies being present. Therefore, Faret recommends, one needs to go to the salons in town where the most beautiful assemblies are.

Given the queen's insignificance before the birth of an heir in 1638, it is interesting to know how she spends her time, because her preferences to a great extent determine social activity at court. That religion plays an important part in her life is clear from her founding the convent Val-de-Grâce, which is approved by Louis XIII until it later becomes the centre of her letter-writing activity.[29] Much of the extant information concerning the queen's life stems from the *Mémoires de Mme de Motteville*. According to this source, the years 1618–20 are the happiest in her marriage to Louis XIII. Yet almost from the moment she sets foot on French soil is she criticized for being childish, capricious, and incapable of focusing on any matter of importance.[30] She is soon asked to send home most of her Spanish ladies because their dress, demeanour, and etiquette give offence to the king. It is probable, according to historical witnesses, that these ladies are dishonest and ruin the queen, in addition to acting as spies for Spain. Moreover, they prevent the king from pushing his favourites, Albert de Luynes and his wife, closer to the queen. This is why certain household decisions become a matter of state.[31] After the death of Luynes, the queen mother, Marie de Médicis, is reconciled with her son and thus troubles the young marriage. The queen is closely observed so as to prohibit her becoming too important to her husband and so as to prevent Spain from having any political influence. After the treaty of Loudun signed by Marie de Médicis, the power of the Huguenots (Orange, Nassau) and therefore of political forces hostile to Spain increases at court.[32]

The queen then spends difficult years:[33] in April 1621, the death of her father deprives her of an interlocutor and an extensive letter correspondence. Her brother knows through his ambassadors that she will not have any political influence on the king and therefore he looks to Marie de Médicis (until her fall and exile in 1631) and to Richelieu. The queen's intimacy with Gaston d'Orléans who counters Richelieu's domestic policy, with Philippe IV, her brother, and with Buckingham will be held against her. She lives those years in an atmosphere of conflict and suspicion. Being lonely, she looks for a friend in the remarried duchess of Luynes, now Chevreuse. The latter, a somewhat irresponsible person, attempts to divert her with entertainment, play, and gallantry. From 1618–19 on, the French ladies around the queen come to organize the royal pastimes. Their choice of readings and topics of conversation, that is, love stories and trivial talk, involve abundant praise of the queen's beauty and the admission of gallants, as well as the *Cabinet satyrique*, an annual publication with contributions of libertine poets, such as Régnier and Maynard. As the Counter-Reformation increasingly disapproves of explicit references to the pleasures of love, such readings further cool the relationship between the king and queen who, in her emotional solitude, becomes even more dependent for company on those French ladies who are chosen by her husband to report to him.

According to Madame de Motteville, the queen's need to be appreciated and her gratitude prevent her from suspecting second thoughts behind any suggestion of amusement and from seeing the competition for influence in which these ladies engage. Madame de Motteville also explains that at the French court remained some of the politeness brought from Italy by Catherine de Medici. The court also found such refinement in the comedies and other works in verse and prose coming from Madrid that it had conceived a high idea of the gallantry which the Spanish had adopted from the Moors. Accordingly, the queen is convinced that men can without offence have tender sentiments for women; that the desire to please women leads men to the greatest and most beautiful actions, gives them intelligence, and inspires liberality and all sorts of virtues; but that on the other hand, women who are the ornament of the world and who are made to be served and adored by men must only suffer their respects.[34] Madame de Motteville clarifies that the queen being so young could not understand that conversation ('la belle conversation'), which is commonly called gallantry ('l'honnête' galanterie'), could ever be reprehensible.[35] It is represented in Paris by the Marquise de Sablé's Platonism and her 'amour à la Précieuse.' Throughout these years, the queen holds her circle: a reunion of princesses and ladies who either sit, as a privilege, or stand around the queen's chair for polite conversation in fashionable gatherings,[36] whose model must be seen, among others, in Guazzo.[37]

II.3 A Literary Precursor: Stefano Guazzo

The limits and restrictions imposed on society at the turn of the sixteenth to the seventeenth century are not only illustrated in the manuals mentioned above, but are also reflected in the French vocabulary that is beginning to be scaled down to that of the 'honnête homme' against what Mlle de Gournay with a Montaignean word names 'uberté,' the 'fertility' of the French language. Marc Fumaroli states that for Pascal, 'conversation' is already becoming an archaism toward the second half of the seventeenth century. Originally, Cicero had distinguished between 'eloquentia' and 'sermo:' one denoting an active and public life, the relationship between an orator and a large audience that he needs to conquer; the other describing a contemplative and private life, 'otium,' and the relationship of interlocutors that are equals or friends who cooperate at answering questions of general human interest in a simple and natural style.[38] 'Conversatio' had described conviviality and decorum of discourses, but had extended to gestures, clothes, habits, attitudes, and looks as much as to speech that composes the mood proper to every small and homogeneous society. The Renaissance would revivify the sociological aspect of the word 'conversatio' and contaminate it semantically with the Ciceronian 'sermo' that appertains to the grammatical and rhetorical vocabulary. This would emerge in the vulgar, and above all, in Italian. Stefano Guazzo, in *La civile conversation* that was published in 1574 and translated in 1579 by Gabriel Chappuys, employs 'conversation' in the sense of 'fréquentation habituelle' as well as in the sense of 'sermo' designating a dialogue among courteous and well-read interlocutors who respect the rules of urbanity. This conversation between a melancholic knight and a doctor, Annibale, develops a philosophy of social interaction notably through speech polished by literature and by that wisdom that derives from contemplating the ancients, other nations, and our personal experience.

According to Guazzo, conversation is the beginning and end of knowledge because through it we are tested as well as our learning, similar to the 'armourer [who] can not assure him selfe of the goodnesse of a corselet, untill such time as he hath seene it prooved with the launce or harquebouse: so neither can a learned man assure him selfe of his learning, untill he meete with other learned men, and by discoursing and reasoning with them, bee acertained of his sufficiencie.'[39] Therefore, conversation should be regarded as the beginning and end of knowledge. This civil conversation can be found everywhere and Annibale maintains 'that to live civilly, is not sayde in respect of the citie, but of the quallities of the minde: so I understand civile conversation not having relation to the citie, but consideration to the maners and conditions which make it civile.'[40]

The characteristic trait of such conversation is harmony like that which is found in diverse organ pipes 'whereof every one giveth a diverse sowne, yet they are all proportioned together, and make one onely bodie: in like sort, albeit there be diverse kindes of entertainemente and conversation, yet in the end we shall perceive that they agree together in such sort, that they seeme in a manner one onely sort, and perchaunce more easie then we thinke for.'[41] Civil conversation also has a mirror function and furthers self-knowledge, where 'a man may not onely cleere himselfe of cowardly abjection, and vaine presumption, but besides, cloath himselfe with the knowledge of himselfe.'[42]

The knight considers women's conversation as useless and dangerous. Annibale replies that this opinion is due to certain men's vanity and dislike of women. Indeed, women's participation is necessary:

And truely, if you marke the order of feastes, playes, and merie meetinges of friendes, you will say, that all those assemblyes are colde and nothing delightfull, if there bee no women at them. For as men in their presence plucke up their spirites, and indevour by woordes, jestures, and all other wayes to give them to understande howe desirous they are of their favour and good will, so you ought to thinke, the object beeing out of their eyes, they will become carelesse, mannerlesse, and lesse readie to commendable enterprises. To bee shorte, women are they whiche keepe men waking and in continuall exercise: yea, I thinke there is no man so lazy and drouzy, but that he will open his eyes when hee heareth talke of women. And so soone as hee spyeth comming a farre of, her whom hee hath placed most neere to his heart, I warrant you he setteth his ruffes, hee turneth his Cappe and feather the right way, hee pulleth up his cloake about his shoulders, hee standeth a tiptoe, he sheweth a joyfull and smyling countenaunce, and hee seemeth to become a newe man, that hee may bee more acceptable to the sight of his mistresse, in whose presence hee chaungeth colour, and looketh pale, by reason that his heart abandoneth his bodie to followe her, beeing drawne as it were by it owne image.[43]

What is more, the ideal lady is the perfect interlocutor:

I say then that this Lady in conversation is singuler, and mervellous: for all the noble partes in her, you shall see her make a most delightfull harmony. For first, to the gravenesse of her wordes, agreeth the sweetnesse of her voyce, and the honestie of her meaning: so that the mindes of the hearers intangled in those three nets, feele themselves at one instant to be both mooved with her amiablenesse and bridled by her honesty. Next, her talke and discourses are so delightfull, that you wyll only then beginne to bee sory, when shee endeth to speake: and wishe that shee woulde bee no more weary to speake, then you are to heare. Yea, shee frameth her jestures so discretely, that in speakyng, shee seemeth to holde her peace, and in holding her peace, to speake ...[44]

This is the conversational model that, according to Fumaroli, will be elaborated by Montaigne. Marie de Gournay certainly may be regarded as a case in point. With François de Sales's *Introduction à la vie dévote* (1609), those humanistic and Christian commonplaces on which the Catholic Church wants to base the general conversation of believers are set over against the love of singularity in Montaigne. The Montaignean model will be preferred by the freethinkers and will take, in Paris, the meaning of a general conversation of believers – the natural conversation that is secular. Under Henri IV and Louis XIII, Parisians are looking for harmony and safety in such conversations for which Montaigne offers the secular model and François de Sales the ecclesiastical one. Both types are practised in the salons; Fumaroli mentions Madame Acarie, Queen Marguerite, the princess Conti, the brothers Dupuy, and the Marquise de Rambouillet. Conversation in these circles is natural, improvised, with a diversity of participants, especially women. In order to be admitted, women are asked to renounce the defaults that are attributed to them, that is, chattering and excessive flirting, as men need to renounce their defaults, such as vanity and arrogance. 'Conversation civile' is spontaneous, improvised, and unpredictable; it is a challenge to the mind, unpedantic, and effaces the gap between cultivated and spontaneous language.[45]

II.4 Women's Conversation according to Court Manuals

Later manuals increasingly reflect the ideology of devotion. François de Grenaille's *L'honneste garçon* should be mentioned here. Grenaille dissuades young men from participating in women's conversation because though it polishes, it also softens and deflects their courage from those difficult and glorious tasks that they should accomplish.[46] If they must talk with ladies it should not be to flirt but only to honour their dignity, the author continues, adding that he is instructing a Christian and not an infidel.[47] The reader should not be surprised at his dissuading young men from ladies' conversation: women are enemies all the more daunting because they are always amiable; men, instead of becoming superior, are hurt by them.[48] As a general rule, company always should enable men to work toward their salvation.[49] *L'honneste fille*, a text that pays homage to Marie de Gournay,[50] is defined by Grenaille as a beautiful young girl who is a champion of rhetoric, making those subjects agreeable in conversation that are not, never tiring any interlocutor because she is good to look at, never proffering anything superfluous because everything she utters is important. In her speech, every word has its weight, its particular energy; no syllable can be lost without her interlocutors' feeling unhappy.[51]

In the preface to *L'honneste femme*, Jacques Du Bosc clearly states the problem that haunts most of these manuals; it is the relationship between 'dévotion' and 'civilité,' concepts which, according to this author, are apparently not opposed. For a lady's edification, it is thus important to choose wisely interlocutors and books. A lady's company must be discreet, silent, and modest, because those ladies who prefer quantity to quality in their talk are not to be entrusted with secrets. In the end, they always betray themselves like butterflies that burn their wings at the candle.[52] According to Du Bosc, while ladies who have no education are uninteresting interlocutors, those who do have these assets are often a little confused, importunate, or aggravating. There is only disorder in their thoughts and constraint in what they say. It seems that their minds do not have enough warmth to digest their reading and one recognizes well from the confusion and inequality of their speech, even though they say good enough things, that it is not sufficient to have marble and porphyry in order to build a palace, if one is not an architect.[53] Du Bosc in this context also warns against the contagious effect of libertine conversation.

II.5 Paradigm Shift

It is evident now that Marie de Gournay experiences a paradigm shift at the threshold to the seventeenth century. In the first half of the seventeenth century, the word 'conversation' is used as a synonym for 'fréquentation,' 'commerce,' 'assemblée,' and yet later it comes to be replaced by 'entretien.'[54] In France, women have conquered a social position that is unprecedented. They move more freely than, for example, in Spain and Italy, and they become the centre of worldly life.[55] Yet gradually, a tendency develops to present knowledge so that it becomes accessible to ladies. This means that women are reduced to representing the uninitiated to whom men are talking down. Logical terms are thus replaced by terms of amorous casuistry that is supposed to be more intelligible to women. Categories such as substance, quantity, or quality are replaced by categories of love, such as beauty, richness, youth, old age, prudery, and stupidity.[56] Basic notions are deemed sufficient for women who, like the 'honnête homme,' should know a little bit of everything. If a woman does possess special knowledge, she should not use it in conversations. Instead she should keep up the appearance of ignorance. Women's role – their obligation to please – thus becomes neatly opposed to the learned woman's position, that of the 'femme savante.' 'L'honnête homme,' then again, needs to please the ladies. Why is this so important? The situation of courtiers who legitimize their existence not by capital or work, but by their social position forces them to be gratifying to women as well as the king and his family. The desire to please therefore becomes the principle of social interaction.[57] Consequently, the conception of women influences social behaviour: ideally, as proffered by Grenaille, rhetoric is associated with the beauty of a young girl. However, given that ladies do not know much and possess, at the most, basic notions on certain subjects, they are flighty in conversation and like to pass rapidly from one subject to the other, because their knowledge is not deemed sufficient for profound thought. How this view of women's talk influences social deportment is reflected in the increasing importance attributed to concepts such as 'galanterie,' 'amour,' and 'apparence.'[58]

Montaigne's conversation is ostensibly private, but may be employed for public ends. Under Louis XIV, conversation becomes the most important social skill. It has been stated that in France, throughout the seventeenth-century, social conduct comes to determine personal identity and individual accomplishment. Therefore the fashioning of self will be regarded as a social event, permitting the ways of social interaction to be theorized and turned into topics of political and philosophical speculation in numerous manuals.[59] The rules of social conduct are encoded and adapted to the demands of courtly politics. Politeness will be used as a means to acquire power in society, such as the deference rituals surrounding the person of the king, to the extent that by the mid-century a view of nobility that gives an entirely new emphasis to education, personal cultivation, and techniques for social interaction will have replaced the medieval code of valor.

III. Marie de Gournay as Reader, Writer, and Conversationalist

What does this paradigm shift mean for Marie de Gournay's work? Let us briefly recall how this author conceives of the process of reading by looking at her preface to the 1595 edition of the *Essais*. This text illustrates how she conceives of herself as a reading subject. The conflict between the reader's observation and her bias constitutes the event of the text. Marie de Gournay's preface is text and meta-text: the author describes the formation of her judgment through reading, proves her judgment in an exhortation to the reader, and then acknowledges this exhortation as a digression in the humanistic fashion. In the dialectic of reading, textual experience becomes personal experience which is again transcended through aesthetic experience: the controlled observation of the text's demands creates the possibility of forming references for what has been internalized in the very process of internalization. This artificial doubling of the reader has been described as 'constitution of the reading subject.'[60]

The dichotomy between object and subject that is necessary for per-

ception and recognition to happen is transferred into the reader's
mind. The reader is engaged by the author's thoughts, temporarily
thinking them instead of her own. Thus, a horizon is formed in her
consciousness which emerges as a new horizon for a new text. Each
text is, therefore, a system of combinations with a place for the person
who is able to realize its particular combination. The reader has to fill
'intentional blanks,' that is, omitted connections in need of concretiza-
tion or simply polysemous words. Out of a list of Montaigne's favour-
ite concepts, such as 'jugement,' 'entendement,' 'intelligence,' 'belle
âme,' the blank that Marie de Gournay decodes in her preface is the
concept of 'suffisance.'[61] It is used by Montaigne to describe men's
competence in all fields of life and is denied women. Marie de Gournay's defence of the Essais against the followers of Malherbe, her point-
by-point refutation of contemporary criticisms, is an art of reading by
which she holds up a new genre and its implied reader: this implied
reader is Gournay herself, a reader who is willing to continue a person-
alized discussion of the topics dear to Montaigne. For her, the contact
with the Essais is an authorization to embark upon the journey toward
the self.

With this in mind, let us look at the Proumenoir de Monsieur de Montaigne (1594).[62] This short novel is above all an answer to many discussions supposedly held by Montaigne and Gournay during one or
several walks. Its central theme is the beginning of a young woman's
writing career; she endeavours to group various literary genres around
a love story in which a young girl sacrifices her love, her origins, her
voice, and her life. The author rewrites a story told in the second Discours des champs faëz by Claude de Taillemont. The original as well as
Gournay's version constitute a play with the concepts of 'amour,'
'amitié' and 'loyauté' that discusses the physical aspects of the passions and that has been interpreted, in Gournay's case, as literary exor-
cism, therapeutic writing, or as a badly entitled piece.[63]

Important in the Proumenoir are the dedicatory letter that provides a
frame to the text and gives insights into the relationship between the
young author and Montaigne, and the digression on women's chastity
that is later removed because it contains foreign language and foreign
authors' names, though for the sake of embellishment purely, as Gournay modestly indicates. This digression pleads for women's education.[64] If rather than asking whether the title misleads the reader or
unduly advertises an unknown author's first work, we look for paral-

lels in literary history, we encounter, for example, Françoise de Graf-figny, who in her *Lettres d'une Péruvienne* develops a story that may rewrite letter 67 of Montesquieu's *Lettres persanes*, that is, the love of Aphéridon and Astarté. Gournay's text thus offers a prolongued con-versation with Montaigne and represents her personal attempt at defining the perfect friendship through a critique of the passions and at continuing this friendship beyond its term.

Instead of emphasizing the author's intellectual dependence, her indulgence in her femininity, her inner revolt against oppression, and her forbidden sexuality,[65] we should underline that Gournay considers her work and herself as a tomb, as ashes, and as a widow. In a letter to Lipsius from 22 May 1596, she says: 'Sir, since the others at this hour do not recognize my face, I fear that you do not recognize my style, thus the loss of my father has transformed me! I was his daughter, I am his tomb: I was his second being, I am his ashes. With him gone, nothing has remained of myself nor of my life, except just that which fortune thought would need to be reserved for me in order to attach my unhap-piness to it.'[66] And in the dedicatory letter to the *Proumenoir* from 1594, she says: 'Father, receive here the adieu of your daughter, glorified and beatified by that title.'[67] On a literary level, Marie de Gournay rewrites the tomb that Montaigne first intended for La Boétie in his essay 'De l'amitié,' and later decided to remove from his work because this author's 'De la servitude volontaire' had become a controversial text. This dedicatory letter, the later removed digressions, the reduced pref-ace, and the successful rewriting of Taillemont's novella all prove her confidence in her independent literary achievement. And on a personal level, she reenacts the emotional heritage from a bygone era and comes to represent this heritage for her contemporaries. If we remember that there will be real danger in defending the free-flowing thought of a free-thinking conversationalist like Montaigne at a time when Théo-phile de Viau is imprisoned for his contributions to the *Parnasse des poètes satiriques* (1622), her courage and daring are considerable.

Le Proumenoir de Monsieur de Montaigne is an explicit as well as an implicit plea for equality. It is a text that arises from (fictitious) conver-sations between two intellectuals; it draws on a literary tradition while adapting this tradition to a female voice which engages in a discussion of some controversial topics, that is, patriarchal authority and female sexuality. In her *Egalité des hommes et des femmes* (1622), Gournay devel-ops the topic that she presented in the (removed) digression of her novel. It has been stated, on the one hand, that she successfully uses the authority of the philosophers, the church fathers, and scripture in order to prove the equality of the sexes.[68] On the other hand, her move has been criticized for incorrect quoting and naive readership where the author with charming passion refuses to recognize the misogynist character of those proofs she quoted in order to underline equality.[69] Yet, as I maintain, Marie de Gournay reacts to the polemical discussion of the 'querelle des femmes' and raises its level by writing a learned treatise from a woman's point of view. She regrets the inadequate education of women that she considers the only cause for inequality. She poses herself as an example of such an education – mentioning her lonely studies during stolen hours and against her mother's will – and as someone who endeavours to overcome this disadvantage.

It has long been recognized that the 'Grief des dames' (1626) is a brief companion piece to Montaigne's essay 'De l'art de conferer.'[70] The originality of this text has been seen in the generous defence of women, whose arguments had been entirely taken from male writing, thus vanquishing male prejudice or proving it wrong.[71] Once again, this manifesto against those men of letters and courtiers who refuse to listen to women's conversation has been criticized for the literary examples being badly chosen without the author recognizing it. Her feminism thus built on misogyny is said to turn against her, because she has grounded it in masculinizing arguments instead of letting it tell her difference.[72] Yet as I see it, this is a manifesto that argues for women's participation in conversations against those men at court who denigrate women's abilities and their character in order to promote their own, at least equally feeble, abilities. Is this 'Grief des dames' a 'feminist' text? Decidedly so, but by being good literature, it avoids being political; by being tastefully erudite, it even is quite in line, for as much as possible given Gournay's personality and intentions, with current conversational fashions. The often quoted beginning: 'Blessed art thou, Reader, if you are not of that sex to which one forbids everything of value, thereby depriving it of liberty'; and the parallel phrase: 'Blessed again are you, since you can be wise without offense,'[73] clearly allude to the problem of the 'femme savante' in a society that is becoming increasingly restrictive. Such sentences, together with Gournay's dialogical constitution of identity as a woman writer, take on a different dimension when seen in the context of the paradigm shift that I have illustrated in the preceding pages and against which Marie de Gournay defends her friendship, her writing, and her career.

NOTES

1 Gournay, *The Equality of Men and Women*, 91. 'Certes Sainct Hierosme escrit sagement en ses Epistres; Qu'en matiere du service de Dieu, l'esprit et la doctrine doivent estre considerez, non le sexe. Sentence qu'on doit generaliser, pour permettre aux Dames à plus forte raison, toute autre Science et toute action des plus exquises et solides, disons en un mot, de la plus haute Classe: et cela suivant aussi les intentions du mesme Sainct, qui par tous ses Ecrits honore et authorise bien fort ce sexe' (*Le Proumenoir de Monsieur de Montaigne*, in Marie de Gournay, *Oeuvres Complètes*, 1:983). I have had to work with the various editions of Gournay's writings listed in the bibliography of this volume, but I quote from the edition by Arnould, the standard reference that is now available.

2 A good survey of Marie de Gournay's (literary) relationship to Montaigne is given by Dotoli, 'Montaigne et les libertins via Mlle de Gournay.'

3 See the articles by Michel Simonin, Andrée Comparot, and Philippe Desan in Arnould, *Marie de Gournay et l'édition de 1595 des Essais de Montaigne*. Of particular interest in this context is Simonin's article, 'Aux origines de l'édition de 1595.'

4 I will go much beyond 'Poétiques dialogiques et réécriture dans l'oeuvre de Marie de Gournay' by Beaulieu and Fournier.

5 Franchetti, 'Marie de Gournay apologiste des *Essais*.'

6 'Adieu de l'ame du roy,' *Oeuvres Complètes*, 1:653. This text embroiled the author in a slander campaign.

7 Bauschatz, 'Imitation, Writing, and Self-Study in Marie de Gournay's 1595 "Préface" to Montaigne's Essays.'

8 See her personal account of discovering the *Essais* in *Oeuvres Complètes*, 2:1863.

9 Desan, 'The Book, the Friend, the Woman.'

10 Rigolot, 'L'amitié intertextuelle,' 57.

11 Gournay, *Le Proumenoir de Monsieur de Montaigne*, ed. Arnould, 1.

12 Burke, 'The Renaissance Dialogue,' 4.

13 Montaigne, *The Complete Essays*, 35. 'Nous ne sommes hommes et ne nous tenons les uns aux autres que par la parole' (Montaigne, *Oeuvres complètes*, I, 9, 37c).

14 Gournay, 'The Ladies' Complaint,' 103. 'Car de l'art de conferer en general, et de ses perfections et deffaux, les *Essais* en traictent jusques au faiste de l'excellence' (*Oeuvres Complètes*, 1:1077).

15 Montaigne, *The Complete Essays*, 1045. 'Le plus fructueux et naturel exercice de nostre esprit, c'est à mon gré la conference' (*Oeuvres complètes*, III, 8, 900b).

16 'Si je n'ai les vertus de mon second Père, j'ai quelques uns des vices qu'il avoue, surtout celui-ci, de m'impatienter vivement d'une conférence confuse' (Ilsley, *A Daughter of the Renaissance*, 27).

17 'Ce n'est pas tant la force et la subtilité que je demande, comme l'ordre' (*Oeuvres complètes*, III, 8, 903c).

18 Montaigne, *The Complete Essays*, 926; *Oeuvres complètes*, III, 3, 800b: 'Ils en ont en ce temps entonné si fort ...'

19 Montaigne, *The Complete Essays*, 927; *Oeuvres complètes*, III, 3, 800b: 'Il ne faut qu'esveiller un peu ...'

20 Faret, 'De la complaisance,' in *L'Honnête homme ou l'art de plaire à la cour*, 70.

21 Ibid., 89. Morvan de Bellegarde (*Réflexion sur ce qui peut plaire ou déplaire dans le commerce du monde* [Paris, 1688]) thinks women to be so sensitive that they misinterpret remarks to their disadvantage that were made in passing, and worry over them; conversations with women therefore often consist in explanations and justifications (see Strosetzki, *Rhétorique de la Conversation*, 73).

22 Faret, *L'honnête homme ou l'art de plaire à la cour*, 89.

23 Ibid., 91.

24 Ibid., 89.

25 'C'est bien là sans doute le grand Theatre de la conversation des femmes, mais l'estrange confusion de monde qui s'y voit, sur tout à ces magnifiques heures du soir, est si importune, que les meilleurs entretiens s'en ressentent' (ibid., 90).

26 Magendie, *La Politesse Mondaine*, 369.

27 Fronde, the name given to the rebellion which took place (1648–52) in France against Mazarin and the court during the minority of Louis XIV. The word *fronde* means a sling (*The Oxford Companion to English Literature*, 1975, 4th ed.).

28 Magendie, *La Politesse Mondaine*, 481.

29 Kleinman, *Anne d'Autriche*, 100.

30 Capefigue, *Anne d'Autriche*, 33.

31 Herbillon, *Anne d'Autriche, reine, mère, régente*, 45.

32 Capefigue, *Anne d'Autriche*, 28.

33 Bertière, *Les Reines de France au temps des Bourbons*, 170.

34 *Mémoires de Mme de Motteville*, 25.

35 Ibid., 26. According to the *Dictionnaire de l'Académie*, 'galanterie' signifies 'Qualité de celui qui est galant; agrément de politesse dans l'esprit et dans les manières. Il se dit plus ordinairment des respects, des soins, des empressements pour les femmes, qu'inspire l'envie de leur plaire. Il se dit également Des propos flatteurs qu'on tient à une femme. Galanterie se dit

From Dialogue to Conversation 131

aussi d'Un commerce amoureux et illicite: "Cette femme a une galanterie avec un tel. Elle a déjà eu plusieurs galanteries." Galanterie se dit en autre Des petits présents qu'on se fait dans la société. Ironiq., la galanterie est un peu forte, se dit d'une action peu honnête, mais que l'on est disposé à pardonner.'

36 Bertière, *Les Reines de France*, 398.

37 Castiglione's *Cortegiano* (translated into French for the first time in 1537 and reedited in 1538) and Della Casa's *Galateo* (translated in 1562) must also be mentioned here.

38 Fumaroli, *Le Genre des genres littéraires français: la conversation*, 6.

39 Guazzo, *The Civile Conversation of M. Steven Guazzo*, 1:39; Guazzo, *La civile conversation*, 1:36.

40 *The Civile Conversation*, 1:56; *La civile conversation*, 1:56.

41 *The Civile Conversation*, 2:114; *La civile conversation*, 2:125.

42 *The Civile Conversation*, 2:115; *La civile conversation*, 2:125.

43 *The Civile Conversation*, 2:235; *La civile conversation*, 2:261.

44 *The Civile Conversation*, 2:241; *La civile conversation*, 2:269.

45 Fumaroli, *Le genre des genres*, 12.

46 Grenaille, *L'honneste garçon*, 229.

47 Ibid., 231.

48 Ibid., 232.

49 Ibid., 233.

50 Grenaille, *L'honneste fille*, 70.

51 Ibid., 264.

52 Du Bosc, *L'honneste femme*, 53 and 63.

53 Ibid., 78.

54 Strosetzki, *Rhétorique de la conversation*, 19–24. See the definition of the *Dictionnaire de l'Académie*: 'conversation – entretien familier; converser – s'entretenir familièrement.' Many 'entretiens' are published in the course of the seventeenth century, such as Costar's *Entretiens de Monsieur de Voiture et de Monsieur Costar* (1654), Bouhours's *Entretiens d'Artiste et d'Eugène* (1671), or Grenaille's *Entretiens du sage Pétrarque* (1673, 1678). In 1668, the chevalier de Méré publishes 'Les conversations' and, according to Fumaroli (*La diplomatie de l'esprit*, 333), in 1677 follows his theory of conversation in a series of essays entitled 'De l'esprit,' 'Des agréments,' and 'De la conversation'; conversation is here defined as 'entretiens' with the aim of 'se divertir.'

55 Strosetzki, *Rhétorique de la conversation*, 139.

56 Ibid., 142. An example is François de Callières, '*La logique des amans ou l'amour logicien*' (1668).

57 Strosetzki, *Rhétorique de la conversation*, 145.

58 A late example of such a text is Fontenelle's *Entretien sur la pluralité des mondes* (1696) where contemporary astronomical knowledge is gallantly offered to a marquise who is being seduced at the same time.

59 See Strosetzki, *Rhétorique de la conversation*, and Goldsmith, *Exclusive Conversations*, 1. Goldsmith discusses the second half of the seventeenth century.

60 Wolfgang Iser, *Der Implizite Leser*, and *Der Akt des Lesens*.

61 Competence, capability, or sufficiency.

62 *Dictionnaire de l'Académie*: 'Proumenoir – Lieu destiné à la promenade et qui est ordinairement couvert.' Emile Littré: 'partie d'un édifice libre et couverte ou d'un jardin destinée à la promenade.' *Trésor de la Langue Française*: 'lieu généralement couvert, aménagé pour la promenade dans un endroit clos, lieu où l'on se promène.' Montaigne, *Essais* III, 3: 'Tout lieu retiré requiert un proumenoir. Mes pensées dorment, si je les assis.' Arnould, *Proumenoir*, 7: 'Le mot "proumenoir" est loin d'être indifférent sous la plume de la lectrice et de la future éditrice des Essais. Il désigne pour elle la conversation itinérante qui a donné naissance au récit; il est pour Montaigne le lieu intime de la réflexion au sein des livres, et donc aussi, peut espérer sa fille d'alliance, celui de la lecture attentive que fera de cet écrit son destinataire unique.'

63 Ilsley, *A Daughter of the Renaissance*, 33, and Schiff, *La fille d'alliance de Montaigne*, 7.

64 'A l'advanture a-on peur que si les dames estudioient l'antique philosophie ne leur fist croire, avec elle, que la continence n'est pas commandee de la raison, ains de la loy civille' (*Oeuvres Complètes*, 2:1356).

65 Venesoen, *Etudes sur la littérature féminine au XVIIe siècle*, 17.

66 'Monsieur, comme les autres mesconnaissent à ceste heure mon visage, je crains que vous mesconnoissiez mon style, tant ce malheur de la perte de mon père m'a transformée entièrement! J'estois sa fille, je suis son sépulcre, j'estois son second estre, je suis ses cendres. Luy perdu, rien ne m'est resté ny de moy-mesme ny de la vie, sauf justement ce que la fortune a jugé qu'il en falloit reserver pour y attacher le sentiment de mon mal' (*Oeuvres Complètes*, 2:1937).

67 Gournay, *Apology for the Woman Writing*, 32. 'Recevez quand à vous, un million de bons jours de vostre fille, glorifiee et beatifiee de ce tiltre' (*Oeuvres Complètes*, 2:1287). Here I would agree with Venesoen, *Etudes sur la littérature féminine*, 21–2.

68 Boase, *The Fortunes of Montaigne*, 57.

69 Venesoen, *Etudes sur la littérature féminine au XVIIe siècle*, 27.

70 Ilsley, *A Daughter of the Renaissance*, 209–10.

71 Schiff, *La fille d'alliance de Montaigne*, 47.

72 Venesoen, *Etudes sur la littérature féminine au XVIIe siècle*, 40.

73 Gournay, *Apology for the Woman Writing*, 101; 'Bien-heureux es-tu, Lecteur, si tu n'es point de ce sexe, qu'on interdit à tous les biens, le privant de la liberté.' 'Bien-heureux derechef, qui peux estre sage sans crime' (*Oeuvres Complètes*, 1:1074).

Dialogues with
History, Religion, and
Science

'Truth Hath the Victory': Dialogue and Disputation in John Foxe's *Actes and Monuments*

Joseph Puterbaugh

I

Controversies of belief and authority in the wake of the Reformation generated the wide publication of catechisms and dialogues in sixteenth-century England. These texts were written and published to edify and persuade on issues of ecclesiastical discipline, church reform, and religious identity.[1] Dialogue, as a literary form, spoke eloquently to Catholics, Protestants, and Puritans engaged in these controversies primarily because dialogue can disguise the source of controversial opinion. By dramatizing voices, authors can deflect direct responsibility for provocative points of view, and place self-condemning speech into the mouths of opponents, a strategy as old as Plato and Lucian.[2] For Protestant and Puritan polemicists, dialogue also allows them to represent reconciliation and order; by showing how two or more voices move toward consensus, dialogue dramatizes the movement of the individual into a wider circle of believers, a movement which is at the centre of Protestant conceptions of spiritual cooperation and godly community.[3]

Perhaps most important, the 'dual' quality inherent in dialogue – both as written text and as re-creation of speech – allows these writers to explore the movement of the Word and its interaction with the unwritten Holy Spirit. Within the fiction of their texts, dialogue opens up space where the individual can validate his or her own authority on matters of faith (an authority guided and secured, of course, by scripture and God's grace). Recent work by historians and literary scholars helps us understand early modern conceptions of religious identity formation, and how religious self-identity emerges in the process of debate, dialogue, and self-definition within religious communities.[4]

Dialogue is deployed by John Foxe in *Actes and Monuments* in a similar fashion. This essay will focus on several key moments of dialogic exchange in Foxe's text in order to show how dialogue functions. I use 'dialogue' here to mean not just the reported speech of direct, vocalized communication between two or more persons, but a dialogue calculated for the printed page, reaching out to the reader in a kind of polemical and ideological colloquy. As we will see, these moments of dialogue function on two levels: they demonstrate how truth is separated from untruth by means of a reformed faith, but they also dramatize how the act of disputation is crucial in the formation of Protestant identity.

Warren Wooden's claim that the scene of dramatization for Foxe is 'less the public disputation, the examination room, or the torture chamber, than the mind and heart of the individual' is too generalized.[5] Whether at formal university disputes, tavern debates, prison conferences, or at the climactic moment of the stake, these public scenes of dialogue are where his martyrs are immortalized.[6] And Foxe surrounds these exchanges with interpretive commentary which, in turn, constructs a dialogue beyond the text, engaging a broader Protestant community in the act of reading.

II

'Dialogue' as a descriptive term and as a literary genre in sixteenth-century England had multiple connotations. The term was used in a variety of contexts, and often used interchangeably with 'discourse,' 'disputation,' 'conference,' 'debate,' or 'conversation.' 'Dialogue' could signify a debate between two or more speakers within a nondramatic, prose narrative; a 'poetic' dialogue (as in Spenser's *Shepheardes Calender*); a method of religious instruction (as in the catechisms and colloquies of Erasmus, Cordier, and others); a method of formal argumentation and public debate (as a component of university training in scholastic disputation and syllogistic logic); a 'conference,' a term used by Protestant and Puritan writers to denote public and private discussion on doctrinal and ecclesiastical issues; and the verbal exchange between characters within a dramatic text (in the modern sense of dialogue as speech reflecting the psychology or emotion of a dramatic character).

Distinctions among these catagories were fluid and overlapping, of course. Thomas Wilson's didactic dialogue, *Discourse Upon Usury* (1572), for example, depicts a group of vividly drawn characters, all with their particular points of view and speech patterns, while the exchange between Richard and Anne in Act I of Shakespeare's *Richard III*, to take an example at the opposite extreme, displays a complex pattern of formal argumentation. It is dialogue's ambiguous position as a literary form (as both literary and dramatic – a hybrid, 'nameless art,' as Aristotle remarked in the *Poetics*) that supplies much of the interest for modern readers, even those explicitly propagandistic and polemical. Despite the understandable modern emphasis on those dialogues that are the most open or provocative, it is important to understand how authority is treated in polemical dialogues, and how the dialogue form either opens up perspectives or tries to establish authorial control for its reader/audience. I will approach Foxe's use of dialogue in *Actes and Monuments* in this way.

Modern readers of the hundreds of nondramatic prose dialogues published in England in the sixteenth and seventeenth century see them mostly (and rightly) as closed-off exercises in propaganda dressed up as dialogue. A few of these texts even end without reconciliation or consensus (although this type of ending has its own polemical strategy). These dialogues are written in moments of negotiation and crisis, and are, in effect, a 'literalization' of the debate at hand. I am tempted to characterize them as 'idealized miniature cultures' (to borrow a phrase from Thomas Greene) in their dramatization of social, religious, and political debates.[7] They are written and published to harmonize social broils or to purge religious error, and to make a text 'dialogue-wise' or 'by way of dialogue' is to show a curing of the body politic, an expunging of poisons, and ultimately a restatement of authority. Such idealization, however, is achieved only tentatively, and in their struggle to smooth over hostility and social instability, these dialogues often paradoxically foreground dissent.

In European models of the *questione d'amore, conversazione*, or *trattato d'amore*, dialogue is conceived as an exercise of wit, suggesting delight in the 'play' of conversation.[8] The dialogues deployed in Elizabethan Protestant polemic, like Foxe's, by contrast, while ostensibly welcoming opinion from multiple points of view, are haunted by the outside world. The element of 'play' is gone. They work hard to construct authority for their speakers, and their speakers struggle to establish authorial control over the dialogue itself. We move into the interrogative mode and a stronger element of didacticism, stressing conversion over conversation. Conversion narratives have been an important component of dialogues from their classical origins, for conversion is at the core of the dialogue's fundamentally pedagogic and therapeutic strategy.[9] Implicit in dialogue is the attempt to persuade the speakers to reject one way of life and accept another, presumably more 'profound,' perspective, and in this sense dialogue implies 'an exchange not just of speeches but of identities.'[10]

In *A Dialogue Between a Vertuous Gentleman and a Popish Priest*, published by the radical printer Robert Waldegrave in 1581, we find a good example of this strategy. A scripture-quoting Gentleman (Christopher Conscience) debates doctrinal issues with 'Parson Neverbegood' as they ride on horseback along a quiet country road. Like much of the propaganda issued from Waldegrave's press, the debate is a pretext for homilies on ecclesiastical order. But it also can be seen as a fictionalized conference of the kind urged by Elizabethan Puritan divines.[11] This dialogue dramatizes the fact that Protestant identity is achieved only through interrogation, and the path toward spiritual regeneration involves the peeling away of false identities as a preparation for entry into the 'mystical body' of fellow Protestants. Dialogue is crucial in this process. The Gentleman's questions and answers finally affect a genuine conversion within the Parson by the dialogue's close, a conversion that literally cures him of his false religion:

PAR: Oh this comfort is great, and these words have stroken me to the heart.
GEN: How doe you (M. Par) me thinkes your collour doth begin to change.
PAR: Oh, oh, oh.
GEN: What [,] are you not wel, that you looke so ill?
PAR: Oh, sicke, sicke.
GEN: Wil you ride to some towne? And we will send your water to some phisition.
PAR: Oh, no, al the Phisitions in England are not able to cure this disease.
GEN: Why (M. Parson) where dothe it greeve you?
PAR: Oh at the heart, at the heart.[12]

The parson suddenly becomes a mouthpiece of reformed doctrine, and this is followed by his tortured confession of the system of simony and bribery that plagues England. The dialogue thus dramatizes the process of edification important to Puritan divines, and dialogue is imagined here as a therapeutic power in the discovery of true Protestant identity.

In another dialogue printed by Waldegrave, *A Dialogue Concerning the Strife of Our Church* (written in the context of the 'subscription struggle' of 1583–4), dialogue is conceived not as a method of edification, nor does it strip away error or false identities. None of the speakers in this imagined debate betweeen Orthodoxos (a divine), Philodoxos (a lawyer), and Philochrematos (a bishop's chaplain), elicit consensus or even a conditional agreement before moving on. The dialogue is composed of short, set speeches; there is little rapid-fire dialogue to suggest an exchange of views or even inquiry into opposing points of view. The dialogue sharpens differences and polarizes opinion.

The vehemence on each side is strong, and it is remarkable, in this piece of Puritan propaganda, that the chaplain's attacks are given such space. In previous years, the writers of such a polemical work might have imagined a reconciliation within the fiction; the three men might have walked off at the end to pray for reform. But the stakes were extremely high in 1584, and the dialogue underlines their differences in order to mark off 'that side which hath the truth' from its opposite. In its attempt to diffuse accusations that Puritans are disruptive and rebellious, this dialogue in fact dramatizes exactly this point: although Orthodoxos spends considerable time pressing his opponents to prove his divisiveness, the dramatic action of the dialogue itself demonstrates precisely the potential for separation and strife in the Puritan cause. Here, the Puritan position stands proudly outside of an 'unreformed' church, and wilfulness is portrayed in the dialogue as something pure and ultimately courageous.[13]

While the dominant visual icon in the *Actes and Monuments* is, of course, the horrific moment of the martyr burned at the stake, I believe Foxe would have us remember prints of dialogue and conference as another key image of the community of Protestant faithful. A woodcut inserted in the section of *Actes and Monuments* describing 'The last examination of Robert Smith' depicts seven men locked in Newgate prison. Smith presses his right hand on the Bible and points to a passage with his left. George Tankerfield holds an open book; John Newman holds a closed book. The mouths of the two older men are also open, signalling that they confer with Smith, while two others hold their tongue, their eyes focused and intense. In the text, Foxe tells us Smith and his fellows 'had godly conference within themselves,' and Smith was diligent in arguing, persuading, and converting many in the course of his imprisonment.[14]

There are other examples. A print labelled 'Certayne Bishops talking with Maister Bradford in prison' depicts John Bradford's encounter with the archbishop of York and the bishop of Chichester in Newgate prison. The bishops face Bradford, their mouths open in mid-argument. One bishop holds his hand out to Bradford, as if urging him to be reasonable. Bradford stands at centre-left of the print, next to the jail keeper. He holds a closed Bible in one hand, looking defiant and strong in the midst of conference. Another print, depicting 'the talke betwene M. Bradford, and two Spanish Fryers,' shows Bradford again engaging opponents with calm determination. Bradford sits to the centre-left of the print, his face once more steady and confident as the friar labelled Alphonsus reaches out to Bradford, urging him to turn away from his 'self-will or wisdom.' The other figure, the king's confessor, looks away, as if dismayed by Bradford's stubbornness. Bradford tells the friars that he will not waiver in his beliefs and in fact engagement in dialogue and conference will only strengthen his 'conviction of religion' because 'it is so certayne and true that it may abide the light, [and] I dare be bold to have it looked on, and conferre it with you, or any man.'[15]

Conferences, disputations, dialogues, and debates fill the pages of Foxe's book, and they are often brilliantly rendered and dramatically satisfying. Indeed, the author's use of vivid dialogue has impressed generations of readers in its dramatic economy and narrative power.[16] The representations of dialogue in his text are comparable to theatrical texts, especially in the examination and trial scenes (the language of the stage is used throughout by Foxe and the martyrs to analogize their situation).[17] But I would like to focus not simply on how Foxe uses dialogue in the dramatic sense, or as transcriptions of historical events, but how he foregrounds the agency of dialogue in the formation of Protestant spiritual experience and eventual martyrdom.

III

Lack of open debate is a sign of corruption in Foxe's eyes. During the time of Pope Innocent III, he tells us in 'A protestation to the whole Church of England' in the opening pages of *Actes and Monuments*, true doctrine was defaced, 'and whereas before truth was free to be disputed amongst learned men, now, liberty was turned into law, argument into authority. Whatsoever the bishop of Rome denounced, that stood for an oracle of all men to be received, without opposition or contradiction; whatsoever was contrary ipso facto, it was heresy.'[18] Foxe's contemporary readers understood the importance of open disputation in propelling church reforms. In *A Conference betwixt a Mother a Devout Recusant and Her Sonne a Zealous Protestant* (published in 1600), the Son in Francis Savage's dialogue cites a debate held at Berne in 1528, a debate that sparked the Reformation across Europe: 'After the rumor of this disputation,' the son tells his mother, 'Reformation followed at Strawsbourge, Basil, and other places, to Gods great glorie.'[19] Look to *Actes and Monuments* for confirmation of this, he continues, where you can read 'what answers have been made by simple women, maides, and girles unto great Bishops and Doctoures in causes of religion & faith, to the great astonishment of their adversaries.'[20]

Foxe's rendering of dialogue in these moments does become almost parodic in its dramatic efficiency. William Haller is right when he notes that we can only marvel at the dramatic flair for expressive speech the martyrs have in Foxe's narrative.[21] But what is central for readers like Savage's son is not simply how Foxe's book records memorable remarks of Protestant faithful, but the process of disputation and its agency as a conversionary force, both within the individual and in the world at large. The polemical force of these moments for Foxe is the legitimacy of the martyrs' claim to engage in disputation on scriptural and doctrinal issues despite their social class or political status. The young university student Julian Palmer is denounced by the Catholic authorities as a 'beardless boy' who dares to 'offer disputation,' and his examiner tries to contain Palmer's responses; the poor miller Edmund Allen, when asked where he finds the liberty to preach and interpret scripture, responds that God gives him authority to engage in debate with priests and schoolmasters; and the iron-maker Richard Woodman, inspired by the Holy Ghost, turns the format of disputation on its head when he quickly becomes the questioner of his own examiners; Alice Driver tells her judges that although she is a poor woman, without university training, 'in the defence of God's truth, and the cause of my master Christ, by his grace I will set my foote against the foote of any of you all.'[22]

Protestants and Catholics repeatedly invoked public disputation as central to the propagation of true doctrine. In Edwardian Cambridge, Cranmer and the Protector both believed that disputation was the best method of dispelling Catholic error, and statutes were enacted for theological debates to be held every other Thursday from one to four o'clock in the afternoon.[23] These debates – the formal argumentation and resolution before an assembly of judges and in the presence of a moderator – were important components of university education in sixteenth-century England. Bachelors of divinity at Oxford were required to engage in disputations at the end of each term, and Cambridge divinity students were required to respond and oppose in a disputation in which a Doctor acted as master and judge.[24] Under Mary, public disputation played an important role in the church's suppression of heresy and the establishment of Catholic uniformity. But what are the dangers of open disputation? Does engagement in dialogue convey to 'heretical' opinions status and legitimacy? These tensions are on display at the 'disputation of Religion' in Convocation a few weeks after Mary's accession in 1553. Controversy quickly overtakes this 'debate of matters of religion' but not only in terms of key issues such as the sacrament of the altar or transubstantiation (each side claims patristic commentary, biblical explication, and appeals to church authority to strengthen their positions on these issues). The true openness of the disputation itself quickly becomes the central issue. In his announcement of the Convocation, Hugh Weston, dean of Westminster under Mary, promises it will be a place where 'all men [can] freely speake their conscience in these matters': but by the third day Weston emphasizes that the debate has been appointed 'not to call the truth into doubt, but that these gainsayers might be resolved of their argument.' As depicted in *Actes and Monuments*, Philpot and other Protestant figures are constantly interrupted and denied full and free expression. At one point, Philpot declares that the strategy of interruption is simply another method of silencing opposing views: 'Master Prolocutor,' Philpot chides Weston and the assembly, 'thinketh that he is in a Sophistrie schoole, where he knoweth right well that maner is, that when the Respondent perceiveth that he is like to be inforced with an argument to the which he is not able to answer, then he doth what he can with cavillation and interruption to drive him from the same.' Philpot repeatedly condemns the lack of open dialogue as the debate unfolds; when he is ordered to silence toward the end of a heated exchange, Philpot concludes by declaring: 'A sort of you here, which hitherto have lurked in corners, and dissembled with God and the worlde, are nowe gathered together to suppresse the sincere truthe of Gods holy worde and to sette forth every false devise, which by the Catholike doctrine of the Scripture, yee are not able to maintaine.'[25] The episode involving Philpot and the Convocation demonstrates how the limits of debate have been reached. The opposing voices have made up their minds on the subject of controversy, and the claim to truth becomes a claim to authority that is made on both sides in a contest between irreconcilable positions.

The disputations at Oxford in 1555 began with a similar intent of quelling controversial opinion through open disputation. In the 'Letter of Warrant' of 1554, written in preparation of the examination and trials of Ridley, Cranmer, and Latimer, Mary ordered that 'certain grave and well learned doctors and others, as well of that our university of Oxford as of our university of Cambridge, [shall] hear, in open disputation ... Cranmer, Ridley, and Latimer; so as their erroneous opinions, being by the word of God justly and truly convinced, the residue of our subjects may be thereby the better established in the true catholic faith.'[26] Mary clearly believed that the authorizing force of public university disputations, conducted in Latin, would bring Cranmer, Ridley, and Latimer to their knees, obliterate the 'residue' of Protestantism in England, and unify the nation. During Edward's reign, Bishop Stephen Gardiner, however, distrusted public disputations involving matters of the church. He believed that opening up key doctrinal issues for debate would inevitably lead to disobedience.[27] Weston cautiously prefaced the examination of Ridley at Oxford by asking liberty of the church to call the truth into question, 'without prejudice to the same.'

In a telling remark that reveals his fear of disputation as a potentially destabilizing force, Weston cautions Ridley as they go forward to use 'short arguments, lest we should make an infinite process of the thing.'[28] The bishop of Gloucester also discounts the role of disputation in determining key points. Ultimate authority, Gloucester insists to Ridley, is to be found only in the church. Heretics in the past were not 'suppressed and convinced' by 'reasoning in disputations.' These voices were silenced through the superior voice of authority of the Catholic Church. Without this voice, all judgment on issues of belief and doctrine become subjective and indeterminate: 'And indeed except we do constitute the church our foundation, stay, and judge, we can have no end of controversies, no end of disputations.'[29] For the reformers, they understood that they were in a position of weakness, as the Marian authorities controlled the conduct of the debates. In his own account of the Oxford disputations, Ridley notes the noise from the partisan crowd, the lapses into English, and a general atmosphere more like a disorderly play than a sober university debate. Ridley understood the skills needed to participate in the types of debates he faced in April 1554, and he published two texts in dialogue form not only to articulate his theological positions but to provide to his readers guidebooks on how to engage Catholic opponents or wavering coreligionists in effective debate.[30]

Foxe is similarly concerned about the presentation of the arguments at the Oxford disputations and how they are published in his book. In the 1563 edition of *Actes and Monuments* the Oxford disputations are presented without marginal commentary, nor are they broken into syllogisms. In the second edition (1570), key arguments are analysed as syllogistic, complete with Foxe's marginal commentary, patristic notation and critical analysis. To take just one example: Weston, during an exchange with Latimer on the Eucharist, turns to the gathered audience and refutes Latimer with a syllogism ('Hear ye people, this is the argument ...'). In the 1563 edition, Latimer answers him immediately, and the disputation continues. But in the 1570 edition, after Weston's argument and before Latimer's response, editorial commentary intrudes: 'This argument [meaning Weston's], because the Major thereof is not universall, it is not formal, and may well be retorted against Weston, thus: ...'[31] These additions clearly show Foxe's desire to prompt the reader (literally from the margins) to be attentive and responsive, and to guide the reader to a proper evaluative position.[32]

Haller is too dismissive when he comments that it is a waste of time to study the obsolete dialectic employed by both sides in these episodes, where syllogism is matched with syllogism, quotation matched with quotation, 'as though it were conceivable that the question could still be settled by such procedures.'[33] But these debates were conducted in disputation form precisely because both sides *did* think these questions could be settled by such procedures; the men on both sides of these debates all received university educations which were deeply influenced by scholastic training in grammar and terminalist logic.[34] In his exchanges with Gardiner, Cranmer employs syllogisms to persuade his listeners on key issues of the visible church, the Eucharist, and the interpretation of scripture. The discovery of the truth of any matter, Cranmer believed, could only be achieved through debate by the word of God: 'The chaff cannot be tried out from the pure corn (that is to say, the untruth discerned from the truth) without threshing, [and] fanning, searching, debating, and reasoning.'[35] Foxe expends much energy ridiculing the logic of the Catholic debaters at Oxford,[36] but often the attempt to argue from deductive proof is met with opposition and dialogue breaks down. In his contest with Latimer, Weston turns away from him and speaks directly to the audience, deducing a syllogism defending his own position by twisting Latimer's response for his own ends.[37] Cartwright, following Weston, tells Latimer, 'I will make you this short argument, by which I was converted from mine errors,' and he constructs a syllogistic proof regarding the true body of Christ – which Latimer rejects and Foxe answers in a marginal note. Glyn, one of the doctors gathered to debate Ridley, attempts something similar when he pulls Ridley's responses out of context and forms syllogisms to defend his own position.[38]

It would be a mistake to characterize these disputations as a clash between an older scholasticism (represented by Catholic authorities) and a humanist rejection of syllogistic argumentation in favour of rhetorical persuasion (represented by Foxe and the Protestant martyrs). Both sides are confident that scriptural citation, patristic commentary, and the deductive force of the syllogism will lead the opposing side to orthodoxy. But there is a tension in these debates between the logic of scholastic dialectic and the power of a truth that is revealed. While the syllogism is deployed to develop thought from *within* interlocutors, building a chain of reasoning through inference, judgment, and deduction, the Protestant dialectic, like that found in the dialogic exchanges of *Actes and Monuments*, also discloses the crucial role revelation plays in the movement toward the light of Truth.[39]

An exchange between Doctor Young and Cranmer on 16 April 1554 provides one example of this tension. 'This disputation,' Young tells Cranmer as he begins, 'is taken in hand, that the truth might appear,' but he quickly adds, 'It is a common saying: "against him that denieth principles we must not dispute."' Young tries to persuade Cranmer to accede to a preliminary point about the body of Christ which Cranmer immediately rejects. But Young continues, as if Cranmer agrees to Young's premise:

YOUNG: Again I demand, whether sense and reason ought to give place to faith?

CRANMER: They ought.

YOUNG: Thirdly, whether Christ be true in all his words?

CRANMER: Yea, he is most true, and truth itself.

YOUNG: Fourthly, whether Christ, at his supper, minded to do that which he spake, or no?

CRANMER: In saying he spake, but in saying he made not, but made the sacrament to his disciples.

YOUNG: Answer according to the truth, Whether did Christ that as God and man, which he spake, when he said, 'This is my body'?

CRANMER: This is sophisticall cavillation: go plainly to work. There is some deceit in these questions. You seek subtileness: leave your crafty fetches.[40]

Note how Young numbers his questions as if they develop into a chain of deduction; Cranmer answers each of them, but Young appears not to speak to Cranmer at all, and instead raises his voice to the gathered audience, until Cranmer breaks from him and condemns his opponent for not engaging in disputation but putting forward arguments unacknowledged by the other side (Young's questions here are annotated by Foxe as Young's 'Socraticall interrogations' and 'sophistical interrogatories').[41]

When Young a few lines later twists Cranmer's definition of figurative speech regarding the sacrament, a frustrated Cranmer answers that 'these are mere sophisms,' and demands that the argument be based on readings in the Bible: 'I look for Scriptures at your hands, for they are the foundations of disputations.' Young asks for agreement from Cranmer that God changes bread into Christ's body. 'This is the truth,' an exasperated Young insists, 'acknowledge the truth: give place to the truth.' 'O glorious words!' is Cranmer's bitter reply: 'you are too full of words.'[42] The exchange ends inconclusively, without the development of ideas as in logical dialectic, suggesting the 'infinite process' so feared by Weston; further, the theological logic like that found in catechism, which should bind both men in its fundamental chains and progressions, breaks down. Dialogic exchange here is a strategy of provocation and persuasion rather than deductive proof. The participants in the Oxford debates literally talk past each other; premises that should bind the disputants go unregarded, deductions and inferences are rejected, argument is characterized as mere sophistry.

Mary decided not to publish accounts of the Oxford debates, and a planned public disputation between Bradford, Sanders, and Rogers was abruptly cancelled.[43] Despite the fact that Ridley and Latimer were condemned as heretics in the course of the Oxford trials – and burned at a stake outside Balliol College, Oxford (Cranmer followed them in March of the following year) – there was something about the disputation format that clearly made the Marian regime uneasy. The reason for this is disputed by historians, but perhaps transmitting the potential instability of the dialogue form to the printed page was an idea too dangerous for Mary to sustain.[44] The effects of the disputations at Oxford were not as profound as Foxe would have his readers believe; while the Oxford trio were of course something of a national sensation,[45] the climate after their deaths darkened considerably. Although Cranmer's burning forever tainted Mary's use of force in the pursuit of heresy, Oxford strengthened its orthodoxy, and the flight of exiles weakened the reform position further. By 1557, a Spanish visitor characterized the colleges as 'Catholic and correct' in religion.[46]

Foxe's retelling of the William Hunter episode has none of the official machinery of the Oxford disputations, but suggests how Foxe deploys dialogue in key moments of his narrative history. Hunter's story is presented in a straight-forward, chronological manner, moving from a small locality to scenes involving representatives of Mary's administrative power.[47] The story begins when the nineteen-year-old Hunter refuses to accept communion in the first year of Mary's reign. He is dismissed from his apprenticeship as a silk-weaver; at a chapel in Brentwood, a summoner hears William read from an English Bible, and his fate is sealed. Hunter is a completely public figure, as presented by Foxe. Apart from his dream, his narrative consists entirely of public examinations – and even his dream foreshadows his public statements at the scene of his death. For the authorities, dialogue with Hunter reveals heresy (after a few questions on the sacrament of the altar, Wood, the vicar, declares Hunter is a heretic), but for martyrs like Hunter, dialogue only brings forward the truth of God's word.

Hunter is characterized as simple and plain speaking. His gentle answers in the course of his dialogic exchanges are sure and confident, in contrast to the summoner's and the vicar's histrionics and Bonner's spiteful replies. In an exchange with Justice Brown, Foxe tells us 'William could not speak a word but [Brown] crossed him, and scoffed at every word.'[48] After trying to reason with him, Bonner even tries the kind of logical proof we saw deployed in the Oxford debates. Bonner takes off his cap and asks Hunter about its 'accidentals' and its 'substance.' But even this approach is turned aside by Hunter's steadfast answers. The bishop's offers of money, office, and flattery also do not persuade, and Hunter's rejection of these rewards are signals to Foxe's lay audience to remain steadfast in the face of such temptations. Bonner tells Hunter that if he will conduct a private dialogue, 'between me and thee,' as he puts it, and recant his sins, Bonner will keep quiet and let Hunter go. But Hunter refuses to violate his conscience. What is stressed here is Hunter's act of public defiance, and the formation of his Protestant identity in the course of these moments of debate. As he awaits his doom in Newgate, Hunter is met by friends, and in a scene that brings us back to the woodcuts of Robert Smith and John Bradford, Foxe tells us that Hunter's friends 'reasoned with him, and he with them, exhorting them to come away from the abomination of popish superstition and idolatry.'[49] Hunter's mid-morning prophetic dream and the sign of God on his final day show how this simple apprentice has been transformed into a soldier of God, a humble man who transcends his locality and is sealed into the chronicles of Protestant martyrdom. As Hunter waits at the stake, there is another important moment of dialogic exchange. Hunter kneels down and reads from the 51st Psalm; Master Tyrell, hearing him read, accuses him of translating falsely and famously comments: 'You translate books as you lift yourselves, like heretics.' 'Well,' Hunter responds simply, 'there is no great difference in those wordes,' and Hunter is brought to the flames.[50]

Foxe's emphasis in this story is on the effect godly belief has on familial relations. Hunter's parents in fact encourage their son's journey to the flames, and in this way Foxe tells us his parents are 'singuler' in that they 'forget themselves' – that is, they release all kinship ties and obligation to become one with their godly identity.[51] Foxe thus designs this narrative to engage in dialogue with a family of readers, incorporating a broader Protestant community.[52] Foxe knows that history is rhetorical in the sense that it is not an unmediated presentation of historical facts and figures, and the annotations, running commentary, and shifting narrative patterns contribute to this rhetorical strategy.[53] It is important for Foxe that we hear the martyrs like Hunter 'speak' for themselves; he gives us 'true copies' of their letters and testaments, and his dialogue is formatted on the page like a theatrical text to give the impression of the 'living speech' of Ridley or Cranmer as unmediated and direct.[54] But Foxe's manipulation of the narrative (inclusion of material not spoken or read at the trial itself, the translation into English) are attempts to control the emotional impact of the proceedings in the mind of his reader. Foxe's marginal notes challenging the conclusions of Tresham, Seton, and Weston, for example, contribute yet another voice to the disputation, answering hyperbole with hyperbole, sarcasm with sarcasm. This commentary attempts to clear away ambiguity and rebuild the missing consensus dramatized by the Oxford debates. Foxe points the reader back to the deductions necessary for true doctrine, and his narration is surrounded by reported speech, transcribed dialogues, and received documents.

It would be a mistake, however, to call Foxe's work 'polyphonic,' as some critics have done. *Actes and Monuments* is a classic example of what Bakhtin would call 'authoritative discourse,' in that Foxe's book is strongly monologic in its desire for narrative authority. The work's underlying hierarchy of discourse is controlled by Foxe's dominant narrative voice, a voice that rises above all others in a position of historical analysis, interpretive mastery, and theological insight. Foxe's book might be more acurately described as 'heteroglossic,' in that his book is a monumental record of the multiple languages – scriptural, royal, heretical, vernacular – that contribute to the community of believers his history invokes.[55] It is the interaction between these languages (whether it be a letter from Bishop Ridley, or a royal command from Queen Mary, or the simple utterance of a poor bricklayer) and Foxe's rhetorical strategy (the interruptions from the margins, the backward and forward jumps in time, and so on) which constitutes the true heteroglossic impulse in *Actes and Monuments*. In this sense, Foxe's book is inexhaustibly dialogic.

In 'A Protestation to the whole Church of England,' Foxe writes that he hopes to 'open up' the transgressions of the Roman Church in his history of Protestant martyrs. 'Of these and a thousand other not one word hath been touched [by former religious historians], but all kept as under benedicite, as in auricular confession.'[56] Foxe's own history, he tells us, by contrast, will work in a public method, and his book is filled with debates, conversations, and examinations. Dialogue and disputation dramatize the dialectical relationship between his book and those who read it. Dialogue, then, opens up space in his narrative where the truth of the Protestant cause can come forward, and thus showcases for Foxe the intersection of text and history.

NOTES

1 See Green, *The Christian's ABC*. Following the Reformation, as Douglas Bruster has noted, 'a new kind of religious authority was sought in the individual's ability to master the answers to fundamental questions' and catechism replaced 'isolated recitation' (review of *The Christian's ABC*). Bruster's comment here is perhaps too schematic; catechisms were an important component of medieval Catholicism in England, along with confession and the sermon. See Duffy, *The Stripping of the Altars*, chapter 2. On early modern English dialogues generally, see Hereford, *Studies in the Literary Relations of England and Germany in the Sixteenth Century*; Wilson, *Incomplete Fictions*; and Puterbaugh, '"Sweet Conversation."'

2 This technique was widely used by Reformation and Counter-Reformation polemicists, especially Luther, More, and Tyndale. See Pineas, *Thomas More and Tudor Polemics*, 22–3 and 77–8. See also Pineas, 'William Turner's Use of the Dialogue Form as a Weapon of Religious Controversy.'

3 See Lake, 'William Bradshaw, Antichrist, and the Community of the Godly.'

4 See Lake and Como, 'Orthodoxy and Its Discontents'; Puterbaugh, '"Your selfe be judge and answer yourselfe"'; Slights, 'Notaries, Sponges and Looking-Glasses'; Questier, *Conversion, Politics, and Religion in England, 1580–1625*; Halley, 'Equivocation and the Legal Conflict over Religious Identity in Early Modern England'; and Lake's 'Puritan Identities.'

5 Wooden, *John Foxe*, 48.

6 Even moments of introspection in Foxe are configured in dialogue, as when George Tankerfield tests his ability to withstand the flame in his private chamber, and the moment evolves into a little dialogue between body and soul (*Actes and Monuments*, 1690). All references to *Actes and Monuments* will be to the 1583 edition, the 4th and last edition published in Foxe's life-time, with any material not in that edition cited in the first edition in which it appears. For a survey of how the corrupt Victorian editions of Foxe's work (edited by S.R. Cattley) have impeded scholarly study, see Freeman, 'Texts, Lies, and Microfilm.' See also Breitenberg, 'The Flesh Made Word: Foxe's *Acts and Monuments*.' On examinations in Foxe and how they are manipulated for maximum effect, see Knott, *Discourses of Martyrdom in English Literature*, 59–69 and 76, note 100. Knott argues that examinations '[displace] torture as the site of combat between individual Christian and the authorities' (50). See also Kendall, *The Drama of Dissent*, 152.

7 Greene, *The Vulnerable Text*, xiii.

8 See Rebhorn, *Courtly Performances*, and Lipking, 'The Dialectic of *Il Corteg-iano*,' 356.

9 The 'turning' in Book VII of the *Republic* is perhaps the most famous classi-cal example. On the therapeutic strategy of Platonic dialogue, see Cush-man, *Therapeia: Plato's Conception of Philosophy*.

10 McCutcheon, 'Heresy and Dialogue,' 367.

11 These controversial practices (also known as 'prophesyings') were urged by presbyterians from the mid-1570s to the end of the century 'to equip [clergy] with the means to preach, and to maintain a general doctrinal agreement' (Collinson, *The Elizabethan Puritan Movement*, 127). The opening pages of *A Dialogue* stresses the importance of the 'right' interpretation of scripture over and above the judgment of the prince: 'O that we knew such an estate to be dangerous, and that such sinnes wil be punished except repentaunce, what shall it profite us to have peace under our prince, and yet live as rebels unto our god?' ('To the godly Reader'). On the role dialogue, both as literary form and as metaphor for 'conference,' plays in the controversies involving 'hotter' protestants and separatists, see Joseph Puterbaugh, '"This gift of

prophecie": Dialogue, Godly Identity and Freedom of Religion in the Separatist Controversies of the Late Elizabethan–Early Stuart church (1575–1615),' in The Puritan Electronic Seminar, ed. Francis J. Bremer, et al. 2000. http://www.millersville.edu/~winthrop/puritan.html.

12 *A Dialogue Between a Vertuous Gentleman and a Popish Priest*, STC 1039, Kv.

13 *A Dialogue Concerning the Strife of Our Church*, STC 6801.

14 *Actes and Monuments*, 1695. So many godly and learned men are imprisoned under Mary, Foxe goes on, 'that almost all the prisons in England were become right christian schools and churches; so that there was no greater comfort for christian hearts, than to come to the prisons to behold their virtuous conversation, and to hear their prayers, preachings, most godly exhortations, and consolations' (1521).

15 *Actes and Monuments*, 1617–18.

16 Hardin Craig puts it well when he writes that 'Foxe's [skill] in the reproduction of vivid dialogue has not been widely recognized by historians of literature, but is attested by centuries of genuine popularity' (quoted in Wooden, *John Foxe*, 62). Wooden notes the 'force and clarity' of Foxe's reported speech (63) and Helen White remarks that the 'pungent dialogue of the Elizabethan dramatists seems less of a miracle after one has read page after page of dialogue and dramatic narrative [in Foxe that is] as brilliant as anything written for the stage' (*Tudor Books of Saints and Martyrs*, 42).

17 Palmer argues that Foxe's use of theatrical dialogue allows him to present 'the true speech of the martyr and legitimate that speech through printer's conventions appropriate to the publication of play texts' ('Histories of Violence and the Writer's Hand,' 89).

18 'A protestation to the whole Church of England,' n.p.

19 Savage, *A Conference betwixt a Mother a Devout Recusant and Her Sonne a Zealous Protestant* (STC 21781, 118). This is a claim echoed by at least one modern historian. See Dickens, *Reformation and Society in Sixteenth-Century Europe*, 120.

20 Ibid., 118.

21 Haller, *Foxe's Book of Martyrs*, 193.

22 *Actes and Monuments*, 1938, 1979, 1997, 2049.

23 Mullinger, *The University of Cambridge*, 112.

24 Curtis, *Oxford and Cambridge In Transition*, 88–9.

25 *Actes and Monuments*, 1410–15.

26 *Actes and Monuments* (1563), 999.

27 In a 1547 letter to Cranmer (regarding issues of the visible and invisible church) Gardiner wrote: 'I cannot call a lie everything [I] like not to believe.

[It] is a very dangerous enterprise to discuss lies from the truth, lest there follow that truth be taken for a lie in some new matter' (quoted in Loades, *The Oxford Martyrs*, 77.

28 *Actes and Monuments*, 1442.

29 Ibid., 1765.

30 See Haller, *Foxe's Book of Martyrs*, 32, 34.

31 *Actes and Monuments* (1563), 983; (1570), 1626.

32 *Actes and Monuments*, 1457–8. Wooden notes Foxe's 'constant interruption from the margin' (*John Foxe*, 115) and Evelyn Tribble describes Foxe as standing 'shoulder to shoulder with Latimer and Ridley defending God's truth' through annotation and authorial projection ('The Peopled Page,' 128, note 32). We should be careful, however, on attributing Foxe's authorship to these marginal notations. Thomas Freeman reminds us that while there is evidence that Foxe did write some of the notes in *Actes and Monuments*, many may have been written by a proofreader in John Day's printshop or possibly by Day himself (e-mail to author, 20 May 2003).

33 Haller, *Foxe's Book of Martyrs*, 37.

34 McGee, 'Cranmer and Nominalism,' 194.

35 Quoted in ibid., 199.

36 Foxe deploys logical argument throughout his text (he reproduces, for example, Bradford's syllogism on the mass as convincing proof [*Actes and Monuments*, 1397–8] but he simultaneously goes to great lengths to show how Catholic arguments are weakened by faulty deduction or incoherent proof. He provides Ridley's own annotation of one of Glyn's badly constructed logical proofs, and at another point he corrects Weston's syllogism in a marginal note of his own (*Actes and Monuments*, 1451). Ridley's answers to Smith on the ascension of Christ are given in syllogisms and supplemented by Foxe's marginal note, also using syllogism (*Actes and Monuments*, 1446).

37 *Actes and Monuments*, 1457–8.

38 Ibid., 1451.

39 I owe this point to Stanley Fish's distinction between Socratic dialectic and Protestant catechesis in *The Living Temple*, esp. 22–45.

40 *Actes and Monuments*, 1438.

41 Cranmer's phrase here – 'sophisticall cavillation' – is an allusion to his *Answer unto a crafty and sophistical cavillation*, published in 1551, which was a reply to a work by Gardiner on the sacrament. On the clash of logic and rhetoric in the syllogism as used by other Protestant polemicists like Penry and Turner, see Kendall, *The Drama of Dissent*, 166–71.

42 *Actes and Monuments*, 1438–9.

43 Ibid., 1469.

44 Loades, *The Oxford Martyrs*, 136, and MacCullough, *Thomas Cranmer*, 568.
45 MacCullough tells the story (580–1) of a Cambridgeshire yeoman, who, after a heated exchange in a tavern with an Anabaptist about the divinity of Christ, decides to travel to Oxford to speak directly with Ridley and Latimer to set his mind at rest. Fortunately a local satisfied his conscience and he did not make the trip. See also Loades, *The Oxford Martyrs*, 171, note 12.
46 Loach, 'Reformation Controversies,' 378–80. See also Dent, *Protestant Reformers in Elizabethan Oxford*, 14–15.
47 The William Hunter narrative first appears in Foxe's *Rerum in Ecclesia gestarum ... Commentarii* (Basel, 1559). In the 1563 edition of *Actes and Monuments*, Foxe translated this material into English and added an account, from official records, of Hunter's final examination by Bonner (1110). A more complete narrative, including Hunter's apprenticeship, the Bible incident at Brentwood, Hunter's dream and his execution are included for the first time in the second edition. The material from official records is dropped, while new material, from William's brother, Robert, is now included, and this 1570 version of the Hunter story appears in all subsequent editions of Foxe (1712–16). Andrew Pettegree notes that Hunter's narrative is in fact a stereotypical one; the Continental writers Haemstede and Crespin also show simple labourers able to confute with monks, scholars, and priests in their movement toward martyrdom ('Haemstede and Foxe,' 288–9; 291, and 293, note 56).
48 *Actes and Monuments*, 1537.
49 Ibid., 1538.
50 Ibid.
51 Tom Betteridge makes the excellent point that the portrayal of Hunter's noble parents is part of Foxe's polemical strategy, meant to fight off charges of social and political instability ('From Prophetic to Apocalyptic,' 292).
52 Breitenberg, 'The Flesh Made Word,' 390, notes how Foxe's text creates an extensive 'dialogue' among those inside and outside the Protestant community.
53 Freeman, 'Texts, Lies, and Microfilm,' 40, notes Foxe's skill is not in invention but in editing and shaping his source material. See also Woolf, 'The Rhetoric of Martyrdom,' 269–70.
54 Palmer, 'Histories of Violence and the Writer's Hand,' 88–9.
55 'Polyphonic' is a term used by Bakhtin in his study of Dostoevsky to suggest how Dosteovesky's novels have no authoritative voice controlling and dominating the multiple voices within the fiction; 'heteroglossia,' the English translation of Bakhtin's *raznorecie* or 'multi-speechedness,' is a complex literary term used by Bakhtin to convey the multiple 'languages'

156   Joseph Puterbaugh

spoken within novels. The play between the author's narrative voice and the styles and conventions of a wide variety of discourse parodied and replicated by the author constitutes, for Bakhtin, a heteroglossic 'give-and-take' between author and language (see Bakhtin, *The Dialogic Imagination*, 301–31. See also Dentith, *Bakhtinian Thought*, 35–8, 42–3).

56 'A protestation to the whole Church of England,' n.p.

Milton's 'Hence':
Dialogue and the Shape of History in
'L'Allegro' and 'Il Penseroso'

W. Scott Howard

Hence loathed Melancholy
Of Cerberus, and blackest Midnight born,
In Stygian cave forlorn
'Mongst horrid shapes, and shrieks, and sights unholy,
Find out some uncouth cell,
Where brooding Darkness spreads his jealous wings,
And the night-raven sings;
There under ebon shades, and low-browed rocks,
As ragged as thy locks,
In dark Cimmerian desert ever dwell.

'L'Allegro' 1–10

Hence vain deluding Joys,
The brood of Folly without father bred,
How little you bestead,
Or fill the fixed mind with all your toys;
Dwell in some idle brain,
And fancies fond with gaudy shapes possess,
As thick and numberless
As the gay motes that people the sunbeams,
Or likest hovering dreams
The fickle pensioners of Morpheus' train.

'Il Penseroso' 1–10[1]

Virtually all of Milton's works of poetry and prose refashion their
respective literary genres and rhetorical modes as they progress.[2] That

distinction is especially true of his well-loved 'twin' poems, 'L'Allegro' (i.e., 'the cheerful man') and 'Il Penseroso' (i.e., 'the contemplative man'). Readers have questioned the generic status of these two texts since their original publication in 1645 and have not unreasonably sought to affiliate the poems with an apparently inexhaustible array of literary forms, themes, and cultural discourses.[3] There has also been considerable discussion as to whether the poems constitute two separate texts, or one longer work.[4] 'L'Allegro' and 'Il Penseroso' first appeared side-by-side in *Poems of Mr. John Milton Both English and Latin Compos'd at several times* and are still customarily published together despite the fact that nothing certain is known about the circumstances and dates of their composition.[5] Though the texts' typographic contiguity in Milton's 1645 volume of poetry (as well as in the revised edition of 1673) underscores the works' formal and thematic inter-relationships, there is little agreement among critics about the exact nature of the companionship between 'L'Allegro' and 'Il Penseroso,' as Finch and Bowen and Gerard H. Cox note in their critiques of the poems' histories of reception.[6]

This aporia concerning the works' placement within and against identifiable literary traditions affirms at least one important point: that 'L'Allegro' and 'Il Penseroso' constitute (both separately and together) a hybrid genre. Given the texts' professed uncertain generic status as well as their widely acknowledged metrical and thematic mirroring of one another, it is striking to note that the poems have not yet been examined in relation to the one Renaissance literary form that epitomizes both the mixing of genres and the dramatization of intertextuality: the dialogue.[7] On the other hand, many studies, following essays by Babb and Samuel, link 'L'Allegro' and 'Il Penseroso' to a genre closely related to the dialogue – medieval debate – and specifically situate the works within the context of Renaissance 'disputations' between Galenic and Aristotelian melancholy.[8] However, all of those readings inevitably subordinate the Galenic temperament of 'L'Allegro' to the Aristotelian disposition of 'Il Penseroso' on the grounds that Milton's poems should be read progressively because they portray respectively his own striving to leave behind the secular world of youthful innocence (i.e., 'L'Allegro') in favour of a life devoted to philosophical meditation and religious service (i.e., 'Il Penseroso').[9] The tradition of 'debate' thus invoked by such arguments does not acknowledge what some critics have more recently perceived to be either dialectical or dialogical tensions between the two texts that interrupt binary taxonomies.[10]

Although an analysis of Milton's companion poems as hybrid works lies beyond the scope of this essay, I propose to investigate their participation in an English tradition of poetic dialogue. I will argue that Milton engages with the genre and modalities of dialectical dialogue as a means for imagining, between and within 'L'Allegro' and 'Il Penseroso,' a pattern for history marked by discursive contiguity and contrariety. That pattern, which traces formal and thematic crossings between and within the poems, outlines Milton's emerging idea of history as a dynamic, often violent, cultural process shaped by contiguous cycles of degeneration and contrary acyclical paths toward progress. While Milton's historical imagination has been theorized in terms comparable to those I have just advanced, his twin poems have not yet been examined for their mutual contribution to the poet's historiographic sense.[11] Rather than subordinating one poem to the other and thereby positing a choice of either/or, I wish to see the nature of the texts' companionship in terms of both/and. The poems' continuous mirroring and refashioning of their generic and modal forms and themes thus signals, I argue, an open, temporal dialectic between two interdependent, fundamental states of being (i.e., mirth and melancholy) represented through two interinvolved literary matrices (i.e., 'L'Allegro' and 'Il Penseroso') of social discourse. This essay therefore posits 'L'Allegro' and 'Il Penseroso' as inherently sociable, dialogic texts that explore complementary and contradicting passions of body and mind, which, from Milton's point of view, together drive the wayward course of human action.

'L'Allegro' and 'Il Penseroso' define their formal and thematic identities, differences and interrelationships through mutual renunciations and invocations, as the above prologues to each poem respectively proclaim. 'L'Allegro' banishes the 'loathed Melancholy' (1) of 'Il Penseroso' in order to invoke the 'goddess fair and free, / In heaven yclept Euphrosyne, / And by men, heart-easing Mirth' (11–13). And 'Il Penseroso' reciprocally banishes the 'vain deluding Joys' (1) of 'L'Allegro' in order to invoke the 'goddess, sage and holy, / ... divinest Melancholy' (11–12). This rhetoric of mutual exclusion engenders, both between and within the works, identity and difference, spatiality and temporality. The 'horrid shapes' (4) of Melancholy inform the condition of Mirth's possibility just as the 'gaudy shapes' (6) of Mirth influence Melancholy's appearances and transformations. And the concluding, internalized 'prophetic strain' (174) that the figure of 'Il Penseroso' envisions within that poem's resting place – the 'peaceful hermitage' (168) – hinges upon a complementary world of externalized motion and change – 'Towered cities ... / And the busy hum of men' (117–18) – that the figure of 'L'Allegro' pursues across a pastoral landscape. Neither text can do without the other even as either strives for autonomy.

As works of dialectical dialogue 'L'Allegro' and 'Il Penseroso,' I believe, involve their respective characters and implied readers in a persistent critique of ideas and experiences of either mirth or melancholy as formulated through binary oppositions. The texts' dialogical representation of that discourse dramatizes two important themes: the interinvolvement of both existential conditions; and the action of the reasoning process. Milton's twin poems underscore not only the many epistemological and metaphorical crossings between discourses of both mirth and melancholy, but (most important) the social dynamics of shared inquiry – so central to the genre and modes of Renaissance dialogue – wherein the movement of thought may be apprehended as a manifestation of physical, intellectual, and spiritual activities that unfold within the realm of human time.

Milton's twin poems thus enact a relentless dialectic of question and answer, commandment and resistance that begins with a single word – 'Hence' – simultaneously signaling both spatial and temporal connotations – that is, away 'from here, from this place' and 'from this time onward.'[12] Milton's 'hence,' I argue, therefore serves as a master trope of dialogism between and within these two works that individually and collectively shape the poetic dialogue as a vehicle for the historical imagination. The contiguous and contrary interinvolvement of the poems on formal and thematic levels reveals Milton's idea of history as a process neither strictly linear nor cyclical, but an open-ended dialectic resembling the structure of a helix that might accommodate both cycles of repetition and contingent transgressions against the patterns of time.

1. On Dialogue: From Genre to Mode

Critical studies of dialogue often begin with an apology for two factors: (1) because works within the genre take so many different shapes and moods a standard definition of dialogue is perhaps impossible to achieve; and (2) that a pervasive lack of theory about the genre (since Aristotle's *Poetics*, 1447b)[13] further complicates any attempt to situate the art form within literary tradition.[14] The dizzying heterogeneity of dialogue's avatars in the Renaissance and early modern eras – including prose works, such as Petrarch's *Secretum* (ca. 1342), John Heywood's, *Witty and Witless* (ca. 1556), and Thomas Becon's *The Sicke Mannes Salue* (1560) and also verse dialogues, such as François Villon's 'Le Debat de Villon et Son Cuer' (ca. 1489), Anne Bradstreet's 'A Dialogue Between Old England and New' (1650) and Henry Vaughan's 'The Evening-watch' (1650) – suggests first of all that the genre may be most productively studied as a mode (rather than a strict form) of literary discourse. Within the context of this essay an epistemological shift from genre to mode, I believe, pays tribute to the most enduring characteristic of literary dialogue whether in prose or verse: the representation of intertextual processes of communication.

Dialogue, thus apprehended, conveys the transformation of shared inquiry into literary discourse. Virginia Cox offers a useful formulation, in this regard, of dialogue as a matrix between language, social practice, fiction, and cognition.[15] Such self-reflexivity underscores dialogue's inherent double structure, which, as it may be multiplied almost endlessly, allows for creative interpolations between and within texts as well as between works and readers. Dialogue hence may be posited as a genre that is always-becoming-other and a literary mode that remains open to the incorporation of newly printed voices. For dialogue's staging of intertextuality involves a double turning: inward (toward the dynamics of fictive discourse) and outward (toward the dynamics of social discourse); in each direction the linguistic movement follows the open, dialectical paths of companionate conversation.[16] Informed by the lacuna in section 1447b of Aristotle's *Poetics* – as noted above – concerning dialogue's inclusion within (or exclusion from) a theory of representation, writers and scholars have sought to posit dialogue as a means for conveying the activity of human reasoning: as plot is to drama, so debate is to dialogue. In tandem with that consequent premise, theorists have further articulated dialogue according to either didactic or dialectical modes of discourse.[17]

Those formulations recapitulate insights first advanced by Torquato Tasso in *Discourse on the Art of the Dialogue*[18] (1585) – a text with which Milton was familiar.[19] Tasso esteems dialectical dialogues – 'The writer of a dialogue must be an imitator no less than the poet; he occupies a middle ground between poet and dialectician' (33)[20] – on the grounds that such open rhetorical structures involve readers in the processes of questioning and reasoning (33): hence (for Tasso) the affinity between dialogue, poetry, and philosophy. Milton's 'L'Allegro' and 'Il Penseroso,' I believe, participate in such a tradition by engaging their readers

in an active interpretation of the formal and thematic inter-relationships between and within the poems. Milton stages in these two works
an intertextual drama about the action of debate and thereby invests
each poem with a principle of dialectical temporality. Although Tasso's
influence upon Milton's oeuvre (from the 1630s onwards) has received
much study,[21] critics have not yet placed 'L'Allegro' and 'Il Penseroso'
within a tradition of dialectical dialogue informed by Tasso's works.

Tasso begins[22] with a reflection upon section 1447b of Aristotle's
Poetics before advancing his own thesis that links Aristotle's epistemology of plot to the representation, in literary dialogue, of intellectual
action – that is, of human reasoning:

> Imitation represents either the actions of men or their discussions, and
> although few deeds are performed without words and few discourses
> without activity, at least of the intellect, nevertheless I judge deeds to be
> very different from discourses. Discourses are proper to speculative men
> and deeds to active men, and there are, therefore, two chief kinds of imi-
> tation: one of action and active men and the other of speeches and men
> who reason. (19)[23]

Whereas Aristotle (1450a–b) draws distinctions between the mimesis
of character, thought, diction, song, and spectacle in order to isolate
and elevate the importance of plot and the arrangement of incidents
(544), Tasso seeks to rejoin a theory of representation with the dynamic
reciprocity between action, character, thought, and rhetorical context:
'one imitates not only the disputation but also the characters of those
who are disputing' (41).[24] Tasso posits dialogue, either in prose or
verse, as a social matrix – that is, a mode of poetic figuration – for
bridging the gap between public and private discourses, and accordingly identifies both civil and speculative ends to the representation of
discussion (23).[25] Dialogue therefore is a hybrid mode for Tasso, one
that occupies a middle ground between poetry and philosophy – that
is: between tropological and dialectical discourses (33) – in order to
script the intertextual drama of thoughts apprehended in the action of
their transformation within a social matrix of debate. That, I will submit, is precisely what it is like to read *both* Milton's 'L'Allegro' *and* 'Il
Penseroso' when the poems are conceptualized as comprising one dialectical dialogue – engaged modally by way of two texts and a plurality of voices/discourses – rather than posited as two distinct works
that make very different interpretive demands upon their readers.[26]

Although many readers have defended the singularity of 'L'Allegro' and 'Il Penseroso,'[27] I would place the texts within a capacious English tradition of poetic dialogue that includes, for example, Edmund Spenser's *The Shepheardes Calender* (1579); Margaret Cavendish's 'A Dialogue Between An Oake, And A Man Cutting Him Downe' (1653); and Andrew Marvell's 'A Dialogue Between the Soul and Body' (1681). Such a tradition of English Renaissance and early modern verse dialogue indeed exists, but (to the best of my knowledge) has yet to be addressed thoroughly by modern scholarship.[28] Other studies in the field focus primarily (if not exclusively) upon the tradition of English prose dialogue.[29] For example, Rosalie Osmond's groundbreaking analysis (1990) of body and soul dialogues arranges seventeenth-century English dialogues – written in either prose or verse – into three categories that each work within and against the conventions of their medieval prototypes: moral and didactic; conversational; and philosophical.[30] K.J. Wilson (1985) and Eugene Purpus (1950) outline genealogies for English Renaissance dialogue that would link texts such as those poems noted above by Spenser, Cavendish, and Marvell to the development of prose dialogues by sixteenth-century writers, including Sir Thomas Elyot, Sir Thomas More, and Roger Ascham.[31] However, Elizabeth Merrill (1911) specifically traces the English poetic dialogue back to 'The Owl and the Nightingale' (ca. 1250) that initiates the genre of 'the contention-poem, which grew out of the direct Latin tradition, partly under French influence.'[32] Merrill accordingly places 'L'Allegro' and 'Il Penseroso' within a context of literary debates between paradigmatic figures (represented by the Owl and Nightingale), but does not offer a sustained interpretation of the texts, noting only that 'the contrast [the poems present] is that between two such opposing ways of life.'[33]

Before proceeding in this essay's next section to a reading of 'L'Allegro' and 'Il Penseroso' with regard to the tradition and theory of poetic dialogue I have thus far presented, it will be useful to refine, in terms of Milton's own tropes of 'contiguity' and 'contrariety,' the notion of 'dialectical dialogue' suited best to the complementary contradictions that shape his companion poems' formal and thematic interrelationships. Both tropes figure prominently in *Areopagitica* (1644), for example, where they inform Milton's critique of the Parliamentary ordinance of 14 June 1643 that restricted the licensing of printing.

Milton's challenge to that statute importantly turns upon a defence of public dialogue and debate engendered by texts that provoke a wide range of interpretations, each of which is figured as a stone used in the construction of a new commonwealth:

> And when every stone is laid artfully together, it cannot be united into a continuity, *it can but be contiguous in this world*; neither can every peece of the building be of one form; nay rather the perfection consists in this, that out of many moderat varieties and brotherly dissimilitudes that are not vastly disproportionall arises the goodly and the gracefull symmetry that commends the whole pile and structure.[34] (my emphasis)

The political architecture for England's 'democratic' future, argues Milton by way of this analogy, rests upon a foundational principle of discursive contiguity – that is, of different opinions expressed and disputed freely concerning matters civil, domestic, or ecclesiastical. To follow Milton's homology one step further, those differing opinions, like the stones to which they are likened, may touch irregularly upon one another to create, by way of their disproportionate overlaps and gaps, 'the goodly and the gracefull symmetry that commends the whole pile and structure.'

Public dialogue and debate also hold intrinsic value because, from Milton's point of view, the knowledge of good and evil are distinct yet finely interwoven – that is, contiguous with each other – as he also writes in *Areopagitica*: 'It was from out the rinde of one apple tasted, that the knowledge of good and evill as two twins cleaving together leapt forth into the World' (2:514). This complementary and yet contradictory relationship between good and evil thus posited as active forces in the world therefore signals both the persistence and hopeful purification of original sin through a related principle of contrariety: 'Assuredly we bring not innocence into the world, we bring impurity much rather: that which purifies us is triall, *and triall is by what is contrary*' (my emphasis) (2:515). Though very closely aligned, Milton's tropes of contiguity and contrariety, in this one tract, respectively concern different realms of human communication and interaction: the first, discourse; the second, experience. Milton's paradoxical idea of contiguity thus involves rhetorical principles of difference and similarity, dissonance and harmony, autonomy and unity, etc., all of which drive the action of public debate. Contrariety, on the other hand, marks for Milton 'the dynamics of meaning'[35] – that is, a transition from dialogue to interpretation, from debate to a reasoned judgment based upon the experience gained from public disputation.

These tropes of contiguity and contrariety complement the logic of Tasso's theory of dialectical dialogue and also underscore, within the context of Milton's political rhetoric, the interinvolved processes of communication at work throughout the companion poems. The following section of this essay offers an analysis of the intertextual activity of companionable inquiry set forth simultaneously (on both spatial and temporal levels of discourse) between and within the twin poems by a single word that begins each work: hence. Milton's formulation of 'hence,' I will argue, signals the chronotope[36] of contiguity and contrariety between and within 'L'Allegro' and 'Il Penseroso.'

2. Contiguity and Contrariety between and within 'L'Allegro' and 'Il Penseroso'

Samuel Johnson's oft-cited appraisal of Milton's twin poems implies a preference for the 'good' Aristotelian melancholy of 'Il Penseroso,' a judgment that prevails in the history of both works' critical reception: 'No mirth can indeed be found in his melancholy; but I am afraid that I always meet some melancholy in his mirth.'[37] 'Il Penseroso' wins every time when the debate between the poems is mediated by any one of five binary taxonomies that predominate in close readings of the relationship between 'L'Allegro' and 'Il Penseroso': mirth/melancholy, secular/spiritual, day/night, innocence/experience, and time/eternity. There are, of course, variations upon these general hermeneutic strategies as well as critiques, as noted above, of such dualistic structures.[38] David Miller, for example, notes that both works 'are more complex than such categories indicate, and together they yield a sense of unity that is not just the unity of complement.'[39] Yet even Miller's attempt to read 'L'Allegro' and 'Il Penseroso' in terms of 'a unified vision' recapitulates a privileging of the 'superiority of the pattern set by "Il Penseroso"' because, as he argues, Milton attains in that poem 'the top rung of the earthly Platonic ladder.'[40] This characteristic subordination of 'L'Allegro' to 'Il Penseroso' across the spectrum of their readings consequently engenders a series of right-hand values that may each be substituted into seemingly endless iterations of antitheses between the texts: cheerful/contemplative, body/mind, outside/ inside, external sight/internal sight, active/passive, natural/supernatural, left (sinister)/right (virtuous), etc. In this fashion, the history of the works' critical reception generally posits the texts' preludes as mutually exclusive invocations: each poem renounces the other in order to secure its own proper place and state of being. 'L'Allegro' expels Melancholy – 'Hence loathed Melancholy' – so that Mirth may celebrate 'in the chequered shade' (96) on a 'sunshine holiday' (98); and 'Il Penseroso' equally drives Mirth away – 'Hence vain deluding Joys' – so that Melancholy may 'keep [her] wonted state' (37) in a land of 'arched walks [and] twilight groves, / And shadows brown that Sylvan loves' (133–4).

Such interpretations, however, turn upon a spatial connotation of the one word that initiates both works – the hinge that announces as it renounces: hence. According·to the *OED*, as early as 1275 'hence' has signified: 'I. Of place. 1. (Away) from here, from this place; to a distance' (1:1289). Critics of Milton's companion poems tend to favour this spatial connotation in support of readings that conclusively praise the eternal 'studious cloister' (156) of 'Il Penseroso' above the temporal, 'unreproved pleasures free' (40) of 'L'Allegro.' Yet that preference for a spatial definition excludes three other primary connotations of 'hence' that have all been in English language use since 1597, a point that has not yet been addressed by the poems' readers. As the *OED* indicates, 'hence' has four primary cases, the third and fourth of which are variations upon the first two. The word's spatial connotation therefore operates within and against the temporal: 'II. Of time. 4. From this time onward, henceforward, henceforth.' The first and second cases underwrite/overwrite one another and thereby condition the possibilities for the third and fourth primary connotations: 'III. Of issue, result, consequences, etc. 5. From this, as a source or origin. IV. 8. *Comb.* a. with sb., as *hence-departure, -going*; b. with pa. pple., as *hence-brought, -got*, etc.; hence-meant, intended, purposed, planned from this place.' These four definitions of 'hence,' I wish to argue, together shape the chronotopic dialogism of contiguity between and contrariety within 'L'Allegro' and 'Il Penseroso' and thereby engender prologues for each poem that are not merely spatial and mutually exclusive invocations, but temporal-and-spatial, mutually inclusive invocations-and-renunciations. Milton's 'hence' thus initiates a dialectical dialogue of question and answer, call and response, between and within each text to the extent that each poem and each state of being paradoxically conditions the possibility of the other's autonomy and interdependence.[41]

Each prologue accordingly welcomes an 'apt and cheerfull conversation'[42] involving not only contiguous relationships between the two poems, but contrary forces within each text because each work's identity depends upon the other's dialogical difference. Just as 'L'Allegro' begins by banishing Melancholy to the space and temporality of 'Il Penseroso,' 'Il Penseroso' banishes Mirth to the space and temporality of 'L'Allegro.' Those reciprocal exclusions paradoxically generate, within each text, the inclusion of each poem's opposite, or contrary. Facilitated by the multiple cases of Milton's 'hence,' each text simultaneously announces and renounces its own contrary, which also becomes the other work's other contrary in a process that Finch and Bowen describe as a 'kind of Mobius strip, a simultaneously two-sided and one-sided loop on which *L'Allegro* and *Il Penseroso* are continually doubling back on one another.'[43] Not only are both texts equally shaped from within by their own unsuccessfully restricted contraries, but they are each also interinvolved with the contiguous contraries of one another's Other. Self-definition becomes self-division and mutual inter-/intra-inscription. The 'horrid shapes' (4) of Melancholy first articulated in the prologue to 'L'Allegro' inform the condition of Mirth's 'gaudy shapes' (6) pronounced by the prologue to 'Il Penseroso' just as the sensibility of Mirth's 'fancies fond' (6) described by 'Il Penseroso' inflects the mood of Melancholy's 'brooding Darkness' (6) within the context of 'L'Allegro.'

This dialectical multivoicing between and within the poems reaches points of intensity during the texts' narratives about different types of towers and enclosed structures. Indeed, many critics argue that the towers mark the epistemological centres of both poems.[44] Towers and other towerlike enclosures appear in three sections of 'L'Allegro' (41–8; 77–80; 117–44) and in two passages of 'Il Penseroso' (85–130; 155–74). Space and time converge upon these architectural structures as they are each composed of the contiguous and contrary 'stones' of the other text's enclosures: Mirth's presence in the towers of 'L'Allegro' turns upon the copresence of Melancholy just as Melancholy's agency in the enclosed structures of 'Il Penseroso' involves the collaboration of Mirth. Neither poem can isolate either sensibility in a pure form because each text and state of being depends upon the existence of their contrary. The inter-involvement of both Mirth and Melancholy in these passages thus enacts an intertextual and dialectical drama of that ongoing disputation and the vigilant reader's active discernment of the inextricable differences and similarities between and within both poems and psychological states.

For example, the central persona of 'Il Penseroso,' following the imperfect illumination of such 'counterfeit gloom' (80), seeks an encounter with Melancholy in 'some high lonely tower' (86). This first tower image in 'Il Penseroso' dialectically complements that of the

'Towers, and battlements ... / Bosomed high in tufted trees' (77–8) in 'L'Allegro'; for here the poem's primary speaker acts from within the enclosure during the night, whereas the central persona of 'L'Allegro' first describes the same tower from an external perspective during the day. The contiguity between these first tower images and contexts in each poem suggests that both texts' personae are simultaneously present in each landscape, each speaker voiced within and against the other's tenor. The contrary influence of Mirth thereby undermines the primary speaker's endeavours in the first tower of 'Il Penseroso' to apprehend pure Melancholy until finally the space of that secluded environment is interrupted by the temporal breaking of a new day: 'Thus Night oft see me in thy pale career, / Till civil-suited Morn appear' (121–2). Mirth's contrariety then moves the central persona of 'Il Penseroso' to flee in search of a more genuinely gloomy environment: 'And when the sun begins to fling / His flaring beams, me goddess bring / To arched walks of twilight groves, / And shadows brown that Sylvan loves' (131–4). The contrary action of dawn's emergence here also touches contiguously upon the appearance of 'dappled dawn' (44) and the persistence of day through respectively the first (41–8) and second (77–80) tower scenes of 'L'Allegro' as both poems continue this intertextual, dialectical drama of the debate between Mirth, Melancholy, the personae of each text, and the poems' readers, all of whom are implicated in the wayward unfolding of the works' representations of the reasoning process.

After several attempts to hide 'from day's garish eye' (141) and the contrary influence of Mirth, the primary speaker of 'Il Penseroso' arrives at the poem's concluding towerlike structures – first 'the studious cloister' (156) and then 'the peaceful hermitage' (168). Yet even here Mirth's dialogic presence within Melancholy's various forms tempers (however slightly) the central persona's experience. In the cloister 'storied windows' (159) cast 'a *dim* religious light' (160) (my emphasis) and the 'full-voiced choir' sings not with melancholic sorrow, but 'with *sweetness*' that dissolves the primary speaker 'into ecstasies' (164–5) (my emphasis). The central persona of 'Il Penseroso' then imagines 'spelling / Of every star that heaven doth shew' (170–1) in the hermitage 'Till old experience do attain / To *something like* prophetic strain' (173–4) (my emphasis). Mirth's dialogical contrariety thus undermines each and every attempt to discover Melancholy's pure essence as Milton's twin poems continue their relentless dialectic of question and answer, commandment and resistance.

3. Milton's 'Hence' and the Historical Imagination

These delights, if thou canst give,
Mirth with thee, I mean to live.
—'L'Allegro' (151–2)

These pleasures Melancholy give,
And I with thee will choose to live.
—'Il Penseroso' (175–6)

From beginning to ending 'L'Allegro' and 'Il Penseroso' dramatize a dialectical dialogue concerning a range of interrelationships between two states of being: mirth and melancholy. Not only do the poems represent that path of inquiry within each work, but they also stage the action of that dialogue as well as of the reader's reasoning process through intertextual patterns of formal and thematic crossings between both texts, patterns that I have examined with regard to Milton's tropes of contiguity and contrariety. The poems' concluding, conditional requests addressed to Mirth and Melancholy, I believe, continue that incessant, dialogic process; for 'These delights' and 'These pleasures' each partake of one another's qualities. Mirth's 'delights' are, to the primary speaker of 'Il Penseroso,' 'gaudy shapes' (6) and 'gay motes that people the sunbeams' (8), as the prologue to that text declares; likewise, Melancholy's 'pleasures' are, to the central persona of 'L'Allegro,' 'horrid shapes' (4) of 'brooding Darkness' (6), as the prologue to that work proclaims. Each text is thus a nodus of delights, pleasures, and shapes contiguous and contrary – the meaning of (or choice for) either: both/and. The companion poems, in this regard, complement the mood of Democritus Junior's (i.e., Robert Burton's) 'The Authors Abstract of Melancholy,' which, while not a verse dialogue, celebrates the intertwining of joy and melancholy through the variable refrain: 'All my joyes to this are folly, / Naught so sweet as melancholy.'[45]

Milton's twin poems stage an intellectual drama in which the action of the reasoning process (including the reader's active participation) plays the key role. 'L'Allegro' and 'Il Penseroso' are therefore sociable, dialogic texts that explore complementary and contradicting passions of body and mind that together shape the course of human action in the world. The poems accordingly conclude with the language of living on the cusp of immanent/imminent change – 'I mean to live' and 'I ... will choose to live' – much like the rhetoric of Eve's last speech to Adam in *Paradise Lost*:

But now lead on;
In me is no delay; with thee to go,

Is to stay here; without thee here to stay,
Is to go hence unwilling; thou to me
Art all things under heaven, all places thou,
Who for my wilful crime art banished hence.
This further consolation yet secure
I carry hence; though all by me is lost,
Such favour I unworthy am vouchsafed,
By me the promised seed shall all restore.[46]

As Eve and Adam accept their charge from Michael 'To leave this Paradise' (12:586) they realize that they stand literally and symbolically on the edge of human history. When they go, 'The world [is] all before them' (12:646); each of their steps forward generates time and space, new actions and new worlds, as Eve's apt articulations of 'hence' here illustrate. She describes their departure first in terms of time and then space – 'to go hence' and 'banished hence' – and then also in terms of both time and space together – 'I carry hence' – because within her rests the promise of 'A paradise within' (12:587) that may only unfold within the drama of human time.

Milton's formulation here of 'hence' (as in the companion poems) thus simultaneously looks backward and forward, invoking temporality and spatiality, and thereby signifies a matrix in the work of literary art within and against which figural discourse constitutes historicity. Milton's use of 'hence' in 'L'Allegro' and 'Il Penseroso,' though far less portentous than in the above passage from *Paradise Lost*, engenders similar consequences for the primary speakers of the twin poems, both of whom are poised, as the texts conclude, on the fold between at least two visions of England's history and (perhaps as well) of the poet's own life.[47]

NOTES

1 *Milton: Complete Shorter Poems*, ed. John Carey, 144–51. 'L'Allegro' 134–44 and 'Il Penseroso' 144–51. All subsequent references to Milton's poetry – with the exception of *Paradise Lost* – correspond with this edition and provide, in parentheses, line numbers for each instance of citation. I wish to thank my colleagues at the South Central Renaissance Conference – John Shawcross, Jim Baumlin, and Jenn Lewin – for their helpful comments on early drafts of this essay, which is dedicated to Sara van den Berg. This chapter informs part of a much extended and differently focused study of

Milton's and Tasso's poetics of dialogue. See Howard, 'Companions with Time: Milton, Tasso and Renaissance Dialogue.'

2 See Lewalski, Paradise Lost *and the Rhetoric of Literary Forms*.

3 For studies of the twin poems with regard to the ode, poetic contests, the medieval debate, eclogues and the pastoral tradition, character writing, the interlude, rural excursions, the argumentative verse essay, the hymn, the invocation, the lyric, and Milton's prolusions, see Carey, *Milton: Complete Shorter Poems*, 134–6; Hunter, *A Milton Encyclopedia*, 4: 191–8; and Hughes, *A Variorum Commentary on The Poems of John Milton*, 2: 223–338.

4 Carey, *Complete Shorter Poems*, 136; Christopher, 'Subject and Macrosubject in "L'Allegro" and "Il Penseroso"'; and Phelan, 'What Is the Persona Doing in "L'Allegro" and "Il Penseroso"?'

5 Hunter, *Milton Encyclopedia*, 4:191.

6 Finch and Bowen, 'The Solitary Companionship of "L'Allegro" and "Il Penseroso"' 3; and Gerard H. Cox, 'Unbinding "The Hidden Soul of Harmony,"' 48.

7 To the best of my knowledge, only one critical text places Milton's companion poems within the tradition of Renaissance dialogue yet makes that association merely by way of a passing allusion in one sentence. See Merrill, *The Dialogue in English Literature*, 28.

8 Babb, 'The Background of "Il Penseroso"'; Samuel, 'The Brood of Folly.' For overviews of this particular critical tradition, see respectively Carey, *Complete Shorter Poems*, 131; and Hurley, *The Sources and Traditions of Milton's 'L'Allegro' and 'Il Penseroso,'* 19–58.

9 See, for example, Brown, '"The Melting Voice Through Mazes Running."' Brown opens his essay with an argument that seems to weigh equally each poem's structural and thematic instabilities, yet finally recapitulates a preference for the 'melancholy pleasure' (10) of 'Il Penseroso.'

10 Finch and Bowen, 'Solitary Companionship'; Patterson, '"Forc'd fingers": Milton's Early Poems and Ideological Constraint'; Council, '"L'Allegro," "Il Penseroso," and the Cycle of Universal Knowledge'; and Miller, 'From Delusion to Illumination.'

11 On Milton's 'historical imagination,' see Loewenstein, *Milton and the Drama of History*, 92–151, and Guibbory, *The Map of Time*, 169–211.

12 'Hence,' in *The Compact Edition of the Oxford English Dictionary*, 1971 ed., 1: 1289. All subsequent in-text parenthetical references correspond with this edition.

13 Aristotle, *Poetics*, trans., Hubbard, 540. All subsequent in-text parenthetical references correspond with this edition. Passage 1447b states: 'The art that uses only speech by itself or verse [that is, rhythmical speech], the verses

being homogeneous or of different kinds, has as yet no name; for we have
no common term to apply to the [prose] mimes of Sophron and Xenarchus
and to the Socratic dialogues, nor any common term for mimesis produced
in verse, whether iambic trimeters or elegiacs or some other such metre.'

14 See, for example, Dryden, *The Works of Lucian*, 45–6.
15 Cox, *The Renaissance Dialogue*, 5–6. All subsequent in-text parenthetical references correspond with this edition.
16 See Siegle, *The Politics of Reflexivity*, 12, and Mukarovsky, *The Word and Verbal Art*, 93.
17 Within a seventeenth-century context, see, for example, Dryden, 'A Defense of an Essay of Dramatic Poesy,' 1:124, and Pallavicino, *Trattato dello stile e del dialogo*, 344. See also Macovski, *Dialogue and Literature*, 3–40; Virginia Cox, *The Renaissance Dialogue*, 2; Snyder, *Writing the Scene of Speaking*, 1–38; Wilson, *Incomplete Fictions*, 1–21; Merle E. Brown, *Double Lyric*, 1–19; and Purpus, 'The "Plain, Easy, and Familiar Way."'
18 Tasso, *Discorso dell'arte del dialogo*, 15–41. All subsequent in-text parenthetical references correspond with this edition.
19 Snyder, *Writing the Scene of Speaking*, 183. On the popularity of Tasso's dialogues in Europe and England during the seventeenth century, see the introduction to *Tasso's Dialogues*, ed. Lord and Trafton, 9; and Brand, *Torquato Tasso*, 205–308. At least one early modern literary work – a dialogue of the dead – suggests Milton's admiration of Tasso's dialogues: *Il Tasso: A Dialogue. The Speakers John Milton, Torquato Tasso.*
20 '... e lo scrittore del dialogo deve imitarlo non altramente che faccia il poeta; perche'egli e quasi mezzo fra 'l poeta e 'l dialettico ...' (32).
21 See Machacek, '*Paradise Lost*, Christian Epic and the Familiar Sublime'; Rhu, *The Genesis of Tasso's Narrative Theory*, 77–98; Kates, *Tasso and Milton*; Hunter, *Milton Encyclopedia*, 8:51–2; and Prince, *The Italian Element in Milton's Verse*, 34–57. On Milton's visit (December 1638) with Giovanni Battista Manso, see Parker, *Milton: A Biography*, 1:173–6.
22 On the biographical contexts and philosophical traditions that influenced Tasso's theory of dialogue, see *Tasso's Dialogues*, 1–3, and Solerti, *Vita di Torquato Tasso*, 1:53–64.
23 'Nell'imitazione o s'imitano l'azioni degli uomini o i ragionamenti; e quantunque poche operazioni si facciano alla mutola, e pochi discorsi senza operazione, almeno dell'intelletto, nondimeno assai diverse giudico quelle da questi; e degli speculativi e proprio il discorrere, si come degli attivi l'operare. Due saran dunque i primi generi dell'imitazione; l'un dell'azione, nel qual son rassomigliati gli operanti; l'altro delle parole, nel quale sono introdotti i ragionanti' (18).

24 'e nell'una e nell'altra non imita solamente la disputa, ma il costume di coloro che disputano' (40).

25 Tasso's concern with interrelated modes (i.e., civil/moral and speculative) as well as themes (i.e., action and contemplation) parallels quite strikingly Milton's complex attitude toward the social interinvolvement of mirth and melancholy in 'L'Allegro' and 'Il Penseroso' and thereby signals the presence, in each of these works, of dialectical tensions between actio/contemplatio and negotium/otium, as exemplified in dialogues by Plato, Cicero, and More as well as in other literary discourses (e.g., satire) and traditions (e.g., utopian writing and pastoral poetry). The affinities and distinctions between mirth and melancholy in Milton's twin poems could also be traced back to Petrarch's thematic in his *Secretum*, which inaugurates the Renaissance tradition of literary dialogue, or to Augustine's *Confessions*, which directly shaped Petrarch's self-reflexive stylistics. On Petrarch's dialogues, see Quillen, *Rereading the Renaissance*, 182–216, and Sturm-Maddox, *Petrarch's Laurels*, 101–30.

26 Fish, *Is There a Text in This Class?* 113, 125–6.

27 Carey, *Complete Shorter Poems*, 1997 ed., 134.

28 See Puttenham, *The Arte of English Poesie*. Puttenham associates English poetic dialogue with the Western tradition of pastoral poetry that begins with *The Idylls* of Theocritus and *The Eclogues* of Virgil where he observes 'in base and humble stile by maner of Dialogue, uttered the private and familiar talke of the meanest sort of men, as shepheards, heywards and such like' (26).

29 See Snyder, *Writing the Scene of Speaking*; Wilson, *Incomplete Fictions*; Ong, *Ramus, Method, and the Decay of Dialogue*; and Purpus, 'The "Plain, Easy, and Familiar Way."'

30 Osmond, *Mutual Accusation*, 115–38.

31 Wilson, *Incomplete Fictions*, 1–21; Purpus, 'The "Plain, Easy, and Familiar Way."'

32 Merrill, *The Dialogue in English Literature*, 26.

33 Ibid., 28.

34 *Areopagitica*, in Milton, *Complete Prose Works of John Milton*, Bush 2:555. All subsequent in-text parenthetical references correspond with this edition.

35 Shoaf, *Milton, Poet of Duality*, 2.

36 On Bakhtin's theory of the 'chronotope,' see Bakhtin, *The Dialogic Imagination*, 84–5, 243. On dialogue, narrative, and temporality, see Mecke, 'Dialogue in Narration (the Narrative Principle),' 201, 205.

37 Johnson, *Lives of the Most Eminent English Poets*, 1:143–4.

38 See Merle Brown, *Double Lyric*; Finch and Bowen, 'Solitary Companion-

ship'; Patterson, '"Forc'd fingers"'; Council, '"L'Allegro," "Il Penseroso,"
and the Cycle of Universal Knowledge'; and Miller, 'From Delusion to Illumination.'

39 Miller, 'From Delusion to Illumination,' 32.

40 Ibid., 32, 36, 37.

41 See Milton, 'Doctrine and Discipline of Divorce,' in *Complete Prose Works of
John Milton*, 2:222–356. All subsequent in-text parenthetical references correspond with this edition. This rhetorical redoubling also complements a
key formulation in Milton's epistemology of divorce. When divorce follows
the rule of charity (229) the resulting separation paradoxically creates interdependent autonomy for both parties, just as 'when by [God's] divorcing
command the world first rose out of Chaos' (273).

42 Ibid., 235.

43 Finch and Bowen, 'Solitary Companionship,' 10.

44 Ibid., 15; Hughes, *Variorum Commentary*, 2.1:241–338; Miller, 'From Delusion to Illumination,' 34.

45 Burton, *The Anatomy of Melancholy*, 1:lxix, 7–8. I would like to thank Bruce
Danner for suggesting this parallel. See also Hurley, *The Sources and Traditions of Milton's 'L'Allegro' and 'Il Penseroso,'* 19–58.

46 Milton, *Paradise Lost*, ed. Fowler, 12:614–23. All subsequent in-text parenthetical references correspond with this edition.

47 On the topic of Milton's self-fashioning in his 1645 collection of poems, see
Swaim, '"Myself a true poem"'; Revard, *Milton and the Tangles of Neaera's
Hair*, 91–127; and Martz, *Milton: Poet of Exile*, 31–59.

Hobbes, Rhetoric, and the Art of the Dialogue

Luc Borot

Thomas Hobbes was educated in an academic culture whose intellectual framework was dominated by rhetoric and dialectic.[1] As translator and teacher, Hobbes was an active participant in that culture. In middle life, he converted to the new science under the influence of Euclid and Galileo, and he wrote his first works on philosophy and political philosophy according to their methods. In later life, he began to write dialogues.[2] He wrote several treatises in dialogue form: the *Seven Philosophical Problems* (1662); *A Dialogue between a Philosopher and a Student of the Common Laws of England* (1664), in which the 'common-law mind' was attacked from the point of view of his theory of law;[3] and *Behemoth, or the Long Parliament*, a history of the civil wars probably written between 1666 and 1668.[4] In 1677 he published *Decameron Physiologicum*, ten dialogues on natural science.[5] A Latin dialogue called *Historia Ecclesiastica* was published in a posthumous collection. It will not be discussed here, as the choice of Latin instead of the vernacular raises problems of genre definitions in Hobbes's philosophy, beyond the scope of this essay. Several polemical works in geometry or theology are near-dialogues, since Hobbes quotes his objectors before stating his own position; yet, as he did not construct these texts as fictional conversations, they cannot be regarded as genuine dialogues. For similar reasons, the *Seven Philosophical Problems* will receive no attention here, since the work does not confront characters embodying different points of view, but merely a questioning voice and an answering one. As he had found the 'geometrical' method to truth in Galileo and Euclid, why did Hobbes resort to dialogical forms? What does it signify in the development of his method? Is it a breach from his philosophical project, or was he resorting to this device, after *Leviathan*,[6] to reach

another kind of audience? After a short presentation of Hobbes's relationship to humanism and rhetoric, this article will discuss the position
of his dialogues in the history and typology of the genre, and finally
suggest an interpretation of his practice.

In relationship to Hobbes's practice of the dialogue, three dimensions of his work must be integrated in the discussion: the importance
of translation and of history,[7] and the centrality of the scientific method
in the development of his works. As a schoolboy of the 1590s, he was
regarded as extremely proficient: he translated Euripides' *Medea* into
Latin verse at the age of fifteen. He then went to Oxford in 1603, before
joining the Cavendish household as preceptor in 1608. At Oxford he
seems to have been influenced by the second scholastic, though his
Latin autobiography dates his rejection of scholasticism and Aristotelianism from his Oxford days.[8] His first book, a translation of Thucydides, only appeared when he was forty. Hobbes's introduction to his
translation was his first statement about history, rhetoric, and politics.[9]
Translation is important in the assessment of Hobbes's rhetorical
approach, because it implies a meditation on audience reception.
Hobbes's justification for the choice of Thucydides and his advocacy of
the Athenian's historical method clearly prove the translator's involvement in historical and rhetorical debates.

Hobbes assumed two essential functions of the humanist scholar: he
translated classical texts, and he trained young noblemen for the state.
Inevitably, he acquainted them with history and rhetoric. The absolut-
ist preceptor was also aware that the civic frame of mind of the rhetorical tradition was likely to draw his pupils away from the interests of
their king, toward republican ideals: Thucydides may have been an
antidote to the dangers of Aristotle's and Cicero's rhetoric. During his
preceptorship, Hobbes also wrote a Latin epitome of Aristotle's *Rhetoric*; the English translation of this text, though Hobbes's authorship is
open to controversy, was the first printed version of the *Rhetoric* in
English.[10] According to Walter Ong, Hobbes's *Rhetoric* was a Ramist
abridgement of Aristotle, and therefore a critical version of the work,
but it has been shown since, that Hobbes's use of rhetorical concepts
ran against the central argument of Ramus's system.[11]

The story of Hobbes's conversion to the method of the new science is
well known. He told it himself, and his biographers have had different
ways of telling it. He reports how he discovered that Euclid's method
should be applied to metaphysics and other philosophical problems,
though things must have been less spontaneous than he pretends: it is

estimated that the *Short Tract on First Principles* was written about 1630 or 1631, and the Latin epitome of the *Rhetoric* about 1633, which means that Hobbes was still teaching Aristotle as he was writing the first draft of his *philosophia prima*.[12]

Hobbes's reformation of philosophy as science rested on the application of a new logic to philosophical method.[13] The *Elements of Law*, published in manuscript in 1640, contain the first published version of Hobbes's ethics, and politics.[14] His anthropology owes much to his debate with the Aristotelian ethics and psychology of the *Rhetoric*. Hobbes's method is an attempt to realize the Euclidian model in a work of moral and political philosophy: in the *Elements*, he is probably as close to his design as ever in his political philosophy, and his attacks on *elocutio* are extremely relevant to his purpose.[15] Rhetoric (as distinct from logic) is more active in his 1642 *De cive* than in the *Elements*, though eloquence receives a regular attack in chapter 12, in a rejection of eloquence and demagogy as seditious means to power.[16]

The recent controversy on the rhetorical status of *Leviathan* focuses on a general interpretation of Hobbes's intellectual development in the 1640s. In *Reason and Rhetoric in the Philosophy of Hobbes*, Skinner writes: '*Leviathan* reverts to the distinctively humanist assumption that, if the truths of reason are to be widely believed, the methods of science will need to be supplemented and empowered by the *vis* ... of eloquence.'[17] After achieving a 'scientific style' distinct from his original 'rhetorical style,' Hobbes returned to old eloquence to adorn his geometrically elaborated science of just and unjust. While conceding that Hobbes's design to reject the sort of linguistic manipulation inherent in rhetoric remains a going concern in *Leviathan*, Skinner develops the idea that the universe of discourse of this masterpiece is more densely characterized by the technique of rhetorical rediscription called 'paradiastole' than the previous versions of his political philosophy.[18] According to him, Hobbes changed nothing in his rejection of the evils of eloquence, but he turned toward the old humanist assumption that *ratio* and *oratio* should work hand in hand. It remains to be proved that this effectively was Hobbes's intention. In pointing out that in chapter 10 of *Leviathan*, Hobbes states that 'the sciences are small power,' whereas 'eloquence is power,'[19] Skinner overlooks that Hobbes does not define all these 'powers' as goods, on the contrary, he needs to define some of these as powers because in chapter 13, in his construction of the state of nature, they appear as means toward ruthless domination. On the other hand, Yves Charles Zarka, in *Hobbes et la pensée politique moderne*, has identified Hobbes's capital invention in *Leviathan*, as residing in his theory of author and representation. Zarka has also located the major link between the theories of language and the civil science in the semiology of power that is at work in the elaboration of the ethics in Part I of *Leviathan*.[20]

Though I acknowledge the growing importance of rhetoric in Hobbes's later works after *Leviathan*, I regard the aforesaid philosophical innovations as the major innovation of *Leviathan*, and the later dialogues as the main achievements of Hobbes as a rhetorician.

Hobbes was writing dialogues when the genre had long begun to decline. Anne Godard describes Girodano Bruno and Galileo, at the turn of the sixteenth and seventeenth centuries, as representatives of the last generation of the dialogical tradition of the fifteenth and sixteenth centuries.[21] Bruno's *Cena delle Ceneri*, for instance, is a mimetic dialogue of a highly subversive nature.[22] It involves characters with meaningful names, in a particular setting, London, on a very significant date, Ash Wednesday.[23] Like Plato and his imitators, Bruno was using the circumstances of the dialogue to convey notions that would be dangerous if he expressed them in words, or that should remain hidden to anyone but the initiates. The fictitious conversation is reproduced as if it had taken place. It could be performed on a stage, though it was never meant to be, since a dialogue is not a play. A dialogue, as Godard explains, either narrates or imitates a conversation, in order to convey abstract controversies through a more realistic medium than several philosophical treatises on contrary positions. It does not mean that the dialogue is meant to address a popular audience: it is an extremely refined form of writing, and much of its import is conveyed through circumstances, not through words.

When did Hobbes begin to write his major dialogues? Did he prepare materials long in advance, as he did for the *Elementa Philosophica*? No recent discovery can answer these questions. In the *Dialogue between a Philosopher and a Student of the Common Laws of England*, he adopts a polemical structure: each speaker embodies a recognizable theoretical position. In *Behemoth*, he follows a didactical strategy instead, with two speakers, a young man and an older one. The younger speaker (A) requests his senior (B) to explain to him the causes and effects of the English revolution, but the young man is not a *tabula rasa*: he proves to be a scholar in history, divinity ... and Hobbesian philosophy. One gradually discovers that both men are so deeply versed in it that it has become their common sense. *Behemoth* could be accurately described as the progression of two minds toward a better perception of the truth of

Hobbes's philosophy, which they already believed to be the true philosophical system. The *Decameron Physiologicum* involves two characters in a debate on first philosophy and the natural sciences. The rhetorical strategy is more initiatory than in Hobbes's first two attempts at writing philosophy in dialogue form: it describes the gradual conversion of a mind from Aristotelianism to the new science.

Hobbes's *Dialogue between a Philosopher and a Student of the Common Laws of England* was first published in 1681, two years after the author's death, in posthumous collections. The character construction and the method seem to confirm that this dialogue was written before *Behemoth*. Cropsey, and Paulette and Lucien Carrive in their English and French editions wonder whether Hobbes effectively finished writing this text, and whether the copy used by the printer reflected a perfected version of the work. My interpretation is that the *Dialogue* was one step on the way to the masterpiece of Hobbesian dialogue called *Behemoth*.[24] As the first chapters of the *Dialogue* reveal, Hobbes was obsessed with the people's ignorance of their duties, and with the rulers' lack of awareness of the grounds of their authority. His dialogue with the lawyer, who alternately sounds like Bacon or Coke, enables him to lay the grounds of consensus between lawyers and philosophers on the rational foundation of natural and positive law, before arguing for the sovereign's ultimate superiority over the lawyers in defining what law is.

The *Dialogue* successively deals with the law of reason, sovereign power, courts, capital crimes, heresy, the writs of *præmunire*, and punishments. Its construction is progressive, from the general grounds of the law to more technical matters. Philosophical didacticism prevails in the construction of the work. Hobbes deliberately engages with a body of doctrine – the works of Coke are often quoted – and with the laws of England – the characters comment on specific laws. It was a work for scholars, lawyers, and magistrates of all rank, but not for the general public.[25]

In the first section, on the law of reason, Hobbes comes to grips with the common lawyer's pretence that his corporation embodies, the 'artificial perfection of Reason' which is '*summa Ratio*,' for '*Nemo nascitur Artifex*.' As the Lawyer argues: 'If all the Reason that is dispersed into so many several heads were united into one, yet could he not make such a Law as the Law of *England* is, because by so many successions of Ages it hath been fined and refined by an infinite number of Grave and Learned Men.'[26] There is such a thing as collective wisdom. One can only note Hobbes's irony in lending his opponent words that sound like his definition of a commonwealth in *Leviathan*: the subjects of the commonwealth are united in one body under one sovereign, whose actions they acknowledge as their own: 'Several heads united into one.'[27] The law of reason is the object of philosophy, and therefore lawyers ought to turn toward philosophy (as it was refounded by Hobbes) to find it out. As philosophy will rationally lead them to the science of just and unjust, philosophy has no lessons in rationality or law to receive from lawyers. The gist of their dissent best appears in this exchange:

PHILOSOPHER: It is not Wisdom but Authority that makes a Law. That the Law hath been fined by Grave and Learned Men is manifestly untrue, for all the Laws of *England* have been made by the Kings of *England*, consulting with the Nobility and Commons in *Parliament*, of which not one of twenty was a Learned Lawyer.

LAWYER: You speak of Statute Law, and I speak of the Common Law.

PHIL.: I speak generally of Law.[28]

The issues of sovereignty imply the definitions of justice and public peace. The shadow of the past wars is obviously in the characters' minds, as Hobbes was introducing the issues that he was to elaborate in less technical terms in *Behemoth*. The problems raised are those of the civil war, and in the space of two pages, the Philosopher of the *Dialogue* voices most of the antirevolutionary criticism that Hobbes was to distil in the first and last dialogues of *Behemoth*.[29] The idea of *Behemoth* may have already dawned in his mind. For instance, the section that has most passages in common with other works is the section on heresy.[30] Its initial discussion is also representative of the spirit of Hobbes's grudge against the common-law mind: the Lawyer opens the debate by quoting from Coke's *Institutes*, from which he lists the points at issue in heresy cases. The first question is who is to be judge of heresy, and only then what is to be considered as heresy. The Philosopher reverses this order, and sets the definition of heresy first, which allows him to require heresy to be defined by law, therefore by the sovereign, as religion is a law of the realm.[31] Hobbes's character tacitly applies chapters 29 and 30 of *Leviathan*, which define the causes of a commonwealth's dissolution and the office of the sovereign. Making laws and teaching the proper religious doctrine are essential for the perpetuation of the sovereign's authority and of the subjects' peace.[32]

Here, as in other works or parts of works on heresy, Hobbes seems to be downplaying the polemical issues surrounding heresy, but he does so in the most polemical way. Initially and etymologically, heresy merely was

> a singularity of Doctrine, or Opinion contrary to the Doctrine of another Man, or Men, and the word properly signifies the Doctrine of a Sect, which Doctrine is taken upon Trust of some Man of Reputation for Wisdom, that was the first Author of the same.[33]

Progressively, Hobbes suggests that since the sovereign is installed to settle all controversies that might arouse sedition, he is the one upon whose 'trust' beliefs should be held. In his summary of the history of heresy as an offence (redescribed here as 'reproach'), the Philosopher manages to get the Lawyer to collect some of the historical and philosophical stages by himself: the men most likely to develop new concepts at the encounter of Christian doctrine with ancient philosophy were those who could best use Aristotle's rhetoric and logic.[34] The Lawyer can accept those philosophical and historical arguments, but he fails to be convinced by the implications of his opponent's philosophy when they bear on the law.

This failure on the Lawyer's part to open his intellect to Hobbesian arguments reveals Hobbes's opinion of legal corporatism. The apparent incompleteness of this work may reflect Hobbes's dissatisfaction with a book that was not going toward any progression of the opponent's mind toward the truth. It is as if the specific characterization designed by Hobbes for this dialogue made it impossible for the work to reach any favourable conclusion. On the other hand, in the subsequent sections of the work, the Lawyer's capacity to step over to Hobbes's side is suggested.

As he must have resorted to the dialogue after his disappointment with the polemical form of his book against Bramhall, by deciding that he would be more comfortable formulating both questions and answers, Hobbes may have interrupted the composition of the *Dialogue* when he discovered that he was unable to construct a persona for another doctrine, that he would be able to bring over to his side. The change of composition in *Behemoth* reveals his preference for a didactic mode, instead of the polemical mode that still dominated the composition of the *Dialogue*.

Some critics doubt that the title *Behemoth* was Hobbes's own choice. In a letter, Hobbes complains that the book was published in 1679 with many mistakes, without his consent, in spite of Charles II's private injunction not to publish it, and with a 'foolish title.'[35] For them, the foolish title must be 'Behemoth,' though Hobbes may have been complaining of the long subtitle. The man who had called his masterpiece *Leviathan* was not incapable of devising a diptych opposing the two biblical beasts symbolizing majesty and brute force. As I have suggested elsewhere, the Hebrew plural 'behemoth' (the beasts) may be an allusion to the people as 'the many-headed multitude,' which was such a nightmare to early modern ideologists.[36]

In the four dialogues of *Behemoth*, A and B recapitulate the history of the two revolutionary decades, trace back the grounds of disobedience to the misconceptions of ancient pagan philosophers and early Christians, and establish and vindicate the grounds of obedience. The first dialogue regresses so far back in history that it has to interrupt its narrative of the revolutionary events on the convening of the Long Parliament. The second dialogue analyses the events leading to the Civil War in 1642. The third narrates the war to the king's execution in 1649 and the last covers the period of the Commonwealth and Protectorate to the Restoration. Apparently, therefore, the work's structure follows the revolution's chronology.

At first sight, *Behemoth* does not answer the definition of a diegetic dialogue: it tells a story, it is not told by a narrator. Yet, it is all about narrating. It is a historical narration by two personae. Also, when the characters need to interrupt their main narrative to delve into the mysteries of priestcraft according to Diodorus of Sicily, they resort to an optional oratorical device, which Cicero calls *digressio*, and which could also be called 'analepsis' by narratologists.[37] The thread is broken, and explanations are provided through a series of framed subnarratives. Some speeches are several pages long, and the dialogue then shifts to plain narrative. A third category should be added to Godard's mimetic and diegetic dialogues: the narrating dialogue, or the dialogical narration. Why did Hobbes decide against a historical narration as such?

Hobbes was not incompetent in plain historical narration: while he was writing *Behemoth*, he was writing *A Historical Narration concerning Heresy and the Punishment thereof*, which was published with his reply to Bramhall's *Catching of Leviathan* in 1682.[38] By the mid- or late 1660s Hobbes did know how to contrive a historical narrative. The common passages between *Historical Narration*, the *Dialogue*, and *Behemoth*, suggest that Hobbes was then involved in two pursuits: the application of his theory to issues of practical government, and the demonstration of the validity of his principles when applied to the interpretation of history. In spite of his admiration for Thucydides, Hobbes was not following his example when he set out to write his account of recent history. He had praised the Athenian's narrative technique and his use of speeches, but he adopted a different strategy: he had chosen a form inherited from humanism and the Reformation. This very choice was a rhetorical statement, but as Hobbes was a critic of his opponents' use of rhetoric to spread their ideological delusions, he was also eager to use the same instrument to pull their verbal constructions to pieces and to edify the people, scholars, and magistrates toward a true understanding of law, sovereignty, and obedience. Here, Skinner's theory of Hobbes's paradiastolic scheme would find a much more complex application: two Hobbesian voices are redescribing the history of the world, of Christendom, and of England to restore the true meaning of events and to speak the truth about the enemies of the truth.

Behemoth is in fact more than a narrative dialogue.[39] It is also a philosophical dialogue between two men who share the same philosophy, and want to prove to themselves that they understand why the other positions are wrong and destructive. The initial exchange points to a didactic piece: after the older man has declared the middle decades of the century to be 'the highest of time,' the younger man, B, begs his senior 'that [has] lived in that time and in that part of [his] age, wherein men used to see best into good and evil,' to tell him the events, and to instruct him 'that could not then see so well,' in the true explanation of 'their causes, pretensions, justice, order, artifice, and event.' To A, the actions of men in that period were characterized by 'all kinds of injustice, and all kinds of folly,' and by 'hypocrisy and self-conceit.'[40] The distribution of matters between the two characters, in Hobbes's philosophical redescription of the history of Christendom and England, looks plain: B keeps the narration going by asking A questions, and he proves his comprehension by adding comments supplementing A's narrative and analysis. In the beginning of the dialogue, B is in charge of commonplaces, catechism, and the Bible. As the dialogue develops, B gradually begins to voice new Hobbesian analyses of the events, which are then confirmed by A. When the dialogue starts, B has strong intimations of Hobbesian principles, but as his reason applies the principles demonstrated by his occasional tutor, he becomes a Hobbesian 'professor,' in the religious sense of the word: a professing and practising believer. For this reason, it is difficult to share M.M. Goldsmith's analysis of the dialogical mode in *Behemoth* in his introduction to Tönnies's edition: 'as Wallis said of Hobbes's scientific dialogues, *Behemoth* is a dialogue between Thomas and Hobbes.'[41]

In dialogue 3, by the time the narration has reached the Civil War, B is able to restate principles from the 'Review and Conclusion' of *Leviathan*, and to apply them to the English rebels:

> Preaching [must] be better looked to, whereby the interpretation of a verse in the ... Bible, is oftentimes the cause of civil war and the deposing and assassinating of God's anointed ... Common people know nothing of right or wrong by their own meditation; they must therefore be taught the grounds of their duty and the reasons why calamities ever follow disobedience to their lawful sovereigns. But to the contrary, our rebels were publicly taught rebellion in the pulpits ... [42]

On many other occasions, in his political treatises as in his dialogues, Hobbes mocks the absurdity of scholasticism, and blames the universities for being a nursery of 'democratical gentlemen'[43] and demagogical clergymen. *Leviathan* and *Behemoth* both explicitly mention the necessity to have Hobbes's thought taught in schools and universities: many gentlemen 'in their youth having read the books written by famous men of the ancient ... commonwealths concerning their polity and great actions; in which books the popular government was extolled by the glorious name of liberty, and monarchy disgraced by the name of tyranny; they became thereby in love with their forms of government.'[44] But political ignorance concerns the meaner subjects as the elite: 'the people in general were so ignorant of their duty, as that not one perhaps of ten thousand knew what right any man had to command him, or what necessity there was of King or Commonwealth ...'[45]

By now, it should be obvious that Hobbes regarded the whole body politic as politically ignorant. Though *Leviathan* was 'short' and 'clear' enough for a sovereign to understand, the danger that the gentlemen's eloquence might raise the Parliament, the people, and even the king against Hobbes's ideas was real, and it was time, *after Leviathan* – and not *in* it, contrary to Skinner's interpretation – to adopt a more pedagogical process of exposition, and my hypothesis is that *Behemoth* is the most powerful manifestation of this strategy. Yet, the field of science also needed the dialogue to create consensus among the learned on the new science.

The *Decameron Physiologicum* begins with a historical narration concerning the confusion of science, philosophy, superstition, and religion. It is a philosophical version of what the *Dialogue* and *Behemoth* had already performed for legal or theological theories. The confusion of physics, astrology, and astronomy, the association of priestcraft with political subversion, are explicitly derived from Diodorus of Sicily, as in Dialogue 2 of *Behemoth*.[46] The other dialogues consist of less ideological, though quite polemical, discussions: motion, vacuum, the system of the world, atoms, gravity and gravitation, the loadstone, or the earth's capacity to produce living creatures are amongst the topics discussed. The method followed in these dialogues depends on both authority (though Bacon, Copernicus, and Kepler are not traditional authorities) and demonstration or experiment, like the exercise in geometry at the start of the dialogue on the system of the world, or the experiments suggested in the dialogues of motion and vacuum. The *Decameron* gets closer than the two others do to a mimetic dialogue since the experiments are described or performed by the characters.

The main interest of this work for our purpose is that it manifests Hobbes's desire to combine his now fully controlled dialogical didactic method with his scientific research. This was a philosophical dialogue occasionally resorting to narration, but managing to abide by its main design. This demonstrates that his practice of rhetoric after *Leviathan* does not reflect any dissatisfaction with science. It therefore perfectly expresses the tension that we have already encountered in the course of this paper: in spite of his belief that he had found out by science the truth about political power and society, though he believed that scientific demonstration was both clearer and simpler than other modes of exposition, he found out that rhetoric and persuasion would be more efficient to convince some categories of people of the validity of his science of just and unjust.

Hobbes may have resorted to dialogue when the humanist dialogue was past its prime, yet the philosophical dialogue was to regain new vigour in the following generations: Leibniz's *New Essays* and Hume's *Dialogues of Natural Religion* were masterpieces of a revived genre. It is therefore difficult to assess whether Hobbes was a latecomer, or a precursor. Hobbes was a master of rhetoric. His style, his translations, and especially his dialogues testify that he was far above most of his contemporaries for his skills in philosophical writing. As he explained in *Leviathan*, he had tried to convince sovereigns by his philosophical treatises. He had realized, through his involvement in the Cavendish milieu, that counsellors often had a negative influence on sovereigns, and he designed strategies to reform the institutions where they were educated, in the fields which were most likely to arouse sedition: religion and the law. The *Dialogue* on the common laws and *Behemoth* are two major stages toward this achievement. The main difference between these two works lies in the intended readerships: *Behemoth* must have been aimed at the middle and upper ranks of English society, as it was important to persuade *all* subjects. If *Leviathan* had been aimed at the philosophers and sovereigns, and *Behemoth* at the subjects, the latter was also meant to rebuke the frame of mind of the counsellors and ministers, whose legal training was directly censored in the *Dialogue*. The status of the *Decameron Physiologicum* is extremely difficult to assess from the point of view of Hobbes's didactic strategies toward English society. Was he endeavouring to persuade scholars? His attempts in treatise form had failed. Was he trying to persuade the amateur scholars and *l'honnête homme*? His polemical verve is not absent from the *Decameron*, but the frequent inadequacy of form and content shows the limitations of his attempt to apply to physics the kind of shift in expository method that had succeeded with law, politics, history, and religion. Hobbes must have entertained some hope to persuade the sovereign, the magistrates, counsellors, clergy, and subjects, but he must have thought that he was doomed to fail as soon as he attempted to silence his fellow scholars.

Anne Godard writes that in the Renaissance, two main dialogical traditions were in conflict: one was 'narrative, referential, doctrinal,' the other 'dramatic, fictional, critical.'[47] Hobbes's dialogues are at the same time narrative, referential, doctrinal, and critical. As they are dialogues, can they avoid dramatization or fiction? These two categories are defined in relationship to reality, whereas the philosopher and scientist aim at the truth, which is a very different category.

NOTES

1 Ong, *Ramus, Method, and the Decay of Dialogue*, and 'Hobbes's and Talon's Ramist Rhetoric in English'; and Wilbur Samuel Howell, 'Ramus and English Rhetoric: 1547–1681.' See also the debate on Quentin Skinner's book *Reason and Rhetoric in the Philosophy of Hobbes* in 'Aux origines de la politique moderne: Hobbes, the Amsterdam debate between Hans Blom, Yves Charles Zarka and Quentin Skinner,' *Le débat* 96 (September–October 1997): 89–120.

2 Biographical information is derived from Schuhmann, *Hobbes: une chronique*, and from the pages on Hobbes in Aubrey, *Brief Lives*. Major contributions on Hobbes's humanist context are in Reik, *The Golden Lands of Thomas Hobbes*, and Johnston, *The Rhetoric of* Leviathan.

3 I shall refer to *A Dialogue between a Philosopher and a Student of the Common Laws of England* as D. Schuhmann follows Aubrey who states that Hobbes began writing it on his suggestion in 1664 (Schuhmann, *Chronique*, 190, 213–14).

4 I shall refer to *Behemoth, or the Long Parliament,* as B. Schuhmann estimates that it was written in 1666–8 (*Chronique*, 197–8).

5 Schuhmann, *Chronique*, 222.

6 I shall refer to *Leviathan, or the Generation, Matter and Forme of a Commonwealth,* as L.

7 For Hobbes's relationship to history, see my 'History in Hobbes's Thought.'

8 Hobbes, 'Thomæ Hobbes Malmesburiensis Vita Carmine Expressa. Authore Seipso,' lxxxvi–lxxxvii. The exceptions to this, if we believe Aubrey, were Aristotle's *Rhetoric* and *History of Animals* (Aubrey, *Brief Lives*, 159).

9 Skinner, *Reason and Rhetoric*, 246–9, analyses Hobbes's application of the method prescribed by the *Rhetorica ad Herennium* for the judicial genre.

10 Chatsworth House, Derbyshire, MS Chatsworth D1 includes the dictation book of William III Cavendish (between 1631 and 1633?), with the Latin summary of Aristotle's *Rhetoric* on which the published English translation of 1637 (the *Briefe* ...) was based. It is in the pupil's hand with additions and corrections in Hobbes's hand. The printed version was *A Briefe of the Arte of Rhetorique, Containing in Substance all that Aristotle hath Written in his Three Books of that Subject, except onely what is not Applicable to the English Tongue, by T.H.* The authoritative edition is *The Rhetorics of Thomas Hobbes and Bernard Lamy.*

11 Ong, *Ramus*, 147–8, and 'Ramist Rhetoric,' 268–9; *L* IX, 147–9. Howell, *Logic and Rhetoric in England 1500–1700*, 383–8, and Zappen, 'Rhetoric in Thomas Hobbes's *Leviathan*, 69.

12 The best critical account of Hobbes's epistemological conversion is in Jean Bernhardt's edition of Hobbes, *Court traité des premiers principes*, 61–87 (commentary). This is a bilingual edition of *A Short Tract on first Principles*, MS Harley 6796, ff. 297–308. See also Schuhmann, *Chronique*, 36.

13 Hobbes, *De corpore*; the text was first published in 1655. It is the first part of the *Elementa Philosophica*, the second being *De homine* (1658), and the third *De cive* (1642). See Sorell, *Hobbes*, and Zarka, *La décision métaphysique de Hobbes*.

14 Hobbes, *The Elements of Law, Natural and Politic*, afterwards *EL*.
15 Skinner, *Reason and Rhetoric*, 257–84. *EL* I.xiii, 64–9, II.viii, 12–15, 175–8.
16 Hobbes, *De cive: The Latin Version*, XII, 12–13.
17 Skinner, *Reason and Rhetoric*, 334.
18 Ibid., 334–46.
19 Ibid., 351–2, referring to *L* X, 151.
20 Zarka, *Hobbes et la pensée politique moderne*, chapters 4–5, 65–123, chapter 9, 197–227.
21 Godard, *Le dialogue à la Renaissance*, 39.
22 Ibid., 7–9.
23 Ibid., 164–8.
24 Another interpretation of Hobbes's evolution, centred on the *Dialogue*, can be found in Saccone, 'The Ambiguous Relation between Hobbes' Rhetorical Appeal to English History and his Deductive Method in *A Dialogue*.' Saccone follows Skinner's view of Hobbes's evolution.
25 Some of Bacon's ideas can be identified among the arguments under attack, but as Hobbes respected Bacon's ideas on science, I agree with Cropsey and L. and P. Carrive that Sir Edward Coke is more probably behind the character constructed by Hobbes (*D* 14–15; *Dialogue des common laws*, introduction, 15–16).
26 *D* 55.
27 *L* XVII, 228.
28 *D* 55.
29 In particular, compare *D* 64–5 with *B* 203–4.
30 *D* 122–32. Hobbes's meditations on church history and heresy are subtly explained by Lessay in 'Hobbes and Sacred History.'
31 *D* 122.
32 *L* XXIX, especially 370–1, XXX, 376–94.
33 *D* 123. Compare with *B* 8–10.
34 *D* 124–5.
35 Schuhmann, *Chronique* 214, 225, quoting Hobbes, letter 208 to John Aubrey, *The Correspondence*, 2:772.
36 See Borot, introduction to *Béhémoth, ou le Long Parlement*, 20–1, for bibliographical details; a part of this introduction was translated by Tom Sorell as 'Hobbes's *Behemoth*,' in Rogers and Sorell, *Hobbes and History*, 137–46, especially for the gloss on *behema/-oth*, 145–6.
37 Godard, *Le dialogue*, 68.
38 Schuhmann, *Chronique*, 197, gives 1668 as the date of composition.
39 It is also a mimetic dialogue: at the beginning and at the end of the dialogues, the characters arrange an appointment to go on with the discussion.

40 *B* 1.
41 *B* xi.
42 *B* 144. He refers to *L* 'General Review and Conclusion,' 728.
43 *B* 26.
44 *B* 3.
45 *B* 4.
46 *B* 90–5.
47 Godard, *Le dialogue*, 45.

The Purpose of Dialogue

Francesco Barbaro's *De re uxoria*: A Silent Dialogue for a Young Medici Bride

Carole Collier Frick

Introduction

In 1416 Lorenzo de' Medici (Il Vecchio), younger brother of Cosimo de' Medici, Pater patriae of Florence, married Ginevra Cavalcanti, the daughter of Giovanni, head of the old aristocratic house of Cavalcanti.[1] Ginevra's age at the time of her wedding is not known, but we can guess that she was perhaps fifteen or sixteen, to Lorenzo's twenty.[2] On the occasion of this young man's betrothal, he was presented with a gift from a friend and contemporary, the Venetian humanist Francesco Barbaro. The gift was a manuscript – a *trattato* written in Latin, which Barbaro had entitled *De re uxoria*, or *Concerning Things about a Wife*.[3] The twenty-six-year-old aristocrat had been in Florence in the previous year, and became acquainted with the circle of humanists there, which included Roberto de' Rossi, the young Medici's tutor. While there, Barbaro likely visited with the Medici brothers, where the topic of Lorenzo's engagement to the Cavalcanti girl arose. Back in Venice, he then conceived the idea for a treatise that would outline the transformation of a new bride into a good wife, and wrote *De re uxoria* in not more than four or five month's time. It was presented to Lorenzo for his edification in Florence during the season of Carnival, in February 1416.[4]

Here, I will use Barbaro's text to examine the transformation of self to which a young upper-class woman learned to aim, as well as the method by which she was to achieve her ideal. Through examples drawn from this treatise and other writers in Florence at this time, I will show how a woman was taught to develop a self-conscious dialogue with herself in order to prevent putting her own person and her family in peril, through any behavioural slips. From the strict management of her body and clothing, to her slow, measured speech, an upper-class wife was instructed to act out the closed nature of her class; to cultivate a corporeal restraint which was impermeable to all.

Upper-Class Marriage

The marriage bond in the Florentine ruling class was arguably the most crucial connection a man would make in his life, because his marriage would link his family to the family of his betrothed and create an enduring alliance. A man's inclusion or exclusion in the social and political milieu of the Florentine oligarchy depended partially on his connection by marriage, the fabric of the ruling class being woven by ties of matrimony which joined one family to another in intricate, binding patterns of kinship.[5] Barbaro, though still single, was of similar social rank in Venice, and understanding this fact very well, addressed just this essential quality of marriage in his work.[6] Given the social and political importance attached to a marriage within the upper class, a Latin treatise on the best way for a man to advise his bride in the wifely arts was probably welcomed with great interest and attention by its males. The literary form of Barbaro's *trattato* to the young Medici male, was a didactic *declamatio*, not a dialogue, as was Alberti's *Libri della famiglia*, written in 1430 on a similar subject, a dozen years or so later. While both Barbaro and Alberti sought to instruct young husbands on marriage, the family, and especially the training of wives, Barbaro intended to create no 'dialogue' with either his audience (Lorenzo de' Medici), or the subject of his treatise (the new wife, Ginevra Cavalcanti). There is only sage counsel and advice, directed toward the husband.

What is especially interesting about Barbaro's *De re uxoria* is that the advice given to Lorenzo and his wife Ginevra is a blend of humanist thought and late medieval Christianity, specifically tailored to serve the aristocratic aims of the upper class.[7] Although the author employs exempla from antiquity, using Greek and Roman sources which value marriage for its role in producing good 'citizens,' he also embraces the ideas of simplicity, honesty, and modesty held by the late medieval church, and even stresses repeatedly the need for true friendship between a husband and wife. This was a partnership of the sort that the Franciscan San Bernardino of Siena taught in his sermons. He preached ' ... of the true friendship which husband and wife must have.'[8] Bernardino, with whom Barbaro kept up a correspondence, goes on to discuss this idea, saying that friendship can be small or great, depending on the reason for the friendship and its usefulness.[9]

In his treatise, Barbaro begins with the *famiglia* and, linking the family to life outside the *casa*, elaborates on the behavioural ideal to which a woman of the upper class should aspire. In his manuscript, the author not only outlined such basic concerns as the ideal age for a wife and her desired physical characteristics, but also discussed her clothing, and even the personal bodily demeanour deemed suitable for her. In addition, he detailed a wife's domestic responsibilities, and then focused on perhaps the most critical aspect of her duties, that is, her proper relationship to her husband and the community at large.

Barbaro's humanist vision of the relationship between husband and wife is firmly rooted within the social complexities of time, place, and class obligations. For the union to succeed, each partner in the marriage must know his or her appropriate role, and carry it out in a diligent manner. While the husband is to assume the humanist ideals of active social participation, his wife is to be sequestered at home with the family, embodying traditional Christian values. By embracing the ideal classical ideal of marriage for males of the upper class, humanist thought forced itself to address the role of the female in the relationship, for whom the same classical paradigms of excellence would not fit. As the Renaissance poet Torquato Tasso wrote, in his 1582 *Discorso della virtù feminile e donnesca*, expanding on ideas first articulated by Thomas Aquinas centuries before, the primary virtues for males are the (classically informed) qualities of courage and eloquence, whereas the primary virtues for females are the (religiously informed) qualities of chastity and obedience.[10] Tasso also establishes a dominant virtue for each sex, the dominant vice being the antithesis of that virtue. In women, the dominant virtue is chastity; the dominant vice is to be unchaste. In men, the dominant virtue is courage; the dominant vice is cowardice. He then defines the most excusable vice in each sex as the dominant vice in the other. Therefore in women, it is most excusable to be a coward, and in men – to be unchaste. From this, the poet extrapolates an entire behavioural ideal based on the appropriate sexually determined virtue. For a woman to embody chastity, it is inappropriate to be eloquent, courageous, magnificent, liberal, or to have public honour. For a man to embody courageousness, it is inappropriate for him to be silent, modest, economical, and chaste. All this is perhaps not surprising. What is unusual here, as we will see, is Barbaro's confidence in the wife's ability to dissimulate – to create an artificial persona through the rigorous development of an interior dialogue with her self.

Self-Fashioning

Many Renaissance writers – from Petrarch to Pico – speak about the mutability of the self. This topic, in and of itself, could be said to justify the entire existence of the 'studia humanitatis.' Greenblatt has written eloquently on a new enthusiasm for the manipulation of human identity in this period.[11] In the Renaissance, as a matter of fact, some scholars have pointed out that the notion of a humanist education as 'formation' became confused with 'transformation.'[12] For men, this transformation of the self was to lead ideally to a complete spiritual metamorphosis. The assertion of the ultimate malleability of the human being, born of one's own free will, would be flirting with heresy, but certainly in texts such as Pico's *On the Dignity of Man*, the thrill of the possibility of transcendence is almost irresistible. He writes that God, the 'Great Artisan,' has said to man, 'You, who are confined by no limits, shall determine for yourself your own nature, in accordance with your own free will, in whose hand I have placed you.'[13] But for the Renaissance wife of the upper-class man thus metamorphosed, the transformational palette took a more pedestrian mien. She was counselled, in a long tradition of writings on women and the family dating back at least to the early Trecento, not to expend her energy in futile pursuit of female spiritual transcendence.[14] Rather, she was to work assiduously on becoming the perfect compliant complement to her husband, an ornament to her class.

In the early years of the fifteenth century, Italian humanist scholars first embraced the Ciceronian model of dialogue. This was a literary avenue of expression completely closed to the wives of the upper ranks, among the most restricted women in early fifteenth-century society. Therefore, only elite males populate these conversations of the early Renaissance. Poggio Bracciolini was the first humanist of the period to base his entire literary reputation on the dialogue form, with his 1428 *De avaritia*. David Marsh has argued that this piece provided a 'significant link' between earlier works of Bruni and Valla.[15] In the dialogues of the Quattrocento, female participants are absent. While Alberti's 1430 dialogic *Libri della famiglia* covers some of the same issues as the *De re uxoria* on the training of wives, no women take part in the conversation which he carries on with his Alberti kinsmen. The inclusion of women, and especially the wives of the upper-class men, was precluded by classical exempla. As preparation for the writing of dialogue demanded an educational grounding in rhetoric, women would logically not have been party to this learned male exchange. Instead, following Augustine, they were to engage in the solitary introspection of self.[16]

However, as the dialogue form is disseminated into the Cinquecento, we do find female voices eventually added. Castiglione's *Il libro del cortegiano* (1528) includes court women within its spirited discussion on life and love at the court of Urbino, and even deploys the duchess of Montefeltro, Elisabetta Gonzaga, as its anchor.[17] Later in the century, female humanists themselves began to speak directly in dialogues they constructed to engage their audiences, often on the Lucianic model. For example, some sixty years later, in 1588, the poet and actress Isabella Andreini (1562–1604) published her popular play *Mirtilla*, a pastoral in imitation of Tasso's earlier *Aminta*.[18] Here, a female protagonist even dominates the conversation in a comic gender-role reversal.

In Barbaro's much earlier treatise however, the fashioning of the female self meets dialogue only in the form of an exemplum detached from medieval/classical forms, and recoupled with Christian notions of female virtue (obedience, humility, silence). Barbaro's primary concern, once he establishes his definition of the marriage bond, is to address the question of the role of the wife within a socially embedded notion of marriage. Not surprisingly, he invests the wife with the responsibility of the family virtue. He writes that by her personal qualities and her exemplary behaviour, the family honour will be upheld and then perpetuated by the properly socialized offspring. Since the wife sets the personal example for the rest of the family, her virtue must be demonstrated by certain qualities which will enable her to shine as a bright lamp, offering her light to the others.[19]

Throughout his work, Barbaro expounds upon five qualities a wife should strive to develop. These are prudence, diligence, frugality, humility, and modesty. Whereas the first three virtues were to be demonstrated 'a casa,' and should be made manifest by a certain shrewdness (*accortezza*) toward the servants and housework, the other two should be apparent in the public eye outside the home. Fascinatingly, he also demands that they be displayed as well in the woman's private relationship with her husband (who was, after all, part of that larger, public world, and her primary link to it). Barbaro writes that modesty is the foundation that preserves and maintains the innate charity between husband and wife. For the wife, the virtue of modesty is made apparent by her face, gestures, words, clothing, the way she eats, and how she goes about her everyday affairs.[20]

Out in public view, a woman should remain covered and hidden ('coperta e nascosta'), not only by concealing her arms and other parts of her body, but her voice as well. A woman should realize that she has two ears with which to hear, one tongue with which to speak (but only a little), and that she should, 'with the greatest mystery, keep her tongue hidden behind the hedge of her teeth and the circle of her lips.'[21] In this way, a woman can move about circumspectly in the public sphere without fear of attracting undue attention, and without compromising her modesty and the reputation of her family. Addressing women in general, Barbaro says that modesty is easily achieved, 'if in their repose, activities, speech, eyes, faces, and finally, in all the movements of their bodies, there is always a certain gentle seriousness, accompanied by that meekness which is suitable to the place, time, and people with whom they find themselves.'[22]

Mirrors

Careful body management then is essential if women are to avoid being considered fickle or thoughtless. Barbaro writes that women should not bustle about ('andar veloce'), nor allow their eyes the vanity of wandering, nor move their hands often without purpose, nor shake their heads, nor indulge in any other distortions of their bodies ('distorcimenti della persona').[23] Instead, they should observe the proper seriousness in each of their gestures and in their behaviour, and be very careful what they say or do. Such conduct will make them feel 'extraordinary dignity and contentment with themselves,' and 'will elicit great praise from men.'[24]

Here, the young Venetian of aristocratic lineage reaches back to Demosthenes for a classical exemplum, which he reworks for the contemporary consumption of his Florentine friend Lorenzo, and other newly married men of their rank. Drawing on the year-long study of Greek he had just completed under the tutelage of the famed Guarino Veronese, he breaks from his usual assumption of a male reader, to address the woman directly. He proposes a 'silent' dialogue for the nubile young woman of upper-class birth.[25] Using Demosthenes, Barbaro advises the woman to develop a self-consciousness about her physical appearance; a type of ongoing visual dialogue with her own mirror, in the privacy of the home. He writes that Demosthenes recommended the use of a mirror to better arrange and correct the gestures of one's actions, so that with one's own eyes, those things could be seen which might not be remembered from his words alone.[26] While not actually employing the term '*dialogo*' to describe this catechistic exercise, his instructions are clear. With the help of the mirror (*specchio*), the young women should consciously (and conscientiously), mould their physical demeanour and bodily behaviour to complement their husbands' outside world. They should 'speculate' on themselves.[27] He adds that he wishes 'women would, every day, and always, with total diligence, consider what is suitable to their position, dignity, sex, and to the honesty of their integrity.'[28] By using their own eyes to view themselves, they should attempt to better adjust the movements of their own body. This solitary dialogue with oneself would serve two goals: continual refinement, and a silent, inward preoccupation with one's self-reflection. Interestingly enough, the city of Venice first produced a newly flat, nondistorting mirror at the beginning of the fifteenth century. This opportunity for a woman to stare intensely at her own newly improved reflection may have stimulated Barbaro's interest in advising this catechistic technique.[29]

At the beginning of the Quattrocento then, no female voice is heard in the renaissance of classical dialogue. Instead, the young upper-class wife was to be visually occupied with a kind of internal dialogue with her own external form. Not engaged in verbal exchange of any kind, she was, instead, to listen. Barbaro counsels on the eloquence of silence for these women, confined to the domestic realm. *Her* transformation was to be manifested physically, in her corporeal behaviour, and continually to be monitored by the militantly silent preoccupation with her reflection. The use of the word 'mirror' as a metaphor for 'exemplum' in medieval and Renaissance thought, has here been dragged back to mundane physical reality for wives. But ironically, by viewing her own mirrored 'self' in a looking-glass, no objective exemplum would be available; no enlightening dialogue forthcoming. There would only be her own subjective determination that she was actually conforming to the extensive dicta set out by Barbaro. As at least one other scholar has noted, Barbaro seems to 'give a lot of credit to women,' and to what they could achieve.[30] Here, a woman could become wise within her own self. She could learn to determine whether or not her behaviour/comportment was appropriate.[31]

Eyes

In *De re uxoria*, Barbaro also offers another classical exemplum as a counterpart to the mirror, for a moral lesson on the ideal management of a married woman's eyes. Barbaro uses Xenophon's story of Tigranes, king of Armenia, as his example. Tigranes, along with his parents and consort (whose name was also Armenia), had met in person with Cyrus, the legendary king of Persia. After they left the king's presence, Tigranes, turned to his 'dearest' Armenia who had remained silent, and asked how Cyrus had appeared to her. She replied, taking immortal God as her witness, that 'I have never taken my eyes from you, Oh Tigranes, and so I cannot know what kind or how much beauty Cyrus could possess.'[32] The consort becomes here emblematic of impeccable wifely behaviour. Her eyes have moved away from herself in the mirror, but only to the face of her husband (the sole possible resting point for a devoted mate, never straying for an instant). She becomes the model of exemplary marital fidelity.

Here, the author displays commonplace notions of the female fragile nature, in his discussion of her delicate sensory apparatus, which must be both protected and controlled. Her eyes and ears are seen as vulnerable – personal conduits by which she could be influenced and corrupted, or ultimately, could corrupt herself. She is taught to limit eye contact and to avert her gaze from people and things outside of home and family, by focusing inwardly instead. In order to preserve her bond of marriage, she is to refuse to meet outsiders eye-to-eye, keeping her own secrets and the secrets of her family from public scrutiny. For a woman to be thought modest, she must consciously restrain her facial expressions, and especially be aware of her eyes and ears, no matter what the place or the occasion. Whereas a woman's modesty can be compromised by the things she hears, a woman's modesty (or lack thereof) can be read by looking into her eyes. Their management, then, was of utmost concern.

Barbaro continues by noting that a person's face is the most telling feature of their innate purity, writing that 'the face is that feature which one can truly take as a certain sign of the image of the heart and mind. In the face then, the secrets of the heart which nature has concealed (within the body), many times can be revealed, even without talking, and (thereby) one can understand many things.'[33] A woman's face can give away the secrets of a less than virtuous heart and mind. Just as in irrational animals, where anger, fear, happiness, and other similar emotions can be read from looking at their eyes and bodily movements, so in human beings one can read these things. Therefore, women need to assiduously demonstrate modesty in their personal demeanour.[34] This physical restraint will serve to intervene between the beholder and the woman, and keep the secrets of her mind and heart internalized. As long as a woman maintains a diligent interior dialogue with herself, she will learn how to be prudent and frugal at home, while being modest, dignified, and serious in public, keeping the reputation of her family beyond reproach. In this way, the virtue of the family that Renaissance culture invested in the reputation of its women, will remain secure, and the family will endure and prosper.

By way of contrast, a very different type of dialogue with one's own eyes was envisioned by Petrarch, who wrote over twenty sonnets in which the first line takes up the power of eyes, Laura's eyes. In Sonnet 63, Petrarch writes a dialogue with his own eyes, telling them to weep and thereby manifest the inward sorrow which is in his heart from being spurned by one whose eyes had held him captive from the first time he saw her. In this dialogue, the poet tells his eyes to show what is in his heart, not to mask it. He addresses his eyes in an internal dialogue, but with the desire to make the internal external. His eyes also answer back and agree to his desire, thereby reintegrating his divided self.[35] In Barbaro's work however, he advises that a woman use a mirror to objectify herself – to deliberately make her own outward self foreign to her inward self, and thereby achieve a calculated split between her true interiority and an artificially manufactured and controlled exteriority, conceived to mask her natural self. She would then be able to achieve the proper closed and protected demeanour thought to be so important for an upper-class woman to project in the public sphere of fifteenth-century Renaissance society.

Conclusions

Barbaro's treatise written to a young husband was couched in a discourse supposedly for an even younger wife, with only indirect references to her partner. Whether or not Lorenzo actually instructed his wife Ginevra according to the classical exempla and proposed interior dialogue set out here is unknown, but certainly the paradigms Barbaro developed were a powerful part of the upper-class male discourse of the Renaissance humanists. The author makes the virtues of the wife identical with familial virtues. He requires the wife's total cooperation in self-discipline in order to maintain the closure of the family, especially outside the home. Since a woman's most important role was in creating the appearance of virtue, her face, her eyes, her movements, and her entire body, had to be moulded carefully. She had to learn to be completely unavailable physically. These fifteenth-century women, using a carefully cultivated private dialogue between their inner and outer selves, were to function, as one historian has termed it, as 'sacred dolls' while in public, playing a passive, yet crucial role within the families of the upper class of Renaissance Italy.[36]

NOTES

1 Lorenzo (1396–1440) was to become the great-uncle of Lorenzo 'Il Magnifico' (1449–92), who would be his namesake, born nine years after his death. Ginevra's family was an ancient Florentine magnate house, which dated from early medieval times. By virtue of its aristocratic past, the Cavalcanti family was barred from the priorate and other high political office, in spite of the fact that the family had passed its prime and was in decline financially. See Brucker, *Renaissance Florence*, 90, 157. For Ginevra's social position, see de Roover, *The Rise and Decline of the Medici Bank*, 19.

2 Lorenzo's young age at marriage was somewhat unusual. In the fifteenth century, men began to wait to establish themselves before beginning a family. By 1427, the year of the Florentine Catasto, it was more typical for a man to be ten to twelve years older than his bride. Lorenzo's older brother Cosimo had been around twenty-four at marriage, closer to the average for the upper-class male, which was from twenty-four to thirty in the years between 1351 and 1427. The average age for an upper-class female was seventeen. See Herlihy and Klapisch-Zuber, *Tuscans and Their Families*, 87.

3 *De re uxoria* became an influential work, which was made available for circulation in manuscript form in the house of Barbaro's teacher of Greek, humanist scholar Guarino Veronese, in Verona in 1428, some twelve years after it was first given to Lorenzo as a wedding gift. In 1513 the first printed version appeared, which was based on a transcription made of the document in Verona by Andre Tiraqueau, and issued by his heirs. The second Latin printing was done in Paris in the following year (1514) by Badius Ascensius, and carried his printer's mark. The standard Latin edition used today is still *Francisci Barbari de re uxoria liber* (1916).

In 1537 the Badius Ascensius printed edition was translated into French by Martin DuPin, and in 1548, appeared in Italian from a translation made

from the Latin manuscript by Alberto Lollio of Ferrara for a Venetian
patron, Federico Barboero. The Italian translation is entitled *Prudentissimi et
Gravi Documenti circa la Elettion della Moglie* (Most Prudent and Serious
Things Concerning the Selection of a Wife). It is this Italian version, printed
in Venice at the press of Gabriel Giolito de Ferrari, that I have used in this
study, in the spirit of Leon Alberti's *Libri della Famiglia*, written in the vulgar Tuscan in 1430. It has been argued by some that Alberti's choice of the
spoken language of Tuscany over Latin was inspired by his desire for a
larger readership, eschewing the example of the ancient Roman dialogues
(see Marsh, *The Quattrocento Dialogue*, 79.) I would further argue that this
early use of the vernacular to reach a broader public could have inspired
the Cinquecento translations of Barbaro's domestic advice manual, into
both French and Italian. For background on Barbaro himself, see the *Dizionario Biografico degli Italiani*, 6:102–3.

4 Sabbadini wrote that in addition to making new friends and inspecting
new humanist manuscripts that were known to be in Florence at this time,
this trip was also profitable for Barbaro's own literary production. Besides
inspiring his *De re uxoria*, Barbaro also subsequently carried on an active
correspondence with his new circle of Florentine friends, who now
included Lorenzo de' Medici, for at least the next four years. Sabbadini
goes on to say that *De re uxoria* was not a political work, but rather a 'happy
and luxuriant early fruit' of Barbaro's labour, inspired by the young Medici's wedding (see Sabbadini, *La Gita di Francesco Barbaro a Firenze nel 1415*,
616, 618).

5 See Martines, *The Social World of the Florentine Humanists 1390–1460*, 57ff, for
an early discussion of the social importance of marriage in the oligarchy.

6 See Swain, '"My excellent and most singular lord,"' 172.

7 Margaret King writes that Barbaro's primary object was to preserve the
'purity' of the noble class ('Caldiera and the Barbaros on Marriage and the
Family,' 31).

8 San Bernadino da Siena, *La Fonte Della Vita*. This passage on friendship was
taken from a sermon entitled 'Come il marito die amare la donna e la
donna il suo marito,' 238–9.

9 A.G. Ferrers Howell, *San Bernadino of Siena*, 130.

10 Torquato Tasso, quoted by Maclean, *The Renaissance Notion of Woman*, 62.

11 Greenblatt, *Renaissance Self-Fashioning*, esp. 2–3.

12 See Thomas Greene, 'The Flexibility of the Self in Renaissance Literature,'
250.

13 Pico della Mirandola, *Oratio de dignitate hominis*. Erasmus also writes on
the desirability of spiritual transcendence (Greene, 'Flexibility of the Self,'

255–6), but others were concerned with the dangers of the Pelagian Heresy, to which Pico della Mirandola himself sails perilously close. This heresy was first asserted by the English monk Pelagius (ca. 360–ca. 422 CE), condemned for heresy at several fifth-century synods for asserting that there was no original sin or need for baptism. He believed that human beings have free will, and that grace was not necessary for salvation. He taught that if humans live in accordance with the laws of human society, it is possible for them to live without sin. Originally an attempt to heighten human responsibility, it fell into the extreme of diminishing divine grace, and was opposed by St Augustine.

14 This tradition would include among others, Francesco da Barberino, *Il Reggimento e costume di donna* (Bologna, 1875); Giovanni Dominici, *Regola del governo di cura familiare*, ed. by D. Salvi (Florence, 1860); the anonymous *Decor puellarum* (Venice, ca. 1471); as well as Alberti's *Libri della famiglia*.

15 See Marsh, *The Quattrocento Dialogue*, 38.

16 Ibid., 3–4.

17 Castiglione, *Il libro del cortegiano* (Milan: Garzanti, 1981). See esp. Book III on the ideal *cortegiana*.

18 For this female-dominated dialogue on the Lucianic, or comic model, see Stortoni and Lillie, *Women Poets of the Italian Renaissance*, 233–43. This play was so well received that it went through six printed editions between 1588 and 1616 (222).

19 Barbaro, *Prudentissimi*, 14: 'Cosi a punto le cose nostre di casa mai non potranno andar bene, se l'accortezza della madre di famiglia non sara come una chiara lampa, che porga col suo esempio la luce a tutti gli altri' (my translations).

20 Ibid., 44: 'Habbiamo hora a trattare della modestia. laquale e come il fondamento che conserva e mantiene la innata charita fra il marito e la moglie ... Questa virtù nel la moglie dal volto, da i gesti, dalle parole, da i vestimenti, dal mangiare, e dal procedere del quotidiano commercio si comprende.'

21 Ibid., 47: 'ci concesse due orecchie per udire assai; e una lingua solar per parlar poco; e quella ancho con pij alto misterio tra la siepe de i denti e il cerchio della labra rinchise.'

22 Ibid., 44: 'se nello stare, nello andare, nel parlare, ne gli occhi, nel volto, e finalmente in tutti gli movimenti del corpo, servaranno sempre una certa gentil gravitate, accompagnata da quella mansuetudine, che si conviene al decoro de i luoghi, de i tempi, e delle persone, con lequali si troveranno.'

23 Ibid.

24 Ibid. '... con che non mediocre dignità e contentezza in se stesse, e non picciola laude venire lor da gli huomini sentiranno ...'

25 King, 'Caldiera and the Barbaros on Marriage and the Family,' 32. On Guarino, see Woodward, *Vittorino da Feltre*, 180.
26 *Prudentissimi*, 'Usava Demosthene con lo aiuto dello specchio di concertare e correggere i gesti de l'attioni, per potere meglio con li occhi proprii discernere quello che orando fuggire.'
27 See Gasché, *The Tain of the Mirror*, 13–17, for the slippery implications of mirrors, self-reflexivity, and transcendence.
28 *Prudentissimi*, 'le donne ogni giorno, e sempre, con somma diligenza considerassero quello che al grado, alla dignitade, al sesso, e al candore della lor integritade si convenga ...'
29 Shapiro, 'Mirror and portrait,' 43.
30 King, 'Caldiera and the Barbaros on Marriage and the Family,' 34, note 53.
31 Timothy Kirchner writes about this newly untethered moral ground in Boccaccio's text, in his 'The Modality of Moral Communication in the *Decameron's* First Day, in Contrast to the Mirror of the Exemplum,' esp. 1035–45.
32 Barbaro, *Prudentissimi*, 45–6: 'Io non ho mai (disse) o Tigrane, levato da te gli occhi miei, e perchè conto alcuno rendere non ti posso, quale, o quanta sia la bellezza di Ciro.'
33 Ibid., 44: 'il volto e quello che tiene in se più, veri, e più certi segni della effigie dell animo nostro. In quello adunque i secreti del core, che la nature ha nascosto, spesse volte si scoprono: facendo anchora senza parlare, intendere di molte cose.'
34 Ibid.
35 Petrarch, *The Sonnets, Triumphs, and other Poems*, 100.
36 See Trexler's classic *Public Life in Renaissance Florence*, 361. Here, Trexler stresses their role as mute displayers of their husbands' wealth. My point is that the bodies on which that wealth was worn, in the form of clothing and jewelry, had to be exquisitely trained to be impassive and still.

Dialogue and German Language Learning in the Renaissance

Nicola McLelland

> So much, virtuous young man ... have I described in this little book, and
> explained the same with certain dialogues and conversations for the sake
> of easier learning ... that one might learn to express very fluently many
> kinds of things, of words and sentences.
>
> Ondrej Klatowsky, *Büchlein* for learning German and Czech.[1]

Introduction

Language study shared no less than other spheres of endeavour in the
popularity of the dialogue in the Renaissance. Indeed, the dialogue
had (and has) an additional practical importance for language practitioners, one which has given it a place in language learning since antiquity. It imitates, more or less convincingly, the form of a spoken
exchange, so that unlike other written forms, it not only presents ideas,
but also *represents* the means – the linguistic forms – that communi-
cates those ideas.[2] The Renaissance language learner could model his
(for it nearly always was *his*) language usage on what he found in the
dialogue.

For the purposes of this essay, I adopt Virginia Cox's maximally simple definition of dialogue as 'an exchange between two or more voices.'[3]
This has the advantage over other more theory-laden approaches of
being maximally inclusive, and avoids the danger of applying literary
or aesthetic criteria to dialogues produced in accordance with quite different demands. I hope to give a representative sample of the many
guises in which the dialogue form occurs within Renaissance language
learning materials, and the different uses to which it can be put. With
one exception, I concentrate on the German-language context, though

the reader will find some references in the notes to the use of dialogues in teaching and learning elsewhere in Europe. In particular, I shall consider how different authors respond to the twofold potential of the dialogue: patently a written text, but also claiming to be a spoken one. We shall also see evidence of a wider dialogue, between two traditions of language learning. The Renaissance saw both a humanist renewal in the teaching of Latin, and the birth of teaching foreign vernaculars as part of formal schooling, and our examples illustrate how the two learn from each other and ultimately change and draw closer together as a result.

It may be useful to begin by placing the language-learning dialogue within the wider context of German vernacular dialogue production in the Renaissance, following Burke's categorization:[4]

1 *The dramatic dialogue*, in which the portrayal of the situation is as important as the participants' speeches themselves (following the tradition of Lucian, and illustrated in the German context by Hutten and in some of the work of Hans Sachs).[5]
2 *The disputation*, represented in the German vernacular by numerous Reformation dialogues of the 1520s in particular. A few are presented as formal disputations; in many more, the same pattern is followed, even if the context is changed: participants express differing points of view on theological and social questions, and one voice is allowed, more or less subtly, to defeat the other(s).[6]

I shall have no more to say about these first two categories here.

3 *The catechistic dialogue*, in which one participant's role is restricted to comments and questions which give cues for the essentially monologic discourse of the other speaker, without any multiplicity of voices in the Bakhtinian sense; the communication represented is unidirectional.[7] The *Lucidarius* (ca. 1190–5), a sort of encyclopedia, is an early example of the master and pupil dialogue in the German vernacular, which remained popular into the fifteenth century and beyond, first printed in 1479. Again, Reformation pamphlets supply examples for the sixteenth century. The form is found in language learning materials too, not least in Donatus's *Ars Minor*, whose use and gradual transformation in the Renaissance is discussed more fully below.
4 *The conversation*, where it is impossible to identify the author with a particular point of view, and in which 'the meaning develops out of

the interaction between the different characters, and the dialogue comes to an end rather than a conclusion' – a definition which embraces the Ciceronian dialogue.[8] Such conversations may be as much about exemplifying a rhetorical ideal, modelling oratory excellence, as about the transmission of knowledge.[9] For Burke, this type of dialogue best demonstrates Bakhtinian dialogicity, but the German-speaking Renaissance offers no obvious examples.[10] Nonetheless, we shall see below numerous instances of model 'conversations' in language learning, where the focus is similarly on an idealized interaction, rather than on the outcome of the dialogue.

First, however, I shall briefly consider the use of the dialogue in debate *about* the vernacular.

Dialogue about Language: The *questione della lingua*

It has been argued that the dialogue lent itself to communication of new ideas to a wider audience still essentially suspicious of *Buchwissen* and which viewed the written word as a poor second to the immediacy of personal contact.[11] It allowed the author both to mimic the immediacy of the personal encounter, and to preempt possible objections or misunderstandings through the questions of an interlocutor. Romance-speaking Europe boasts numerous dialogues of this type which debate the pressing *questione della lingua*.[12] Yet Germany offers no comparable texts for the period. The *questione della lingua* will only become the matter of hot debate in the seventeenth century, and even then we find nothing resembling the dialogues of Romance-speaking Europe in the sixteenth century – at best, parts of Harsdörffer's *Frauenzimmer Gesprächspiele* (1644–9), in which questions on art, language, and literature are discussed, might qualify.

If we expand our view of German to include the language of Low Countries, however (well into the seventeenth century and beyond, *Teutsch/Deutsch*, or *Duyts(ch)* were used on both sides of the present-day language border as umbrella terms which included both Dutch and German), we do find one example of the dialogue used to reflect on the cultivation of the vernacular, the *Twe-spraack vande Nededuitsche letterkunst* (1584), the first attempt at a complete *ars grammatica* of Dutch.[13] However, even this offers a unidirectional explanation of correct Dutch usage by teacher to willing listener:·it is catechistic, rather than a conversation in Burke's sense. It aims to set down rules for Dutch spelling and the avoidance of foreign words, though it also has sections on derivational morphology, syntax, and prosody. The participants, Gedeon and Roemer, probably represent Gedeon Fallet and Roemer Fischer, both members of the Amsterdam 'In liefd bloeyende' language society.[14] As in the *Dialogue de l'ortografe e prononciacion françoese*, these prominent real-life figures vouch for the merit of what is said, and perhaps also for the supposed veracity of this record of their 'encounter.' In the shape of the off-duty teacher Gedeon, the author presents his arguments in ordinary conversation with Roemer, thus making his views more acceptable to the adult middle-class readership whom Roemer represents.[15] The words of the two 'speakers' also actually illustrate the subject of the chapter, the fashionable use in Dutch conversation of foreign loanwords in place of their native equivalents, a controversial topic both in the Low Countries and later in Germany.[16] It begins:

> The First Chapter. On native base words and foreign terms
> Roemer and Gedeon
> Roemer and Gedeon. *Bonjour*, nephew, G. Good day, *cousin*. R. Hey, see how our tongue is finely out of tune! G. Everyone Germanises and obscures others' words. R. What does that mean? G. When I say good day instead of *bonjour* that is not Germanised, and *cousin* for nephew is obscured: nephew [*neef*] is our own German word and *cousin* is a French bastard. R. And isn't *bastard* a bastard as well? G. No in truth. R. Why, isn't it French as well? G. Yes, but they inherited it from the Germans.[17]

The sense of a real conversation is undercut by the division into chapters, which makes the text as much a conventional book, the source of learnèd knowledge, as a supposed record of a conversation. It also makes self-conscious use of the visual, written medium, for the foreign words that are the focus of discussion are highlighted for the reader by the use of a different typeface. The text is a demonstration par excellence of the position of the Renaissance dialogue 'zwischen Schriftlichkeit und Mündlichkeit.'[18]

In the remainder of this paper, I shall consider two further manifestations of the dialogue within Renaissance language learning: first, the catechistic elementary Latin grammar, and its transformation as the vernacular increasingly penetrates it; and secondly, some examples of the model conversation.

The Catechistic Dialogue and Its Transformation within Formal (Latin) Language Learning

It is impossible to discuss the use of the dialogue form in language learning without mentioning the prototypical formal language-learning text in Germany, Donatus's *Ars Minor*. Written in the fourth century AD, it takes the form of questions and answers between master and pupil and became the standard elementary Latin grammar across Europe. The text would have been learned off in chunks, and learners would have been tested orally in class, delivering their lines to the master, whose questions merely gave the cues to the answers he was already expecting. It begins: 'How many are the parts of speech? Eight. What are they? Noun pronoun verb adverb participle conjunction preposition interjection.'[19] Ironically, the beginning learner must learn Latin's complexities by taking a role in a Latin dialogue where he may not even understand all that he is saying. This certainly posed difficulties, and by the early Renaissance there was a growing tendency to give either interlinear or parallel German translations of the *Ars Minor* – marking both a transition to a pedagogy more based around a written text[20] and a humanist concern for catering to young learners' needs. The most elaborate example of such a glossed *Ars Minor* is Konrad Bücklin's 1473 manuscript.[21] Each 'chunk' of Latin text is followed by a word-for-word rendering in German, and then by a more fluent translation:

Textus *zuo latin* (Text in Latin)
Nomen quid est. parsoracionis cum casu corpus aut rem proprie communiter ue signifcans. proprie vt Roma Tyberis. communiter vt vrbs flumen.
Die ußlegung (The explanation)
Quid *was* est *ist* Nomen *der nam* parsoracionis *ain tail der rede* cum casu *mit der vallenden stim* corpus *lyb* aut *oder* rem *das ding* proprie *aigentlich* aut *oder* communiter *gemainlich* significans *betütend ist* proprie *aygentlich* vt *als* Roma *Rom* Tyberis *Tyfer* Communiter *gemainlich* vt Vrbs *als die stat* flumen *als das wasser*.
Der sin jn tütschem (The meaning in German)
Was ist der Nam. Ain tail der rede mit der geschicht lyb oder das ding aygentlich oder gemeinlich betütend ist. Aygentlich als Rom und Tyfer gemainlich als die stat und das wasser.
[What is the Noun? A part of speech with case, signifying a body or thing, properly or commonly. Properly as in Rome and Tiber. Commonly as in the town and the water.][22]

This text indicates the changing use of the *Ars Minor*. Originally a tool for essentially oral teaching and learning, where the dialogic form assisted the memorizing of a fixed set of material in a fixed order, it has become a text to be read. The layout presupposes a visual engagement with the text, as the Latin and vernacular versions are compared with the assistance of the word-for-word translation, and the one elucidates the other. The mediated 'dialogue' between the two language versions now takes precedence over the dialogic form of the original text. Such a layout no doubt encouraged at least the beginnings of reflection on the grammatical structure of the vernacular too,[23] and indeed the later fifteenth century sees a proliferation of texts that explicitly teach the rudiments of grammar first with respect to the vernacular, and then proceeding to the Latin.[24]

In such heavily glossed versions of the *Ars minor*, demanding visual comparison, the dialogic form of the text loses its raison d'être as an aid to orally based learning. It is not surprising, then, that in the numerous grammars inspired by the *Ars Minor*, and written to meet the requirements of the growing numbers of town schools and *Winkelschulen* of the fifteenth and sixteenth centuries, the dialogue framework is abandoned. While the *Exercitium* of 1485 still uses such phrases as *Quero* ... ('I ask') and *Dico* ('I say') which make the oral function of the text explicit, Johannes Coclaeus's *Quadriuium Grammatices* from 1511 has shifted to visual reception only, with phrases such as *Vides (candide lector)* ('You see, [fair reader]').[25] The increasing focus on visual presentation is also reflected in the growing use of tabular layout (it may seem unthinkable to us, but for centuries paradigms were learned as stretches of discourse, not as tables of 'endings') – a development associated with and certainly strengthened by Ramism[26] in Germany, but which already predates Ramus.

Thus the developing interest in the analysis of German is accompanied by a move away from the catechistic dialogue grammar towards monologic texts – both arguably natural consequences of the growing access to written German.

The Dialogue in Learning German as a Foreign Language: German-Italian Language Manuals

The increasing focus on the vernacular as mother tongue in the previous example may serve as a convenient bridge to vernacular language learning. Here the model dialogue, simulating the oral discourse which is pupils' learning objective, has a firm place in vernacular language learning long before the Renaissance – the earliest examples are brief snippets of conversation in German-Romance vocabulary lists from the ninth and eleventh centuries.[27] By the fifteenth century, we find a well-preserved tradition of language manuals for Italian merchants learning German,[28] quite independent of the tradition of explicit grammar teaching (which in Europe essentially remains tied to the study of Latin, and so accessible only to a small elite, until the sixteenth century).[29]

The most sophisticated exponents of the tradition, preserved in manuscripts from the 1420s, fall into two parts: a word-list section, and a dialogue section.[30] The dialogues are lively exchanges involving tough haggling over prices,[31] and make relatively few allowances for a learner's potential difficulties with the wide range of structures and vocabulary of natural language, though there is a clear emphasis on the vocabulary of the cloth trade. In considering how the dialogues might have been used in learning, we are again faced with their paradoxical position between orality and written form. In all cases, the dialogues are bilingual. An Italian line is followed by its German translation, as in the following example, from a 1424 manuscript held at the Bavarian State Library, Cod. it. 261:

Dio te salue, Bortolomio. *Got gruezz dich, Batholme.* ['God greet you, Bartholomew.']
O misier, vui si' 'l ben vegnudo! *O herr, ir seit got bilchum!* ['Oh, sir, you are most welcome.']
El è asay ch' io no ve ho vezudo. *Ez ist langt daz ich euch nicht han gesehen.* ['It's a long time since I saw you.'][32]

We must assume some form of visual comparison of the two written versions, whether the two are read alternately; or the German is read, and the Italian referred to where necessary; or the Italian is read and an attempt is made to produce the German, before checking against the given translation; or a combination of all three. (In fact, an inspection of a late manuscript from the same tradition, Canon. It. 291 held in the Bodleian, suggests that the German version which follows the Italian may sometimes have been filled in at a different time or by a different hand to the Italian, suggesting possible use as a sort of exercise book.) The *Sprachbuch* is not just a crutch for memory, to recall the phrases needed; rather, its format invites a reader/writer (who may or may not have been the one individual) to engage in an intertextual dialogue, between two languages in their written forms, as well as to read each dialogue as a sample of oral usage. Indeed, the full parallel translations (rather than merely glossing individual new or difficult words) suggests at least some focus on how different forms of the words could be put together to build sentences in the target language, compared to the mother-tongue.[33] For instance, the word-list section before the dialogue contains lists of verb conjugations, including the imperative, as well as adjectives in all three forms of comparison; in more than one manuscript (Modena Biblioteca, Estense It. 405; Canon. It. 291 in the Bodleian), these are even explicitly headed as such (*capitollo di verbi, capitollo dî conperativi*, 'chapter of verbs, chapter of comparatives').[34] This focus on form is matched by the high frequency of comparatives and imperatives in the dialogues themselves, as the following example shows (I have italicized imperatives and adjectives, also used adverbially):

- *Show* me the 'Barchent' [type of mixed cotton-linen cloth] with the crown on it.
- I won't show you any *bad* one, so help me God. I'll show them all to you and you take the one which pleases you *best of all*. And the one which will be *of most use* to you to carry.
- You speak *well*, you cannot speak *badly*. Do you have *good* 'falessi' and *good* 'bochasin'?
- Haven't I said so? I have *the very best* there is in this town.
- *Bring* it here! *Let* me see it! ...
- You are offering it at *too high* a price. I can surely get it *more easily* elsewhere.
- That's fine by me if it is *as good as* this here.
- I think it is *better still* at two [ducats] per hundredweight.[35]

It seems likely, then, that study of the dialogues included some focus on form, if only on those few forms which are listed (in some cases explicitly labelled) in the vocabulary section. However, while significant, this is certainly not comparable with the parsing and analysis associated with the learnèd Latin-based grammatical tradition – for instance, there is no attention paid to inflectional morphology at all.

These dialogues have attracted greater notice for their lively, natural style. A German apprentice exchanges notes with his Italian counterpart on how to give abuse in each other's language ('Do you know how to say yet "The devil's plague on you!"?');[36] the merchants chaff each other about the relative value of health and riches.[37] The young merchant's son strikes a good deal with his father's client; and we hear that the young learner of German, Peter, spends his spare time courting a girl with the tacit approval of his master – a matter of prestige for an adolescent male. Such exchanges in part help win over the reader by portraying positively an interlocutor with whom he identifies.

Most sophisticated of all, however, is the use of the dialogue form to show German-Italian negotiations in practice, imparting at least as much pragmatic competence as grammatical. In the following examples, Bartholomew (B), the son of an Italian merchant, acts on behalf of his father; G is the German buyer, and U the *unterchauffel* who checks the German merchants' deals. We learn the following pragmatic rules:

1 It is normal to be evasive about where you have been.

> B: Where have you been so long, that I haven't seen you?
> G: Here and there in many places.[38]

2 Germans are known for their fondness for drink.

> B: Won't you have a drink?
> G: I don't know, it is too early. It is not my custom to drink so early.
> B: That is amazing. For that isn't the German custom.
> G: Just you say too that the Germans are drunkards. And the Italians don't fall behind when they come to it. But the Germans have the reputation.

3 Negotiate hard. Negotiations for the purchase of cloth are protracted, and both parties insist throughout that to agree to the other's price would mean ruin. The Italian refuses the German's offer with the claim that it would mean losing his capital:

> B: I'd gladly give it to him, but I'd lose the proper capital.

Even when agreement has been reached, the German claims to have been 'tortured' in the negotiations:

> G: Yes, with great torture I have got my rights.

If necessary, remember with Bartholomew that is better not to sell at all than to sell at a bad price: *Ez ist pesser underbeilen nichcz verchauffen ben ubel verchauffen* ('it is sometimes better not to make a sale than to make a bad sale').

4 Germans expect a *zugab* (something thrown in free), as the German *unterchauffel*, fetched from the *deutczen hauzz* to oversee the deal, explains to Bartholomew:

> U: It is the German custom that they must always get something extra. ... By my troth, a German doesn't feel he has made a purchase if he doesn't get something extra.

5 Bartering (*stechen*) is accepted – the merchants agree not only on a purchase, but also on an exchange of goods.

Given that today's cross-cultural studies are only now beginning to focus on pragmatic failure as an obstacle to successful business communication, rather than grammatical difficulties,[39] the rich pragmatic and cultural content of these dialogues is impressive.

The Decline of the Dialogue in the Sprachbücher

The later *Sprachbücher* all reduce their use of dialogue to some degree. Already in the Heidelberg manuscript,[40] dated to the early fifteenth century, Meister Iorg's three dialogues have been reduced to a single, rather banal synthesis, and in the printed *Sprachbücher* of Adam von Rottweil (1477ff.),[41] only some conversational phrases remain. This may reflect a lack of understanding of their value as models of specifically oral language use, with all its pragmatic and cultural complexities, and an increasing emphasis instead on correct, context-free mastery of a given set of lexis and phrases. Certainly the legacy of the *Sprachbücher* is their contribution to the tradition of bilingual and plurilingual vocabularies, which become increasingly popular into the sixteenth and seventeenth centuries. A quadrilingual Latin-Italian-Czech-German manuscript held in the Vatican (Codex. Palat. lat. 1789) may serve as one example of this very widespread development. The manuscript, no earlier than mid-fifteenth century, has a German-Italian *Sprachbuch* as its basis,[42] and begins with phrases for greetings and simple conversation. For instance, the question 'Where were you?' is followed by a battery of possible answers in the four languages: 'I went

for a walk. – At church. – In the square. – At home. – At school. – In a
service. – I've been here, there and everywhere.'[43] After chapters of
vocabulary arranged by semantic field, a final chapter offers *spruche*
(largely short declaratives such as 'I am glad that I have sold my cot-
ton,' or 'The tax burdens the merchants who come to Venice with their
goods'). Supposedly conversational material is reduced to the level of
bite-size pieces, which were apparently to be learnt off at the rate of
one or more a day, for they begin, after a prayer:

> I shall begin to say my sayings. In the name of the Father, of the Son and
> of the Holy Ghost, and I shall begin to speak first thus.[44]

Real-life lessons of how to negotiate successfully are here replaced by
random, decontextualized sentences, which often take the shape of
worthy didacticism. Thus the *spruche* continue from above:

– All things are hard to learn at first.
– Whoever wants to be a good German, let him be open and speak
  loudly [!]
– I hope that I will become cleverer than Peter and less despised than
  him.
– If I were to learn more diligently than I do, I could do more than I
  can and my master would receive greater honour from me than from
  Peter.[45]

Again, as with the trilingual *Ars Minor*, it is likely that the loss of the
dialogic form here went hand in hand with a greater focus on the written text, and, arguably, on formal accuracy, as each *spruch* had to be
learned in its relation to the versions in each of the other three languages.

Schoolboy Latin Dialogues

If the dialogue element was reduced in plurilingual vocabularies, it
enjoyed renewed vigour in formal Latin language teaching, where
grammar had once reigned supreme. The humanist pedagogue Juan
Luis Vivès (1492–1540) advocated the teaching of Latin as a living language, and believed that pupils learned languages best through practising speaking and listening rather than through grammatical rules.
His twenty-five Latin dialogues for beginners (*Linguae latinae exercita-*

tio, first published in 1539), present scenes from the everyday life of their intended audience, well-to-do schoolchildren, from getting up in the morning, to greetings, the way to school, a lesson, or a meal. They were immensely popular and were much imitated. Both they and Erasmus's (1467–1536) more advanced *Colloquia familiaria* (first printed in 1518, revised and reprinted by Erasmus up to 1533) were translated into the various European vernaculars and reprinted many times.[46]

There is some doubt as to how such Latin dialogues would have been used. Vivès envisaged learners rehearsing his dialogues with each other, first word for word, and then gradually improvising in their own words – his focus was on presenting the necessary words and idioms to talk about all aspects of life. Breva-Claramonte argues, however, that Vivès's Latin dialogues allowed the teaching not just of vocabulary in context, but also of some rudiments of grammar (gender, number, diminutives), and idiomatic structures. In particular, the repetition of key words in different cases or verbal forms enabled learners to become alert to the function of the different endings.[47] Mack goes further still, suggesting (for the English context) that Erasmus's dialogues were to be 'analysed, parsed and varied' like any text to practise the forms of accidence.[48]

The Melding of Two Traditions: Ondrej Klatowsky

Our last example of the dialogue in Renaissance language learning combines the focus on schoolboy life from the humanist dialogues in the tradition of Vivès on the one hand, with the bilingual approach and trade orientation of the *Sprachbücher* on the other. Ondrej Klatowsky's *Ein Buechlein, in Böhmischer und Deutscher Sprach/ wie ein Boehem Deutsch/ deß gleichen ein Deutscher Boehemisch lesen/schreiben und reden lernen soll* was a popular bilingual manual for learning German and Czech, first printed in Prague in 1540.[49] It contains some three dozen dialogues, in addition to several poems in the early pages and, towards the end, examples of commercial correspondence and bookkeeping. The dialogues begin with schoolboy topics reminiscent of Vivès, but then move on to the minutiae of buying and selling cloth, which strongly suggests indebtedness to the *Sprachbuch* tradition.

Klatowsky explicitly states that he has used the dialogue form to make learning *dest leichter* ('easier' 147v). How, then, did Klatowsky's dialogues make learning easier? First, the choice of speakers and situations is designed to appeal. Klatowsky's dialogues, like those of the *Sprachbuch* tradition, are bilingual demonstration dialogues between interlocutors with whom the learners can identify, and whom they are implicitly invited to imitate closely in their German language use. The encounter with the language begins on the level of the learners' interests: the early dialogues deal with the trials and tribulations of everyday schoolboy life, reflecting the learners' first exposure to the language in the school environment; they give learners the German vocabulary they need to meet Klatowsky's requirement that pupils should not speak their native language during their breaks (41r, also 33r).

Furthermore, Klatowsky pays attention to form, too, to make learning *dest leichter*, for his dialogues are clearly graded. Hand in hand with the introduction of more specialized vocabulary in the later dialogues, and with gradually increasing length, his conversations allow exposure to certain grammatical structures before others, even if these are not explicitly discussed. The early dialogues have only two interlocutors, so that the *du* form is used (34v–35r); *Vom außbitten zum spielen* then introduces the *ir* form in plural usage, as Kasspar's friends persuade him to ask the master for a break, and the next dialogue, *Unterredung mit dem Meister*, introduces *ir* in formal, polite usage, as Kasspar uses it to address the master (37r ff.). The ensuing *verku^{e}ndigung / wie er seinen Schulgesellen erlaubnu^{e}ß zu spielen erbetten hat* (39r ff.) contains noticeably more complex sentences, particularly subordinate clauses, as Kasspar reports what the master said. The later dialogues then concentrate more on specialist vocabulary than on additional structures.

Klatowsky's dialogues also include limited explicit treatment of some grammatical features of the language. We cannot be sure whether Klatowsky's learners had any exposure to formal Latin-based grammatical training, though there is a reference to the learning of Latin in addition to Czech and German (17v). However, the book does seem to betray a modest, Latin-influenced explicit focus on form. First, the introductory dialogue, between a German and a Czech learner, explicitly presents the letters and their pronunciation, just as we would expect to find a *de literis* section at the beginning of a formal Latin grammar. Second, the learners also list for each other the noun + article in six forms in both German and Czech. Since the number six corresponds neither to the four needed in German, nor the seven (with the addition of the instrumental) required in Czech, one again suspects at least a superficial influence of Latin grammar, with its six cases. (Early grammarians of German frequently list six cases, with vocative given as *o* + noun, and ablative consisting of *von* + dative.)

Overall, however, Klatowsky still has more faith in non-grammar-based methods than in explicit grammar teaching, advocating *ubung ein Meister aller Kunst*, 'practice, the master of all art' (17r) (again, this is reminiscent of Vivès). Both through the interlocutors of his dialogues and in his poems, he emphasizes that learning is easy with diligent practice – it is important to make a *kleinen Anfang*, 'a small beginning' (2v), and then to study industriously. His model Czech and German speakers exemplify the correct attitude to language learning, as each expresses his desire to 'learn to read, write and speak well' the other's language (2r), and they repeatedly reassure each other that with application the task is not difficult. 'Practice learns everything in its time, which the art [of grammar] cannot get to the bottom of.'[50] The popularity of Klatowsky's approach is attested by the fact that his book was still being reprinted as late as 1641.[51]

Dialogue Meets Grammar

Klatowsky's little book shows points of contact between the two traditions of formal grammar and vernacular language learning. The emergence some three decades later (from 1573 onwards) of the first grammars of German, aimed at foreign learners of the language, marks the gradual merging of these two historically distinct traditions. Now the vernacular language too becomes subject to thorough, explicit grammatical analysis, and this in turn affects how it may be taught. Thus we conclude by noting the dialogues of Albert Ölinger, whose grammar of German for French learners appeared in 1574.[52] Ölinger had already produced a set of twelve German dialogues, though they were printed only after the grammar, in 1587.[53] His *Duodecim dialogi* are in fact translations of some of Vivès's Latin dialogues, and present the Latin and French on one page, the German on a facing page.[54] Ölinger's adoption of them reflects a belief that what is successful in teaching Latin will also apply for the German vernacular. But for Ölinger, as for an increasing number of his contemporaries (and in contrast to Vivès), this extends to the study of the grammar of the language too, as the publication of his *Vnderricht der Hoch Teutschen Spraach* shows. The vernacular is seen now as no less rich and systematic than Latin, and so equally amenable to formal grammatical analysis.

Conclusion

The catechistic form of the *Ars minor* tradition, and the use of the dialogue to discuss controversial matters in the *Twe-spraack* have much in common with the dialogue elsewhere in the Renaissance, and are equally indebted to classical antiquity. However, the centrality of dialogues as demonstration pieces is probably unique to language learning. Here we have seen that attention is not on the product, but on the process – on the model use of the language (lexical, grammatical, and even pragmatic).

Some manifestations of the language-learning dialogue died in the increasingly book-based culture of the Renaissance. The elementary Latin grammar moved away from the dialogic form of the *Ars minor* once it became a text for visual study; and the *Sprachbücher* reverted to word-lists for consultation, especially where the number of languages to be compared increased, requiring a visual engagement with the text. But elsewhere, the dialogue adapted readily. The opening of the *Twe-spraack* both imitates the use of foreign words in speech, and draws our attention to them in the written text by the use of a different typeface. Meister Iorg's dialogues exploit the written form to allow comparative analysis of parallel texts in two languages – dialogue between texts – and, as documents of spoken usage, also illustrate the pragmatic complexities of cross-cultural communication in a remarkably sophisticated manner. The dialogue also thrives on the possibility of intertextual connections to other written materials: to a translation of the same text in another language; to word-lists presented earlier; or to a more or less formal grammatical analysis of some aspects of its language. Ultimately, indeed, the changing role of the model conversation in both Latin and vernacular language learning reflects another fruitful dialogue – the increasing permeability between the grammar-based approach of Latin study and the oral practice-based approach of vernacular language learning.

NOTES

1 'So viel hab ich/ Tugentsame Ju^{e}ngling/ ... in diesem Bu^{e}chlein beschrieben/ dasselbe auch mit mancherley Dialogen und Unterredung von dest leichterer lehrnung wegen erkla^{e}rt./ ... damit man vielerley sachen uberflu^{e}ssig/ aussprechen der Wo^{e}rter und Sententz lernen mo^{e}ge/ ... .' The

first edition appeared in 1540 but I cite here from the 1641 edition, *Ein Büechlein, in Böhmischer und Deutscher Sprach*, 147v.
2 Virginia Cox, *The Renaissance Dialogue*, 5.
3 Ibid., 1.
4 See Burke, 'The Renaissance Dialogue.'
5 Gewerstock's study, *Lucian und Hutten*, seeks to establish a line of continuity from Lucian to the dramatic dialogues of Hutten and Sachs, and thence to the emergence of the vernacular drama as a genre in its own right.
6 On the reformation dialogue, see Kampe, *Problem 'Reformationsdialog*,' and Campbell, 'The Dialogue as a Genre of German Reformation Literature, 1520–1530.' Campbell's study considers some ninety-five dialogue pamphlets from the period.
7 See Burke, 'The Renaissance Dialogue,' 3. Similarly, K.H. Ludwig Pölitz, cited in Kalmbach, *Der Dialog im Spannungsfeld von Schriftlichkeit und Mündlichkeit*, 151, and Cox, *The Renaissance Dialogue*, 2, 4.
8 Wilson, *Incomplete Fictions*, 28–9.
9 Ibid., 34–43. The polemic Reformation dialogues, while less overtly sophisticated than Burke's 'conversations,' can likewise model for an alert audience how to argue a particular view of the controversies they discuss. See Kampe, *Problem 'Reformationsdialog*,' 117.
10 This may explain why the Bakhtinian notion of dialogicity has not, as far as I am aware, been used to approach dialogues in the German Renaissance. Germanists have fruitfully applied it to earlier, medieval German literature, however: see, for instance, Groos, *Romancing the Grail*; Groos, 'Dialogic Transcriptions'; Stevens, 'Heteroglossia,' 241–55; and Kasten, 'Bachtin und der höfische Roman.'
11 See Kalmbach, *Der Dialog*, 139ff, who notes Sebastian Brant's mockery of useless books in his *Narrenschiff* (Basel, 1494).
12 The classic in Italy is Speroni's *Dialogo delle lingue* (1542); Spain produced Juan de Valdés's *Diálogo de la lengua* (1535); in France, Jacques Peletier du Mans's *Dialogue de l'ortografe e prononciacion françoese* (1550) brings together well-known figures to discuss orthographical reform. See Waswo, *Language and Meaning in the Renaissance*, 141–2; Lepschy, *Renaissance and Early Modern Linguistics*, 16, 55.
13 The writers of this work see the *Nederduits(ch)* or *Nederlands* they describe as part of 'our common German language' (onze alghemene Duytsche taal, 501ff.), which also included High German. It is influenced by Erasmus of Rotterdam's well-known *De recta Latini Graecique Sermonis pronuntiatione dialogus*, where a chance conversation between Ursus (Bear) and Leo (Lion) is used to teach the correct pronunciation of Latin and Greek (for details of

editions, see *Twe-spraack*, 14); see Lambrecht's dialogue between *meester* and *leerknecht* on the correct spelling and pronunciation of Dutch (Lambrecht, *Nederlandsche Spellijnghe*).

14 *Twe-spraack*, 14.

15 Ibid., 16.

16 For the situation in the Low Countries, see Van der Wal, *Geschiedenis van het Nederlands*, 195–8; and Van den Toorn et al., eds, *Geschiedenis van de nederlandse taal*, 149–60; for the German context, Von Polenz, *Deutsche Sprachgeschichte vom Spätmittelalter bis zur Gegenwart* 2: 77–134.

17 *Twe-spraack*, 82–3. Roemer ende Gedeon.
    Bon jours Neef, G. ghoeden dagh *Cozyn*. R. ey ziet hoe fyn staat onze tong *discoord* G. elck verduitscht en verduistert anders wóórd. R. wats dat te zeggen? G. als ick voor *bon jours* ghoeden dagh zeg / is dat niet verduitscht / en voor Neef *Cozyn* is immers verduistert: want Neef een eighen Duits wóórd is / en *Cozyn* een Franzoys basterd. R. en *basterd* is dat niet mede een basterd? G. Neen in trouwen. R. hoe zo / ist niet óóck Fransóys? G. Ja / maar zy hebben t'zelfde vanden Duitschen gheërft. (Thanks to Lieke Schreel for the English translation.)

18 Kalmbach, *Der Dialog*, 69.

19 'Partes orationes quot sunt? Octo. Quae? Nomen pronomen uerbum aduerbium participium coniunctio praepositio interiectio.' I use the edition in Holtz, *Donat et la tradition de l'enseignment grammatical.*

20 Ong, *Orality and Literacy*, 112–38.

21 See Ising, *Die Anfänge der volkssprachlichen Grammatik in Deutschland und Böhmen.*

22 Ibid., 26.

23 Some focus on the vernacular is all the more likely in the case of Glareanus's trilingual *Ars Minor* (Nurmberg: Johannes Guldenmundt, after 1532), edited in Ising, *Die Anfänge*. Intended for the bilingual German-Czech context of Bohemia, this text puts the Latin alongside two vernaculars. It seems more than likely that this encouraged not just the use of each vernacular by its native speakers as a crutch for the Latin, but also at least limited comparison of the two vernaculars with each other (even if these do remain slaves to the Latin word order).

24 See, for example, the *Exercitium puerorum grammaticale per dietas distributum*, printed in 1485 in Antwerp, with the first High German edition six years later, in 1491 in Hagenau: extracts in Müller, *Quellenschriften und Geschichte des deutschsprachlichen Unterrichts bis zur Mitte des 16. Jahrhunderts*, 17ff. For a detailed study of the growing role of the vernacular in materials for teaching Latin grammar in the Renaissance, see Puff, '*Von dem schlüssel aller Künsten/ nemblich der Grammatica.*'

25 Müller, *Quellenschriften*, 43.
26 Ong, *Ramus, Method, and the Decay of Dialogue*, 150–1.
27 Penzl, 'How German Was Taught in the 9th and 11th Centuries.' The texts are also excerpted in Braune and Ebbinghaus, *Althochdeutsches Lesebuch*, 8–11.
28 The earliest of this group is a manuscript from 1424, edited in Pausch, *Das Älteste Italienisch-Deutsche Sprachbuch* (=Cod.12514 of the Austrian National Library). One may presume that the tradition is rather older, reaching back into the Middle Ages. Compare *A Book for Travellers*, a fourteenth-century French-Flemish compilation printed by Caxton around 1473, cited in Watts, 'Learning English through Dialogues in the 16th Century.'
29 Though the first grammars of any European vernaculars, of Italian and Spanish, date from 1437–41 and 1492 respectively, they had 'little or no influence' (Lepschy, *Renaissance and Early Modern Linguistics*, 29).
30 Pausch, *Das Älteste Italienisch-Deutsche Sprachbuch*, 38.
31 Compare the emphasis on haggling in the dialogues for French learners of English discussed by Watts, 'Learning English through Dialogues,' 226.
32 I follow the edition in Höybye, 'Glossari italiano-tedesco del Quattrocento, Maistro Zorzi,' 172ff.
33 The full translations mean that Germans learning Italian could also use the *Sprachbücher*. However, the portrayal in the dialogues of Meister Iorg as a teacher of German (with a school in St Bartholomew's Square in Venice, presumably the author of the dialogues: see Rossebastiano Bart, *Vocabulari Veneto-Tedeschi del secolo XV* introduction) suggests that they were not originally intended for this purpose.
34 Ibid., vol. 3.
35 Cod. it. 261 in Höybye, 'Glossari italiano-tedesoo,' 174ff. For reasons of space, I give only the German.

– *Zaig her* den parchant fon der chron.
– Ich mag euch chain *pösen* zaigen, also helff mir Got. Ich bird in euch all-sampt zaigen und ir bert nemen den der euch *aller paz* gefelt. Und den der euch *aller nutz* sey ze furn.
– Du sagst *wol*, do mogst nicht *poz* sagen. Hastu *gueten* falessi und *gueten* bochasln?
– Han ich euch nicht gesagt? ich han den *aller pesten* der in diser stat ist.
– *Pring her! Lass* in sehen!
[there follows a discussion of price, where numerals – also prominent in the vocabulary section – are frequent]
– Du peucz in *zetewr*. Ich mag in wol anderswo *leichter* haben.

– Ez ist mir liebt ob er *alz guet* ist alz der.

– Ich gelaub er sey *noch pesser* zwen auff ein zentar.

36 Sastu anchora dir: te nascha el vermochan? Chanstu noch sprechen: daz dir der huncz burm wachs? Ibid., 204.

37 Ibid., 196.

38 Ibid., 172; see also 199. The following extracts are taken from 177, 181, 192, 184, 187f., 190ff. Again, I cite only the German.

    1) B: Wo seit ir alz lang gebesen daz ich [supply: euch] niht han gesehen?
       G: Hin und her an fil enten.

    2) B: Wölt ir nicht ein trinch tun?
       G: Ich waizz sein nicht, ez ist ze frue. Es ist nicht mein gebonhait alz frue ze trinken.
       B: Das ist wol ein bunder. Darumb ez ist nicht der deuczen gebanhait.
       G: Sprich nur du auch also daz die deuczen trunchen sein. Und die walich fallen nicht benn si dar zu chumen. Wol daz die deuczen den nomen haben.

    3) B: Ich gebs im gern, aber ich verlur dez rechten haubtguetcz. G: Jo, mit gross[er] marter han ich mein recht gehabt. [The emendation is Höybye's.]

    4) U: Ez ist der deuczen gebanheit daz sie muessen albeg zugab haben. ... Pey mein trewn, ez duncat ein deuczen er hiet nicht chauff gemacht ob er nicht zugab hiet.

39 For a readable introduction to studies in intercultural communication from a pragmatics perspective, see Scollon and Scollon, *Intercultural Communication*.

40 Pal. Germ. 657, in *Ein italienisch-deutsches Sprachlehrbuch des 15. Jahrhunderts*.

41 Rottweil, *Deutsch-italienische Sprachführer*.

42 It is the work of Duke Johannes of Bavaria, born 1430 – possibly later, if the surviving manuscript is a copy of the original. See Höybye, 'Glossari italiano-tedeschi del Quattrocento II,' which contains a partial edition.

43 Ibid., 167. The following extracts are taken from 179, 170.

44 Ich wil anheben sprechen meyne spruch. Im namen des Vaters, des Suns und des heiligen Geistes, und wil zu irsten sprechen also (170).

45 Al dingt sint swer lernen zum irsten. – Wer wil werden eyn guter deutscher der sey offenbar und rede laute. – Ich han hoffnung das ich werde kluger dan Peter und mynder versmeet den her. – Flisse ich mich pas zu lernen denn ich thu, ich kunde mer dene ich kan und meyn meyster entphing grosser ere von mir wen von Peter (170–1).

46 Caravolas, *Précis d'histoire* I (1450–1700), 281, and *Anthologie I: A l'ombre de Quintilien*, 239–43 on Erasmus, 267–84 on Vivès. See also Bömer, *Die lateinischen Schülergespräche der Humanisten*. Erasmus's more sophisticated dialogues, aiming to model elegant Latin, satirize superstitions, and inculcate good morals, inspired fewer imitators (Gewerstock, *Lucian und Hutten*, 129ff). As Wilson (*Incomplete Fictions*, 57) notes, Vivès's approach has precedents already in practical Latin *Dialogbüchlein* with German glossings of the late Middle Ages (see Bodemann and Grubmüller, 'Schriftliche Anleitung zu mündlicher Kommunikation.'

47 Breva-Claramonte, 'A Re-analysis of Juan-Luis Vivès' (1492–1540) *Exercitatio Linguae Latinae.'*

48 Mack, 'The Dialogue in English Education of the XVIth Century,' 199.

49 The book entered several editions, well into the seventeenth century (1540, 1567, 1595, 1641). Though the title suggests it is equally useful for learning German or Czech, it was probably originally used for teaching German, for while the dialogues themselves are bilingual throughout, the Czech always precedes its German translation, and the speakers in the first dialogue, between a German and a Czech boy, are identified in Czech only, as *Némec* and *Czech.*

50 lesen\ schreiben und wol reden lehrnen (2r); Ubung lernet es alles zu seiner zeit \ das die Kunst nicht ergruenden mag (17r).

51 See note 1.

52 Ölinger, *Vnderricht der Hoch Teutschen Spraach.* On the early grammars of German, see McLelland, 'Albertus (1573) and Ölinger (1574): Creating the First Grammars of German.'

53 Ölinger, *Duodecim dialogi apprimi eleganted clarissimi D. Ioan. Luduicic Viuis Valentini.* See Meier, 'Oelingerania,' 568.

54 The use of both French and Latin alongside the German is probably simply taken over from the source (a bilingual French-Latin edition had appeared in 1560, see Caravolas, *Précis d'histaire*, 281), but may also reflect the desire to attract as wide a readership as possible.

The Subject of
Dialogue

Renaissance Dialogue and Subjectivity

Eva Kushner

The thoughts which follow attempt to situate themselves at the meeting point of two problematics central to the study of the early modern period. The first, both literary and philosophical, concerns a genre, the dialogue, so widespread during the Renaissance that it seems to represent a fundamental and innovative aspect of its intellectual life. The second, also both literary and philosophical, is the problematic of subjectivity, of vital interest to us because it is important to know whether it is true, as has long been thought, that the concept of the human person emerges from the Renaissance expanded, liberated, strengthened; or whether this concept enters into conflict with one which, put forward by Stephen Greenblatt and Michel Foucault especially, seems to have imposed itself in recent decades. It hypothesizes that in the sixteenth century, and especially before Descartes, subjectivity in the modern sense cannot be thought to have existed. What can we learn in this connection from the study of dialogue, both in terms of the authors' sense of their own subjectivity, and of the way in which they imagine – if indeed they imagine it – their own subjectivity?

One of the main characteristics of dialogue, so obvious that it has seldom been discussed, at least in theoretical terms, is the author's initial self-projection into two voices, preceding more complex fragmentation to come. What has often been emphasized is the importance of the mimesis to which we owe, in Renaissance texts that are in dialogue form, so many historically real or at least verisimilar characters. What has seldom been stressed but seems fundamental, is that as the importance of mimesis grows and replaces the formal rigidity of medieval *disputatio* the externalized representation of inner dialogue comes to play a major part among dialogical models. In any case, the two phenomena – the representation of inner dialogue and that of a discussion among several speakers deemed to have actually taken place – are in fact intimately linked. Rhetorically, but we might also say psychologically, the author identifies with each speaker in turn, thus enlivening his discourse. For example, in Pasquier's *Monophile*, as also in the framing dialogues of Marguerite de Navarre's *Heptaméron*, speakers relate so closely to the respective doctrines of love they embody that they easily achieve *ekphrasis*. But this animation would be less dynamic and less instrumental to mimesis if the author were not able to assume through imagination the viewpoint of others, divergent from his or her own.

Experimentally, let us consider this inner accompaniment of mimesis as the fundamental phenomenon underlying the most successful dramatizations, even those in appearance most impersonal. Petrarch's *Secretum* is the very prototype of dialogues textualizing the division of the self. We can of course trace the device back to the *consolatio* tradition, particularly Boethius's *De consolatione philosophiae*; and to the affinities of the *Secretum* with St Augustine's *Confessions* as well as his *Soliloquies*, in which he invokes an absent God. Petrarch dramatizes the conflict he feels between the natural desires of the self (represented by Franciscus) and the divine call (embodied by Augustinus) to renounce all terrestrial objects so as to devote himself solely to the salvation of his soul. The two protagonists discuss mortality, love, and glory. The fact that they have equal entitlement to speaking time bears witness to a humanistic determination to underscore everything that contributes to the knowledge of human personality. Impetuous, Franciscus shows no regret as he recalls his passions and their stubborn survival in him. Even when, at the end of the dialogue, Augustinus persuades him of the need to think of nothing but his spiritual needs, the reader understands that the inner division will never end because Franciscus cannot renounce his spiritual identity. And Petrarch did integrate into his text the return of the eternal problem which has become coextensive with the self, as he has Franciscus stating: 'I shall be as true to myself as I can, collect the scattered fragments of my soul, and diligently aim at self-possession. But even as we speak, many important matters, though they are of this world, await my attention.'[1]

Let us take in Petrarch an example other than the *Secretum*, however, where the projection of the self into two characters representing opposed forces is too immediately obvious. *De librorum copia* is dialogue 43 in *De remediis utriusque fortune*, part of a subgroup of four dialogues dealing with intellectual matters: books, authors, academic and professional titles. Two allegorical characters confront each other in *De librorum copia*, Joy and Reason, the latter, of course, in the role of killjoy. While in the *Secretum* Franciscus and Augustinus are given approximately equal speech time, so that there is no doubt that the voice of earthly satisfaction will indeed be heard, here, in accordance with a catechetical dialogue model, Joy, the opponent, cannot get more than a sentence in at any time. But let us not be deceived: it is a sentence brimming over with energy because it resonates with all of Petrarch's nostalgia for precisely this earthly possession against which Reason warns him. The sentence also is litanically repeated throughout the dialogue; there is complete identification between the voice of the speaker and the joy of possessing such an abundance of books. It could be said that the brevity of the sentence expresses by way of contrast the immensity of and the self-sufficiency of the world of books: 'There are vast quantities of books ... there is a huge abundance of books ... immense is the quantity of books.'[2] In this refrain, Petrarch gathers his whole resistance against the voice of reason; one can imagine that this rhetorical trick could give much pleasure to Erasmus, whose *De copia* features long lists of expressions with only minute variations among them. Petrarch knows that his dialogue is but paradox since at the age of sixty-two he aspires to nothing except to devote himself even more to the world of books. To resist the voice of reason is for him a deep personal joy, underpinned by a mosaic of quotations from classical authors. He begins with Seneca's *De tranquillitate animi*, from which he draws the basic theme of the number of books owned by the Egyptian king Ptolemy Philadelphus, as well as the theme of the vice which consists in taking into account only the external aspect of books. But there is more. Petrarch's personal energy also invests itself in the discourse of Reason. That is where we see that he is discussing with and within himself, as when he complains about the inexactitude of scribes which threatens the integrity of books. 'Even if the integrity of books were fully assured, who could remedy the ignorance of scribes and their indolence which corrupts and confuses everything, in fear of which I imagine already many brilliant minds have turned away from great creative projects.'[3]

The structure of the following dialogue, *De scriptorum fama*, is exactly the same, and just as disturbing in its simplicity. Once again Joy, expressing the natural impulses of the self, obstinately repeats the same sentence with slight variations: 'I write ... I write books ... I write passionately ...'[4] It is precisely this ardour Reason tries to assuage and to defuse by demonstrating the vanity of books. But it is clear, as it already was in the *Secretum*, that passion (whether it is directed toward possessing books by others or toward writing them oneself) and the self are consubstantial and inseparable. In the end, is it Joy that elicits Reason to save the self from the excess of its own humanity?

Two other closely related subjects will be debated in the *Four Dialogues* under the sign of the division of the self: academic titles in *The Master's Degree*, the degree that gave access to teaching at the university; and *Various Academic Titles*. Both texts are animated by the theme of aspiration to glory, so strong in Petrarch; while inherited from antiquity it is aggressively appropriated by him and even today retains its power since few temptations depend as heavily as it does upon the interdependence of human beings. In order to be famous one has to be chosen as such by others. Thus, if the desire for glory is in no way laudable from the point of view of an ascetic spirituality it at least forces us to recognize our dependence upon others and thus imposes limits to our pride. This in turn enables Petrarch to live in an ambiguous peace with his love of glory. Reason insists upon other values such as quest of truth and excellence of style, superior to glory because inwardly motivated. But Joy persists in its preference for the flattering admiration of others ...

Marguerite de Navarre also chooses the medium of dialogue to project her inner division so as to reduce it after experiencing, contemplating, and resolving it. In a text such as the *Dialogue en forme de vision nocturne* the division is not simple, because it does not consist, as in Petrarch's case, in a rational self confronting a worldly and selfish one. There is only one self, overcome with pain, conscious of its dependency under the severe theological influence of Guillaume Briçonnet, aspiring only to self-examination and, ultimately, renunciation. The division into two speakers (the Queen and the soul of her niece Charlotte who died at the age of eight) is thus a device that we know in advance is designed to reduce human rebellion in the face of death, but that will succeed in at least fully expressing that rebellion. Briçonnet had written to Marguerite that the Christian must desire death, because the ultimate joy will be that of mystical union. What is demanded is a kind of suicide of the self. 'Charlotte' reproaches 'Marguerite' for even her best intentions, contending that they are still driven by self-seeking 'car en vos faicts vous mesmes vous cerchez.'[5] Robert Cottrell has excellently grasped both the necessity and the powerlessness of the dialogue form: 'Like most of Marguerite's poems, the *Dialogue* dramatises the dilemma of a self that longs for the experience of Christ as all but resists the experience of self as nothing. In her poetry, Marguerite tries to find a poetic form and a language capable of translating this dilemma. The spiritual and psychological problem becomes a poetic problem ... In the tradition of the pseudo-Dionysius and Briçonnet she seeks to manipulate language in such a way that it will undermine discursive modes of thought and thus weaken reason and the will, two of the pillars that support the self in its illusion of independence ... In a sense a poem by Marguerite is a statement of the impossibility of poetry in the same way that the Christian's insight that Christ is all is a denial of the autonomy of the self without which there would have been no insight in the first place.'[6] Here, the poem is in the form of dialogue, which is also both necessary and condemned by dint of all that strengthens and prolongs the resistance of the self. Marguerite de Navarre excels in the art of creating beings endowed with an air of reality and bearing witness to her own participation, such as the Cross in her *Petit oeuvre dévot et contemplatif*. In the *Heptaméron*, the voices of the ten speakers are in many ways all Marguerites's even as they express divergent doctrines of love. We cannot but recognize that there is a paradox here, which Marguerite experiences and projects in all her writings: her very intensity is her personal way of detaching herself from living intensively.

Any reflection upon the role of subjectivity in the Renaissance dialogue would be incomplete if it did not take into account Thomas More's *A Dialogue of Comfort against Tribulation*, written in 1534 while More was imprisoned in the Tower of London. (He was executed on 6 July 1535.) The material details of its composition – the author's solitude, the deprivation of writing materials, the absence of a library (which makes astonishing the richness of the text in classical and contemporary references More drew entirely from his memory) and all the harassment of which he was the victim – leave no doubt as to the fact that authorial subjectivity was at stake in the most existential way. The personal motives which impelled More to write this dialogue are multiple and complex. 'On the most elemental level, in his solitude, he needed to keep his mind occupied. Second ... he wanted to give comfort to his family and friends. Beyond this ... he wanted to "prepare the minds of Englishmen ... to withstand ... the ... persecution which he foresaw ... against the ... Catholic faith."'[7] Indisputable biographical proofs show that More was desperately afraid of physical pain, that he was terrified by the perspective of being beheaded or, even worse, eviscerated. Even spicy stories he tells sometimes reveal a secret obsession with decapitation (as for example in II/16 the story of the widow who wanted to be beheaded so as to qualify for canonization).

More's *Dialogue* is an excellent example of the way in which an author's self projects its inward hesitancies. As a humanist More naturally knew texts such as Seneca's *De remediis fortuitorum*, where reason argues, as it does here in III/18, that for a wise man exile does not exist, since he does not totally identify with any terrestrial sojourn; and Boethius's *Consolation* where Philosophy denounces the vanity of worldly goods, and depicts misfortune as a blessing in disguise. Uncle Anthony evidently represents the persona of More himself in the dialogue; his intellectual horizon and his experience closely resemble those of the historical More, even if the dialogue is supposed to have taken place in Buda under the threat of the Turks rather than in England under the threat of Henry VIII. But who is Vincent? A possible answer is that he represents More's daughter, to whom the dialogue may even have been dictated, and who may have sporadically transcribed it following her visits to her father's prison. But what concerns us here more specifically is the textualization of the inner rift. It is to the young man that More entrusts his doubts and fears; thus, Vincent remarks that in addition to depriving the captive of his freedom, prison 'hath many more displeasures and very sore griefs knit and adjoined thereto';[8] and it is Vincent who utters words of wisdom and consolation. This shows the extent to which, here also, the subject's inner conflict is wholly inscribed into the process of argumentation, on both sides of a divide which he has created so as to represent, entrap so to speak, and finally bring into submission the rebellious self; that is why he is both Anthony and Vincent.

Let us now consider the case of Erasmus, who very seldom depicts himself as the centre of the text except in certain poems and letters. He prefers doxographic genres such as the treatise, the colloquy, and the commentary, where strong evidence of subjective engagement can nevertheless be found, and studied systematically. In a text that is not in dialogue form, *De pueris instituendis*, we can immediately detect the fundamentally practical and experiential character of Erasmus's philosophy of education. He speaks with moving compassion of the suffering of children who are too brutally punished; and with enthusiastic inspiration of the magnificent opportunity offered by motherhood and fatherhood to shape the child's personality tenderly and wisely from the very beginning of its life. This orientation, no doubt nourished by Erasmus's own suffering as an illegitimate child (whether in actuality or imagined later in life) can for the most part be linked with his sense of the value and uniqueness of the individual person. He was witness to and probably also victim of the horrifying punishments inflicted upon pupils by the not infrequently sadistic masters of his time. His affectivity calls upon the reader to sensitize him or her, in turn, to the needs of the child. He does not dwell excessively on unhappy situations; the *De pueris instituendis* mostly insists upon the crucial importance of devoting as much attention as possible to the child, and choosing an excellent tutor for it. To be sure, the main purpose of education is the intellectual formation of the child. But what is innovative in Erasmus's thought is that he insists on the educational process taking place in a happy atmosphere, and not just in order to make this happiness ultimately the tool of moral progress. Erasmus is also haunted by the fragility of the child's body. He reacts with indignation to the sight of children disguised in ceremonial costumes, which restrain their movements, and treated almost like monkeys in a circus. Thus, by his sympathy toward children, and by dint of the strength of his indignation against what harms them, Erasmus becomes the first champion of the rights of the child, beginning with its right to childhood. In that spirit he selects problematics relating to the development of the human person which are of a general nature but at the same time engage his attention in a profoundly personal way. Our tools for ascertaining this double motivation are stylistic criteria, necessary but, by themselves, insufficient.

But we also know, through *De pueris instituendis* as well as the *Enchiridion militis christiani*, the extent to which Erasmus believed in the extraordinary diversity of human beings, and in the depth of their singularity. He asserts in *De pueris instituendis* that everyone's being depends on the talents imparted by nature.[9] In the *Enchiridion*, Erasmus stresses the importance of submitting one's life to Christ. It is essential to note that this offering does not consist in denying the self, but in cultivating it. To be liberated in Christ does not mean to abandon what one is but to freely offer what one is as an individual. If that were not the case, if conversion meant obliterating personal difference, the picture drawn by Foucault of the universe of resemblance that imprisons minds in the sixteenth century would also apply to Erasmus's doctrine of the soul. But this is not the case. By insisting on the diversity of persons the *Enchiridion* also insists on the diversity of their power to interpret scripture. The exhortation to know oneself and to live spiritually in full knowledge of one's spirituality bears witness to Erasmus's manner of linking the humanistic cultivation of self with the Christian imperative to renounce all one possesses. Within the human being, whose heart is a 'turbulent republic,'[10] Erasmus distinguishes between the 'inner' and the 'outer' person. With Plato he gives to reason the power to dominate the passions; but he thinks with Aristotle that they should be reined in rather than obliterated; and this is another aspect of taking individual personality into account. Erasmus discusses at length the theme of variations among personalities with respect to the control of emotions and passions. He reviews, not without relying on stereotypes, differences between the sexes and among temperaments and nations. Most striking in this respect is his insistence upon spiritual survival, upon the will to be 'Christian with all one's heart and soul.'[11] In distancing himself from Plato, what Erasmus finds in Aristotle and Origen is a soul experiencing emotions, sensations, feelings; an entity intermediate between the spiritual which is divine and the physical, exposed to sin. 'The soul constitutes us as human beings.'[12] It animates our will to choose freely. Obstinately, Erasmus strives to adapt his doctrine to every human being.

Is there any relationship between this active acceptance of singularity, and the engagement of Erasmus's own singularity in the practice of dialogue? In my view the relationship is obvious but has not been theorized precisely because Erasmus is personally too involved to objectively assess the extent of his own subjectivity; and because the master rhetorician that he is would be delighted rather than indignant in encountering it. In the *Colloquies*, the discourse of the self is often shared between two speakers holding opposite views with respect to the problem at hand; one defends Erasmus's viewpoint, the other attempts to invalidate it. This opponent is rarely an absolute embodiment of evil; the alternative he or she represents might even be tempting. In order to overcome this opposition Erasmus employs argumentative devices ranging from irony to sarcasm, always marked by a passionate desire, which overdetermines the discussion, to speak and be recognized in and through the text. In *Puerpera*, Eutrapelus endeavours to persuade Fabulla, and in the end persuades her, of the importance of breastfeeding. Erasmus is not the only champion of this cause, already defended in *De liberis educandis* attributed to Plutarch, and later by Vives in *De institutione feminae christianae*, by Elyot in *The Governor*, by More in *Utopia*. It is the mode of Erasmus's engagement in the text that appears more personal than theirs. The dialogue begins with a discussion (and soon an affirmation) of the merits of motherhood. Obviously, the author sympathizes with Fabulla against the male viewpoint of Eutrapelus, who, as soon as he hears that Fabulla is not breastfeeding her baby, attacks her violently: not to breastfeed the baby and to entrust it to a wet nurse is tantamount to killing it. What distinguishes Erasmus's discourse from those of the others on this point is the down-to-earth character of the description of the child, and the litany-like repetition of the word 'mother,' which undoubtedly reflects an unconscious identification of the abandoned child that Erasmus himself was with the unjustly weaned baby. 'If you want to be a complete mother, take care of your baby's little body so that after his mind has begun to find itself, it may have the support of good and serviceable bodily organs. Every time you hear your baby squall, believe that he is asking of you ... What if he calls you 'half-mother' instead of 'mother' when he can talk? ... He is nourished not only with milk but by the fragrance of the mother's body as well ... To take some kind of nurse for a baby still warm from its mother is a kind of exposure.'[13] It is the emphasis of this text upon physical phenomena relative to the mother as well as the child, and upon the physical basis of the very first emotions in life, which may constitute signs of a subjectivity ready to manifest itself even if the argument could be won without this surge of the self.

Nor is it by chance that the third and longest part of the colloquy deals with the relationship between body and soul. Eutrapelus must persuade Fabulla that the child's health absolutely demands the presence of a mother, since the body and the soul of the child are so intimately linked that the care given to its body will have an impact on its eternal destiny. The Aristotelian doctrine of a soul which is, so to speak, the soul of the body, fits in well with the Erasmian image of the desiring, crying infant, an image returning at the end of the colloquy as Eutrapelus pictures, with expressions that again dwell on the body, the feelings of the child rejected by its mother.

Thus the physicality of the imagined body is in harmony with Erasmus's philosophical stance. A similar conjuncture occurs in the colloquies where Erasmus so vividly imagines the sufferings of women imprisoned in forced marriages that a visceral compassion seems to project him, and the reader, into their situation and thereby to espouse the Christian compassion which is his theological preference. In *Coniugium impar* Gabriel, who has just attended the wedding of a young woman with a man much older than her and visibly afflicted by a horrible disease, gathers in his description of it the entire spectrum of disgust. Of course Erasmus is only too familiar with illness, which perpetually threatens the integrity of his body. This seems to lead him to project his obsession with the ailing body onto the young woman's torturer (the forced marriage being torture for her); and this lends the force of subjectivity to the description of the torturer as well as that of the feelings of the victim. All senses are unpleasantly affected, especially the sense of smell: 'Meanwhile, enter our handsome groom: nose broken, one foot dragging after the other ... scurvy hands, a breath that would knock you down, lifeless eyes, head bound up, bloody matter exuding from nose and ears.'[14] Depictions of ugliness are not unknown in Erasmus's century; what may be unique in his vision is the manner in which the revulsion of all his senses at the sight of the fate of the young bride is mobilized in the service of a humanitarian ideal, against the social ambitions of the young woman's parents, perpetrators of the forced marriage.

In order to underscore his categorical disapproval of the subjection of women Erasmus does not hesitate to bring into play an allusion to a classical author which has sadistic and necrophilic connotations. To wed this young bride to this decrepit bridegroom is worthy of Moezentius, who, according to Vergil, would tie corpses to living bodies, hand to hand, mouth to mouth. But Moezentius himself would not have been savage enough to tie this young woman to this quasi-corpse. One hyperbole follows another. Gabriel defies Petronius to try and imagine the caresses the woman must endure.[15] Obviously, when it comes to denouncing such abuse, Erasmus combines the whole arsenal of his personal sensitivity with his literary experience.

Here is another example: the case of women entering or not entering convents against their own will. In *Virgo misogamos*, Catarina has committed herself, against the opposition of her parents, to become a nun; Eubulus tries to dissuade her from it. In *Virgo poenitens*, where we encounter the same protagonists, Catarina will be forced by nuns and monks to enter a convent. In the first colloquy, Erasmus in no way criticizes the project of a life wholly devoted to religion; but he does criticize situating it in a specific convent. It is Eubulus's function to unveil the secret vices of this institution. What triggers a passionate reaction on Erasmus's part is the relationship, perceived by Eubulus, between a total abandonment of one's will and slavery pure and simple. Once again it is the author's experience, in this case that of an inflexible hierarchy, which animates his discourse; yet the central character with whom he identifies is a woman. Altogether, Gabriel declares, slavery as it existed in the ancient world has been abolished. But monastic life is a new form of slavery. The habit worn by the monks and nuns, one from which they cannot separate without being severely punished, is not that which Christ bequeathed to them, and that is purity of heart. The length of Gabriel's discourse, so different from the sharp, brief responses in the tradition of Lucian of Samosata practised by Erasmus in his other colloquies, signals the depth of his disapproval vis-à-vis monastic vows and practices.

In *Virgo poenitens* the same characters appear, but Catarina has changed her mind: she no longer wishes to enter the convent. This enables the author to denounce the real culprit – the religious order – in opposition to the apparent culprits of the first dialogue, the young woman's parents, who only wanted to spare her a cruel disappointment. In the second dialogue, they would prefer to see her stay at the convent. Once again, Erasmus's subjectivity identifies with a young woman, her solitude and her terrors. Through Catarina, he is the fictionally innocent observer, and involuntary actor, who under Eubulus's questioning brings to light the demonic actions of the monks and nuns. This device enables Erasmus to withhold his indignation so as to let it explode at the climax: the apparition, probably brought by the holy community, of a ghost who might be Satan. This scene, like that of the monastic vows made to resemble as much as possible those of marriage, is the dramatization of a deceit, and Erasmus hates nothing as much as deceit, a hatred which here is undoubtedly made more violent by the remembrance of his own monastic vows.

The *Dialogues* of Juan Luis Vivès adhere more closely than Erasmus's *Colloquies* to their vocation as pedagogical tools. His biography is less well known than Erasmus's, which makes any hypotheses concerning the mode of his presence in the text more problematic. Here, however, is an example, which can be considered close to reality: the dialogue on drunkenness. Horace's Vth epistle is given as the source of a dialogue which, while praising good food, good wine, and a pleasant host, condemns eating to excess, and other excesses, lack of courtesy, and unpleasant habits. With respect to this second aspect Horace's text is very succinct. Four brief lines describe the impeccable tablecloth, the plates and glasses so sparkling with cleanliness that one could mirror oneself in them, and friends so discreet that not a word spoken at the banquet will be revealed outside. The manner in which Vivès expands these few lines is striking. The cause of sobriety is defended by a character named Abstemius. As in Erasmus's writings, moral conviction coalesces with affective tastes and reactions that are personal. Vivès detests drunkards; therefore he prefers the company of a cat or a dog to that of a drunkard. Like Erasmus he has an acutely developed sense of smell which warns him of undesirable visitors; but his moral sense is even more developed and alert and it warns him of any loss of humanity, that is, any loss of self-control.

So far we have only discussed the inner division from which the dialogue springs, inciting the author to imagine perspectives different from his or her own. Have we neglected the philosophical, and more specifically the 'Ciceronian' dialogue, which features a larger number of participants whose perspectives are differentiated, and a more systematic exploration of the position of the Other and therefore also of oneself? The history of the dialogue in France between 1550 and 1560, which I have called the 'dialogue of dialogues,'[16] offers us a richly interdiscursive corpus in this regard. Pontus de Tyard's *Premier Curieux* (1557) shows decisively the extent to which subjectivity is not only present even in the most academic discussions, but profoundly engaged, since the quest for truth and the establishment of its criteria are at the very heart of the author's concerns. In my view, the time of emergence of modern subjectivity, and that of the preparation of the scientific revolution, coincide. Are these two phenomena not related? Let us question Tyard's text. The *Premier Curieux* features three characters. At first sight, it would appear that the Curieux represents the spirit of research, observation, and experimentation; that Hieromnime defends ecclesiastical positions; and that the Solitaire, the author's fictitious persona, will arbitrate. But the meaning of the triad is less simple; the argumentation incorporates the issues of the scientific revolution and thus represents Tyard's thought in process of transformation. In other words, he involves himself personally in the debate; or rather, the debate is in him. As the discussants explain their respective attitudes with respect to the quest for truth, metadiscursive indications occur and are examined, in such a way that the current epistemological process is unveiled. Biographical details interspersed in the dialogue point to a sort of provincial academy. These are well known. What we should observe most attentively is the conscious textualization of the choices that the theatre of the world proposes to the philosophical mind. Early modern subjectivity is on the alert here because it observes and describes itself in the process of becoming aware of itself as an entity called upon to appropriate the approaching mathematizable universe. The dialogue is process rather than affirmation of elusive truths; that is why it expresses an inner plurality typical of the later Tyard as opposed to the Neoplatonic and Petrarchan Tyard of the 1549–55 period, a plurality which announces for the dialogues to come a role of semaphore among subjects no longer limited to communicating only, or mostly, within the 'universe of resemblance.'

NOTES

1 Petrarch, *Secretum*, 144.
2 Librorum copia magna est ... ingens est copia librorum ... Immensa copia librorum est (Petrarch, *Four Dialogues for Scholars*, 30–2).
3 Ibid., 35. Utque ad plenum auctorum constet integritas, quis scriptorum inscitiae inertiaque medebitur corrumpenti omnia miscentique, cuius metu multa iam, ut auguror, a magnis operibus clara ingenia reflexerunt ... (ibid., 34).
4 Scribo ... Scribo libros ... Scribo ardenter ... (ibid., 50–4).
5 Marguerite de Navarre, *Dialogue en forme de vision nocturne*, 586.
6 Cottrell, *The Grammar of Silence*, 45–6.
7 Miles, Introduction to More, *A Dialogue of Comfort against Tribulation*, xxvi.
8 Ibid. 192. My translation.
9 Erasmus, *Declamatio de pueris statim ac liberaliter institudendis*, 453.
10 Erasmus, *Enchiridian*, 42.
11 Ibid., 46.
12 Ibid., 52.
13 *The Colloquies of Erasmus*, 282–3. 'Si tota mater esse vis, cura corpusculum infantuli tui, quo posteaquam sese explicuit ex vaporibus, mentis igniculis, bonis et commodis organis utatur. Quoties audis puerum tuum vagientem, crede illum hoc abste flagitare ... Ubi iam erit fandi potens, quid si te pro matre vocet semimatrem? ... Alitur enim non solum lacte, sed et fragrantia materni corporis ... Nam prorsus conductitiam nutricem infantulo adhuc a matre tepenti asciscere genus est expositionis ...' 467–8.
14 Erasmus, *Colloquies*, 405. 'Interim prodiit nobis beatus ille sponsus, trunco naso, alteram trahens tibiam ... manibus scabris, halitu graui, oculis languidis, capite obiuncto, sanies et e naribus et ex auribus fluebat' (*Opera Omnia*, 593).
15 Ibid.
16 See Kushner, 'Le dialogue en France de 1550 à 1560.'

Bibliography

Primary Sources

Alberti, Leon B. *I libri della famiglia*. Edited by Ruggiero Romano and Alberto Tenenti. Turin: Einaudi, 1969.

Andreae, Johann Valentin. *Christianopolis*. Edited by Edward H. Thompson. Dordecht: Kluwer, 1999.

– *Christianopolis: An Ideal State of the Seventeenth Century*. Edited and translated by Felix Emil Held. New York: Oxford University Press, 1916.

Aretino, Pietro. *Aretino's Dialogues*. Translated by Raymond Rosenthal. New York: Marsilio, 1994.

– *Le carte parlanti*. Edited by Giovanni Casalegno and Gabriella Giaccone. Palermo: Sellerio 1992.

– *La cortigiana*. In *Tutte le commedie*, edited by G.B. De Sanctis. Milan: Mursia, 1973.

– *Lettere*. Vol. 1, bk. 1. Rome: Salerno, 1997.

– *Il piacevol ragionamento de l'Aretino: Dialogo di Giulia e di Madalena*. Edited by Claudio Galderisi. Rome: Salerno, 1988.

– *Ragionamento delle corti*. Edited by Fulvio Pevere. Milan: Mursia, 1995.

– *Ragionamento~Dialogo*. Edited by Carla Forno, with an introduction by Giorgio Bàrberi Squarotti. Milan: Rizzoli, 1988.

– *Tutte le commedie*. Edited by G.B. De Sanctis. Milan: Mursia, 1973.

Aristotle. *Poetics*. Edited by S.H. Butcher. 4th edition. London: Macmillan, 1917.

– *Poetics*. Translated by M.E. Hubbard. In *A New Aristotle Reader*, edited by J.L. Ackrill, 540–56. Princeton: Princeton University Press, 1987.

Ascham, Roger. *English Works of Roger Ascham: Toxopholis, Report of the Affaires and State of Germany, The Scholemaster*. Cambridge: Cambridge University Press, 1904. Reprint, 1970.

Augustine of Hippo. *Confessions.* Edited by James J. O'Donnell. Oxford: Clarendon, 1992.

– *Confessions.* Edited by Gerard Watson. London: Hoddes and Stoughton, 1997.

– *Soliloquies.* Edited by Joel C. Relihan. Warminster, UK: Aris and Phillips, 1990.

– *'De utilitate credendi,' 'De vera religione,' 'De fide rerum quae non videntur' di Agostino d'Ippona.* Edited by Onorato Grassi et al. Rome: Città nuova; Palermo: Augustinus, 1994.

Averell, William. *A Marvelous Combat of Contrarities.* London: J. Charlewood, 1588.

Bacon, Francis. *New Atlantis.* In *The Great Instauration and New Atlantis,* edited by J. Weinberger, 37–81. Arlington Heights, IL: Harlan Davidson, 1980.

Barbaro, Francesco. *Francisci Barbari de re uxoria liber.* In *Atti e memorie della regia accademia di scienze, lettere ed arti in Padova,* edited by Attilio Gnesotto, n.s., 32 (1916): 6–105.

– 'On Wifely Duties.' Part 2 of *De re uxoria.* Translated by Benjamin G. Kohl. In *The Earthly Republic: Italian Humanists on Government and Society,* edited by Benjamin G. Kohl and Ronald G. Witt, with Elizabeth B. Welles, 189–228. Philadelphia: University of Pennsylvania Press, 1978.

– *Prudentissimi et gravi documenti circa la elettion della Moglie (De re uxoria).* Translated by Alberto Lollio. Venice: Gabriel Giolioto de Ferrari, 1548.

Barberino, Francesco da. *Il Reggimento e costume di donna.* Bologna, 1875.

Boethius. *Consolation of Philosophy.* Translated by Joel C. Relihan. Indianapolis: Hackett, 2001.

Brant, Sebastian. *Narrenschiff.* Basel: Johann Bergmann, 1494.

Bruni, Leonardo. *Dialogi ad Petrum Histrum.* In *Prosatori latini del Quattrocento,* edited by Eugenio Garin, 44–98. Milan and Naples: Ricciardi, 1952.

– *The Humanism of Leonardo Bruni.* Edited by Gordon Griffiths, James Hankins, and David Thompson. Binghamton, NY: The Renaissance Society of America, 1987.

Burton, Robert. *The Anatomy of Melancholy.* Edited by Thomas C. Faulkner, Nicolas K. Kiessling, and Rhonda L. Blair. 6 vols. Oxford: Clarendon, 1989.

Campanella, Tommaso. *The City of the Sun.* Translated by Daniel J. Donno. Berkeley and Los Angeles: University of California Press, 1981.

Castiglione, Baldassare. *The Book of the Courtier.* Translated by Leonard Eckstein Opdycke. New York: Horace Liveright, 1929.

– *The Book of the Courtier.* Translated by Charles S. Singleton. Garden City, NY: Doubleday, 1959.

– *The Book of the Courtier.* Edited by Daniel Javitch. New York: W.W. Norton, 2002.

– *Le Courtisan, nouvellement traduit de langue italique en françois.* Translated

probably by Jacques Colin d'Auxerre. Paris: Jean Longis and Vincent Sertenas, 1537.
– *Le lettere*. Edited by Guido La Rocca. Vol. I. Milan: Mondadori, 1978.
– *Lettere inedite e rare*. Edited by Guglielmo Gorni. Milan: Ricciardi, 1969.
– *Il libro del cortegiano*. Edited by Ettore Bobora. Milan: Mursia, 1972.
– *Il libro del cortegiano*. Introduction by Amedeo Quondam. Notes by Nicola Longo. Milan: Garzanti, 1981.
– *Le livre du courtisan*. Translated by Gabriel Chappuis. Edited by Alain Pons. Paris: G. Lebovici, 1987.
– *La seconda redazione del* Cortegiano. Edited by Ghino Ghinassi. Florence: Sansoni, 1968.
Cavendish, Margaret, Duchess of Newcastle. *The Description of a New World, Called The Blazing World*. In *The Blazing World and Other Writings*, edited by Kate Lilley, 119–230. Harmondsworth: Penguin Classics, 1992. Reprint, 1994.
Cecil, William, Lord Burghley. *A Pack of Spanish Lies Sent Abroad in the World: First Printed in Spain in the Spanish Tongue, and Translated Out of the Original, Now Ripped Up, Unfolded, and by Just Examination Condemned, as Containing False, Corrupt, and Detestable Wares Worthy to be Damned and Burned*. London: Christopher Barker, 1588.
Cervantes, Miguel de. *Dialogue of the Dogs*. In *Exemplary Stories*, translated by Lesley Lipson, 250–305. Oxford: Oxford University Press, 1998.
Cicero. *De oratore*. Translated by H. Rackham. Cambridge, MA: Harvard University Press, and London: William Heinemann, 1977.
– *On the Ideal Orator (De oratore)*. Translated by James M. May and Jokob Wisse. Oxford: Oxford University Press, 2001.
Cortés, Hernán. *Letters from Mexico*. Translated and edited by Anthony Pagden. New Haven: Yale University Press, 1986.
Daunce, Edward. *A Brief Discourse Dialoguewise, Showing How False and Dangerous their Reports Are which Affirm the Spaniards intended Invasion to be for the Reestablishment of the Romish Religion*. London: R. Field, 1590.
– *A Brief Discourse of the Spanish State, with a Dialogue annexed entitled Philobasilis*. London: R. Field, 1590.
Decor puellarum. Venice, ca. 1471.
The Deliquium: or, The Grievances of the Nation Discovered in a Dream. London: n.p., 1681.
Della Casa, Giovanni. *Galateo*. Edited by Ruggiero Romano. Turin: Einaudi, 1975.
A Dialogue at Oxford between a Tutor and a Gentleman, formerly his Pupil, concerning Government. London: printed for R. Janaway, 1681.
A Dialogue between a Knight and a Cleric. London: Thomas Berthelet, 1533. Original Latin ed., Thomas. Berthelet, 1531.

A Dialogue between a Vertuous Gentleman and a Popish Priest. London: printed by Robert Waldegrave, 1581.

A Dialogue between the Duchess of Portsmouth and Madam Gwyn at Parting. London: printed for J.S., 1682.

A Dialogue between Two Porters. London: printed for A. Banks, 1681.

A Dialogue betwixt Sam the Ferriman, Will a Waterman, and Tom a Bargeman upon the King's calling a Parliament to meet at Oxford. London: printer unknown, 1681.

A Dialogue concerning the Strife of Our Church. London: printed by Robert Waldegrave, 1584.

A Dialogue upon Dialogue: or L'Estrange, No Papist nor Jesuit but the Dog Towzer. London: printed for H.B., 1681.

A Dialogue wherein is Plainly Laid Open, the Tyrannical dealing of L. Bishops against God's Children. La Rochelle: Robert Waldegrave, 1589.

Díaz, Bernal. *The Conquest of New Spain*. Translated by J.M. Cohen. Harmondsworth Penguin, 1963.

Dizionario Biografico degli Italiani. 38 vols. Rome: Instituto della Enciclopedia italiana, 1960– .

Dominici, Giovanni. *Regola del governo di cura familiare*. Edited by D. Salvi. Florence: 1860.

Dryden, John. *A Defense of an Essay of Dramatic Poesy*. In *Essays of John Dryden*, edited by W.P. Ker. 2 vols. Oxford: Clarendon, 1926.

– *The Life of Lucian*. In *Prose 1691–1698*, vol. 20 of *The Works of John Dryden*. Edited by A.E. Wallace Maurer. Berkeley and Los Angeles: University of California Press, 1989.

– *The Works of Lucian*. London: Samuel Briscoe, 1711.

Du Bosc, Jacques. *L'honneste femme*. 2nd ed. Paris: Jean Jost, 1633.

Ein italienisch-deutsches Sprachlehrbuch des 15. Jahrhunderts: Edition der Handschrift Universitätsbibliothek Heidelberg Pal. Germ. 657 und räumlich-zeitliche Einordnung des deutschen Textes. Edited by Martina Blusch. Frankfurt: Peter Lang, 1992.

Elyot, Thomas. *The Book Named the Governor*. 1531. Edited by John M. Major. New York: Teachers College Press, 1969.

– *Of the Knowledge which Maketh a Wise Man*. 1533. Edited by Edwin Johnston Howard. Oxford, OH: Anchor, 1946.

– *Pasquil the Plain*. 1533. In *Four Political Treatises*. Facsimile reproductions and introduction by Lillian Gottesman, 41–100. Gainesville, FL: Scholars' Facsimiles and Reprints, 1967.

Erasmus, Desiderius. *Adagia. Adages [i] to Iv100*. Vol. 30 of *Collected Works of Erasmus*. Translated by Margaret Mann Phillips. Toronto: University of Toronto Press, 1982.

- *Antipolemus*, or *Dulce bellum inexpertis*. 1515. Translated by Vicesimus Knox. N.p., 1795.
- *Colloquia*. Vol. 3 of *Opera omnia Desiderii Erasmi Roterodami*, edited by L.-E. Halkin, F. Bierlaire, and R. Hovem. Amsterdam: North-Holland, 1972.
- *The Colloquies of Erasmus*. Translated by Craig R. Thompson. Chicago: University of Chicago Press, 1965.
- *The Correspondence of Erasmus, Letters 446–593 (1516–17)*. Vol. 4 of *Collected Works of Erasmus*. Edited and translated by R.A.B. Mynors and D.F.S. Thomson. Toronto: University of Toronto Press, 1977.
- *The Correspondence of Erasmus, Letters 993 to 1121 (1519–1520)*. Vol. 7 of *Collected Works of Erasmus*, edited and translated by R.A.B. Mynors. Toronto: University of Toronto Press, 1987.
- *Declamatio de pueris statim ac liberaliter instituendis*. Edited by Jean-Claude Margolin. Geneva: Droz, 1966.
- *De recta Latini Graecique sermonis pronuntiatione dialogus*. Basel: Frobeniana, 1528.
- *Enchiridion militis christiani*. In vol. 66 of *Collected Works of Erasmus*, edited by John W. O'Malley. Toronto: University of Toronto Press, 1983.
- *The Praise of Folly and Other Writings*. Edited and translated by Robert M. Adams. New York and London: W.W. Norton, 1989.
- *Ten Colloquies*. Edited by Craig R. Thompson. New York: Library of the Liberal Arts, 1957.
Faret, Nicolas. *L'honnête homme ou l'art de plaire à la cour*. 1925. Reprint, Geneva: Slatkine, 1970.
Foxe, John. *Actes and Monuments of these latter and perillous days*. London: John Day, 1563.
- [*Acts and Monuments.*] *The First (Second) Volume of the Ecclesiastical History*. London: John Day, 1570.
- [*Acts and Monuments.*] *The First (Second) Volume of the Ecclesiastical History*. London: John Day, 1576.
- [*Acts and Monuments of matters most special and memorable*]. London: John Day, 1583.
- *Rerum in Ecclesia Gestarum Commentarii*. Basel: Nicolaum Brylingerum and Ioannem Opporinum, 1559.
Gibbon, Charles. *Not So New as True, Being a Very Necessary Caveat for All Christians to Consider Of*. London: T. Orwin, 1590.
A Glass of the Truth. London: Thomas Berthelet, 1531.
Gournay, Marie le Jars de. *Apology for the Woman Writing*. Edited by Richard Hillman and Colette Quesnel. Chicago: University of Chicago Press, 2002.
- *The Equality of Men and Women*. In *Apology for the Woman Writing*, 69–97.

– *Fragments d'un discours féminin.* Edited by Elyane Dezon-Jones. Paris: Corti, 1988.
– 'Grief des dames.' ('The Ladies' Complaint'). In *Apology for the Woman Writing,* 97–105.
– *Oeuvres complètes.* 2 vols. Edited by Jean-Claude Arnould. Paris: Champion, 2002.
– *Preface to the Essays of Michel de Montaigne.* Translated and edited by Richard Hillman and Colette Quesnel. Tempe, AZ: Medieval and Renaissance Texts and Studies, 1998.
– *Proumenoir de Monsieur de Montaigne.* Edited by Constant Venesoen. Geneva: Droz, 1993.
– *Le Proumenoir de Monsieur de Montaigne.* Edited by Jean-Claude Arnould. Paris: Champion, 1996.
Grenaille, François de. *L'honneste fille.* Paris: J. Paslé, 1639–40.
– *L'honneste garçon.* Paris: Quinet, 1642.
– *L'honnête fille.* Edited by Alain Vizier. Paris: Champion, 2003.
Guazzo, Stefano. *La civile conversation.* Translated by Gabriel Chappuys. Lyon: J. Beraud, 1579.
– *The Civile Conversation of M. Steven Guazzo.* Translated by G. Pettie and B. Young. New York: AMS Press, 1967.
Harsdörffer, Georg Philipp. *Frauenzimmer Gesprächspiele.* 1644–9. Edited by Irmgard Böttcher. Tübingen: Niemeyer, 1968.
Hobbes, Thomas. *A Briefe of the Arte of Rhetorique, Containing in Substance all that Aristotle hath Written in his Three Books of that Subject, except onely what is not Applicable to the English Tongue by T.H.* London: Th. Cotes for Andrew Crooke, 1637.
– *Behemoth, or the Long Parliament.* Edited by F. Tönnies. Introduction by M.M. Goldsmith. 1889. Reprint, London: Frank Cass, 1969.
– *Béhémoth, ou le Long Parlement.* Vol. 9 of *Œuvres de Hobbes en français.* Edited and translated by Luc Borot. Paris: Vrin, 1990.
– *The Correspondence.* 2 vols. Edited by Noel Malcolm. Oxford: Clarendon, 1994.
– *Court traité des premiers principes* (A Short Tract on First Principles). Edited and translated by Jean Bernhardt. Paris: Presses Universitaires de France, 1988.
– *Decameron Physiologicum, or Ten Dialogues of Natural Philosophy.* London: William Cooke, 1678.
– *De cive: The Latin Version.* Vol. 2 of *Philosophical Works of Thomas Hobbes.* Edited by Howard Warrender. Oxford: Clarendon, 1983.
– *De corpore.* Edited by Karl Schuhmann. Hobbes Latinus 1. Paris: Vrin, 1999.
– *A Dialogue between a Philosopher and a Student of the Common Laws of England.* Edited by J. Cropsey. Chicago: University of Chicago Press, 1971.

– *Dialogue entre un philosophe et un légiste des Common Laws d'Angleterre*. Vol. 10 of *Œuvres de Hobbes en français*. Edited and translated by Lucien Carrive and Paulette Carrive. Paris: Vrin, 1990.

– *The Elements of Law, Natural and Politic*. Edited by F. Tönnies. 1889. Reprint, London: Frank Cass, 1969.

– *Leviathan, or the Generation, Matter and Forme of a Commonwealth*. Edited by C.B. Macpherson. Harmondsworth: Penguin, 1968.

– *The Rhetorics of Thomas Hobbes and Bernard Lamy*. Edited by John T. Harwood. Carbondale and Edwardsville: Southern Illinois University Press, 1986.

– 'Thomæ Hobbes Malmesburiensis Vita Carmine Expressa. Authore Seipso.' In vol. 1 of *Thomæ Hobbes Malmesburiensis Opera Philosophica quae Latine Scripsit Omnia*, edited by Sir William Molesworth, lxxi – xcix. London: Bohn, 1839.

Johnson, Samuel. *Lives of the Most Eminent English Poets*. 3 vols. London: John Murray, 1854.

Klatowsky, Ondrej. *Ein Buechlein, in Böhmischer und Deutscher Sprach/ wie ein Boehem Deutsch/ deß gleichen ein Deutscher Boehemisch lesen/schreiben und reden lernen soll*. Prague: Barthmle Netolický, 1540; Ollmuotz: Nicolaus Hradetzky, 1641.

Lambrecht, Joos. *Nederlandsche Spellijnghe*. Ghent: Lambrecht, 1550. Reprint, Ghent, 1882.

Lefèvre d'Étaples, Jacques. *Prefatory Epistles of Jacques Lefèvre d'Etaples and Related Texts*. Edited by Eugene F. Rice. New York: Columbia University Press, 1972.

L'Estrange, Roger. *The Casuist Uncas'd in a Dialogue betwixt Richard and Baxter, with a Moderator Between Them for Quietness Sake*. London: printed for H. Brome, 1680.

– *Citt and Bumpkin in a Dialogue over a Pot of Ale, concerning Matters of Religion and Government*. London: printed for H. Brome, 1680.

Lucian. *Toxaris, or Friendship*. In vol. 5 of *Lucian*, translated by A.M. Harmon, 101–207. Loeb Classical Library. London: William Heinemann, 1936.

Lupton, Thomas. *Too Good to Be True*. London: H. Bynneman, 1580.

Marguerite de Navarre, *Dialogue en forme de vision nocturne*. Edited by Renja Salminen. Helsinki: Suomalainen Tiedeakatemia, 1985.

– *L'Heptaméron*. Edited by Michel François. Paris: Garnier, 1975.

– *The Heptameron*. Translated by P.A. Chilton. Hamondsworth: Penguin Books, 1984.

– *Heptaméron*. 2 vols. Edited by Renja Salminen. Helsinki: Suomalainen Tiedeakatemia, 1997.

– *L'Heptaméron*. Edited, with an introduction, by Gisèle Mathieu-Castellani. Paris: Librairie génerale française, 1999.

– *Pater noster* et *Petit oeuvre dévot*. Edited by Sabine Lardon. Paris: Champion, 2001.

Milton, John. *Complete Prose Works of John Milton*. 6 vols. Edited by Douglas Bush. New Haven: Yale University Press, 1959.

– *Milton: Complete Shorter Poems*. Edited by John Carey. 1968. Reprint, London: Longman, 1997.

– *Paradise Lost*. Edited by Alastair Fowler. 1968. Reprint, London: Longman, 1971.

Montaigne, Michel de. *The Complete Essays*. Edited by Donald M. Frame. Stanford: Stanford University Press, 1958.

– *The Complete Essays*. Translated by Michael A. Screech. Harmondsworth: Penguin, 1991.

– *Essais*. Edited by Pierre Villey. Paris: Presses Universitaires de France, 1978.

– *Oeuvres complètes*. Paris: Gallimard, 1962.

More, Thomas. *Dialogue concerning Heresies*. 1529. Vol. 6, parts 1 and 2, of *The Yale Edition of the Complete Works of St. Thomas More*. Edited by Thomas Lawler, Germain Marc'hadour, and Richard Marius. New Haven: Yale University Press, 1981.

– *A Dialogue of Comfort against Tribulation*. 1534. Edited by Miles Leland. Bloomington: Indiana University Press, 1965.

– *A Dialogue of Comfort against Tribulation*. Vol. 12 of *The Yale Edition of the Complete Works of St. Thomas More*. Edited by Louis L. Martz and Frank Manley. New Haven: Yale University Press, 1976.

– *Selected Letters*. Edited by Elizabeth Frances Rogers. New Haven: Yale University Press, 1961.

– *Translations of Lucian*. Vol. 3, part 1, of *The Yale Edition of the Complete Works of St. Thomas More*. Edited by Craig R. Thompson. New Haven: Yale University Press, 1974.

– *Utopia*. Vol. 4 of *The Yale Edition of the Complete Works of St. Thomas More*. Edited by E. Surtz and J.H. Hexter. New Haven: Yale University Press, 1965.

– *Utopia*. Translated and edited by Robert M. Adams. New York: W.W. Norton, 1992.

– *Utopia*. Edited by Clarence Miller. New Haven: Yale University Press, 2001.

– *L'Utopie de Thomas More*. Edited by André Prévost. Paris: Nouvelles éditions Mame, 1978.

Motteville, Françoise Bertaut de. *Mémoires de Mme de Motteville*. Paris: Fontaine, 1982.

Neville, Henry. *Plato Redivivus*. In *Two English Republican Tracts* (1681), edited by Caroline Robbins, 61–200. Cambridge: Cambridge University Press, 1969.

Ölinger, Albertus. *Duodecim dialogi apprimi eleganted clarissimi D. Ioan. Luduicic*

Viuis Valentini, ex Latini et Gallico Idiomate in Germanicum linguam fideliter translati. Speyer: Bernardi Albini, 1587.
– *Underricht der Hoch Teutschen Spraach.* Strasbourg, 1574. Reprint, Hildesheim: Olms, 1975.
Pallavicino, Sforza. *Trattato dello stile e del dialogo.* Rome: G. Casoni, 1662.
Pasquier, Etienne. *Le Monophile.* Milan: Cisalpino, 1957.
Peletier du Mans, Jacques. *Dialogue de l'ortografe e prononciacion françoese.* Poitiers: J. e E. Marnef, 1550; 2nd ed. Lyon: de Tournes, 1555; rpt. of the 1555 edition Geneva: Droz, 1966.
Périers, Bonaventure de. *Cymbalum Mundi: Four Very Ancient and Facetious Poetic Dialogues.* Translated by Bettina L. Knapp. New York: Bookman, 1965.
Petrarch, Francesco. *Four Dialogues for Scholars.* Edited and translated by Conrad H. Rawski. Cleveland: Western Reserve University Press, 1967.
– *Secretum.* Edited, with an introduction by Davy A. Carozza and H. James Shey. New York: Peter Lang, 1989.
– *The Sonnets, Triumphs, and other Poems.* Translated by Robert MacGregor London: Bell, 1912.
Pico della Mirandola. *Oratio de dignitate hominis.* In *Latin Writings of the Italian Humanists,* edited by F.A. Gragg, 215–18. New York: Scribners, 1927.
Plato. *The Dialogues of Plato.* Vol. 1. Translated by B. Jowett. Oxford: Clarendon, 1891.
– *Protagoras and Meno.* Translated by W.K.G. Guthrie. Boston: Penguin Books, 1966.
A Pleasant Battle Between Two Lap Dogs of the Utopian Court. London: Printed for R.B., 1681.
A Pleasant Discourse Between two Sea-men. London: Printed for T. Davies, 1681.
Plutarch. *Moralia.* Edited by Giuliano Pisani. Pordenone: Edizioni Bibilioteca dell'Immagine, 1989.
Puttenham, George. *The Arte of English Poesie.* 1589. Cambridge: Cambridge University Press, 1936.
Rainolds, John. *The Sum of the Conference between John Rainolds and John Hart Touching the Head and the Faith of the Church.* London: J. Wolfe, 1584. Reprint, London: G. Bishop, 1588.
Ramus, Petrus [Pierre de La Ramée]. *Dialecticae institutiones.* Paris: n.p., 1543.
The Return of the Renowned Cavaliero Pasquil of England. London: J. Charlewood, 1589.
Rottweil, Adam von. *Adam von Rottweill, Deutsch-italienische Sprachführer.* Edited by Vito R. Giustiniani. Tübingen: Niemeyer, 1987.
Sabbadini, Remigio. *La Gita di Francesco Barbaro a Firenze nel 1415.* Trieste: G. Caprin, 1910.

The Sack of Rome, Executed by the Emperor Charles' Army. London: A. Jeffes, 1590.

St German, Christopher. *St. German's Doctor and Student.* Edited by T.F.T. Plucknett and J.L. Barton. London: Selden Society, 1974.

– *Salem and Bizance.* London: T. Berthelet, 1533.

San Bernadino da Siena. *La Fonte Della Vita: Prediche volgari scelte e annotate da Giacomo Vaifro Sabatelli.* Florence: Libreria Editrice Fiorentina, 1964.

Savage, Francis. *A Conference betwixt a Mother a Devout Recusant, and Her Sonne a Zealous Protestant.* Cambridge: John Legat, 1600.

Sidney, Philip. *A Defence of Poetry.* Edited by J.A. van Dorsten. Oxford: Oxford University Press, 1966.

Sigonio, Carlo. *De dialogo.* Venice: Giordano Ziletti, 1562.

Sophronistes: A Dialogue persuading the People to Reverence and Attend the Ordinance of God, in the Ministry of their Own Pastors. London: T. Orwin, 1589.

Spenser, Edmund. *A Vewe of the present state of Irelande.* In *Spenser's Prose Works*, edited by Rudolf Gottfried. Vol. 10 of *The Works of Edmund Spenser: A Variorum Edition.* Edited by Edwin Greenlaw, Charles Grosvenor Osgood, Frederick Morgan Padelford, and Ray Heffner, 39–232, and Commentary 278–439. Baltimore: Johns Hopkins University Press, 1949.

– *A View of the Present State of Ireland.* Edited by Andrew Hadfield and Willy Maley. Oxford: Blackwell, 1997.

Speroni, Sperone. *Apologia dei dialogi.* In vol. 1 of *Trattatisti del Cinquecento*, edited by Mario Pozzi, 683–724. Milan: Riccardo Ricciardi, 1978.

– *Dialogo delle lingue.* Vinegia: Alda, 1542.

– *Dialogo della rettorica e Aplogia dei dialogi.* In vol. 1 of *Opere*, edited by Mario Pozzi, 1: 202–42, 266–425. Rome: Vecchiarelli, 1989.

Starkey, Thomas. *Thomas Starkey: A Dialogue between Pole and Lupset.* Edited by T.F. Mayer. London: Royal Historical Society, 1989.

Il Tasso: A Dialogue. The Speakers John Milton, Torquato Tasso. London: R. Baldwin, 1762.

Tasso, Torquato. *Discorso dell'arte del dialogo.* Translated by Carnes Lord and Dain A. Tafton. Berkeley and Los Angeles: University of California Press, 1982.

– *Discorso della virtú feminile e donnesca.* In *The Renaissance Notion of Woman*, edited by Ian Maclean. Cambridge: Cambridge University Press, 1980.

– *Discourse on the Art of the Dialogue.* In *Tasso's Dialogues: A Selection*, 15–42.

– *Tasso's Dialogues: A Selection.* Translated and edited by Carnes Lord and Dain A. Trafton. Berkeley and Los Angeles: University of California Press, 1982.

Temporis Filia Veritas: A Merry Device called the Troublesome Travail of Time. N.p., 1589.

Twe-spraack vande Nederduitsche letterkunst. 1584. Edited by Geert R.W. Dibbets. Maastricht: Van Gorcum, Assen, 1985.

Tyard, Pontus de. *Premier curieux.* In *The Universe,* edited by John C. Lapp, 1–126. Ithaca: Cornell University Press, 1950.

– *L'Univers ou Discours des parties et de la nature du monde.* Lyon: Jean de Tournes, 1557.

Udall, John. *The State of the Church of England laid open in a Conference between Diotrephes a Bishop, Tertullus a Papist, Demetrius a Usurer, Pandochus an Innkeeper, and Paul a Preacher of the Word of God.* London: Robert Waldegrave, 1588.

Valdés, Alfonso de. *Diálogo de las cosas ocurridas en Roma.* Edited by José F. Montesinos. Madrid: Ediciones de 'La Lectura,' 1928. Rpt. Madrid: Epasa-Calpe, 1956.

Valdés, Juan de. *Diálogo de la lengua.* 1535. Edited by Cristina Barbolani. Madrid: Cátedra, 1982.

Valla, Lorenzo. *De professione religiosorum.* Edited by Mariarosa Cortesi. Padua: Antenore, 1986.

Vivès, Juan Luis. *De institutione feminae christianae.* Edited by C. Fantazzi. Chicago: University of Chicago Press, 2000.

– *Linguae latinae exercitatio.* Basel: Robertus Winter, 1539.

Vox populi: or, The People's Claim to their Parliament's Sitting. London: printed for F. Smith, 1681.

Secondary Sources

Allen, Michael J.B. *The Platonism of Marsilio Ficino.* Berkeley and Los Angeles: University of California Press, 1984.

Allen, Peter R. '*Utopia* and European Humanism: The Function of the Prefatory Letters and Verses.' *Studies in the Renaissance* 10 (1963): 91–107.

Altman, Joel B. *The Tudor Play of Mind: Rhetorical Inquiry and the Development of Elizabethan Drama.* Berkeley and Los Angeles: University of California Press, 1978.

Arnould, Claude. *Marie de Gournay et l'édition de 1595 des Essais de Montaigne.* Paris: Champion, 1996.

Astell, Ann W. 'Rhetorical Strategy and the Fiction of Audience in More's *Utopia*.' *The Centennial Review* 29, no. 3 (1985): 302–19.

Aubrey, John. *Brief Lives.* Edited by Richard Barber. Woodbridge: Boydell, 1982.

Auerbach, Erich. *Mimesis: The Representation of Reality in Western Literature.* Translated by Willard Trask. Princeton: Princeton University Press, 1953.

254 Bibliography

Babb, Lawrence. 'The Background of "Il Penseroso."' *Studies in Philology* 37 (1940): 257–73.

Bakhtin, Mikhail. *The Dialogic Imagination: Four Essays*. Edited by Michael Holquist. Translated by Caryl Emerson and Michael Holquist. Austin: University of Texas Press, 1981.

– *Rabelais and His World*. Translated by Hélène Iswolsky. Cambridge, MA: MIT, 1968. Reprint, Bloomington: Indiana University Press, 1984.

Bakhtin, Mikhail, and V.N. Voloshinov. *Marxism and the Philosophy of Language*. Translated by L. Matejka and I.R. Titunik. New York: Seminar, 1973.

Baron, Hans. 'The Genesis of Bruni's *Dialogi*.' In *The Crisis of the Early Italian Renaissance*, 225–44. Princeton: Princeton University Press, 1966.

Bauschatz, Cathleen. 'Imitation, Writing, and Self-Study in Marie de Gournay's 1595 "Préface" to Montaigne's Essays.' In *Contending Kingdoms*, edited by Mary-Rose Logan and Peter Rudnytsky, 346–64. Detroit: Wayne State University Press, 1991.

Beaulieu, Jean-Pierre, and H. Fournier. 'Poétiques dialogiques et réécriture dans l'oeuvre de Marie de Gournay.' *Neophilologus* 82, no. 3 (1998): 357–67.

Bedouelle, Guy. *Lefèvre d'Etaples et l'intelligence des Écritures*. Geneva: Droz, 1976.

Bénouis, Mustapha Kemal. *Le dialogue philosophique dans la littérature du seizième siècle*. The Hague: Mouton, 1976.

Berrong, Richard M. *Rabelais and Bakhtin: Popular Culture in Gargantua and Pantagruel*. Lincoln: University of Nebraska Press, 1986.

Bertière, Simone. *Les Reines de France au temps des Bourbons*. Paris: Fallois, 1996.

Betteridge, Tom. 'From Prophetic to Apocalyptic: John Foxe and the Writing of History.' In *John Foxe and the English Reformation*, edited by David M. Loades, 210–32. Aldershot: Scolar Press, 1997.

Bevington, David M. 'The Dialogue in *Utopia*: Two Sides to the Question.' *Studies in Philology* 58 (1961): 496–509.

Boase, Alan. *The Fortunes of Montaigne*, New York: Octagon Books, 1970.

Bodemann, Ulrike, and K. Grubmüller. 'Schriftliche Anleitung zu mündlicher Kommunikation. Die Schülergesprächbüchlein des späten Mittelalters.' In *Pragmatische Schriftlichkeit im Mittelalter. Erscheinungsformen und Entwicklungsstufen*, edited by Hagen Keller, Klaus Grubmüller, and Nikolaus Staubach, 177–93. Munich: Fink, 1992.

Boesky, Amy. 'Bacon's *New Atlantis* and the Laboratory of Prose.' In *The Project of Prose in Early Modern Europe and the New World*, edited by Elizabeth Fowler and Roland Greene, 138–53. Cambridge: Cambridge University Press, 1997.

Bolotin, David. *Plato's Dialogue on Friendship: An Interpretation of the Lysis, with a New Translation*. Ithaca: Cornell University Press, 1979.

Börner, Aloys. *Die lateinischen Schülergespräche der Humanisten. Auszüge mit Einleitungen, Anmerkungen und Namen- und Sachregister. Quellen für die Schul- und Universitätsgeschichte des 15. und 16. Jahrhunderts*. Berlin: J. Harrwitz Nachfolger, 1897.

Borot, Luc. 'History in Hobbes's Thought.' In *The Cambridge Companion to Hobbes*, edited by Tom Sorell, 305–28. Cambridge: Cambridge University Press, 1996.

– Introduction to *Béhémoth, ou le Long Parlement*. Vol. 10 of *Oeuvres de Hobbes en français*. Edited and translated by Luc Borot. Paris: Vrin, 1990.

Bradshaw, Brendan, and Eamon Duffy, eds. *Humanism, Reform and the Reformation: The Career of Bishop Fisher*. Cambridge: Cambridge University Press, 1989.

Brand, Charles P. *Torquato Tasso*. Cambridge: Cambridge University Press, 1965.

Braune, W., and E. Ebbinghghaus. *Althochdeutsches Lesebuch*. 17th edition. Tübingen: Niemeyer, 1994.

Breen, John M. 'Imagining Voices in *A View of the Present State of Ireland*: A Discussion of Recent Studies Concerning Edmund Spenser's Dialogue.' *Connotations* 4 (1994–5): 119–32.

Breitenberg, Mark. 'The Flesh Made Word: Foxe's *Acts and Monuments*.' *Renaissance and Reformation* 25, no. 4 (1989): 381–407.

Breva-Claramonte, Manuel. 'A Re-analysis of Juan-Luis Vivès' (1492–1540) *Exercitatio Linguae Latinae*.' In *Papers in the History of Linguistics*, edited by Hans Arsleff, Louis G. Kelly, and Hans-J. Niederehe, 167–77. Amsterdam: Benjamins, 1987.

Brown, Eric C.'"The Melting Voice Through Mazes Running."' *Milton Studies* 40 (2002): 1–18.

Brown, Merle E. *Double Lyric*. New York: Columbia University Press, 1980.

Bruce, Donald. 'Spenser's Irenius and the Nature of Dialogue.' *Notes and Queries* 39 (1992): 355–7.

Brucker, Gene. *Renaissance Florence*. 1969. Berkeley and Los Angeles: University of California Press, 1983.

Bruster, Douglas. Review of *The Christian's ABC*. *Early Modern Literary Studies* 3, no. 3 (January 1998): 9.1–14.

Burckhardt, Jacob. *Die Cultur der Renaissance in Italien: Ein Versuch*. Basel: Schweighauser, 1860.

Burke, Peter. 'The Renaissance Dialogue.' *Renaissance Studies* 3, no. 1 (March 1989): 1–12.

Cairns, Christopher. *Pietro Aretino and the Republic of Venice*. Florence: Olschki, 1985.

Campbell, Fiona. 'The Dialogue as a Genre of German Reformation Literature, 1520–1530.' PhD diss., St Andrews University, 2000.

Capefigue, Jean P. *Anne d'Autriche*. Paris: Amyot, 1861.

Caravolas, Jean-Antoine. *Anthologie I: À l'ombre de Quintilien*. Vol 2 of *La didactique des langues*. Montréal: Les Presses de l'Université de Montréal; Tübingen: Gunter Narr, 1994.

– *Précis d'histoire I (1450–1700)*. Vol 1 of *La didactique des langues*. Montréal: Les Presses de l'Université de Montréal; Tübingen: Gunter Narr, 1994.

Carron, Jean-Claude. 'La Renaissance du dialogue.' In *De la littérature française*, edited by Denis Hollier and François Rigolot, 171–4. Paris: Bordas, 1993.

Cave, Terence. *The Cornucopian Text: Problems of Writing in the French Renaissance*. Oxford: Clarendon, 1979.

Cazauran, Nicole. 'La nouvelle exemplaire ou le roman tenu en échec.' *Cahiers Textuels* 10 (1992): 21–3.

Charlier, Yvonne. *Érasme et l'amitié d'après sa correspondance*. Paris: Les Belles Lettres, 1977.

Chojnacki, Stanley. *Women and Men in Renaissance Venice*. Baltimore: Johns Hopkins University Press, 2000.

Christopher, Georgia B. 'Subject and Macrosubject in "L'Allegro" and "Il Penseroso."' *Milton Studies* 28 (1992): 23–35.

Cian, Vittorio, ed. 'Dizionarietto biografico.' In *Il libro del cortegiano del conte Baldesar Castiglione*, 503–40. Florence: Sansoni, 1947.

Collinson, Patrick. *The Elizabethan Puritan Movement*. Berkeley and Los Angeles: University of California Press, 1967.

Comito, Terry. *The Idea of the Renaissance Garden*. New Brunswick, NJ: Rutgers University Press, 1978.

Copeland, Rita. *Rhetoric, Hermeneutics, and Translation in the Middle Ages: Academic Traditions and Vernacular Texts*. Cambridge: Cambridge University Press, 1991.

Cosenza, Mario Emilio. *Biographical and Bibliographical Dictionary of the Italian Humanists and of the World of Classical Scholarship in Italy, 1300–1800*. 6 vols. Boston: Hall, 1962–7.

Costa, Dennis. 'Domesticating the Divine Economy: Humanist Theology in Erasmus's *Convivia*.' In *Creative Imitation: New Essays on Renaissance Literature in Honor of Thomas M. Greene*, edited by D. Quint et al., 11–29. Binghamton, NY: Medieval and Renaissance Texts and Studies, 1992.

Cotgrave, Randall. *Dictionarie of the French and English Tongues*. London, 1611. Reprint, Columbia: University of South Carolina Press, 1970.

Cottrell, Robert. *The Grammar of Silence: A Reading of Marguerite de Navarre's Poetry*. Washington: Catholic University of America Press, 1986.

Coughlan, Patricia. '"Some secret scourge which shall by her come unto England": Ireland and Incivility in Spenser.' In *Spenser and Ireland: An Interdisciplinary Perspective*, edited by Patricia Coughlan, 24–45. Cork, Ireland: Cork University Press, 1989.

Council, Norman B. '"L'Allegro," "Il Penseroso," and the Cycle of Universal Knowledge.' *Milton Studies* 9 (1976): 203–19.

Cox, Gerard H. 'Unbinding "The Hidden Soul of Harmony."' *Milton Studies* 18 (1983): 45–62.

Cox, Virginia. *The Renaissance Dialogue: Literary Dialogue in its Social and Political Contexts. Castiglione to Galileo.* Cambridge: Cambridge University Press, 1992.

Crawford, Bartholomew Vincent. 'The Non-Dramatic Dialogue in English Prose.' PhD diss., Harvard University, 1918.

Curtis, Mark H. *Oxford and Cambridge in Transition, 1558–1642.* Oxford: Clarendon, 1959.

Cushman, Robert E. *Therapeia: Plato's Conception of Philosophy.* Westport, CT: Greenwood, 1976.

Cusson, Marie. 'La lecture est-elle un dialogue?' *Protée* 27, no. 2 (1999): 7–13.

Day, John T., Jr. 'Elizabethan Prose Dialogue.' PhD diss., Harvard University, 1977.

Deakins, Roger Lee. 'The Tudor Dialogue as a Literary Form.' PhD diss., Harvard University, 1964.

– 'The Tudor Prose Dialogue: Genre and Anti-Genre.' *Studies in English Literature, 1500–1900* 20 (1980): 5–23.

Defaux, Gérard. 'Against Derrida's "Dead Letter": Christian Humanism and the Valorization of Writing.' *French Forum* 13, no. 2 (1988): 167–85.

– *Marot, Rabelais, Montaigne: l'écriture comme présence.* Paris and Geneva: Champion-Slatkine, 1987.

– *Montaigne et le travail de l'amitié.* Orléans: Paradigmes, 2001.

Demure, Catherine. 'L'*Utopie* de Thomas More: entre logique et chronologie, l'enjeu du sens.' In *Logique et littérature à la Renaissance: Actes du colloque de la Baume-les-Aix, Université de Provence, 16–18 septembre 1991*, edited by Marie-Luce Demonet and André Tournon, 165–77. Paris: Champion, 1994.

Dent, Christopher M. *Protestant Reformers in Elizabethan Oxford.* Oxford: Oxford University Press, 1983.

Dentith, Simon. *Bakhtinian Thought.* London: Routledge, 1995.

de Roover, Raymond. *The Rise and Decline of the Medici Bank.* Cambridge, MA: Harvard University Press, 1963.

Desan, Philippe. 'The Book, the Friend, the Woman: Montaigne's Circular

Exchanges.' In *Contending Kingdoms*, edited by M.-R. Logan and P. Rudny-tsky, 225–62. Detroit: Wayne State University Press, 1991.

Dotoli, Giovanni. 'Montaigne et les libertins via Mlle de Gournay.' In *Montaigne et Marie de Gournay, actes du colloque international de Duke*, edited by Tétel, 105–41.

Duffy, Eamon. *The Stripping of the Altars: Traditional Religion in England c.1400–1580*. New Haven: Yale University Press, 1992.

Eliade, Mircea. *The Sacred and the Profane*. New York: Harcourt Brace Jovanovich, 1959.

Elliott, Robert C. 'The Shape of Utopia.' In *Utopia*, edited by R.M. Adams, 181–95. New York: W.W. Norton, 1975.

Ferreras, Jacqueline. *Les dialogues espagnols du XVIᵉ siècle ou l'expression littéraire d'une nouvelle conscience*. Paris: Didier Erudition, 1985.

Ferroni, Giulio. 'Pietro Aretino e le corti.' In *Pietro Aretino nel Cinquecentenario della nascita*, edited by E. Malato et al., 23–48.

Finch, Casey, and Peter Bowen. 'The Solitary Companionship of "L'Allegro" and "Il Penseroso."' *Milton Studies* 26 (1991): 3–24.

Fish, Stanley. *Is There a Text in This Class?* Cambridge: Cambridge University Press, 1980.

– *The Living Temple*. Berkeley and Los Angeles: University of California Press, 1978.

– *Self-Consuming Artifacts: The Experience of Seventeenth-Century Literature*. Berkeley and Los Angeles: University of California Press, 1972.

Floriani, Piero. 'Dall'amore cortese all'amor divino.' In *Bembo e Castiglione: Studi sul classicismo del Cinquecento*, 169–186. Rome: Bulzoni, 1976.

– 'Il dialogo e la corte nel primo cinquecento." In *La corte e il 'Cortegiano.' I. La scena del testo*, edited by Carlo Ossola, 83–96. Rome: Bulzoni, 1980.

– 'I personaggi del *Cortegiano*.' *Giornale storico della letteratura italiana* 156 (1979): 161–78.

Fontana, Alessandro, and Jean-Louis Fournel. 'Piazza, Corte, Salotto, Caffé.' In *Letteratura Italiana V: Le questioni*, edited by A. Asot Rosa, 624–52. Turin: Giulio Einaudi, 1986.

Forno, Carla. *Il 'libro animato': teoria e scrittura del dialogo nel Cinquecento*. Turin: Tirrenia Stampatori, 1992.

Foucault, Michel. *Les mots et les choses*. Paris: Gallimard, 1979.

Fowler, Elizabeth, and Roland Greene, eds. *The Project of Prose in Early Modern Europe and the New World*. Cambridge: Cambridge University Press, 1997.

Fraisse, Jean-Claude. *Philia. La notion d'amitié dans la philosophie antique: essai sur un problème perdu et retrouvé*. Paris: Vrin, 1974.

Franchetti, Anna Lia. 'Marie de Gournay apologiste des *Essais*: la préface de 1599.' *Montaigne Studies* 8 (1996): 173–7.

Freccero, Carla. 'Politics and Aesthetics in Castiglione's *Il cortegiano*: Book III and the Discourse on Women.' In *Creative Imitation: New Essays on Renaissance Literature in Honor of Thomas M. Greene*, edited by David Quint. Binghamton, NY: Medieval and Renaissance Texts and Studies, 1992.

Freeman, Thomas. 'Texts, Lies, and Microfilm: Reading and Misreading Foxe's "Book of Martyrs."' *Sixteenth Century Journal* 30, no. 1 (1999): 23–46.

Fumaroli, Marc. *Le genre des genres littéraires français: la conversation*. Oxford: Clarendon, 1992. Reprinted as 'L'art de la conversation, ou le Forum du royaume,' in *La diplomatie de l'esprit*, 283–320. Paris: Hermann, 1994.

– 'Montaigne et l'éloquence du for intérieur.' In *Les Formes brèves de la prose et le discours discontinu (XVIᵉ–XVIIᵉ siècles)*, edited by Jean Lafond, 27–50. Paris: Vrin, 1984.

Gasché, Rodolphe. *The Tain of the Mirror: Derrida and the Philosophy of Reflection*. Cambridge, MA.: Harvard University Press, 1986.

Gewerstock, Olga. *Lucian und Hutten: Zur Geschichte des Dialogs im 16. Jahrhundert*. Berlin: Emil Ebering, 1924. Reprint, Berlin: Kraus, 1967.

Ghinassi, Ghino. 'Fasi dell'elaborazione del *Cortegiano*.' *Studi di filologia italiana* 26 (1967): 158–61.

– 'Postille sull'elaborazione del *Cortegiano*.' *Studi e problemi di critica testuale* 3 (1971): 171–8.

Girardi, Raffaele. *La società del dialogo: Retorica e ideologia nella letterature conviviale del Cinquecento*. Bari: Adriatica, 1991.

Godard, Anne. *Le dialogue à la Renaissance*. Paris: Presses universitaires de France, 2001.

Godzich, Wlad, and Jeffrey Kittay. *The Emergence of Prose: An Essay in Prosaics*. Minneapolis: University of Minnesota Press, 1987.

Goldsmith, Elizabeth. *Exclusive Conversations: The Art of Interaction in Seventeenth-Century France*. Philadelphia: University of Pennsylvania Press, 1988.

Gómez, Jesús. *El diálogo en el Renacimiento*. Madrid: Catedra, 1988.

Goodman, Nelson. *Ways of Worldmaking*. Indianapolis: Hackett, 1978.

Gordon, Jill. 'Dialectic, Dialogue, and Transformation of the Self.' *Philosophy and Rhetoric* 29, no. 3 (1996): 259–78.

Goyet, Francis. *Le Sublime du lieu commun: L'Invention rhétorique dans l'Antiquité et à la Renaissance*. Paris: Champion, 1996.

Grafton, Anthony, and L. Jardine. *From Humanism to the Humanities: Education and the Liberal Arts in XVIth- and XVIIth-Century Europe*. London: Duckworth, 1986.

Green, Ian. *The Christian's ABC: Catechisms and Catechizing in England c.1530–1740*. Oxford: Clarendon, 1996.

Greenblatt, Stephen. *Renaissance Self-Fashioning: From More to Shakespeare*. Chicago: University of Chicago Press, 1980.

Greene, Roland. 'Fictions of Immanence, Fictions of Embassy.' In *The Project of Prose in Early Modern Europe and the New World*, edited by Elizabeth Fowler and Roland Greene, 176–202. Cambridge: Cambridge University Press, 1997.

Greene, Thomas M. '*Il Cortegiano* and the Choice of a Game.' In *Castiglione: The Ideal and the Real in Renaissance Culture*, edited by R.W. Hanning and D. Rosand, 1–15. New Haven: Yale University Press, 1983. Reprint, in *The Vulnerable Text: Essays in Renaissance Literature*, by Thomas M. Greene, 46–60. New York: Columbia University Press, 1986.

– 'The Flexibility of the Self in Renaissance Literature.' In *The Disciplines of Criticism*, edited by Peter Demetz, Thomas Greene, and Lowry Nelson, Jr, 241–64. New Haven: Yale University Press, 1968.

– *The Light in Troy: Imitation and Discovery in Renaissance Poetry*. New Haven: Yale University Press, 1982.

– *The Vulnerable Text: Essays on Renaissance Literature*. New York: Columbia University Press, 1986.

Groos, Art. 'Dialogic Transcriptions.' In *Chrétien de Troyes and the German Middle Ages*, edited by Martin Jones and Roy Wisbey, 257–76. London: Institute of Germanic Studies, 1993.

– *Romancing the Grail: Genre, Science and Quest in Wolfram's 'Parzival.'* Ithaca: Cornell University Press, 1995.

Guellouz, Suzanne. *Le dialogue*. Paris: Presses universitaires de France, 1992.

Guggisberg, Hans R., Frank Lestringant, and Jean-Claude Margolin, eds. *La Liberté de conscience (XVIᵉ–XVIIᵉ siècles)*. Geneva: Droz, 1991.

Guibbory, Achsah. *The Map of Time*. Urbana: University of Illinois Press, 1986.

Guidi, José. 'Baldassar Castiglione et le pouvoir politique.' In vol. 1 of *Les écrivains et le pouvoir en Italie à l'époque de la Renaissance*, edited by André Rochon, 243–78. Paris: Université de la Sorbonne Nouvelle Press, 1973.

– 'Le jeu de cour et sa codification dans les différentes rédactions du *Courtisan.*' In *Le pouvoir et la plume: Incitation, contrôle et répression dans l'Italie du XVIᵉ siècle*, 97–115. Paris: Université de la Sorbonne Nouvelle, 1982.

Guillén, Claudio. *Literature as a System*. Princeton: Princeton University Press, 1977.

Hadfield, Andrew D. 'The Course of Justice: Spenser, Ireland, and Political Discourse.' *Studia Neophilologica* 65 (1993): 187–96.

– 'Who Is Speaking in Spenser's *A View of the Present State of Ireland*? A Response to John Breen.' *Connotation* 4 (1994–5): 233–41.

Haller, William. *Foxe's Book of Martyrs and the Elect Nation*. London: Jonathan Cape, 1963.

Halley, Janet E. 'Equivocation and the Legal Conflict over Religious Identity in

Early Modern England.' *Yale Journal of Law and the Humanities* 3, no. 33 (1991): 33–52.

Headley, John M. 'Campanella, America, and World Evangelization.' In *America in European Consciousness, 1493–1750*, edited by Karen Ordahl Kupperman, 243–71. Chapel Hill: University of North Carolina Press, 1995.

Herbillon, E.C. *Anne d'Autriche, reine, mère, régente*. Paris: Tallandier, 1939.

Hereford, Charles. *Studies in the Literary Relations of England and Germany in the Sixteenth Century*. Cambridge: Cambridge University Press, 1886.

Herlihy, David, and Christiane Klapisch-Zuber. *Tuscans and Their Families*. New Haven: Yale University Press, 1985.

Hexter, J.H. *More's Utopia: The Biography of an Idea*. Princeton: Princeton University Press, 1952.

– 'Thomas More and the Problem of Counsel.' In *Quincentennial Essays on St. Thomas More*, edited by Michael J. Moore, 55–66. Boone, NC: Albion, 1978.

Hirzel, Rudolf. *Der Dialog: ein literarhistorischer Versuch*. 2 vols. Leipzig: S. Hirzel, 1895.

Holstun, James. *A Rational Millennium: Puritan Utopias of Seventeenth-Century England and America*. New York: Oxford University Press, 1987.

Holtz, Louis. *Donat et la tradition de l'enseignement grammatical: Étude sur l'"Ars Donati" et sa diffusion (IVe–IXe siècle) et édition critique*. Paris: Centre National de la Recherche Scientifique, 1981.

Howard, W. Scott. 'Companions with Time: Milton, Tasso and Renaissance Dialogue.' *The Comparatist* 28 (2004):

Howell, A.G. Ferrers. *San Bernadino of Siena*. London: Methuen, 1913.

Howell, Wilbur Samuel. *Logic and Rhetoric in England 1500–1700*. Princeton: Princeton University Press, 1956. Reprint, New York: Russell and Russell, 1961.

– 'Ramus and English Rhetoric: 1547–1681.' *Quarterly Journal of Speech* 37 (1951): 299–310.

Höybye, Poul. 'Glossari italiano-tedesco del Quattrocento, Maistro Zorzi.' *Studi di Filologia Italiana* 22 (1964): 167–204.

– 'Glossari italiano-tedeschi del Quattrocento II.' *Studi di Filologia Italiana* 32 (1974): 143–203.

Hughes, Merritt Y. *A Variorum Commentary on The Poems of John Milton*. 6 vols. New York: Columbia University Press, 1972.

Huizinga, Johan. *Erasmus of Rotterdam*. Translated by F. Hopman. London: Phaidon, 1952.

– *Herfsttij der middeleeuwen*. Harlem: H.D. Tjeenk Willink, 1919.

– *The Waning of the Middle Ages: A Study of the Forms of Life, Thought, and Art in France and the Netherlands in the XIVth and XVth Centuries*. Garden City, NY: Doubleday, 1954.

Hunter, William B., Jr., ed. *A Milton Encyclopedia*. 8 vols. Lewisburg, PA: Bucknell University Press, 1978.

Hurley, Harold C. *The Sources and Traditions of Milton's 'L'Allegro' and 'Il Penseroso.'* Lewiston, NY: Edwin Mellen, 1999.

Hyatte, Reginald. *The Arts of Friendship: The Idealization of Friendship in Medieval and Early Renaissance Literature*. Leiden: E.J. Brill, 1994.

Ilsley, Marjorie Henry. *A Daughter of the Renaissance*. The Hague: Mouton, 1963.

Iser, Wolfgang. *Der Akt des Lesens*. Munich: Fink, 1976.

− *Der Implizite Leser*, Munich: Fink, 1972.

Ising, Erika, ed. *Die Anfänge der volkssprachlichen Grammatik in Deutschland und Böhmen: Dargestellt am Einfluß der Schrift des Aelius Donatus* De octo partibus orationis ars minor *(Teil I: Quellen)*. 1473. Berlin: Akademie, 1966.

Jardine, Lisa. *Erasmus, Man of Letters: The Construction of Charisma in Print*. Princeton: Princeton University Press, 1993.

Jeanneret, Michel. *A Feast of Words: Banquets and Table Talk in the Renaissance*. Chicago: University of Chicago Press, 1991.

− 'La lecture en question: sur quelques prologues comiques du seizième siècle.' *French Forum* 14, no. 3 (1989): 279–89.

Jechova, Hana. 'Le dialogue dans les littératures tchèque et polonaise entre le Moyen Âge et la Renaissance.' *Revue de l'Université d'Ottawa* 43 (1973): 205–34.

Johnston, David. *The Rhetoric of* Leviathan: *Thomas Hobbes and the Politics of Cultural Transformation*. Princeton: Princeton University Press, 1986.

Jones-Davies, M.T., ed. *Le dialogue au temps de la Renaissance*. Centre de recherches sur la Renaissance. Paris: Jean Touzot, 1984.

Journal of the History of Ideas 59, no. 4 (October 1998).

Kahler, Erich. *The Inward Turn of Narrative*. Translated by Richard and Clara Winston. Princeton: Princeton University Press, 1973.

Kahn, Victoria. *Rhetoric, Prudence and Skepticism in the Renaissance*. Ithaca: Cornell University Press, 1985.

Kalmbach, Gabriele. *Der Dialog im Spannungsfeld von Schriftlichkeit und Mündlichkeit*. Tübingen: Niemeyer, 1996.

Kampe, Jürgen. *Problem 'Reformationsdialog': Untersuchungen zu einer Gattung im reformatorischen Medienwettstreit*. Tübingen: Niemeyer, 1997.

Kasten, Ingrid. 'Bachtin und der höfische Roman.' In *Bickelwort und wildiu mære. Festschrift für Eberhard Nellmann*, edited by Dorothee Lindemann, Berndt Volkman, and Klaus-Peter Wegera, 51–70. Göppingen: Kümmerle, 1995.

Kates, Judith. *Tasso and Milton*. Lewisburg, PA: Bucknell University Press, 1983.

Kautsky, Karl. *Thomas More and His* Utopia. 1890. Reprint, New York: Russell and Russell, 1959.

Kendall, Ritchie D. *The Drama of Dissent: The Radical Poetics of Nonconformity.* Chapel Hill: University of North Carolina Press, 1986.

Kent, Dale. *The Rise of the Medici.* Oxford: Oxford University Press, 1978.

King, Margaret L. 'Caldiera and the Barbaros on Marriage and the Family: Humanist Reflections of Venetian Realities.' *The Journal of Medieval and Renaissance Studies* 6 (1976): 19–50.

– *Women of the Renaissance.* Chicago: University of Chicago Press, 1991.

Kinney, Arthur F. *Humanist Poetics: Thought, Rhetoric, and Fiction in Sixteenth-Century England.* Amherst: University of Massachusetts Press, 1986.

Kirchner, Timothy. 'The Modality of Moral Communication in the *Decameron*'s First Day, in Contrast to the Mirror of the Exemplum.' *Renaissance Quarterly* 54 (2001): 1035–73.

Kleinman, Ruth. *Anne d'Autriche.* Paris: Fayard, 1985. Reprint, 1993.

Knott, John R. *Discourses of Martyrdom in English Literature 1563–1694.* Cambridge: Cambridge University Press, 1993.

Kristeller, Paul O. *The Classics and Renaissance Thought.* Martin Classical Lectures. Vol. 15. Published for Oberlin College. Cambridge, MA: Harvard University Press, 1955.

– *Renaissance Thought II.* New York: Harper and Row, 1965.

– 'Thomas More as a Renaissance Humanist.' *Moreana* 65–6 (1980): 5–22.

Kushner, Eva. 'Le dialogue en France au XVIe siècle: quelques critères génologiques.' *Canadian Review of Comparative Literature* 5 (spring 1978): 141–53.

– 'Le dialogue en France de 1550 à 1560.' In *Le dialogue au temps de la Renaissance,* edited by M.T. Jones-Davies, 151–67. Paris: J. Touzot, 1984.

– 'The Dialogue of the French Renaissance: Work of Art or Instrument of Inquiry?' *Zagadnienia Rodzajów Literackich* 20, no. 39 (1977): 23–35.

– 'Epilogue: The Dialogue of Dialogues.' In *The Dialogue in Early Modern France, 1547–1630: Art and Argument,* edited by Colette H. Winn, 259–83. Washington, DC: The Catholic University of America Press, 1993.

– 'Réflexions sur le dialogue en France au XVIe siècle' *Revue des sciences humaines* 38 (1972): 485–501.

– 'The Renaissance Dialogue and its Zero-Degree Fictionality.' In *Fiction Updated: Theories of Fictionality, Narratology, and Poetics,* edited by Calin-Andrei Mihailescu and Walid Hamarneh, 165–172. Toronto: University of Toronto Press, 1996.

– 'Le rôle structurel du "locus amoenus" dans les dialogues de la Renaissance.' *Cahiers de l'Association internationale des études françaises* 34 (1982): 39–57.

Lake, Peter. 'Puritan Identities.' *Journal of Ecclesiastical History* 35, no. 1 (1984): 112–23.

– 'William Bradshaw, Antichrist, and the Community of the Godly.' *Journal of Ecclesiastical History* 36, no. 4 (1985): 570–89.

Lake, Peter, and David Como. 'Orthodoxy and Its Discontents: Dispute Settlement and the Production of "Consensus" in the London (Puritan) Underground.' *Journal of British Studies* 39 (2000): 34–70.

Langer, Ullrich. *Divine and Poetic Freedom in the Renaissance: Nominalist Theology and Literature in France and Italy.* Princeton: Princeton University Press, 1990.

La Rocca, Guido. 'Un taccuino autografo per il *Cortegiano.*' *Italia medioevale e umanistica* 23 (1980): 341–73.

Lecler, Joseph. 'Liberté de conscience: Origine et sens divers de l'expression.' *Recherches de Science Religieuse* 54 (1966): 370–406.

Lepschy, Giulio, ed. *Renaissance and Early Modern Linguistics.* Vol. 4 of *History of Linguistics.* London: Longman, 1998. Translation of 1992 Italian edition.

Lerer, Seth. *Boethius and Dialogue: Literary Method in the* Consolation of Philosophy. Princeton: Princeton University Press, 1985.

Lessay, Franck. 'Hobbes and Sacred History.' In *Hobbes and History,* edited by G.A.J. Rogers and Tom Sorell, 147–59. London: Routledge, 2000.

Lettieri, Michael, Salvatore Bancheri, and Roberto Buranello, eds. *Pietro Aretino e la cultura del Rinascimento.* Vol. 2 of *Pietro Aretino nel Cinquecentenario della nascita. Atti del Convegno di Roma-Viterbo-Arezzo (28 settembre–1 ottobre), Toronto (23–24 ottobre), Los Angeles (27–29 ottobre).* Rome: Salerno, 1995.

Leushuis, Reinier. *Le Mariage et 'l'amitié courtoise' dans le dialogue et le récit bref de la Renaissance.* Florence: Olschki, 2003.

Levao, Ronald. *Renaissance Minds and Their Fictions: Cusanus, Sidney, Shakespeare.* Berkeley and Los Angeles: University of California Press, 1985.

Levy, William Albert. 'Philosophy as Literature: The Dialogue.' *Philosophy and Rhetoric* 9, no. 1 (winter 1976): 14–27.

Lewalski, Barbara. Paradise Lost *and the Rhetoric of Literary Forms.* Princeton: Princeton University Press, 1985.

Lewis, C.S. *English Literature in the Sixteenth Century (Excluding Drama).* Vol. 3 of *The Oxford History of English Literature.* Oxford: Clarendon, 1954.

Lipking, Lawrence. 'The Dialectic of *Il Cortegiano.*' *PMLA* 81 (1966): 355–62.

Loach, Jennifer. 'Reformation Controversies.' In Vol. 3 of *The History of the University of Oxford,* edited by James McConica, 363–96. Oxford: Clarendon, 1986.

Loades, David M. *The Oxford Martyrs.* New York: Stein and Day, 1970.

Loewenstein, David. *Milton and the Drama of History.* Cambridge: Cambridge University Press, 1990.

Lord, Carnes, and Dain A. Trafton. Introduction to *Tasso's Dialogues.* Translated and edited by Carnes Lord and Dain A. Trafton. Berkeley and Los Angeles: University of California Press. 1982.

Lyons, John D. *Exemplum: The Rhetoric of Example in Early Modern France and Italy*. Princeton: Princeton University Press, 1990.

MacCullough, Diarmaid. *Thomas Cranmer: A Life*. New Haven: Yale University Press, 1996.

Machacek, Gregory. '*Paradise Lost*, Christian Epic and the Familiar Sublime.' *Cithara* 40, no. 1 (2000): 37–49.

Mack, Peter. 'The Dialogue in English Education of the XVIth Century.' In *Le Dialogue au temps de la Renaissance*, edited by Marie-Thérèse Jones-Davies, 189–209. Paris: Jean Touzot, 1984.

Maclean, Ian. *The Renaissance Notion of Women*. Cambridge: Cambridge University Press, 1980.

Macovski, Michael. *Dialogue and Literature: Apostrophes, Auditors, and the Collapse of Romantic Discourse*. Oxford: Oxford University Press, 1994.

Magendie, Maurice. *La politesse mondaine et les théories de l'honnêteté*. 1925. Geneva: Slatkine, 1970.

Malato, Enrico, et al. eds. *Pietro Aretino nel Cinquecentenario della nascita. Atti del Convegno di Roma-Viterbo-Arezzo (28 settembre–1 ottobre), Toronto (23–24 ottobre), Los Angeles (27–29 ottobre)*. Vol. 1. Rome: Salerno, 1995.

Maley, Willy. 'Dialogue-Wise: Some Notes on the Irish Context of Spenser's *View*.' *Connotations* 6 (1996–7): 67–77.

Mandrou, Robert. *Des humanistes aux hommes de science (XVIᵉ et XVIIᵉ siècles)*. Vol. 3 of *Histoire de la pensée européenne*. Paris: Seuil, 1973.

Marc'hadour, Germain. 'Thomas More: de la conversation au dialogue.' In *Le Dialogue au temps de la Renaissance*, edited by Marie-Thérèse Jones-Davies, 35–53. Paris: J. Touzot, 1984.

Margolin, Jean-Claude. 'L'Art du dialogue et de la mise en scène dans le *Julius exclusus (c. 1513)*.' In *Le Dialogue au temps de la Renaissance*, edited by Marie-Thérèse Jones-Davies, 213–35. Paris: J. Touzot, 1984.

Marsh, David. *The Quattrocento Dialogue: Classical Tradition and Humanist Innovation*. Cambridge, MA: Harvard University Press, 1980.

Martines, Lauro. *Power and Imagination: City-States in Renaissance Italy*. New York: Knopf, 1979. Reprint, Baltimore: Johns Hopkins University Press, 1988.

– *The Social World of the Florentine Humanists 1390–1460*. Princeton: Princeton University Press, 1963.

Martz, Louis. *Milton: Poet of Exile*. New Haven: Yale University Press, 1980.

McCutcheon, Elizabeth. *My Dear Peter: The Ars Poetica and Hermeneutics for More's Utopia*. Angers: Moreanum, 1983.

- 'Thomas More, Raphael Hythlodaeus, and the Angel Raphael.' *Studies in English Literature 1500–1900* 9, no. 1 (1969): 21–38.

McCutcheon, R.R. 'Heresy and Dialogue: The Humanist Approach of Erasmus and More.' *Viator: Medieval and Renaissance Studies* 24 (1993): 357–84.

McGee, Eugene K. 'Cranmer and Nominalism.' *Harvard Theological Review* 57 (1964): 189–216.

McKinnon, Dana G. 'The Marginal Glosses in More's *Utopia*: The Character of the Commentator.' *Renaissance Papers* (1970): 11–19.

McLean, Andrew. 'Thomas More's *Utopia* as Dialogue and City Encomium.' In *Acta Conventus Neo-Latini Guelpherbytani*, edited by S.P. Revard, F. Radle, and M. Di Cesare, Binghamton, NY: Medieval and Renaissance Texts and Studies, 1988.

- 'Early Tudor Prose Dialogues: A Study in Literary Form.' PhD diss., University of North Carolina at Chapel Hill, 1971.

McLelland, Nicola. 'Albertus (1573) and Ölinger(1574): Creating the First Grammars of German.' *Historiographica Linguistica* 28 (2001): 7–38.

Mecke, Jochen. 'Dialogue in Narration (the Narrative Principle).' In *The Interpretation of Dialogue*, edited by Tullio Maranhao, 195–215. Chicago: University of Chicago Press, 1990.

Meerhoff, Kees. *Rhétorique et poétique au XVIe siècle en France: Du Bellay, Ramus et les autres*. Leiden: E.J. Brill, 1986.

Meier, J. 'Oelingerania.' *Beiträge zur Geschichte der deutschen Sprache und Literatur* 20 (1894): 567–71.

Merrill, Elizabeth. *The Dialogue in English Literature*. Yale Studies in English, vol. 42. New Haven: Yale University Press, 1911. Reprint, New York: Burt Franklin, 1970.

Michel, Alain. 'L'influence du dialogue cicéronien sur la tradition philosophique et littéraire.' In *Le Dialogue au temps de la Renaissance*, edited by Marie-Thérèse Jones-Davies, 9–24. Paris: J. Touzot, 1984.

Miles, Leland. Introduction to *A Dialogue of Comfort against Tribulation*, by Thomas More. Bloomington: Indiana University Press, 1965.

Miller, David M. 'From Delusion to Illumination.' *PMLA* 86, no. 1 (1971): 33–9.

Mukarovsky, Jan. *The Word and Verbal Art*. Translated and edited by John Burbank and Peter Steiner. New Haven: Yale University Press, 1977.

Müller, Johannes. *Quellenschriften und Geschichte des deutschsprachlichen Unterrichts bis zur Mitte des 16. Jahrhunderts*. Gotha. 1882. Reprint, with an introduction by Monika Rössing-Hager, Hildesheim: Olms, 1969.

Mullinger, J.B. *The University of Cambridge: From the Royal Injunctions of 1535 to the Accession of Charles the First*. 1884. Reprint, New York: Johnson Reprint, 1969.

Murphy, J.J. *Rhetoric in the Middle Ages: A History of Rhetorical Theory from Saint Augustine to the Renaissance*. Berkeley and Los Angeles: University of California Press, 1978.

Niemann, Gottfried. *Die Dialogliteratur der Reformationszeit nach ihrer Entstehung und Entwicklung*. Leipzig: C. Voigtländes, 1905.

O'Brien, Brian. 'J.H. Hexter and the Text of *Utopia*: A Reappraisal.' *Moreana* 29, no. 110 (June 1992): 19–32.

Olin, John C. 'Erasmus's *Adagia* and More's *Utopia*.' In *Erasmus, Utopia, and the Jesuits: Essays on the Outreach of Humanism*, New York: Fordham University Press, 1994.

Ong, Walter. 'Hobbes's and Talon's Ramist Rhetoric in English.' *Transactions of the Cambridge Bibliographical Society* 1, no. 3 (1951): 260–9.

– *Orality and Literacy: The Technologizing of the Word*. London: Routledge, 1982.

– *Ramus: Method, and the Decay of Dialogue*. Cambridge, MA: Harvard University Press, 1958.

Ordine, Nuccio. '*Le Sei giornate*: struttura del diagolo e parodia della trattatistica sul comportamento.' In *Pietro Aretino nel Cinquecentenario della nascita*, edited by E. Malato et al., 673–716.

Osmond, Rosalie. *Mutual Accusation*. Toronto: University of Toronto Press, 1990.

Ossola, Carlo. *Dal* Cortegiano *all'*Uomo di mondo: *Storia di un libro e di un modello sociale*. Turin: Einaudi, 1980.

Palmer, Daryl. 'Histories of Violence and the Writer's Hand: Violence and Text in Foxe's *Acts and Monuments*.' In *Reading and Writing in Shakespeare*, edited by David M. Bergeron, 82–115. Newark: University of Delaware Press, 1996.

Parker, William Riley. *Milton: A Biography*. 2 vols. Edited by Gordon Campbell. Oxford: Clarendon, 1996.

Paternoster, Annick. *Aptum: Retorica ed ermeneutica nel dialogo rinascimentale del primo Cinquecento*. Rome: Bulzoni, 1998.

Patrizi, Giorgio. 'Il libro del cortegiano e la trattatistica sul comportamento.' In vol. 3, bk. 2 of *Letteratura italiana*, edited by A. Asor Rosa, 855–90. Turin: Einaudi, 1984.

Patterson, Annabel. '"Forc'd fingers": Milton's Early Poems and Ideological Constraint.' In *The Muses Common-Weale*, edited by Claude J. Summers and Ted-Larry Pebworth, 9–22. Columbia: University of Missouri Press, 1988.

Pausch, Oskar. *Das Älteste Italienisch-Deutsche Sprachbuch. Eine Überlieferung aus dem Jahre 1424. Nach Georg von Nürnberg*. Vienna. Döhlau, 1972.

Penzl, Herbert. 'How German Was Taught in the 9th and 11th Centuries.' *The German Quarterly* 57 (1984): 392–401.

Pettegree, Andrew. 'Haemstede and Foxe.' In *John Foxe and the English Reformation*, edited by David M. Loades, 278–94. Aldershot: Scolar Press, 1997.

Pevere, Fulvio. '"Vita è il non andare in corte": il *Ragionamento delle corti* di Pietro Aretino.' *Critica letteraria* 20, Fasc. 2, no. 75 (1992): 218–40.

Phelan, Herbert J. 'What Is the Persona Doing in "L'Allegro" and "Il Penseroso"?' *Milton Studies* 22 (1987): 3–20.

Pigman III, G.W. 'Versions of Imitation in the Renaissance.' *Renaissance Quarterly* 33 (1980): 1–32.

Pineas, Rainer. *Thomas More and Tudor Polemics*. Bloomington: Indiana University Press, 1968.

– 'Thomas More's Use of the Dialogue Form as a Weapon of Religious Controversy.' *Studies in the Renaissance* 7 (1960): 193–206.

– 'William Turner's Use of the Dialogue Form as a Weapon of Religious Controversy.' *Journal of the Rocky Mountain Medieval-Renaissance Association* (January 1983): 97–105.

Polenz, Peter von. *Deutsche Sprachgeschichte vom Spätmittelalter bis zur Gegenwart*. Bd. II. 17. und 18. Jahrhundert. Berlin: Walter de Gruyter, 1994.

Preto-Rodas, Richard A. *Francisco Rodrigues Lobo: Dialogue and Courtly Lore in Renaissance Portugal*. Chapel Hill: University of North Carolina Press, 1971.

Prévost, Albert. 'Avant-propos.' In *L'Utopie de Thomas More*, edited by André Prévost, 64–8. Paris: Nouvelles éditions Mame, 1978.

Price, A.W. *Love and Friendship in Plato and Aristotle*. Oxford: Oxford University Press, 1989.

Prince, Frank T. *The Italian Element in Milton's Verse*. 1954. Oxford: Clarendon, 1962.

Puff, Helmut. '*Von dem schlüssel aller Künsten/ nemblich der Grammatica.*' *Deutsch im lateinischen Grammatikunterricht 1480–1560*. Tübingen: Francke, 1995.

Pugliese, Olga Zorzi. *Il discorso labirintico del dialogo rinascimentale*. Rome: Bulzoni, 1995.

– 'L'evoluzione della struttura dialogica nel *Libro del cortegiano*.' In *Il sapere delle parole: Studi sul dialogo latino e italiano del Rinascimento*, edited by Walter Geerts et al., 59–64. Rome: Bulzoni, 2001.

– 'Liminality and Ritual in the Renaissance Attitude Toward Antiquity.' *Altro Polo* 6 (1984): 15–22.

– 'Love and Death and Their Function as Frames in *The Book of the Courtier*.' In *Love and Death in the Renaissance*, edited by Kenneth R. Bartlett et al., 135–44. Ottawa: Dovehouse Editions, 1991.

– 'Sperone Speroni and the Labyrinthine Discourse of Renaissance Dialogue.' In *Imagining Culture: Essays in Early Modern History and Literature*, edited by Jonathan Hart, 57–72, 200–1. New York: Garland, 1996.

Purpus, Eugene R. 'The "Plain, Easy, and Familiar Way": The Dialogue in English Literature, 1660–1725.' *ELH* 17 (1950): 47–58.

Puterbaugh, Joseph. '"Sweet Conversation": Argument and Experiment in the Dialogue as a Literary Form in Sixteenth-Century England.' PhD diss., Claremont Graduate University, 1999.

– '"Your selfe be judge and answer yourselfe": The Formation of Protestant Identity in *A Conference betwixt a Mother a Devout Recusant and her Sonne a zealous Protestant.*' *Sixteenth Century Journal* 31, no. 2 (2000): 419–31.

Questier, Michael. *Conversion, Politics, and Religion in England, 1580–1625.* Cambridge: Cambridge University Press, 1996.

Quillen, Carol. *Rereading the Renaissance.* Ann Arbor: University of Michigan Press, 1998.

Quint, David. 'Humanism and Modernity: A Reconsideration of Bruni's Dialogues.' *Renaissance Quarterly* 38 (1985): 423–45.

Quondam, Amedeo. 'Nel giardino del Marcolini: Un editore veneziano tra Aretino e Doni.' *Giornale storico della letteratura italiana* 157 (1980): 65–83.

– 'On the Genesis of *The Book of the Courtier*,' translated by Paul Bucklin, in Baldesar Castiglione, *The Book of the Courtier*, edited by Daniel Javitch, 283–95. New York: W.W. Norton & Company, 2002.

– *'Questo povero Cortegiano': Castiglione, il libro, la storia.* Rome: Bulzoni, 2000.

Rebhorn, Wayne. *Courtly Performances: Masking and Festivity in Castiglione's Book of the Courtier.* Detroit: Wayne State University Press, 1978.

Reik, Miriam. *The Golden Lands of Thomas Hobbes.* Detroit: Wayne State University Press, 1977.

Renaudet, Augustin. *Préréforme et humanisme à Paris pendant les premières guerres d'Italie (1494–1517).* Paris: Librairie d'Argences, 1953.

Revard, Stella P. *Milton and the Tangles of Neaera's Hair.* Columbia: University of Missouri Press, 1997.

Reynolds, Ernest E. *Thomas More and Erasmus.* London: Burns and Oates, 1965.

Rhu, Lawrence. *The Genesis of Tasso's Narrative Theory.* Detroit: Wayne State University Press, 1993.

Rigolot, François. 'L'amitié intertextuelle: Etienne de la Boétie et Marie de Gournay.' In *L'Esprit et la Lettre: Mélanges offerts à Jules Brody*, edited by Louis van Delft, 57–66. Tübingen: Narr, 1991.

– 'The *Heptameron* and the Magdalen Controversy: Dialogue and Humanist Hermeneutics.' In *Critical Tales: New Studies of the 'Heptameron' and Early Modern Culture*, edited by John D. Lyons and Mary B. McKinley, 218–31. Philadelphia: University of Pennsylvania Press, 1993.

– 'The Rhetoric of Presence: Art, Literature, and Illusion.' In vol. 3 of *The Cambridge History of Literary Criticism*, edited by Glyn P. Norton, 161–7. Cambridge: Cambridge University Press, 1999.

Rigolot, François, et al., eds. 'The Renaissance Crisis of Exemplarity.' *Journal of the History of Ideas* 59, no. 4 (October 1998).

Rogers, G.A.J. and Tom Sorrell, eds. *Hobbes and Arstory*. London: Routledge, 2000.

Roskill, Mark W. *Dolce's* Aretino *and Venetian Art Theory of the Cinquecento*. CAA Monograph 15. New York: New York University Press, 1968. Reprint, Toronto: University of Toronto Press, 2000.

Rossebastiano Bart, Alda, ed. *Vocabulari Veneto-Tedeschi del secolo XV*. Turin: L'artistica Savigliano, 1983.

Sabbadini, Remigio. *La Gita di Francesco Barbaro a Firenze nel 1415*. Trieste: G. Caprin, 1910.

Saccone, Giuseppe Mario. 'The Ambiguous Relation between Hobbes' Rhetorical Appeal to English History and His Deductive Method in *A Dialogue*.' *History of European Ideas* 24, no. 1 (1998): 1–17.

Samuel, Irene. 'The Brood of Folly.' *Notes and Queries* 203 (1958): 430–1.

Schiff, Mario. *La fille d'alliance de Montaigne: Marie de Gournay*. 1910. Reprint Geneva: Slatkine, 1978.

Schoeck, R.J. '"A Nursery of Correct and Useful Institutions": On Reading More's *Utopia* as Dialogue.' *Moreana* 22 (1969): 19–32. Reprinted in *Essential Articles for the Study of Thomas More*, edited by R.S. Sylvester and G.P. Marc'hadour, 281–9. Hamden, CT: Archon, 1977.

– 'Telling More from Erasmus: An *Essai* in Renaissance Humanism.' *Moreana* 23, no. 91–2 (1986): 11–19.

Schuhmann, Karl. *Hobbes: une chronique. Cheminement de sa vie et de sa pensée*. Paris: Vrin, 1998.

Scollon, Ron, and Suzanne Wong Scollon. *Intercultural Communication: A Discourse Approach*. Oxford: Blackwell, 1995.

Shannon, Laurie. *Sovereign Amity: Figures of Friendship in Shakespearean Contexts*. Chicago: University of Chicago Press, 2001.

Shapiro, Marianne. 'Mirror and Portrait: The Structure of *Il libro del Cortegiano*.' *Journal of Medieval and Renaissance Studies* 5 (1975): 37–61.

Shoaf, R.A. *Milton, Poet of Duality: A Study of Semiosis in the Poetry and the Prose*. New Haven: Yale University Press, 1985.

Shuger, Deborah. 'Irishmen, Aristocrats, and Other White Barbarians.' *Renaissance Quarterly* 50, no. 2 (1997): 494–525.

Siegle, Robert. *The Politics of Reflexivity*. Baltimore: Johns Hopkins University Press, 1986.

Skinner, Quentin. *Reason and Rhetoric in the Philosophy of Hobbes*. Cambridge: Cambridge University Press, 1996.

– 'Sir Thomas More's *Utopia* and the Language of Renaissance Humanism.' In

The Languages of Political Theory in Early Modern Europe, edited by Anthony Pagden, 123–57. Cambridge: Cambridge University Press, 1987.

Slights, Camille Wells. 'Notaries, Sponges and Looking-Glasses: Conscience in Early Modern England.' *English Literary Renaissance* 28, no. 2 (1998): 231–46.

Sloterdijk, Peter. 'Postface à l'édition française.' In *Règles pour le parc humain.* Paris: Éditions Mille et une nuits, 2000.

– *Regeln für den Menschenpark: Ein Antwortschreiben zum Brief über den Humanismus.* Frankfurt: Suhrkamp, 1999.

Smith, Charles George. *Spenser's Theory of Friendship.* Baltimore: Johns Hopkins University Press, 1935.

Smith, Christine. *Architecture in the Culture of Early Humanism: Ethics, Aesthetics, and Eloquence 1400–1470.* Oxford: Oxford University Press, 1992.

Snyder, Jon R. *Writing the Scene of Speaking: Theories of Dialogue in the Late Italian Renaissance.* Stanford: Stanford University Press, 1989.

Solerti, Angelo. *Vita di Torquato Tasso.* 3 vols. Turin: Loescher, 1895.

Sorell, Tom. *Hobbes.* London: Routledge, 1986.

Starobinski, Jean. *Montaigne en mouvement.* Paris: Gallimard, 1983.

Stern-Gillet, Suzanne. *Aristotle's Philosophy of Friendship.* Albany: State University of New York Press, 1995.

Stevens, Adrian. 'Heteroglossia.' In *Chrétien de Troyes and the German Middle Ages,* edited by Martin Jones and Roy Wisbey, 241–55. London: Institute of Germanic Studies, 1993.

Stierle, Karlheinz. 'L'Histoire comme exemple, l'exemple comme histoire.' *Poétique* 10 (1972): 176–98.

Stortoni, Laura Anna, and Mary Prentice Lillie, eds. *Women Poets of the Italian Renaissance: Courtly Ladies and Courtesans.* New York: Italica, 1997.

Strosetzki, Christoph. *Rhétorique de la conversation: Sa dimension littéraire et linguistique dans la société française du XVIIe siècle.* Papers on French Seventeenth Century Literature. Paris: Biblio 17, 1984.

Sturm-Maddox, Sara. *Petrarch's Laurels.* University Park: Pennsylvania State University Press, 1992.

Swaim, Kathleen M. '"Myself a true poem."' *Milton Studies* 38 (2000): 66–95.

Swain, Elisabeth Ward. '"My excellent and most singular lord": Marriage in a Noble Family of Fifteenth-Century Italy.' *Journal of Medieval and Renaissance Studies* 16 (1986): 171–95.

Tétel, Marcel. *Marguerite de Navarre's Heptaméron: Themes, Language, and Structure.* Durham, NC: Duke University Press, 1973.

Tétel, Marcel, ed. *Montaigne et Marie de Gournay, actes du colloque international de Duke (31 mars – 1er avril 1995).* Paris: Champion, 1997.

Todorov, Tzvetan. *Les genres du discours.* Paris: Seuil, 1978.

Trexler, Richard A. *Public Life in Renaissance Florence*. Ithaca: Cornell University Press, 1980.

Tribble, Evelyn. 'The Peopled Page: Polemic, Confutation, and Foxe's Book of Martyrs.' In *The Iconic Page in Manuscript, Print, and Digital Culture*, edited by George Bornstein and Theresa Tinkle, 109–23. Ann Arbor: University of Michigan Press, 1981.

Vallée, Jean-François. 'Les voix imprimées de l'humanisme: Un dialogue entre *L'Utopie* et le *Cymbalum mundi*.' PhD diss., Université de Montréal, 2000.

Van den Toorn, Martin C., W.J.J. Pijnenburg, J.A. van Leuvensteijn, and J.M. Van der Horst, eds. *Geschiedenis van de nederlandse taal*. Amsterdam: Amsterdam University Press, 1997.

Van der Wal, Marijke. *Geschiedenis van het Nederlands*. Utrecht: Het Spectrum, 1992.

Venesoen, Constant. *Études sur la littérature féminine au XVIIe siècle*. Birmingham, AL: Summa, 1990.

Vianello, Valerio. *Il 'giardino' delle parole: Itinerari di scrittura e modelli letterari nel dialogo cinquecentesco*. Rome: Jouvence, 1993.

Vickers, Brian. *In Defence of Rhetoric*. Oxford: Oxford University Press, 1988.

Von Polenz, Peter. *Deutsche Sprachgeschichte von Spätmittelatter bis zur Gegenwart*. Bd. II. 17. und 18. Jahrhundert. Berlin: Walter de Gruyter, 1994.

Vulcan, Ruxandra Irina. *Savoir et rhétorique dans les dialogues français entre 1515 et 1550*. Ars Rhetorica 7, Hamburg: LIT, 1996.

Walzer, Michael. 'A Critique of Philosophical Conversation.' *The Philosophical Forum* 21, no. 1–2 (fall–winter 1989–90): 179–92.

Warner, J. Christopher. *Henry VIII's Divorce: Literature and the Politics of the Printing Press*. Woodbridge, Suffolk: Boydell, 1998.

Warren, Finton B. *Vasco de Quiroga and His Pueblo-Hospitals of Santa Fe*. Washington, DC: Academy of American Franciscan History, 1963.

Waswo, Richard. *Language and Meaning in the Renaissance*. Princeton: Princeton University Press, 1987.

Watkins, Renée Neu, ed. *Humanism and Liberty: Writings on Freedom from XVth-Century Florence*. Columbia: University of South Carolina Press, 1978.

Watts, Richard. 'Learning English through Dialogues in the 16th Century.' In *Historical Dialogue Analysis*, edited by Andreas H. Jucker, Gerd Fritz, and Franz Lebsanft, 215–41. Amsterdam: Benjamins, 1999.

Wegemer, Gerard. 'Ciceronian Humanism in More's *Utopia*.' *Moreana* 27, no. 104 (1990): 5–26.

– 'The Rhetoric of Opposition in Thomas More's *Utopia*: Giving Form to Competing Philosophies.' *Philosophy and Rhetoric* 23, no. 4 (1990): 288–306.

White, Helen. *Tudor Books of Saints and Martyrs*. Madison: University of Wisconsin Press, 1963.

White, Thomas I. 'Legend and Reality: The Friendship between More and Erasmus.' In *Supplementum Festivum: Studies in Honor of Paul Oskar Kristeller*, edited by J. Hankins, J. Monfasani, and F. Purnell Jr., 489–504. Binghamton, NY: Medieval and Renaissance Texts and Studies, 1987.

Wilson, Kenneth J. *Incomplete Fictions: The Formation of English Renaissance Dialogue*. Washington, DC: Catholic University of America Press, 1985.

Winn, Colette. *The Dialogue in Early Modern France, 1547–1630: Art and Argument*. Washington, DC: Catholic University of America Press, 1993.

Wooden, Warren W. *John Foxe*. Boston: Twayne, 1983.

Woodward, William Harrison. *Vittorino da Feltre and Other Humanist Educators*. 1897. Reprint, New York: Bureau of Publications, Teachers College, Columbia University, 1963.

Woolf, D.R. 'The Rhetoric of Martyrdom: Generic Contradiction and Narrative Strategy in John Foxe's *Acts and Monuments*.' In *The Rhetoric of Life-Writing in Early Modern Europe*, edited by Thomas Mayer and D.R. Woolf, 243–82. Ann Arbor: University of Michigan Press, 1995.

Zaercher, Véronique. *Le Dialogue rabelaisien: Le* Tiers livre *exemplaire*. Geneva: Droz, 2000.

Zappen, James P. 'Rhetoric in Thomas Hobbes's *Leviathan*: Pathos versus Ethos and Logos.' *Rhetorica* 1 (1983): 65–92.

Zarka, Yves Charles. *La décision métaphysique de Hobbes*. Paris: Vrin, 1998.

– *Hobbes et la pensée politique moderne*. Paris: Presses universitaires de France, 1995.

Zavala, Silvio. *Thomas More in New Spain: A Utopian Adventure of the Renaissance*. London: The Hispanic and Luso-Brazilian Councils, 1955.

List of Contributors

Luc Borot studied at the École Normale Supérieure. He is currently professor of early modern British civilization in the English Department of Université Paul-Valéry, Montpellier (France). He is a member of the Institut de Recherches sur la Renaissance, l'Âge Classique et les Lumières, supported by the Centre national de la recherche scientifique. His research focuses on Hobbes, on the first English revolution, and on various aspects of British seventeenth-century culture.

Robert Buranello has published articles on Leonardo Bruni, Sperone Speroni, and the literature of Italian immigration, and is coeditor of *Pietro Aretino e la cultura del Rinascimento*, Vol. 2 (1995). He is assistant professor of Italian at the College of Staten Island, City University of New York.

Nina Chordas earned her PhD in English at the University of Oregon and is currently assistant professor of English at the University of Alaska Southeast in Juneau. Her research focus includes Renaissance and Soviet utopias, as well as Renaissance humanism in Eastern Europe.

Carole Collier Frick is an associate professor in the Department of Historical Studies at Southern Illinois University, Edwardsville. Her monograph *Dressing Renaissance Florence. Families, Fortunes and Fine Clothing* was published in 2002. She has also written on gender issues in fifteenth-century art, the family, and the urban marketplace.

Dorothea Heitsch is associate professor of French at Shippensburg

University in Pennsylvania. She has published essays on Montaigne, Montaigne and Nietzsche, and Marie de Gournay. She is the author of *Practising Reform in Montaigne's* Essais (2000).

W. Scott Howard teaches courses on Shakespeare, Milton, poetics, and historiography at the University of Denver, where he is associate professor of English. He is currently completing *John Milton's Divorce Tracts: Texts and Contexts*, a coedited collection of Milton's complete writings on divorce.

Eva Kushner is Professor Emerita of French and Comparative Literature at the University of Toronto. Her most recent books are *The Living Prism: Itineraries in Comparative Literature* (2001) and *Pontus de Tyard et son oeuvre poétique* (2001). She directs the critical edition of the complete works of Pontus de Tyard being published by Champion and the Renaissance subseries of the Comparative History of Literatures in European Languages published by Benjamins.

Nicola McLelland is a lecturer in German at Trinity College, Dublin. She wrote her dissertation on Ulrich von Zatzikohoven's *Lanzelet*. Her research interest is the history of linguistic reflection in early modern Germany; she is currently focusing on Justus-Georg Schottelius.

Olga Zorzi Pugliese is professor of Italian and Renaissance Studies at the University of Toronto, where she chaired the Department of Italian Studies from 1997 to 2002. Her book-length publications on the Renaissance include Italian and English editions of two treatises by Lorenzo Valla, a study on Renaissance dialogue, and a coedited volume of proceedings. She is currently working on the manuscripts of Castiglione's *Il libro del cortegiano*.

Joseph Puterbaugh, adjunct instructor of English Language and Literature at Whittier College, is the author of several articles on the dialogue as a literary form in sixteenth-century England. He also teaches screenwriting and film analysis at Columbia College, Hollywood.

François Rigolot, Meredith Howland Pyne Professor of French Literature, chairs Renaissance Studies at Princeton. His major books include *Les Langages de Rabelais* (1972, new edition, 1996), *Poétique et onomastique* (1977), *Le Texte de la Renaissance* (1983), *Les Métamorphoses de Mon-*

taigne (1988), *Louise Labé Lyonnaise ou la Renaissance au féminin* (1997), *L'Erreur de la Renaissance* (2002), and *Poésie et Renaissance* (2003). He is also the editor of Louise Labé's complete works, and Montaigne's *Journal de voyage*. In 2002 the French government made him a Knight of the Ordre National du Mérite.

Jean-François Vallée is professor of literature and communication at the Collège de Maisonneuve and is currently a postdoctoral fellow at the Université de Montréal. He has published on dialogue, utopia, Thomas More, and Bonaventure Des Périers. He is now editing a collection of essays on 'prudence' in sixteenth- and seventeenth-century France.

J. Christopher Warner is associate professor of English at Le Moyne College. He has published numerous studies in the fields of English Renaissance literature and printing history, including essays on the Thomas More circle, Edmund Spenser, and Lady Mary Wroth. He is also the author of the forthcoming book *The Augustinian Epic: Petrarch to Milton*.

Index Nominum

Abraxa, 34
Abstemius, 239
Acarie, Barbe Jeanne Avrillot (Marie de l'Incarnation), 123
Accolti, Bernardo (Unico Aretino), 9, 87
Adolph, 6
Alberti, Leon Battista, x, xii, 194, 196, 204n14
Allen, Edmund, 143
Allen, P.S., 6
Allen, Peter R., 52
Alphonsus, 142
Altman, Joel B., 75n1
Ames, Michael, 34
Andreae, Johann Valentin, xv, 37
Andreini, Isabella, 197
Anne of Austria, 117, 118
Annibale, 121
Anthony (*Dialogue of Comfort against Tribulation*), 65, 234
Anthony (*Shipwreck*), 6
Antonia, 98, 99
Aquinas, Thomas, 195
Aretino, Pietro, x, xvi, 95–100, 102, 105
Ariosto, Alfonso, 8

Aristippus, 65–6
Aristotle, 4, 29, 44, 88, 139, 160–2, 176, 177, 181, 236
Armenia, 200
Arthur, Prince, 68
Ascham, Roger, xii, 65–6, 163
Astell, Ann, 51
Augustine, St, 3, 99, 108n20, 197, 230–1
Averell, William, 70

Babb, Lawrence, 158
Bacon, Francis, xv, 17, 35, 36, 179, 185
Bakhtin, Mikhail, xi, xvi, 17, 23n65, 107n8, 150, 155n55, 173n36, 221n10
Balthesar the Barber, 70
Barbaro, Francesco, xviii, xix, 193–5, 197–201
Barberino, Francesco da, 204n14
Barker, Francis, 36
Baron, Hans, 4
Bartholomew, 212, 214–15
Becon, Thomas, 161
Bembo, Pietro, x, 9, 84–5, 98–9, 103–4
Bennion the Button-maker, 70
Bénouis, Mustapha Kemal, x, xii
Bensalemites, 35

Bernardino of Siena, San, 194–5
Berthelet, Thomas, 68
Betteridge, Tom, 155n51
Bevington, David M., 40n14
Bibbiena, Bernardo, 81, 87, 89
Boadiglia, 89
Boccaccio, x, 8, 10–12, 86
Boethius, 230, 234
Bolotin, David, 57n7
Bonner, Bishop Edmund, 149
Bowen, Peter, 158, 167
Bradford, John, 141–2, 148–9
Bradstreet, Anne, 161
Bramhall, Bishop John, 181–2
Brand, Charles P., 172n19
Breen, John M., 75n5
Breitenberg, Mark, 155n52
Breva-Claramonte, Manuel, 217
Briçonnet, Guillaume, 232–3
Brown, Merle, E., 172n17
Bruce, Donald, 75n5
Bruni, Leonardo, x, xii, xiv, 3–4, 6, 9, 196
Bruno, Giordano, 178
Buber, Martin, xi
Buckingham, George Villiers, first duke of, 119
Budé, Guillaume, x, 46, 52
Bücklin, Konrad, 210
Burke, Peter, xxiin26, 8–9, 18n12, 75n5, 207–9
Burton, Robert, 169
Busleyden, Jerome, 46, 53

Campanella, Tommaso, x, xv, 27, 34
Campbell, Fiona, 221n6
Canale, Paolo, 92n14
Canossa, Ludovico, 82
Cardinal Morton, 46–7, 63
Carrive, Lucien, 179

Carrive, Paulette, 179
Cartwright, Nicholas, 146
Castagneto, countess of, 89
Castelvetro, Lodovico, xii
Castiglione, Baldassare, x, xiv, xvi, 5, 7–11, 30, 79–89, 97–8, 103–4, 115, 131n54, 197
Catarina, 238–9
Catherine of Aragon, xv, 67–8
Cavalcanti, Ginevra, xix, 193–4, 201, 202n1
Cavalcanti, Giovanni, 193
Cavendish, Margaret, xv, 37, 163, 185
Cecil, William, Baron Burghley, 69
Cervantes, Miguel de, x, 75n2
Charles II, king of England, 64, 71–2, 182
Charlier, Yvonne, 57nn5, 13
Charlotte, 232
Christopher Conscience, 140
Cian, Vittorio, 80, 86
Cicero, ix, xii, 4, 30, 42–4, 54, 63, 74, 86, 100, 108n20, 120, 176, 182
Coccio, Francesco, 100–5
Coclaeus, Johannes, 211
Coke, Sir Edward, 179–80
Columbus, Christopher, 32
Comito, Terry, 97
Conti, princesse de, 123
Copernicus, Nicolas, 185
Cordier, Maturin, 138
Costa, Dennis, 6
Cottrell, Robert, 232
Cox, Gerard, H., 158
Cox, Virginia, xi–xii, xxin9, 30, 35, 67, 106n3, 161, 172n17, 206
Craig, Hardin, 153n16
Cranmer, Thomas, 143, 145–8, 150
Crawford, Bartholomew V., 75n4
Cropsey, J., 179

Cyrus, king of Persia, 200

Dagoucin, 13
Daunce, Edward, 68
Day, John T., ix, 75n5
Deakins, Roger Lee, ix, 66, 75n4
Defaux, Gérard, 57nn5, 8
Della Casa, Giovanni, 86, 131n54
Demosthenes, 198–9
Demure, Catherine, 49
Descartes, René, xx, 229
Desmarais, 46, 53
Des Périers, Bonaventure, 75n2
Diodorus of Sicily, 182, 185
Dolce, Lodovico, 100–5
Dominici, Giovanni, 204n14
Donatus, xix, 207, 210
Driver, Alice, 143
Dryden, John, ix, 172n17
Du Bosc, Jacques, 116, 123–4
Duffy, Eamon, 151n1
Dupuy, brothers, 123

Edward VI, king of England, 145
Eliade, Mircea, 112n45
Elizabeth I, 37, 70
Elliott, Robert C., 49
Elyot, Thomas, xii, 65–6, 74, 163, 236
Erasmus, Desiderius, x, xiv, xx, 5–7,
    44–6, 51–4, 56, 138, 217, 234–40
Este, Ippolito, 85
Eubulus, 238–9
Euclid, xviii, 175–6
Eudoxus, 37–9, 65
Eulalius, 6
Euripides, 44, 176
Eutrapelus, 236–7

Fabulla, 236–7
Fallet, Gedeon, 209

Faret, Nicolas, 116–18
Fazio, 84
Ferreras, Jacqueline, ix
Ferroni, Giulio, 97
Ficino, Marsilio, x, 54
Finch, Casey, 158, 167
Fischer, Roemer, 209
Fish, Stanley, 154n39
Fisher, John, 13, 22n47
Floriani, Piero, 80
Fontana, Alessandro, 96
Fontenelle, Bernard de, 132n58
Forno, Carla, xxiin30, 97
Foucault, Michel, xx, 229, 235
Fournel, Jean-Louis, 96
Fowler, Elizabeth, 31
Foxe, John, xvii, 137–9, 141–3, 146–51
Fraisse, Jean-Claude, 57n7
Francis, 3
Freeman, Thomas, 154n32, 155n53
Fregoso, Federico, 82
Fregoso, Ottaviano, 9, 81–2, 85, 87,
    90
Froben, John, 52
Fumaroli, Marc, 120, 123

Gabriel, 237–9
Gadamer, Hans-Georg, xi
Galilei, Galileo, xviii, 175, 178
Gardiner, Bishop Stephen, 145–6
Geldenhauer, Gerard, 53
Gellius, Aulus, 44
Genoese, 35
Gewerstock, Olga, xxiin21, 221n5
Ghinassi, Ghino, 80, 82, 85
Gibbon, Charles, 69
Giles, Peter, 45–7, 49–53, 55
Girardi, Raffaele, xxiin30
Giustiniani, Giovanni, 100, 102–5
Gloucester, bishop of, 145

Glyn, 147
Gnatho, 65
Godard, Anne, xiii, 178, 182, 186
Godzich, Wlad, 39n11
Goldsmith, Elizabeth, 132n59
Goldsmith, M.M., 183
Gómez, Jesús, x
Gonzaga, Cesare, 81
Gonzaga, Elisabetta, 86, 197
Gournay, Marie de, xvi, xvii, 113–14,
    116–17, 120, 122–8
Graffigny, Françoise de, 127
Grapheus, 53
Green, Ian, 151n1
Greenblatt, xx, 196, 229
Greene, Roland, 31, 40n16
Greene, Thomas, 139
Grenaille, François de, 116, 123–4
Guazzo, Stefano, 115, 120–1
Guellouz, Suzanne, xii
Guidi, José, 80, 86
Gwyn, Nell, 64, 72–3

Hadfield, Andrew D., 75n5
Haller, William, 143, 146
Harpocrates, 65
Harrington, James, 74
Harsdörffer, Georg Philipp, 208
Held, Felix E., 41n26
Henri de Guise, 15
Henri de Navarre, Henri IV of
    France, 15, 122
Henry VIII, king of England, xv, 67–
    8, 74, 234
Hereford, Charles, 151n1
Hexter, J.H., 45, 49
Heywood, John, 161
Hieromnime, 240
Hircan, 12–13
Hirzel, Rudolf, xxin2, 75n4

Hobbes, Thomas, x, xviii, 17, 175–86
Holbein, Hans, 53
Holstun, James, 31, 34
Horace, 239
Hospitaler, 35
Huizinga, Johan, 42, 49
Hume, David, 185
Hunter, William, xvii, 149–50,
    155n47
Hutten, Ulrich von, x, 58n18, 207
Hyatte, Reginald, 57n5
Hythloday, Raphael, 33, 45–55, 63–4,
    72

Irenius, 37–9, 65
Iser, Wolfgang, 132n60

Jacques, Francis, xi
James Stuart, duke of York, 71–2
Jardine, Lisa, 51, 53–4
Jean Paul, 42
Jechova, Hana, xxin13
Jerome, St, 114
Johnson, Samuel, 165
Jones-Davies, M.T., xxiin24
Juliano, Magnifico, 9
Jupiter, 81
Justice Brown, 149

Kahler, Erich, 17, 18n13
Kahn, Victoria, 6
Kampe, Jürgen, 221n6
Kasspar, 218
Kendall, Ritchie, 154n41
Kepler, Johann, 185
Kéroualle, Louise de, duchess of
    Portsmouth, 64, 72
Kinney, Arthur, 75n1
Kittay, Jeffrey, 39n11
Klatowsky, Ondrej, 206, 217–19

Kristeller, P.O., 28
Kristeva, Julia, xi
Kushner, Eva, ix, xi, 75n4

La Boétie, Etienne de, 13, 114, 127
La Mothe Le Vayer, François de, 114
Langer, Ullrich, 20n28
La Rocca, Guido, 81–2, 90
Latimer, Hugh, 145–8
Lattantio, 71
Laura, 201
Lefèvre d'Etaples, Jacques, 13, 22n48
Leibniz, Gottfried Wilhelm, 185
Lepschy, Giulio, 221n12
L'Estrange, Roger, 72–3
Leushuis, Reinier, xxiin32
Levao, Ronald, 28, 32
Levy, Albert William, 96, 107n9
Lewis, C.S., 58n21
Lipsius, Justus, 114, 127
Lobo, Francisco Rodrigues, 30
Louis XIII, king of France, 118, 122
Louis XIV, king of France, 125
Lucian, ix, 5, 8, 19n14, 43, 137, 207, 239
Lucifer, 72
Lupset, Thomas, 46, 52, 65
Luynes, Albert de, 119

MacCullough, Diarmaid, 155n45
Machiavelli, Niccolò, x
Mack, Peter, 217
Maley, Willie, 75n5
Mandrou, Robert, 54
Marcolini, Francesco, 99–105
Margolin, Jean-Claude, 19n21
Marguerite de Navarre, x, xiv, xx, 10–13, 230, 232–3
Marguerite de Valois, 123
Marsh, David, xii, xxin8, 196

Martial, 44
Marvell, Andrew, 163
Mary I, queen of England, 144, 148–9, 151
Maynard, François, 119
McCutcheon, Elizabeth, 52, 55, 75n1
McKinnon, Dana, 59n28
McLean, Andrew, 59n29, 75n4
Medici, Cosimo de', 193
Medici, Giuliano de', 84–5
Medici, Lorenzo de', 193, 194, 198, 201, 202n1
Médicis, Marie de, 119
Meerhoff, Kees, 16
Meister Iorg, 215, 220
Menander, 44
Mercury, 81
Merrill, Elizabeth, xxiin21, 75n4, 163
Michelangelo Buonarroti, 11
Miller, David, 165
Milton, John, xvii, xviii, 157–70
Moezentius, 238
Montaigne, Michel de, xiv, xvii, 3, 5, 13–16, 112, 114–15, 117, 122, 125–8
Montesquieu, Charles de Secondat, Baron de, 127
More, Thomas, x, xii, xiv–xv, xx, 27, 30–4, 42–55, 63–6, 74, 163, 233–4, 236
Motteville, Françoise Bertaut de, 119–20

Nanna, 99
Nash, Thomas, 70
Neville, Henry, 74
Newman, John, 141
Niccoli, Niccolò, 3, 5–6
Niemann, Gottfried, xxin12

O'Brien, Brian, 45

Oisille, 12–13
Olin, John C., 44
Ölinger, Albert, 219
Olivier, Jacques (Alexis Trousset), 114
Ong, Walter, 16, 173n29, 176
Ordine, Nuccio, 99
Orestes, 54
Origena, 236
Orléans, Gaston de, 119
Orthodoxos, 141
Osmond, Rosalie, 163
Ossola, Carlo, 9
Ovid, 88

Paleotto, Camillo, 84
Pallavicino, Gasparo, 9, 81, 85, 90
Pallavicino, Sforza, 172n17
Palmer, Julian, 143
Parlamente, 11–13
Parma, Fabrizio da, 101
Parson Neverbegood, 140
Pascal, Blaise, 120
Pasquier, Nicolas, 116, 230
Pasquil, 65, 70
Patrizi, Francesco, 4
Peletier du Mans, Jacques, 221n12
Peter, 214, 216
Petrarch, ix, xii, xiv, xx, 3, 5, 54, 161,
    196, 201, 214, 230–2
Petronius, 238
Pevere, Fulvio, 100, 103–4
Philippe IV, king of Spain, 119
Philocrematos, 141
Philodoxos, 141
Philpot, John, 144
Pia, Emilia, 86, 88
Piccardo, Pietro, 100–3
Pico della Mirandola, Giovanni, 196,
    203n13
Pineas, 75n5

Pippa, 99
Pirithous, 54
Plato, ix, xiv, 3, 27, 30–2, 43–4, 65–6,
    74, 82, 108n20, 115, 137, 178, 236
Plutarch, 44, 82, 236
Poggio Bracciolini, Gian Francesco,
    x, xii, 196
Pole, 65
Pontano, Giovanni, x, xii
Preto-Rodas, Richard A., xxin11, 30
Price, A.W., 57n7
pseudo-Dionysius, 233
Ptolemy Philadelphus, 231
Purpus, Eugene, 163, 172n17, 173n29
Puttenham, Richard, 173n28
Pylades, 54
Pythagoras, 44

Quint, David, 4
Quintilian, 14
Quiroga, Vasco de, 31, 33
Quondam, Amedeo, 80, 102, 111n39

Rabelais, François, x, 17
Rainolds, John, 69
Rambouillet, Catherine de Vivonne
    de Savelli, Marquise de, 123
Ramus, Petrus, 16, 211
Raphael, 11
Régnier, Mathurin, 119
Reynolds, E.E., 44
Richelieu, Armand du Plessis, Cardi-
    nal de, 119
Ridley, Nicholas, 145, 147–8, 150–1
Robinson, Ralph, 63
Rogers, John, 148
Rossi, Roberto de', 3, 193
Rottweil, Adam von, 215

Sabbadini, Remigio, 203n4

Sablé, Madeleine, Marquise de, 120
Sachs, Hans, 207
Sales, François de, 122, 123
Salutati, Coluccio, 3–4
Samuel, Irene, 158
Sanders, Laurence, 148
Satan, 239
Saturn, 89
Savage, Francis, 143
Schoeck, R.J., 40n14, 54, 75n1
Schurman, Anna Maria van, 114
Seneca, 231, 234
Seton, John, 150
Shaftesbury, Anthony Ashley Cooper, 71–2
Shakespeare, 139
Shannon, Laurie, 57n5
Shuger, Deborah, 41n30
Sidney, Sir Philip, 28–9
Sigonio, Carlo, xii
Silva, Don Michel de, 9–11
Skinner, Quentin, 40n14, 183–4
Sloterdijk, Peter, 42
Smith, Charles George, 57n5
Smith, Christine, 4
Smith, Robert, 141, 149
Snap-short, 64
Snyder, Jon, x, xii, 30, 172nn17, 19, 173n29
Socrates, 15, 32, 44
Solitaire, 240
Spenser, Edmund, x, xv, 27, 37–9, 65, 138, 163
Speroni, Sperone, x, xii, 8, 84, 92n18
Starkey, Thomas, 65
Stern-Gillet, Suzanne, 57n7
St German, Christopher, 76n12
Strosetzki, Christoph, 130n21

Taillemont, Claude de, 126–7

Tankerfield, George, 141
Tasso, Torquato, x, xii, 29, 161–2, 165, 195, 197
Terence, 44
Theseus, 54
Thompson, Craig R., 5
Thucydides, 176, 183
Tigranes, king of Armenia, 200
Timaeus, 44
Todorov, Tzvetan, xi
Tönnies, Ferdinand, 184
Toxophilus, 65
Tresham, William, 150
Trexler, Richard, 205n36
Tribble, Evelyn, 154n32
Turpilius, 51
Tutty, 64, 73
Tyard, Pontus de, xx, 240–1
Tyrell, Henry, 150

Udall, John, 69
Utopus, King, 34, 46

Valdés, Alfonso de, 71
Valdés, Juan de, 221n12
Valla, Lorenzo, x, xii, 4, 84, 196
Vaughan, Henry, 161
Vergil, 238
Veronese, Guarino, 198
Vianello, Valerio, xxiin30
Viau, Théophile de, 127
Vickers, Brian, 4
Villon, François, 161
Vincent, 65, 234
Vivès, Juan Luis, x, xix–xx, 216–18, 236, 239–40
Voloshinov, V.N., 107n8
Vulcan, Ruxandra Irina, xiii

Waldegrave, Robert, 140

Warren, Finton, 40n12
Waswo, Richard, 221n12
Wegemer, Gerard, 48
Weston, Hugh, 144, 146, 148, 150
White, Helen, 153n16
Wilson, Kenneth J., xii, 33, 66, 75nn4,
   5, 163, 172n17, 173n29
Wilson, Thomas, 138, 151n1
Winn, Colette, xii
Wooden, Warren, 138, 153n16,
   154n32

Woodman, Richard, 143

Xenophon, 200

Young, John, 147–8

Zaercher, Véronique, xxiin31
Zarka, Yves Charles, 177–8
Zavala, Silvio, 40n12

Index Rerum

Actes and Monuments, xvii, 138–9, 141–4, 146–7, 150–1
Additions to Doctor and Student, 68
'L'Allegro,' 157–70
Alphabet de l'imperfection et malice des femmes, 114
Aminta, 197
Antidotum, 84
Apologia dei dialogi, 8, 84
Apologie de Raimond Sebond, 114
Areopagitica, 163–4
Ars minor, xix, 207, 210–11, 216, 220
Asolani, 9, 98
Avis, 115

Behemoth, xviii, 175, 178–86
Berne, 143
Blazing World, xv, 37
Brief Discourse Dialoguewise, 68
Brief Discourse of the Spanish State, with a Dialogue annexed entitled Philobasilis, 68
Buechlein, in Böhmischer und Deutscher Sprach, 217

Cabinet satyrique, 119
Carte parlanti, 95, 106n3

Casuist Uncas'd in a Dialogue betwixt Richard and Baxter, 73
Catching of Leviathan, 182
Cena delle Ceneri, 178
Chiliades, 44
Christianopolis, xv, 37
Citt and Bumpkin in a Dialogue over a Pot of Ale, 73
City of the Sun, xv, 27, 34–5
Civile conversation, 121
Colloquia familiaria, 217
Colloquies, 5, 236, 239
Conference betwixt a Mother a Devout Recusant and Her Sonne a Zealous Protestant, 142
Confessions, 230
Coniugium impar, 237
conversation, 113–25
Convivium Religiosum, 6
Cortegiano, Il libro del, xiv, xvi, 7–13, 30, 79–81, 88, 90, 97–8, 103–4, 197
Cortigiana, 95 6

De avaritia, 196
'Debat de Villon et Son Cuer,' 161
Decameron, x, 8, 10–12, 86

Decameron Physiologicum, 175, 179, 184–6

De cive, 177

De consolatione philosophia, 230, 234

Defence of Poetry, 28–9

De institutione feminae christianae, 236

De l'art de conferer, 115, 128

De liberis educandis, 236

De librorum copia, 230–1

Deliquium: or, The Grievances of the Nation Discovered in a Dream, 72

De oratore, 4, 95

De pueris instituendis, xx, 234–5

De remediis fortuitorum, 234

De remediis utriusque fortune, 230

De re uxoria, xviii, 193, 196, 200, 202–3n3

De scriptorum fama, 231

Des trois commerces, 115

De tranquillitate animi, 231

dialogism, 17

Diálogo de las cosas acaecidas en Roma, 71

dialogue: catechistic, 210; and civic humanism, 4; and courtliness, xiii, xv, 95–112; and exemplarity, xiv, 3–24; and fiction, 30, 33; and friendship, xv, 42–62; and gender, xiii; and history, xvii, xviii, 157–74; and humanism, xiii; and imperialism, 27–41; interior, 193–205; inward turn of, xiv, 3–24; and literary history, xv, 63–76; and pedagogy, xiii, xix, 206–25; and philosophy, 30; and print culture, xiii, xvii, 79–94, 113–33; and religion, xiii, xvii, 137–56; and rhetoric, xiii, xv, xviii, 4, 175–89; and science, xiii, xvii; and subjectivity, xiii, xiv, xx, 229–41; Utopia, xiii, xv, 27–41

Dialogue at Oxford between a Tutor and a Gentleman, 73

Dialogue between a Knight and a Cleric, 68

'Dialogue Between an Oake, And A Man Cutting Him Downe,' 163

Dialogue between a Philosopher and a Student of the Common Laws of England, 175, 178–82, 185

Dialogue Between a Vertuous Gentleman and a Popish Priest, 140

'Dialogue Between Old England and New,' 161

Dialogue between Pole and Lupset, 65

Dialogue between the Duchess of Portsmouth and Madam Gwyn at Parting, 72

'Dialogue between the Soul and the Body,' 163

Dialogue between Two Porters, 73

Dialogue betwixt Sam the Ferriman, Will a Waterman, and Tom a Bargeman, 73

Dialogue concerning Heresies, 65–6

Dialogue concerning the Strife of Our Church, 140

Dialogue de l'ortografe e prononciacion françoese, 209

Dialogue en forme de vision nocturne, x, 232–3

Dialogue of Comfort against Tribulation, xx, 65–6, 233–4

Dialogue of the Common Laws, xviii

Dialogue philosophique dans la littérature française du seizième siècle, xii

Dialogue upon Dialogue: or, l'Estrange, No Papist nor Jesuit but the Dog Towzer, 72

Dialogue wherein is Plainly Laid Open, the Tyrannical Dealing of L. Bishops, 69
Dialogues, 239
Dialogues of Natural Religion, 185
Discorso della virtù feminile e donnesca, 195
Discours des champs faëz, 126
Discourse on the Art of the Dialogue, 29, 161
Discourse Upon Usury, 138
Doctor and Student, 68
Duodecim dialogi, 219

Egalité des hommes et des femmes, 117, 127
Elementa Philosophica, 178
Elements of Law, 177
Enchiridion militis christiani, 235
Encomium Moriae, 45
entretien, 131n54
Essais, xiv, 13–14, 113, 115, 125–6
'Evening-watch,' 161
exclusion crisis, xv, 71–2
exemplarity, 22n50
exemplum, 7, 19n24
Exercitium puerorum grammaticale per dietas distributum, 211, 222n24

Four Dialogues, 232
Frauenzimmer Gesprächspiele, 208

galantry, 120, 130n35
Gentilhomme, 116
Glass of the Truth, 68
Governor, The, 236
'Grief des dames' (The Ladies' Complaint), 113, 115, 128

Heptaméron, x, xiv, 10–13, 230, 233

Historia Ecclesiastica, 175
Historical Narration concerning Heresy and the Punishment thereof, 182
Hobbes et la pensée politique moderne, 177
L'honnête homme ou l'art de plaire à la cour, 116
L'honneste Femme, 116, 123
L'honneste Fille, 116, 123
L'honneste Garçon, 116, 123

Incomplete Fictions, 66
Institutes, 180
Introduction à la vie dévote, 122
in utramque partem, 4, 6, 13, 24n67, 63

Laelius (De amicitia), 43
Lettres d'une Péruvienne, 127
Lettres persanes, 127
Leviathan, xviii, 175, 177–8, 180, 182, 184–6
Libri della famiglia, 194, 196
Linguae latinae exercitatio, 216–17
locus amoenus, 99
Lucidarius, 207
Lysis (On Friendship), 43

Martin Marprelate controversy, 69
Marvelous Combat of Contrarities, 70
Marxism and the Philosophy of Language, 107n8
Master's Degree, 232
Medea, 176
Mémoires de Mme de Motteville, 118
Mirtilla, 197
Monophile, 230

New Atlantis, xv, 35–6
New Essays, 185

Northern humanists, xv, 43–4, 54
Not So New as True, 69

Of the Knowledge which Maketh a Wise
    Man, 65–6, 74
On the Dignity of Man, 196

Pack of Spanish Lies Sent Abroad in the
    World, 69
Paradise Lost, 169
Parnasse des poètes satiriques, 127
Pasquil the Plain, 65, 74
'Il Penseroso,' 157–63, 165–70
Petit oeuvre dévot et contemplatif, 233
Philippics, 102
Piacevol Ragionamento de l'Aretino.
    Dialogo di Giulia e di Madalena,
    106n2, 109n24
Plato Redivivus, 74
Pleasant Battle Between Two Lap Dogs
    of the Utopian Court, 64, 71–4
Pleasant Discourse between two Sea-
    men, 73
Poems of Mr. John Milton Both English
    and Latin Compos'd at several times,
    158
Poetics, 139, 160–2
Praise of Folly, 44
Premier curieux, xx, 240
Project of Prose, 31
Protestation to the whole Church of
    England, 151
Proumenoir de Monsieur de Mon-
    taigne, 116, 127, 132n62
Puerpera, 236

Quadriuium Grammaticus, 211
Quarrel of the Ancients and the
    Moderns, 114
'Querelle des femmes,' 114

Ragionamento delle corti, xiv, 95–7, 99–
    100, 103
Ramus and Talon Inventory, 16
realism, 9, 21n38
Reason and Rhetoric in the Philosophy
    of Hobbes, 177
Republic, xiv, 27, 32
Return of the Renowned Cavaliero Pas-
    quil of England, 70
Rhetoric, 176–7
Rhetoricae Distinctiones, 16
Rhetorics of Thomas Hobbes and Ber-
    nard Lamy, 176–7
Richard III, 139
Rome, xv, 96–7, 100, 142, 210

Sack of Rome, Executed by the Emperor
    Charles' Army, 71
Salem and Bizance, 68
Second Philippic, 100
Secretum, xii, xiv, xx, 3, 5, 161, 230–2
Sei giornate, xvi, 95, 97–8, 103
Seven Philosophical Problems, 175
Shepheardes Calender, 138, 163
'Shipwreck' (Colloquies), 6
Short Tract on First Principles, 177
Sicke Mannes Salue, 161
Sophronistes, 69
Spanish Armada, xv
Sprachbuch, 212, 215, 217, 220
sprezzatura, 87–9
State of the Church of England laid open
    in a Conference, 69
Sum of the Conference between John
    Rainolds and John Hart, 69

Il Tasso: A Dialogue. The Speakers John
    Milton, Torquato Tasso, 172n19
Temporis Filia Veritas, 70
Tiber, 210

Tiers Livre, x
Toxaris, 43
Toxophilus, 65–6
Twe-spraack van de Nededuitsche letterkunst, 208, 220

Underricht der Hoch Teutschen Spraach, 219
Unterredung mit dem Meister, 218
Urbino, 8, 10–11, 79, 85, 87, 98, 197
Utopia, xiv–xv, xx, 27, 30–1, 34–5, 42–6, 49–51, 53–6, 63, 65–6, 74, 236
utopia, 27–9, 31–3, 37, 56
Utopia, island of, 45–6, 64, 72

Various Academic Titles, 232

Venice, 96, 102
Venus, 6
A Vewe of the Present State of Ireland, xv, 27, 37–8, 65
Verkuendigung wie er seinen Schulgesellen erlaubnuess zu spielen erbetten hat, 218
Virgo misogamos, 238
Virgo poenitens, 238–9
Vom außbitten zum spielen, 218
Vox populi: or, The People's Claim to their Parliament's Sitting, 71

Witty and Witless, 161